Administrative Management of
PHYSICAL EDUCATION
and
ATHLETIC PROGRAMS

Administrative Management of
PHYSICAL EDUCATION
and
ATHLETIC PROGRAMS

CLAYNE R. JENSEN
Brigham Young University
Provo, Utah

Lea & Febiger   1983   •   *Philadelphia*

GV
343.5
.J46
1983

Lea & Febiger
600 Washington Square
Philadelphia, PA 19106
U.S.A.

Library of Congress Cataloging in Publication Data

Jensen, Clayne R.
    Administrative management of physical education
and athletic programs.

    Bibliography: p.
    Includes index.
    1. Physical education and training—Management.
2. School sports—Organization and administration.
I. Title.
GV343.5.J46   1983   613.7'068   82-23933
ISBN 0-8121-0817-5

PRINTED IN THE UNITED STATES OF AMERICA

Print Number 3 2 1

PREFACE

Every one of the 50 states includes physical education as one of the subjects taught in the public schools, and competitive athletics and intramural sports are important aspects of the educational system of every state and territory. In addition to the programs in public schools, most colleges and universities sponsor physical education and athletics. This means that every year the great majority of the youth of this country participate in physical education and many of them are involved in school athletics.

Because of the extensive participation in these activities and the large amount of time and funds spent in their support, these programs must be administered efficiently so as to fulfill important purposes with respect to the individuals involved and to society as a whole.

This book is aimed toward improving physical education and athletic programs at all school levels by helping those who manage them to implement better content and procedures. The book takes cognizance in a related fashion only of curricular content, teaching methods, and counseling. The main focus is on effective *planning, organization,* and *management.*

The Book Is Divided into Five Sections

Part I deals with the philosophic foundations of administrative leadership. This section is designed to help the reader better understand the need for and the means of developing a sound philosophic basis for effective administration.

Part II emphasizes methods and procedures that will help guarantee success in any kind of management position. The content is "success oriented."

Part III deals with management techniques and processes that enhance efficiency and positive results.

Part IV provides pertinent information about administration as it relates to the specific content of physical education and athletics. It is designed to help the reader gain insight into what really needs to be done and how to approach it.

Part V consists of related information that every administrator in this field needs in order to function effectively as a well-informed, insightful, and integrated member of the profession.

In sum, the material in this book has been carefully selected to help current and potential administrators gain the knowledge, skills, and insights that are needed to effectively administer high quality physical education and athletic programs. The information is purposely presented in a manner that can be easily understood.

Special appreciation is expressed to the following individuals for contributing to the book and for their critical reviews of certain sections: Linda Carpenter, Joyce Harrison, Bruce Holley, Boyd Jarman, Betty Vickers, and Pete Witbeck.

Provo, Utah

Clayne R. Jensen

CONTENTS

vii

Contents • **xi**

Part I
PHILOSOPHIC BASIS OF ADMINISTRATIVE LEADERSHIP

Chapter **1**

RATIONALE FOR THE STUDY OF ADMINISTRATION

In a book about administration, it seems important at the outset to discuss the rationale for studying the topic, and to establish certain meanings relative to it. Furthermore, we need to examine the nature of administration and how it functions in the educational system, and to describe some of its basic tools.

One might ask, "Why study administration?" Especially, why should college students study the topic when administrative assignments for them are not imminent, and many of them have no intention of pursuing administration as a career. Certainly, the study of administration has more direct and immediate value for one who is preparing to become an administrator or is already an administrator and wants to improve. However, all teachers and coaches should have a basic understanding of administrative theory and practice. This is especially true because every teacher and coach has some administrative responsibilities, such as student records, selection and ordering of books and class materials, and helping with selection and ordering of equipment and supplies. Furthermore, all else being equal, a teacher who has knowledge and insight about administrative processes will be able to work more effectively with those in administrative positions.

Physical educators are more likely to have administrative assignments than most other teachers because of the related out-of-class programs that must be administered, such as interschool athletics and intramural activities. Athletic coaching has administrative aspects because the coach must be able to deal effectively with other members of the coaching staff, members of the team, those who care for equipment and facilities, the school administrators, parents of athletes, and other members of the public. Athletics includes activities pertaining to finances and public relations that do not exist to the same degree in the assignments of most other teachers.

Good administrative procedures in connection with physical education and athletics have been made even more important by the effects of Title IX. This act has escalated the need for men and women to share facilities and

3

use those facilities more effectively. It has also enlarged the programs and thereby contributed to the financial squeeze that is being felt in many schools. Therefore, a need has developed for more adequate budgeting and better financial management. Furthermore, with the national trend toward school consolidation, physical education and athletic departments have become larger and more complex, therefore requiring better administrators. It is also interesting that in their later professional years a high proportion of physical educators and coaches pursue administrative work outside their own discipline. Many become deans of students, guidance counselors, school principles, and superintendents.

NATURE OF EDUCATION

Education, in the broad sense, can be defined as any act or experience that has a formative effect on the mind, character, or physical ability of an individual. In other words, it is the process of positive change. In this sense, education never ends, because we learn from experience throughout our lives. *Formal education* is the process by which society, through schools, colleges, universities and other institutions, deliberately transmits its cultural heritage—its accumulated knowledge, values, and skills—from one generation to another. Formal education involves planned programs and distinct methods for the purpose of accomplishing educational objectives.

Physical education is an element of the total field of education, and it can be viewed in two different ways: education *through* the physical and education *of* the physical. Education *through* the physical can cause changes in the total individual—knowledge, values, skills—as a result of participation in muscular activities. Much can be learned about our environment, about others, and about ourselves through this form of participation. Furthermore, it can significantly influence the development of one's personality and ability to function effectively in society. Education *of* the physical causes development of the physiologic systems. It emphasizes the body's ability to perform efficiently. The total thrust of the physical education program ought to emphasize both these aspects in proper balance. The need for effective administration of educational programs is obvious, especially when one considers the important role that education serves in society and the tremendous amount of public and private resources devoted to it. However, exactly what is meant by the term administration is not so obvious. Let us analyze what the term includes and what methods and techniques are involved.

MEANING OF ADMINISTRATION

A meaningful way to describe certain aspects of administration is by use of the term management. Every organization or business must be managed, and if it is managed well, it stands a better chance of success.

The complexity of management varies in accordance with the size and nature of the organization. Let us relate this idea to the educational system. A teacher in a one-room school would have teaching as the primary responsibility. But even in this simple educational setting, there would be certain administrative duties. The facility would have to be provided and cared for, supplies and equipment kept on hand, student records maintained, and certain student information submitted to a higher authority. A budget would have to be worked out to cover the teacher's salary and the expenses of the facility and equipment. There would be public relations considerations, involving parents and local citizens. The school would operate under some form of local authority, such as a committee, council, or board, and this would involve an administrative relationship between the teacher and the higher authority. Therefore, it is apparent that even in the simple setting of the one-room school, the teacher, being the sole employee, would need to devote a portion of his time to the managerial functions inherent in the situation.

As one-room schools became less prevalent and more than one teacher was employed, it was apparently decided that most of the administrative tasks should be handled by one of the teachers, and that a portion of his time should be given for this purpose. Such a person has become prevalently known as the principal. As the educational system became even more complex, each state created a state department of education with a state superintendent in charge. Each state became subdivided into school districts with a district superintendent appointed to administer the educational programs of the district.

In a similar fashion, colleges and universities became large and complex. They were organized into colleges and departments, with an administrative head over each unit. Each of these steps of development resulted in administrative positions that had previously not existed.

In a general sense, the areas of administrative duties are the same under today's large and complex system as they were in the one-teacher school. But, the complexity and involvement of each aspect of administration has increased immensely.

Even in our present educational arrangement, no school employee is totally free of administrative tasks and procedures. Those in full-time teaching positions must still provide some managerial leadership. For example, they must make sure that the facilities are properly scheduled and ready for use and that the necessary supplies and equipment are readily available. Student data must be recorded and processed. Adequate attention to public relations is expected, including relationships with parents, other teachers, administrators, and the public. Physical educators and athletic coaches normally have more public relations involvement than do other teachers.

Even though a teacher cannot be totally separated from management responsibilities, his involvement should be carefully controlled in order to maximize teaching. Administrative tasks should be handled as much as possible by those in administrative positions. Supposedly, those given administrative assignments are prepared to handle these tasks, whereas those given full-time teaching assignments are supposedly well prepared to teach.

Even though many of the responsibilities of an administrator are managerial in nature, an educational administrator is certainly more than a manager. In addition to direct management of the organization, he must (1) be an educational leader who will provide both enthusiasm and direction to the instructional program; (2) be an insightful leader on both curricular and noncurricular matters; (3) provide broad and far reaching leadership toward overall planning, including budget, personnel, and facilities; (4) help define and interpret goals and provide continuing leadership toward achieving them; (5) provide opportunities for improvement of employees; and (6) give positive leadership to public sentiment.

In actual fact, some administrative positions are largely managerial with the focus on the efficiency of the daily operation; whereas other administrative positions are much broader in scope. To give examples, the chairman of a physical education division in a high school has primarily managerial responsibilities. The principal of the same school is also involved in management, but on a broader basis. The principal, additionally, has to give adequate attention to the overall objectives of the educational system of which his school is a part and to how his school fits into the system and contributes toward the objectives. He must be analytical about the organizational divisions within the school and how well they function in relationship to each other. He is concerned about the balance of educational experiences the students receive, as well as the quality of those experiences. The well-being of the employees, their productivity, and their continuous professional improvement is of concern to him. These are administrative responsibilities which extend beyond direct managerial functions. In a like manner, the superintendent's responsibilities are broader and more far-reaching than those of the principal. The superintendent's job involves less attention to the direct and specific aspects of management and more emphasis on the broader aspects of educational administration.

SOME ELEMENTS OF ADMINISTRATION

In education, the philosophies of those in leadership positions have significant influence on the nature of programs, their underlying purposes, established goals, and methods employed. The decisions the leaders make are, in a sense, expressions of their philosophic concepts toward education and life. Therefore, it is of crucial importance for educational leaders to have personal philosophies that emphasize the objectives and desired results of the educational system. More will be said about this important topic in subsequent chapters.

Ideas about education in general, and physical education and athletics in particular, have developed from analysis of social and individual needs and from experiences with the total environment, including educational, social, economic, religious, and political aspects. Ideas originate as untested, unrefined, and unvalidated notions. These notions, along with opinions and intuitions, form general concepts, which help formulate theories, principles, and laws, which in turn, help to form the basis of our programs and our procedures.

Unproved and untested ideas become verified through reasoning, constructive and critical thinking, analysis, evaluation, interpretation, and the testing of hypotheses. All of these are valuable methods of the administrative process. These methods help us determine and apply useful goals, standards, criteria, policies, principles, and procedures. These elements of administration are discussed in more detail.

Goals

The term goals is often used as all-inclusive of aims, objectives, and expected outcomes. For example, it would be logical to state a broad and remote goal labeled *the aim*, and then state several more specific goals labeled *objectives*, followed by numerous immediate goals called *expected outcomes* (or expected results). Such a structure of goals gives definite purpose and direction to the program and to those involved with it (Figure 1-1).

Having clearly stated goals that are both challenging and realistic is of utmost importance. Administration without them is similar to going on a trip with no destination in mind and, therefore, no determined route to follow. Socrates expressed it well when he said, "for a ship without a destination, no wind is favorable."

Figure 1-1. Hierarchy of goals in education.

Goals may be expressed from different points of view. For example, goals are set by administrators, teachers, students, and those who sponsor the educational program. There can be goals for the educational program as a whole and goals for specific areas such as physical education and athletics. In addition, each individual has some personal goals that relate to the situation which should be considered in the total plan.

Goals that are carefully thought through and properly stated have a strong element of stability. They should not be thought of, however, as static and never-changing. As circumstances change, it naturally becomes necessary to update goals. One of the challenges of educational leaders is to maintain the right balance between keeping goals current with changing circumstances and maintaining sufficient stability and continuity.

Goals should be stated in terminology that is understood by those involved. They should be clear, concise, and meaningful. Goals should express concepts to which people relate, which motivate, and cause them to aspire to achieve. They should be measurable, and a time frame for their accomplishment should be stated. Each goal should include the implied *action*, expected *results*, and *time frame.*

It is apparent that a comprehensive treatment of goals is complex; but when the goals are dealt with properly at each level and in connection with each aspect of the program, the process becomes simplified. Loucks[1] and Swanson[2] added considerably to the understanding of the importance of goals in physical education.

Aims. An aim may be defined as a broad statement of purpose or a desired result to point toward. It is a remote level of achievement toward which efforts are directed. In education, an aim is usually thought of as a broad, inclusive, and remote goal stated in a manner that gives a general direction to the broad spectrum of educational programs. The following is an example of how an aim might be stated for a department of physical education and athletics.[3]

> The overall aim of the department is to provide the highest quality programs and leadership possible in the areas of physical education and competitive athletics for the benefit of the total student body. Further, the aim is to contribute maximally to the self-fulfillment of each student and to help develop each student's potential to the fullest.

Objectives. Educational objectives are desired goals for which one strives in the attainment of knowledge, skills, and appreciations. The achievement of specific objectives leads toward the aim, which is more general and more remote. Objectives are related to the aim but they are not synonymous with it. They are steps toward achievement of the aim. Following are some examples of intermediate objectives.[1]

1. To sponsor a strong and well balanced program of interschool athletics for both boys and girls with proper emphasis on the development of each individual participant.

2. To sponsor a high quality and varied program of physical education instruction consisting of interesting and beneficial activities arranged in logical sequence and proper graduation of difficulty.

Expected Outcomes. Expected outcomes are statements of anticipated immediate results. They serve as short-range goals on which to focus. They are steps toward the attainment of objectives, which are broader and more long-range. An expected outcome in a beginning swimming class might be for each student to *swim 100 yards nonstop by a specified date.* For a basketball team, an expected outcome might be the achievement of *shooting 50% or better from the field during early season.* A track athlete might have an expected outcome of *running the mile in 4 minutes 30 seconds by a particular date in mid-season.*

Standards

As used in education, the term standard refers to a defined level of performance against which other performances or achievements are compared. The standard may be quantitative or qualitative. For example, it might be determined that ninth grade boys should be able to run the 100-yard dash in *13.2* in order to receive a rating of *good.* This means 13.2 seconds is the standard for a *good* rating. Some universities hold to the rule that a student must meet a standard of a *3.0 GPA* (grade point average) in order to *qualify for graduate school.* In his 12-minute run test, Kenneth Cooper established the standard of *1.6 miles* for men between ages 30 and 40 years to receive a rating of *excellent* in relationship to cardiovascular fitness level. Each teacher determines certain standards or levels of performance a student must meet in order to earn a particular grade. In a well-developed educational program, many standards of achievement and behavior are applied. Standards evolve from criteria, and they serve as guides toward excellence. They help to evaluate student achievement, teacher success, and curriculum effectiveness. In educational programs, only reasonable and useful standards should be applied, and they should be primarily for the benefit of students and not for other reasons.

Criteria

Criteria are measures of data that form the basis for establishing standards. As with standards, criteria may be either quantitative or qualitative. The reason some universities have the standard of 3.0 GPA for entrance into graduate school is that a substantial amount of *data* has been gathered and evaluated that supports the idea that students with less than a 3.0 GPA have marginal chances for success. These data are the criteria on which the standard is based. Likewise, in order for Kenneth Cooper to establish 1.6 miles as the standard of *excellence* in the 12-minute run for men between ages 30 and 40, a large amount of data were gathered and became the criteria for the standard.

A defined set of criteria can form the basis for making judgments or evaluations. For example, leadership can be evaluated with increased objectivity if the evaluation is based on specifically stated and valid leadership criteria. The same would be true in the case of judging or evaluating social adjustment, basketball playing effectiveness, or other characteristics where objective and precise measuring methods are not applicable.

Policies

A policy is considered a governing statement: a statement that defines the procedure to be followed under given circumstances. Policies are usually closely related to the underlying philosophies of those who establish them. They are also related to the nature of the particular organization and the circumstances. The primary purpose of policies is to serve as guides in the administrative procedure. Some policies are strict in nature and not subject to exception, whereas others are considered guidelines and are subject to exception for good reason. A school district might have the policy of *keeping parents informed about student absenteeism,* but the exact procedures for implementing the policy might vary from one school to another. Furthermore, the exactness with which each school implements the policy might vary. Perhaps it is a policy of a particular university that *faculty members who are not going to be reemployed will be notified by March 1st,* otherwise reemployment can be assumed. The exact procedure in notifying each person affected by this policy might vary within the different administrative units, but the basic policy would be consistent throughout.

It is important to have clearly stated policies that are understood by all concerned. Further, it is important to have a strong element of consistency in their application. Whenever an exception is made to a policy, there must be sufficient reason to justify it. Lack of consistency can result in confusion and have a demoralizing effect.

Following are sample policies taken from a college policy manual[1]:

1. Even though available facilities and teachers must be taken into account in determining the class schedule, these factors should not dictate the content of the program. Instead, the program needs should dictate the availability of facilities and teachers insofar as this is feasible. This is an important element in the long-range planning of the organization.

2. Classes that need not be taught every semester should be placed on a rotation schedule, which results in an optimum combination of economy for the university and convenience for the students.

3. When a teacher will be absent from class, both the reason for absence and the substitute arrangements must be approved by the department chairman.

Procedures

Proper administrative procedures are of crucial importance both in terms of efficiency and acceptability. Procedures that are clearly defined and applied consistently become *standardized.* Once standardized, a procedure is automatic and generally accepted by those concerned. Procedures that have been carefully thought out, properly refined, and tried and tested, provide a distinct advantage toward overall efficiency. However, not all procedures can be standardized, because sometimes a procedure must be tailor-made to fit a unique or infrequent situation.

To aid the administrative effort, many organizations have a *procedure manual,* and this contributes significantly toward standardizing the procedures and communicating them to others in the organization. It is highly desirable for the procedures to be understood and supported by those involved with them or affected by them. Here are some procedural statements[1] of the kind found frequently in procedural manuals pertaining to physical education.

1. All physical education classes for which students must dress into activity uniforms are expected to start five minutes after the regular beginning time and end ten minutes prior to the scheduled ending time. This is to allow for dressing and showering.

2. In the case of an accident that results in injury to a student, the instructor or supervisor in charge is fully responsible for the administration of emergency care in accordance with the procedures described in the American Red Cross First Aid Manual. Further, he/she is expected to exercise prudence and sound judgment in relationship to all aspects of the situation.

Principles and Laws

A principle may be defined as a fundamental truth, a uniform result, or a universal guide. Often principles serve as cornerstones for a particular body of knowledge. They can form the basis for defining methods and procedures or for conduct and behavior.

Principles are used in a variety of ways in education. For example, some principles give direction to the overall educational effort, such as the *seven cardinal principles* stated by the U.S. Commission of Education in 1917. For many years, these principles served as a guiding light for the public education programs of America. They are still referred to often, and they are still basically sound. Certain physiologic and mechanical principles (or laws) are applied in athletic conditioning and performance. Examples are the *law of use* as it applies to the human organism (with proper use, the organism improves, while in the absence of use, it deteriorates), and the *principles of leverage* as they apply to movement of body parts and the application of external objects. Furthermore, the field of education has *leadership principles* and *principles of conduct* (often stated in the form of ethics).

Theories

A theory is one step beyond an assumption or hypothesis. It is a guide, which has some evidence in its support, but is still not validated. Theories are useful in education in the formulation of administrative practices. Sometimes, a theory gradually evolves into a standard procedure, a policy, or a principle, after sufficient evidence has been accumulated to support it. In other cases, theories become discarded because attempts to prove their validity and usefulness are unsuccessful. Theory can be viewed as a starting point; it has no practical presuppositions and no guarantee of success. On the contrary, actual practice always presupposes some theory. Standardized procedures, policies, principles, and laws all have theory as their starting point.

BIBLIOGRAPHY
1. Jensen, C.R.: Policy and Procedure Manual. Brigham Young University, Provo, UT, College of Physical Educaton, 1981.

2. Loucks, D.H.: New professionals reorder objectives. JOPER, *50*(7):64, 1979.

3. Swanson, J.: Developing and implementing objectives in physical education. JOPER, *50*(3):68, 1979.

Chapter *2*

A SOUND PHILOSOPHY

To be really useful, an educational administrator must be professionally ethical and moral. He must believe, represent, and foster desirable attitudes, concepts, and practices. He must contribute strength to the educational system and to his colleagues and students. This means that perhaps the most important characteristic an administrator has is his personal philosophy, because this influences all else that he does. In striving to be an effective administrator, the phrase "know thyself" is certainly applicable.

The term philosophy is derived from both Latin and Greek, and it means "love of truth" or "love of wisdom." It implies the need to find the real truths and values in life and apply them correctly.

Philosophy has two important themes: first, to gain a greater understanding of life and of the universe in which we live; and second, to sharpen one's ability to think clearly and logically. Both these aspects are of vital importance to an educational administrator.

Philosophers are viewed as deep thinkers who have unusual insights and express superior wisdom. Philosophers think more analytically than the ordinary person, concentrating on life's fundamental values and vital issues. The serious philosopher approaches a hypothetic question much like a scientist approaches a scientific problem.

Most people have personal beliefs or ideas about life, just as they have favorite remedies for aches and pains. However, the philosophic beliefs of some people are fuzzy and poorly defined, because they are unknowledgeable or have not really analyzed matters thoroughly. Others express definite beliefs based on superficial thought, emotional reaction, or incorrect information. Still others have deep and well-defined beliefs based on thorough knowledge and careful analysis.

Some people try to make a distinct separation between *philosophy* and *science*, and thus, individuals are often labeled "philosophers" or "scientists," but not both. Such clear separation is not totally appropriate. Every scientist should be a philosopher in the sense that he should carefully con-

13

sider the reasons for pursuing scientific discovery and the application of the results. Further, every philosopher should be a scientist in the sense that he should take an organized and systematic approach to philosophic inquiry, and his inquiry should be inclusive of important scientific facts and concepts. Through the scientific approach, discoveries are made about matter, composition, and energy. Through the philosophic process, decisions are made about where, when, and for what purposes those discoveries should be used. A scientist who has no concern for the purposes of his discoveries could be considered irresponsible, while a philosopher who fails to test his beliefs through critical investigation is equally lacking.

In order to comprehend more clearly the nature and meaning of philosophy, it is helpful to know the processes involved. These include the following[3]:

1. *Metaphysics,* which attempts to answer the question, "what is reality?" It includes a study of the science of being, the science of fundamental causes and processes, the nature of the mind and the body, and the nature of self. As Aristotle said, "it is associated with principles of being."

2. *Epistemology,* which is concerned with knowledge—its sources, authority, validity, principles, and limits.

3. *Logic,* which deals with reason: what constitutes sound reasoning and logical thought, what are the characteristics of it and the criteria by which it is measured?

4. *Ethics,* which is associated with morals: what is right and wrong, the criteria for determining good and bad, and an understanding of the foundation on which moral character rests. Ethics attempts to answer the question "what is the highest good?"

5. *Aesthetics,* which is pertinent to taste and discriminates between beauty and ugliness. Its basis is appeal and quality of form or technique.

6. *Politics,* which is a study of the various forms of government and social structure, such as anarchism, aristocracy, communism, democracy, and socialism. Much of the behavior of humans is politically related in terms of cause and results.

Within the framework of the processes listed above, philosophers utilize the following methods for arriving at philosophic beliefs: *reason, observation, experience, intuition,* and *revelation.*[4]

Reason is probably the predominant method in philosophic analysis. The principle tools of reason are the inductive and deductive processes. The deductive process begins with a general idea or principle and uses reason to arrive at (deduce) specific conclusions based on the general principle. Inductive reasoning builds on specific ideas or facts to arrive at a general concept or principle.

Discovering truth through *observation* is the most scientific approach. Observation of physical results, events, and discoveries through the five senses seems inconsistent with the theoretic analysis of the philosophic process. Observable truth, however, is essential to philosophy as well as to science.

It is hard to distinguish *experience* from observation in that both these sources of truth involve the senses. Experience, however, involves learning through active participation, as one might learn that the rays of the sun are hot because he has felt the heat on his body. Observation, on the other hand, separates the person from direct experience, in the way that a spectator in a sport is separated from the participants on the playing field.

Intuitive learning is a nebulous concept in the minds of many scholars. One's intuition is that form of native intelligence which enables a person to become the initiator of ideas, the thought process from which comes both the desire and ability to investigate. It relates to the spirit or soul of man.

Some philosophers believe that truth may be gained through *revelation* from a higher power—an extraterrestrial source. Many believe that revelation is the only pure form of truth since it comes from the only perfect source, the supernatural being, or "God."

BUILDING A PERSONAL PHILOSOPHY

The question here is not whether each of us has a philosophy, but rather what the philosophy includes. With a weak or poorly developed philosophy, a person lacks clear understanding and direction. Certainly life cannot be successful and satisfying without a philosophy that leads to a purposeful existence.

It is often useful for a person to put in written form what he truly believes about the various aspects of life, because putting thoughts into writing contributes exactness to one's ideas and concepts. This process forces decisions about one's philosophy that might otherwise never be made. It is recommended that each prospective administrator follow this procedure, and in doing so, apply the following guidelines.

Some Suggested "DOs"

Keep asking these questions as you write your beliefs.
1. Why do I believe this, if there are worthy contrary beliefs?
2. Is this a "best guess," an expedient opinion, or do I really believe it?
3. Is this a prejudiced belief? A narrow one? A closed-minded one?
4. Is this a belief that is attuned to the past, the present, or the future?
5. Is this a belief that is too restricted in some way (time, place, condition, or circumstance)?
6. Beneath and beyond all rationalization, why do I believe this?
7. Is this a necessary or important belief for me to hold?
8. What facts or near-facts support this belief?
9. Is this belief probably permanent or will it likely change with increased experience and exposure to additional facts and new ideas?

Some Suggested "DON'Ts"

1. Don't start wondering in general, "What *do* I believe?" Be exact and proceed with an orderly design.
2. Don't think that a written account of your philosophy has to be fancy or

filled with "big words." It is possible to be complex but express yourself in simple terms.

3. Don't believe that you have to agree with the "great minds," or the half-great, or your friends, or even the instructor. Just be yourself.
4. Don't write anything that is not sincere or truthful. In philosophy, loss of integrity is loss of everything.
5. Don't be ashamed of beliefs that may be linked to the idealistic, the beautiful, the artistic, or any other area that symbolizes a sensitivity and awareness of life, thought, and experience above the common and the mediocre.
6. Don't make hard work of the process. Let the words come easily. After all, you are only writing about the things you believe.
7. Don't just skim the surface. Dig deep into your basic beliefs and concepts, and don't stop digging just because you hit hard-pan.

Building (or perfecting) a personal philosophy involves putting one's thoughts into a logical order, beginning with the most basic items. For example, how did I come to exist, for what reasons am I here? In light of this, what are my responsibilities and what contributions should I strive toward? Some helpful suggestions follow[4]:

1. Am I evolved from a lower form of life? Am I a child of God? Am I an individual unrelated to other beings or any form of divinity? Am I inherently important; if so, for what?

2. Am I here (a) simply to exist; (b) to contribute to the betterment of mankind; (c) to better myself through constant progress and self-realization; (d) to suffer, to have experiences, to pursue pleasure?

3. Where am I going? (a) toward maximum accomplishment of self; (b) to achieve as much pleasure as possible until death—the end; (c) to become like Christ (or some other God-like being); (d) to attain perfection toward eternal progress and eternal life; (e) to suffer in this life as a means of gaining future glory?

Once a person's basic premise is fairly well established, it is helpful to continue with such questions as these:

4. How can I accomplish my goals?
5. Do I have responsibilities to others or to society? If so what are they?
6. How should I incorporate elements of my philosophy into my profession and my associations with other people?
7. Are my daily actions consistent with my beliefs?

Answers to questions such as these will go a long way toward perfecting the fundamental aspects of your philosophy. The nature and strength of these aspects will have a firm influence on your daily actions and your responses to life's various situations.

THE IMPORTANCE OF VALUES

Assuming, as we have, that the term "beliefs" includes the several areas covered in and by philosophy (purpose, values, and the like), then one's quest to know what one believes is not easy. In fact, in-depth thinking and analysis become necessary.

The task of ferreting out what one believes with reference to physical education is not easy, even for one who is a specialist in the field. This leads to even larger questions, such as the purposes of education in general, and those of life itself. But, for any particular individual, the purposes of life, of education, and of physical education depend upon his *system of values*. For that matter, the methods of instruction he chooses are dependent on his values, as are the activities selected for the program.

Let us investigate further the significance of *values*. Do you think some phase of administration, or some activity in the program, or some method of instruction, or some technique of discipline is desirable because:

1. It satisfies the individual?
2. It is developmental to the person?
3. It calls for interaction between the individual and the environment?
4. It is based on the greatest good for the greatest number?
5. It is in and of itself desirable?
6. It is good for society?
7. It contributes to some purpose of a deity?

Obviously, no major purpose, no program of activities, and no method of instruction, can serve all of these results. Thus you must choose, and your choices will be based on your system of values.

If you wish to refine your system of values you must ask the question, "Why?" "Why have you selected a particular idea or held to a certain premise?" If you have the fiber to persist in this line of questioning, you begin not only to think crisply but to really understand. Moreover, because there are often good reasons for selecting any one of several alternatives, you begin to understand yourself better, and become more tolerant, more understanding, and find more respect for others and their views.

A person's values shape and color his life by influencing the way he thinks and acts in both personal and professional relationships. Indeed, the kind of person that an individual is as an employee, neighbor, friend, and parent, is strongly influenced by the sum total of his system of values or lack of one.

Some of our values change as we grow and expand our understanding. More experience, further education, and broader exposure alter our thinking, thus changing our values. In turn, our values affect our experiences, and in fact, determine which experiences we have by the choices we make.

It is said that values cannot be taught. But certainly teaching values is possible in the sense that values may be influenced by one's experiences. And one of the processes of education is to provide carefully selected experiences. However, it is also true that people do not consistently adopt values simply by being instructed to do so. The development of values results from a complex interaction between a person and his experiences.

It is, therefore, important for teachers, administrators, and others who influence educational programs to make value-based decisions in educational settings. Values influence such things as (1) one's objectives in education, (2) the selection of learning experiences and how they are arranged, (3) the relative emphasis on different subject matter, (4) the provision of facilities and equipment in support of the various areas of education, (5) teaching methods, (6) the administrative organization and procedures, and (7) the standards by which employees are to conduct themselves.

The fact that no two people have exactly the same value system indicates the complexity of the topic, and because of their complexity, values defy comprehensive classification. Certain groups of values are identifiable, however, and some meaningful distinctions can be made. Values may be expressed as *intrinsic* or *extrinsic; subjective* or *objective; individual* or *social; absolute* or *relative.*[3]

Intrinsic versus *extrinsic* values provide an interesting contrast. Intrinsic values are those which have worth in and of themselves and do not depend on extraneous factors. These are the more permanent and less changing values in life, and they relate mostly to nonphysical qualities. They form the moral and spiritual fiber upon which society depends, superseding prestige, fame, wealth, or influence. Intrinsic values play a significant role in education, community, and family life.

Extrinsic values are those which lead to something of greater worth and are instruments for attaining another end. For the most part, these values lie in the practical affairs of everyday life: physical items such as clothes, automobiles, and sporting equipment; and also such things as the accumulation of money, power, and facts of practical use. A youngster, for example, earns money in order to finance his education. The work he does represents a value which is extrinsic toward the end of gaining an education. Some aspects of education are instrumental (extrinsic) toward achieving a desired lifestyle or fulfilling lifelong aspirations. Conversely, some view education as an intrinsic value, because it results in the development of the person, and the person is an eternal being.

Some philosophers feel that all values are basically intrinsic because even in using something as a means to something else, the individual gains some basic worth. Others feel that all values are extrinsic because it is impossible to achieve or apply a value that does not lead to something else. Obviously, there is no clear cut division between intrinsic and extrinsic values. It is a matter of relative emphasis.

Values may also be labeled as *subjective* or *objective.* A person emphasizing subjective values would be relatively nonmaterialistic. He would hold that truly valuable things exist in the mind in the form of knowledge, attitudes, appreciations, and ideals. He would contend that significance, worth, and beauty exist in the mind rather than in the object.

Conversely, objective values are those which exist in the material world, whether or not they are observed. Such values do not depend on the imagination, hopes, or aspirations of the individual. They exist independently and need only to be discovered. Objective values emphasize that beauty and worth are inherent in the object or the thing itself and not in one's mental perception.

Values are also classified as *individual* or *social*. Since only individuals can have values, this terminology is somewhat inaccurate. In a given society, however, there becomes a unity of values among individuals; these values become prominent characteristics of the society and are sometimes labeled "social values." They are concerned with such factors as respect for the rights and property of others, respect for the law, volunteer service to others, and particular standards of social conduct.

One of the most clear cut classifications is *absolute* versus *relative*. Values that are absolute are universal and unchanging. The advocates of absolute values believe that they have always existed and will continue to exist indefinitely. Absolute values are not related to time nor circumstance. These values are often related to a supreme being or deity, and they include such things as truth, virtue, love, and goodness. Other people relate absolute values to the natural order, emphasizing that the laws of nature are consistent, predictable, and everlasting; therefore, they are universal and absolute.

Relative values fluctuate with circumstances and time. One who takes the position that all values are relative would emphasize that the world is in a constant state of physical and social change, and therefore, values must remain adjustable.

Within the framework of the philosophic dichotomies there are people who live by *positive* thoughts as opposed to those who emphasize the *negative*. Positive thinkers look for the inevitable good. They are optimistic in the face of adversity, and are easily encouraged and often encourage others. Conversely, the negative thinkers look for the worst. Such persons tend to destroy optimism, enthusiasm, and creative ideas by always finding reasons to feel reserved, reluctant, and discouraged.

As adults who are especially concerned with the development of young people, it is imperative that we understand the importance of providing positive models. Furthermore, as parents, teachers, and administrators, we have a responsibility to provide an abundance of developmental experiences for children and youth (as well as adults), which contribute toward sound values. The development of values is a major function of education.

Each of us has established a value system which guides and directs us in all of our activities and influences our behavior. It forms the basis for our aspirations, dedications, and actions. To a large extent, our system of values dictates the meaning of life, forming the foundation of what we are and what we hope to become. It determines our most marvelous intentions and structures our actions.

But we must recognize that our system of values is never complete or final. It is always more or less in a state of development and flux, due to new experiences and changing circumstances. In view of this, each of us must consistently try to keep our values on track, developing in a manner that will be for our good and the good of others whose lives we influence.

BIBLIOGRAPHY

1. Davis, E.C.: Toward a Better Philosophy. Englewood Cliffs, NJ, Prentice-Hall, 1971.

2. Harper, W.A.: The Philosophical Process in Physical Education. 3rd Ed. Philadelphia, Lea & Febiger, 1977, p. 336.

3. Hartvigsen, Milton F.: Unpublished papers on establishing a personal philosophy. College of Physical Education, Brigham Young University (updated, 1981).

4. Vickers, B.: Lecture notes on Philosophy of Physical Education and Athletics. Brigham Young University, 1981.

5. Ziegler, E.F.: Physical Education and Sports Philosophy. Englewood Cliffs, NJ: Prentice-Hall, 1977.

6. Ziegler, E.F.: Philosophical perspective. JOPER, *51*(11):40, 1980.

Chapter *3*

LEADERSHIP STYLES
AND METHODS

Leadership is an intriguing quality that is found in people of various ages, male and female, members of different races, and from various cultural and economic backgrounds. No segment of society has a hold on leadership. But, what is a leader? What qualities differentiate such persons from others in the organization? Why do certain leadership approaches function well in some situations and not in others? These are interesting questions and they relate to only a few of the concepts that will be dealt with in this chapter.

A typical dictionary definition of leadership includes such descriptions as the following: one who directs others, such as a person who goes before to guide or to show the way; one who conducts; one who has authority to preside.

The emphasis in these descriptions is on guiding, directing, and presiding. Some specialists on leadership, however, stress that the leader is a *persuader* or an *enabler*. In this context, a leader could be one who persuades others to seek particular objectives; one who has the human qualities that bind a group together and motivate it toward goals; or one who demonstrates the art of coordinating and stimulating individuals and groups to achieve desired ends. Leadership may also be described as the capacity to help others achieve their own desires. British Field Marshall Montgomery described leadership as "the capacity and will to rally people to a common purpose."

Unfortunately, some effective leaders produce negative results because of divisive intent or a confused sense of values. Adolf Hitler is an example of this. Of course, in education, our efforts should always be towards *positive* influence.

Leadership is more than just authority. It is more than enthusiasm or inspiration. In the most serious sense, leadership is a tool for achieving objectives, and its success must be judged in terms of what is accomplished. Leadership is *influencing* the actions of individuals and organizations. The key word is "influence." A person may be well liked and admired, but if he does not influence results, he is ineffective.

Some of the definitions of leadership found in the literature that emphasize *influence* include the following:

1. Leadership is an influence process, the dynamics of which are a function of the personal characteristics of the leader and followers and of the nature of the specific situation.[14]
2. Leadership is the process of influencing the activities of an organized group in efforts toward goal setting and goal achievement.[17]
3. Leadership is getting people to do what the leader wants them to do because he has influenced or inspired them to believe it is what they want to do.[9]

Exerting significant influence in an organization is a complex process. Influence is exercised through an intricate system of authority, responsibility, persuasion, and communication. Given the exertion of influence, each level of leadership still leaves an area of discretion to the level below. Even the lowest ranking employee exercises some judgment in determining particular actions.

In addition to the influence of direct leadership, employees are also governed by policies, operating procedures, organizational loyalty, and other factors. This emphasizes the importance of a leader who can create an environment that will produce the desired responsiveness on the part of others. One of the most successful forms of leadership is the creation of conditions conducive to motivation and effective performance by the employees. Accordingly, the truly effective leader, instead of being "the boss," is a resource to the organization, an expert in communication, and a catalyst to his fellow workers. His functions include facilitating, as well as directing, and maintaining a healthy flow of communication up, down, and across the organization, instead of merely issuing orders.

Leadership can be either *direct* or *indirect*. Direct leadership is immediate contact between the leader and those being led. Indirect leadership is when the leader purposely influences people without having contact with them.

An example of direct leadership is a department chairperson administering a program in which he influences how well other employees perform their responsibilities. From such a position, the leader is expected to direct the program and account for its accomplishments. Another example of direct leadership is a person who gives public speeches, thereby changing people's knowledge, concepts, and feelings about certain matters. A teacher is a direct leader who regularly influences people's lives along a set pattern toward educational goals.

Examples of *indirect* leadership are an educator who writes materials that influence those who read them, or one who communicates indirectly to a large number of people through a small number who might be referred to as his "disciples." Another form of indirect leadership is the role model. Both colleagues and students are influenced by models with whom they relate. One who has achieved unusual professional success is often identified as a model by others who aspire to the same kind of success. Outstanding teachers and coaches serve as worthy models for students and also for others in the profession. The effective administrator serves as a model for others who aspire to administrative positions.

ELEMENTS OF LEADERSHIP SITUATIONS

Every leadership situation has four basic elements.
1. The leader—with his abilities, personality traits, responsibilities, and authority.
2. The followers—with their abilities, personalities, and responsibilities.
3. The situation—with its special features.
4. The purpose or task—with which the individuals, program, or organization is concerned.

Analysis of these elements shows that people who emerge as leaders in one setting might not emerge, or at least not to the same degree, in other circumstances. Leadership is, after all, a functional relationship between the *leader*, the *followers*, the *situation*, and the *purpose or task*. Thus, different circumstances call for different leadership qualities.

FORMS OF LEADERSHIP

The basic forms of leadership can be labeled *autocratic, participative*, and *laissez faire* (the latter two are democratic in nature). The main distinctions between autocratic and democratic leadership are seen in the contrasts between totalitarian and democratic governments. But, less pure forms of these contrasting styles can be found in various organizations, and among individual leaders in the same organization.

Autocratic

The characteristics of *strict autocratic* (authoritarian) leaders have been documented as having protective and paranoid tendencies, combined with a lack of security, frequently bolstered by arbitrary displays of authority. Also, they tend to be remote from other members of the group and demand to have activities and attention centered on them. The apparent stability of the group is somewhat artificial, and is maintained largely under threat. Typically, there is a tight authoritative structure in which any deviation or disloyalty is met with chastisement. Negative expression against the organization or leader is viewed particularly seriously, although some "constructive criticism" of organizational practices is usually allowed.

The autocratic leader insists on exercising the decision-making power. He is often seen as "heavy handed" and "hard-boiled." He issues the orders and expects subordinates to be unfaltering in their subservience. Typically, such a leader is a hard worker and a hard driver.

Many autocratic leaders threaten and use negative sanctions to enforce their authority. They may show little concern for the needs and problems of others. Subordinates often respond to such leadership by being tense, subtly resentful of the "system," and quarrelsome among themselves.

A modification of strict autocratic leadership is known as *benevolent authoritarianism*. Its practitioners employ positive techniques toward gaining support by providing incentive awards to followers, hoping that this will produce the desired obedience. Although subordinates may respond more positively to this style, they still do not share in important decision making.

Authoritarian leaders of either the strict or modified pattern usually insist on exact compliance with rules and regulations, and they place heavy emphasis on mechanical considerations of operational efficiency. In fact, adherence to rules frequently becomes so important to the authoritarian that the achievement of organizational goals is subordinated to procedural perfection.

Participative

Participative leadership represents an intermediate position between the extremes. Under this style, members of the group are participants or contributors to decision making, but the one in the leadership position makes or strongly influences the final decision, after taking into consideration input from the others. The leader shares authority and decision making with his subordinates, but ultimately, he retains the authority and the associated responsibility.

Directions are issued and adherence is expected under this system, but the expectations are likely to be accompanied by positive rewards as well as negative sanctions, with emphasis on the positive. Goal achievement is stressed at least as fully as adherence to rules and procedures.

With participative leadership, decision making sometimes follows a time-consuming and cumbersome process. The advantage, however, is that it adds stability since it does not depend too much on the power of only one person. There are checks and balances that do not exist in autocratic leadership.

Certain dangers should be avoided with leadership that is highly participative. It can become almost leaderless, unstructured, and chaotic. While subordinate tension may be reduced by minimizing heavy-handed rule enforcement, it is also true that productivity may be adversely affected by too much emphasis on the participative technique.

The preferred degree of participative leadership is one in which the leader exercises enough command to move things along at the desired pace and keep the organization responsive and alive, while, showing adequate sensitivity toward other members of the organization and permitting sufficient involvement and influence by them.

Laissez Faire

This pattern of leadership allows extensive freedom to act without interference from the leader. The leader is available to serve as a resource person and to assist in accomplishing individual or group goals. He will generally provide materials, information, guidance, and support when needed, but little uninvited direction. The leader encourages co-workers to set their own objectives, make their own decisions, and proceed on their own. He often appears to be a bystander, observer, or subtle mediator without getting deeply involved in the activities of the group.

Management authorities and behavioural scientists generally agree that the probability for disorganization, instability, low output, and chaos is just too great to advocate the laissez faire technique. However, there are unique circumstances, where such an approach can work effectively. Possible examples would be a group of competent and dedicated researchers, a mature departmental faculty at a university, a law firm staff, or a medical staff in a clinic.

Leadership Continuum

A continuum graph is a helpful method of viewing the complete range of leadership styles from one extreme to the other. This concept has been presented in a variety of forms by different writers and lecturers. Figure 3-1 is the author's version of a leadership continuum illustrating the range from the extreme autocratic to the extreme democratic approach. At one end is the autocratic administrator who makes all the decisions, which the other employees are expected to accept. He not only sets the goals for the group and makes the final decisions, but also discourages subordinate participation. At the other end is the extreme democratic administrator, who not only permits but actually encourages extensive participation by subordinates.

CONTRASTING LEADERSHIP PATTERNS

Within the three leadership methods just discussed, there are specific patterns which have distinguishable characteristics. A leader might, for example, be basically either autocratic or democratic and still exhibit certain characteristics included in the patterns described here. The contrasting patterns represent extremes, and most leaders function somewhere in between. The study of these patterns can help an administrator better understand the strengths and weaknesses of his own approach and help him to visualize the alternative approaches that could be considered.[5]

An interesting distinction exists between *failure avoidance* and *success seeking*. The failure avoidance strategy is based on the idea that one succeeds by simply avoiding failure. Accordingly, such a leader emphasizes adherence to rules and regulations. Change tends to be discouraged, because one measure of success is the smoothness of the operation and the absence of problems. Accomplishment of significant results often becomes hidden and neglected in the failure avoidance process. There is a tendency to accept relatively low productivity as long as it is above the failure level.

The success seeking style is just the opposite. Such a leader views success as relative and favors the highest possible level of achievement. Innovation and goal accomplishment is the principle task; and he sees problem solving, reasonable risk-taking, and dynamic change as both sources and results of

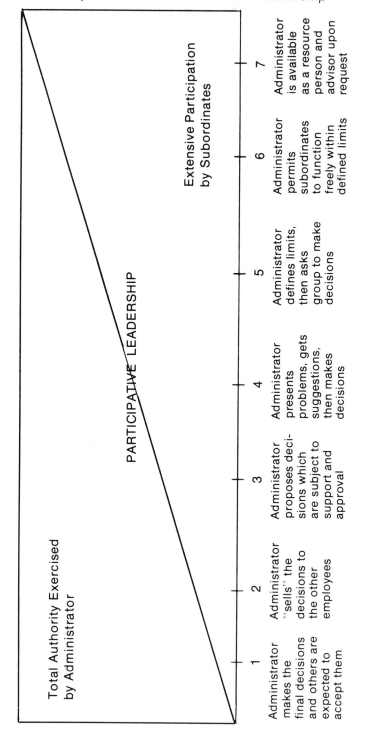

Total Authority Exercised by Administrator

Extensive Participation by Subordinates

PARTICIPATIVE LEADERSHIP

1	2	3	4	5	6	7
Administrator makes the final decisions and others are expected to accept them	Administrator "sells" the decisions to the other employees	Administrator proposes decisions which are subject to support and approval	Administrator presents problems, gets suggestions, then makes decisions	Administrator defines limits, then asks group to make decisions	Administrator permits subordinates to function freely within defined limits	Administrator is available as a resource person and advisor upon request

Figure 3-1. A continuum graph, illustrating the range from extreme autocratic to extreme democratic leadership in decision making.

organizational vitality and ultimate success. A leader who stresses this style does not expect the operation to always run smoothly. Adherence to defined procedures and regulations is relatively unimportant if the expected results are achieved.

Another interesting contrast is the *integrated innovator* and the *detached director*. The integrator's procedure is socially oriented. He wants to be "one of the group" who exercises his leadership as a fully involved member. He strives for close and congenial associations and attempts to move the group with him towards the desired goals by serving as the moving and directing force from within the group.

The detached leader takes the opposite approach. By assuming a distant boss–employee relationship, he directs the group toward the goals from an arm's length position. He may or may not be authoritative, but he definitely does not integrate and he is not socially oriented in his approach.

Two other opposite approaches in leadership involve *negative strategies,* which employ fear and threat in the motivation of employees, and *positive strategies,* which exhibit incentives and rewards as a means toward accomplishment. Leadership experts generally agree that even if the effectiveness of the two were equal, the positive approach would certainly be preferred. However, on some occasions, with certain individuals the hard-line negative approach becomes necessary in order to produce desired results.

Some leaders are *task oriented* and others are *relations oriented*. The task-oriented leader focuses on the completion of work with emphasis on well-defined projects or units of work. This kind of leader feels that the quantity and quality of work is the main consideration. It is the end to which all efforts are focused, and from the beginning, the emphasis is on the final result rather than the methods, processes, and relationships involved. Conversely, the relations-oriented person gives primary consideration to personnel. This is based on the idea that concern for individuals and relationships is a worthy end in itself, and in addition, it will produce the best overall results in productivity.

Another interesting difference in leadership styles is *functional* versus *formal*. Functional leadership depends greatly on highly workable relationships between the leader and others in the organization, which earn cooperation and support for the leader. By this method, the functional leader's authority is reinforced by the members of the organization. In contrast, the formal leader claims the authority that comes with the position he holds, and utilizes the authority in a structured manner to enforce rules and policies. His formal authority enables him to have things done his way because "the boss says so."

LEADERSHIP MODELS

The process of reducing complex human behaviors into "leadership models" results in a substantial loss of individual detail. No person exactly fits any leadership stereotype, yet a description of leadership models provides guidelines by which one can analyze and understand his own leadership behavior. Although every leader is in some degree a prisoner of his personal heritage, few are so constrained that new alternatives are entirely closed to them. The particular models discussed here are *climbers, conservers, zealots, advocates, statesmen, philosophic leaders, experts, innovators, symbolic models, charismatic leaders, reformers,* and *administrators.* The basic characteristics of these models have been identified and explained in the literature on leadership.[2,5,7,11]

Climbers, as the name implies, are self-propelled in their quest for improved status. They are energetic in seeking out avenues of personal progress and self-aggrandizement. They tend toward empire building. When a frontal assault is blocked, the climber will likely regroup and then try to move in a different direction to increase his sphere of influence and recognition. Climbers tend to be abrasive to others, because of their aggressive approach. Many climbers, however, are effective leaders because they are "doers" who efficiently attack the situation.

Conservers are almost exact opposites of climbers. They tend to maintain the status quo. Conservers resist and even resent change, since it has an unsettling effect on well structured procedures and relationships. Conservers are more interested in security and stability than power and progress. They want to trim their management unit to a simplified, clear-cut package and then hold it intact. They prefer organizations that rely extensively on formal regulations and protocol.

Zealots have visions of greatness both for themselves and their programs, and they manifest an evangelistic zeal for the improvement of the organization—as they see it. They are generally aggressive, determined, and hard-driving. Unlike climbers, zealots have the interest of the organization primarily at heart. Unlike conservers, they are impatient and want to improve and innovate. The aggressiveness of zealots sometimes irritates people who do not share their visions. Opposition, however, means relatively little to zealots, who are more noted for aggressiveness than human relations. They are excellent instruments for stirring up an apathetic organization or getting a new one off the launching pad. They make better task force leaders than overall administrators, because they place their "sacred objectives" first and foremost, often to the neglect of far-reaching and more important goals.

Advocates are concerned with improvement of the organization, especially the part they represent. They are tigers at fighting for their personnel and programs. Unlike zealots, who are basically loners, advocates are usually responsive to the ideas and influences of their superiors, peers and subordinates. Unlike climbers, who are ever self-serving, advocates will at times promote programs that do not benefit them personally, but have long-term favorable implications for the organization. Whereas zealots tend to take on all adversities, advocates usually engage in conflict only if supported by their colleagues. Externally, they defend their group or department in a partisan manner. Internally, they tend to be fair and impartial.

Statesmen are found in practically every organization. They have a strong inclination to intercede in conflict and politics, and they try to stand above parochial interests. They seek to reconcile conflicts and disagreements by pointing to the overall objectives or mission of the organization, or by emphasizing the fair and equitable side of the situation. Statesmen who are located in the rank and file of the employees perceive themselves as spokesman for the group, usually in carrying messages to or negotiating with the management. Statesmen who are in administrative positions perceive themselves as spokesmen for the organization.

Experts are people who are recognized for their specialized knowledge. People look to them for expert opinion and professional guidance. What they say as teachers, lecturers, or writers takes on unusual significance. Recognition as an expert increases a person's influence in almost every respect. Each professional field has its own group of experts who exert a strong influence within the profession and beyond it. Each organization also has individuals who are more or less recognized as experts and whose influence is felt accordingly.

Philosophical leaders place emphasis on philosophic ideas and ideals. Leaders of this kind can have significant influence on both goals and program results. Here again, each professional field has its own philosophic experts, and each organization has personnel who exercise this kind of leadership.

Innovators have the ability to envision or develop better methods, techniques, and procedures. Some innovators are energetic doers who can bring about positive changes. Their approach is to search out or create better methods or products and apply them. Innovative leadership is an important characteristic among both teachers and school administrators. An adequate amount of it can make the difference between the educational program being alive and interesting or dormant and drab.

Agitators and reformers want people to turn against the present system or methods and either accept the proposed reform or search out or create a new system. They are often associated with political, social, and religious unrest. They oppose the system, and their objective is to weaken it to the point that reformation will occur. Reform efforts are not limited to governments and churches. They go on often in less obvious settings, including the educational system. Even though reformation efforts are often distasteful, they sometimes produce constructive results, and there are cases when it seems that no other approach can bring about the desired changes.

Symbolic leadership has little application in the educational system; however, it is not totally lacking. Sometimes faculty members play a modified role of symbolic leadership, and occasionally a school board will have a member who is more symbolic than functional. International examples of symbolic leaders include the Queen of England and the Emperor of Japan (since World War II). Symbolic leaders derive their strength from tradition and association with the position. Whoever holds the position fills essentially the same leadership purpose regardless of the individual's characteristics or ability. Many believe that symbolic leadership provides a stabilizing influence.

In terms of leadership, charisma is defined as a "personal magic." The *charismatic* leader captures the imagination of his followers, inspiring their loyalty and enthusiasm. He leads and influences others by means of his personal appeal, not necessarily because of his expressed beliefs.

Administrative leadership is not a model in itself; it is a leadership function. Administrative leadership can have strong elements of any of the various models already discussed. The administrative leader provides a framework within which the other forms of leadership can be applied. He has a coordinating and supporting role in addition to implementing management procedures and furnishing direction toward the desired goals. The administrator is responsible for controlling the environment within which others work.

It is often assumed that those in administrative positions make the greatest leadership contributions, but this is not necessarily true. Some people actually have more positive influence from nonadministrative positions. This is not meant to minimize the importance of administrators. The point is to clarify that nonadministrative positions can often be just as important in terms of overall contribution. Some seek administrative assignments while others prefer to apply their influence in other ways.

IMPORTANT LEADERSHIP CHARACTERISTICS

Although the traits discussed here are certainly not all-inclusive, they stand among the more important leadership characteristics necessary to successful administrators. These traits apply regardless of the particular leadership model one might resemble.

Ability

Ability is the extent to which a person has developed himself within the limits of his capacity. A high level of ability implies that one learns quickly, applies himself effectively, and is generally well-informed. Even though we have inherent limits, our development within these broad limits is fundamental to success. Few of us come close to approaching our capacities. Usually, those who are eventually selected to fill important positions have worked hard to develop themselves through education and practical experience.

Confidence

With the right combination of talent and preparation, a person can consistently experience success, which develops awareness that he can perform well. With this awareness comes increased confidence, and this in turn, motivates a person to tackle larger and more significant tasks. The development of confidence at each new level helps to form a base for another step up the leadership ladder. Others in an organization recognize and appreciate well-founded confidence. This makes them feel more comfortable about the person in the leadership role. Conversely, when one loses confidence or displays false confidence, colleagues' faith and support usually falter.

Ambition

A key element in successful leadership is ambition, a trait that includes vitality, aggressiveness, and drive. The word ambition is used here in a positive context. It is not to be confused with false ambition or ambition with ulterior motives. The drive to work extra hours, indulge in difficult tasks, identify and solve problems, and consistently strive for better methods and more productivity, are marks of an ambitious person. Ambition demonstrated in these ways is vital to the success of an organization. It is certainly an important element in leadership, and it can contribute to one's opportunities for advancement.

Willingness to Risk Failure

The constant talk about job security and pension benefits among many people leads one to believe that they are more concerned with security than opportunity. As one person stated, "many people seem more afraid of life than of death." A leader must believe in himself and his ability and be willing to run reasonable risks in order to move things along in the proper direction and with the proper pace. An administrator who is self-protective and unwilling to accept calculated risks lacks the "crisp" approach that most people appreciate in an administrator. On the other hand, foolhardiness, reckless decision making, and irresponsible procedures are unacceptable. The appropriate balance is needed between risk-taking and a fair chance for success. If those in leadership positions become too cautious, the organization will go flat. Conversely, if they take unintelligent risks, the consequences can be disastrous.

One of the most frequent risks by an administrator is possible loss of favor among his colleagues when he makes a decision that is right but unpopular. Fortunately, "right decisions" usually become popular, if the reasons behind the decisions are understood. At any rate, if a leader has to choose between what is right and what is popular, he ought to have the courage to choose what is right.

Another form of risk is speaking out forthrightly on issues. Truth and honesty are undermined by falsehoods, and sometimes, by silence. As Emerson said, "All that is necessary for evil to prevail is for good people to remain silent."

Desire to Lead

Unless a person wants to be a leader, he likely will not be one. This is not to imply that desire alone will make an effective leader, but without it, a person is apt to lack the necessary persistence.

An athlete could never run a 4-minute mile without a strong desire. A sales manager cannot inspire his employees to surpass last year's record unless he has a strong will to attain that goal. A school administrator cannot influence teachers and students to do better unless he feels compelled in that direction. Every potential leader must want to succeed as a leader. Consistent desire for success is fundamental.

Integrity

Integrity is a complex concept and, therefore, difficult to evaluate. The superficial aspects of integrity are easy to appraise, but integrity in the deeper sense reaches far into a person's sense of values and relates to numerous other aspects of life: how he deals with his fellow beings, his attitude and conduct on the job, fairness with his employer, honesty as a neighbor, friend and family member, and finally, integrity with himself. True integrity, in the full sense, is a deep-rooted characteristic; a significant element of one's personality. It is basic to one's fitness as an educational leader.

Additional Characteristics

Following are additional characteristics that are important in educational leaders. Each administrator ought to try to cultivate and apply these traits.
1. A cooperative attitude and the ability to create congenial relationships.
2. A sincere interest in human service and in the positive development of individuals and of society as a whole.
3. Personality traits that are appealing to other people, along with strong character traits induce respect.
4. A strong sense of personal responsibility and high moral standards in all areas of human relationships.
5. A keen insight into the kinds of educational opportunities that people need in order to achieve success, enrichment, and fulfillment.
6. The ability to work effectively with people of various ages, beliefs, and backgrounds, without interference because of race, sex, religion, or other differences.
7. The specific knowledge, skills, and insights necessary to administer the particular specialized area of education.
8. A basic conviction that all human being have worth and dignity, and a determination to help them improve the quality of their lives.
9. The ability to think clearly and logically, to understand and analyze problem situations and to arrive at intelligent conclusions.
10. Skill in communicating effectively with others, both orally and in writing.

11. Such personal qualities as warmth, patience, empathy for the needs and feelings of others and a sense of humor, all of which contribute to the ability to get along.
12. Emotional and psychologic maturity. The successful leader should understand himself and others, be free from irrational prejudice, and be able to manage disagreement and opposition constructively.
13. The ability to be a self-starter: be able to clearly identify goals and move directly and forcefully toward them.
14. Integrity, honesty, and loyalty to the organization and to its goals and philosophy.
15. The ability to make difficult decisions without stalling or equivocating and then stand by them.
16. To be both visionary and practical; have high goals and a clear vision of what might be possible in the future while at the same time, maintaining a realistic sense of practical problems that must be overcome.
17. Flexibility in the sense of growing and changing with time, rather than clinging to outmoded views, attitudes, and practices.
18. A point of view that emphasizes cooperation and mutual support rather than competition and jealousy.

BIBLIOGRAPHY

1. Baldridge, J.V.: Policy Making and Effective Leadership, 1st Ed. San Francisco, Josey-Bass Publishers, 1978.

2. Banovetz, J.M.: Leadership Styles and Strategies, *In* Managing the Modern City. Washington, D.C., International City Management Association, pp. 109, 118-121.

3. Brown, D.G.: Leadership Vitality: A Workbook for Academic Administrators. Washington, D.C., American Council on Education, 1979.

4. Cronin, J.M., and Pancrazio, S.B.: Women as educational leaders. Phi Delta Kappan 60:583, 1979.

5. Gilligan, A.: Relationship between interactive style and effective leadership. Phi Delta Kappan, 61:567, 1980.

6. Hart, L.B.: Moving Up! Women and Leadership, New York, AMACOM, 1980.

7. Hodges, R.M.: Social context of leader-subordinate relations; an investigation of the effects of group cohesiveness. J App Psych, 65:192, 1980.

8. Hollander, E.P.: Leadership Dynamics: A Practical Guide to Effective Relationships. New York, Free Press, 1978.

9. Kohn, M.: Dynamic Managing. Menlo Park, CA, Cummings Publishing Co., 1977, p. 356.

10. Mathews, W.C.: Leadership in sport, physical education, and athletics. Physical Educator, 37:106, 1980.

11. Levinson, H. and Lang, C.: Executive. Cambridge, MA, Harvard University Press, 1981.

12. Milner, K.E., and Tetu, R.G., Jr.: Leadership behavior, JOPER, 50:22, 1979.

13. Parker, B.: School managers need charisma. Education Digest, *45*:6, 1980.

14. Richards, M.D., and Greenlaw, P.S.: Management Decision Making, Homewood, IL, Richard D. Irwin, 1972, p. 166.

15. Sayles, L.R.: Leadership: What Effective Managers Really Do—And How They Do It. New York, McGraw Hill, 1979.

16. Scheidel, T.M., and Crowell, L.: Discussing and Deciding: A Deskbook for Group Leaders and Members. New York, Macmillan, 1979.

17. Snodgill, R.M.: Leadership, membership, and organization. Psychological Bulletin, *52*:4, 1978.

18. Spiva, U.V. (ed.): Leadership plus Administration in School Management: Selected Readings. Sherman Oaks, CA, Banner Books, 1978.

Part II
THE ART OF
ADMINISTERING

Chapter 4

WHAT AN
ADMINISTRATOR DOES

Just what is an administrator? In a general sense, he is a person who gets things done through other people. He is one who gives direction to the organization and to the utilization of its resources.

The term administrator is broad and can be used interchangeably with other terms. Whether an individual is labeled school principal, athletic director, police chief, hospital manager, or shop superintendent, he is an administrator. *Management* is the term often used in profit seeking organizations, whereas *administration* is the term usually used in education and other nonprofit programs.

In the broad sense, the administrator is responsible for providing effective and consistent leadership for those activities needed to reach the organization's goals. The functions the administrator performs to accomplish this can be grouped into the following categories: (1) planning, (2) organizing, (3) staffing, (4) directing, and (5) controlling.

PLANNING

The planning function involves establishing goals and arranging them in logical order from immediate to long-range. It includes deciding what to do, how to do it, when to do it, and who should do it. Planning provides the strategies to be followed to achieve goals. It is like a recipe for the cook or a road map for the motorist. It results in a mapped-out course of where to go and how to get there.

The importance of planning can be illustrated more clearly by analyzing profit organizations than educational institutions, because profit organizations have the dollar and cent standard with which to measure success, whereas the standards for measuring educational success are less objective and less precise. Thune and House found some phenomenal results when they analyzed planning as it occurred in 6 different industries and 36 different firms.[12] Their results seem to have highly useful implications for all kinds of organizations, including education. They compared companies that had formal planning approaches with companies that did not. They found the following to be true: (1) Firms that did formal planning were more successful than firms that planned informally. (2) Those companies that did formal planning performed more successfully after the formal planning approach was instituted. (3) On the average, sales increased by 38%, earnings per share rose 64%, and stock prices rose 36% within 2 years after formal planning began.

Planning should accomplish two broad objectives:

1. Because it allows rationality and order within an organization, planning should enable the administrator to foresee and control situations more effectively.
2. It should help an administrator shape the future of the organization.

A well-managed educational environment has order, although it is not perfect order by any means. This type of management is influenced by the past, as well as by present trends and predictions for the future. If historical patterns were repeated exactly, then planning would be easy. But since this is not the case, the administrator needs the benefit of all the information he can acquire to aid in planning.

The Time Factor

One common element of all forms of planning is the time factor. Planning involves establishing goals to be achieved within a certain time and translated into specific, measurable outcomes. Intermediate targets should be defined to serve as indicators that orderly progress toward the goals is taking place within the desired time schedule.

A clearly defined plan results in a commitment to a specific course. It is important that the plan cover a long enough period to allow the commitment to be fulfilled.

Flexibility, however, is crucial in planning, since planning deals with the future, and the future is not perfectly predictable. Sometimes, it becomes necessary to revise the plan before the final goals can be reached. It would be foolish to continue working with an obsolete plan; therefore, periodic review of the plan and timely updating is of utmost importance.

Management by Objective

Although it is correct to say that management by objective (MBO) combines selected aspects of all functional areas in administration, it is more meaningful to view it as a philosophy of administration—a way of operating an organization. Setting appropriate and meaningful objectives is of crucial importance in the MBO process. It involves mutual formulation of objectives by administrators at different levels, mutual evaluation of performance toward the objectives, and determining the reasons for success or failure.

At regular intervals, the administrator and his co-workers participate in deciding what results are to be achieved and what will constitute acceptable performance. The administrator then delegates responsibilities to his subordinates, who must take the appropriate initiative at their levels to achieve the results agreed upon. It is not that the chief administrator does not help—he is required by his agreement to supply certain kinds of assistance—but the subordinates take the main responsibility for what they have agreed to do. Periodically, program results are jointly measured and compared with the objectives.

Several potentially significant benefits can be derived from using the MBO approach. It usually insures that the motivation and sense of accomplishment of people up and down the administrative line remains high because each person participates in determining the goals and how to achieve them. This enhances each one's self-esteem and this is no small consideration. Furthermore, MBO enables management personnel at the different levels to understand the purposes of the organization and the plan. Also, the MBO approach focuses the thoughts and efforts of people on results instead of activities.

MBO is a subtle approach to helping people arrange and perform their activities in accordance with the plan. It discourages impressions among employees that all that is important is reporting on time and appearing active. A further advantage of MBO is that it enables an administrator to evaluate subordinates on the basis of measurable results which relate to the objectives. Also, focusing on results makes decisions about salary and promotions more objective.

Regardless of the techniques employed, planning is not foolproof, and sometimes good plans go awry. With adequate planning , however, an organization can better control its own destiny instead of being controlled by random events. Planning gives structure to the organization's program and the activities of the individual employees. A realistic plan that is well conceived and properly managed will usually be achieved on a reasonable time schedule.

ORGANIZING

Organizing involves identifying the responsibilities to be performed, grouping the responsibilities into departments or divisions, and specifying organizational relationships. The purpose is to achieve a coordinated effort by the total organization. The primary focus is on definition of responsibilities and relationships. Among key questions are the following: (1) How many different tasks make up a particular job? (2) Which particular tasks fit together logically into one position? (3) Which job positions fit together logically to form a division or department? (4) How do the divisions and departments fit together to form the total organization?

In education, jobs and responsibilities are almost always grouped into divisions or departments according to specialty. Sometimes, however, a faculty member's specialty laps over two or more departments, thus causing him to have a split assignment. Also, some staff positions, such as secretaries or financial managers, do not relate to a particular educational discipline, so their placement in the organization is determined by different criteria.

Span of Control

One important question in organizing is how many employees should report directly to the particular administrator. Obviously, there is a limit to the number of persons an individual can supervise or work with effectively. For years, management theorists and practitioners have analyzed this problem. Common sense indicates that the optimum span of control is contingent on the particular administrator, the subordinates, and the work being performed, and not on some magic number. The amount of time the administrator has for supervising employees is one important consideration. If he is required to perform a series of duties that takes time away from his supervisory function, the span of control must be smaller. Other important factors include (1) the abilities of both the administrator and the subordinates, (2) the degree of coordination the particular kind of work requires, and (3) the frequency of new problems that arise within the administrator's realm and the potential difficulty of those problems. The effective span of control then, varies with the situation. A common fault among administrators is to try to cover a span that is too broad. When this happens, the administrator can improve his effectiveness by narrowing his span, thus relinquishing some of the control to others in the organization.

Authority and Responsibility

Authority can be defined as the right to decide or to act within specific limits. From an administrative point of view, this includes the right to control people and situations and to allocate the organization's resources toward accomplishment of the objectives.

In an educational or business organization, the governing board represents the owners. They grant authority to the chief executive, who in turn, delegates authority to others. When authority is delegated, an obligation is placed on the recipient to exercise it properly. He becomes obligated to perform certain actions and to see that others perform at an acceptable level.

Delegating authority to a subordinate does not relieve the administrator of overall accountability. He is still responsible for accomplishing the objectives of the organization and accounting for the use of its resources.

Centralization versus Decentralization

As an organization grows it becomes increasingly difficult for one person to manage everything. Therefore, it becomes necessary to rely increasingly on subordinate administrators. Eventually, the administrator has to choose between: (1) losing command by trying to directly control too much (refusing to delegate) or (2) retaining orderly control by delegating authority and responsibilities within the organization (decentralization). If a head football coach tries to coordinate all phases of the game, he does a mediocre job at best in all the different areas. A solution is to delegate the defensive responsibilities to the best qualified assistant and so forth. Through delegation the coach retains orderly control, in a general sense, over the various aspects of the program, but he gives up direct involvement in all of the decision making.

Centralization and decentralization can be considered the extreme ends on a continuum with numerous intermediate points. Effective decentralization is dependent on: (1) the ability of the top administrator to delegate authority (and responsibility) to subordinates, and (2) the ability of the subordinates to accept and handle it well (Chapter 5 includes a further discussion of the delegation of authority).

STAFFING

An organization is composed of people carrying out specific responsibilities which lead toward set goals. Effective staffing means filling the jobs available with the right people. Personnel specialists can help in staffing by recruiting and screening people, but the ultimate responsibility for effective staffing rests with the administrator.

Position descriptions and specifications are essential in staffing. The descriptions detail the responsibilities associated with the various positions, and the specifications describe the personal qualifications required. Normally, the statement of qualifications includes the required educational level, professional experience, personality characteristics, rank, salary, and tenure status. Obviously, some positions are easier to write descriptions and specifications for than others, but regardless of the position, the best job description that can be prepared will be more useful than no description at all. Once it is clear what the job includes, it is easier to take an effective approach toward finding the right person.

Two general sources of personnel may fill a particular position—personnel from within the organization and applicants from outside. Most administrators agree that promoing from within can be a positive morale factor. It seems both logical and fair that first consideration should be given to the organization's own people. However, sometimes problems or situations prevent this approach. For example, it is unwise to advance a person who is not well qualified. This can result either in low productivity or eventual failure for the individual. The result is undesirable for both the organization and the person. Also, promoting an unqualified employee can have a negative effect on morale. Furthermore, it is sometimes impossible to promote from within because of personality conflicts or jealousies.

The correct procedure is to attract the strongest applicants possible for a given position and then make an objective selection of the one that seems best prepared. If it turns out to be a stalemate between two applicants, and one is an employee of the organization, then why not promote from within.

Personnel Development

A related function of staffing is personnel development or in-service training. This is discussed in more detail in Chapter 7, but it should be pointed out here that continued improvement of employees is an important function for two reasons: (1) to help employees perform their present responsibilities more effectively, and (2) to better prepare them for promotion when the opportunity comes.

Personnel development relates to the important concept that "the best way to get rid of a poor teacher is to make him into a good one." Although this is idealistic, it should be the first consideration and should receive an honest effort.

The personnel development program should be evaluated periodically to determine whether it is meeting the needs of the organization. Simply having development programs provides no guarantee of effectiveness, and the time and cost involved in such programs can be substantial. The results of personnel development activities should be reflected in measurable performance, both of the individuals and the organization.

An organization can offer the opportunities and provide the appropriate climate for personnel development, but the individuals must seize these opportunities and turn them into the desired results. This requires employee motivation, and in the absence of adequate motivation, development activities will be unsuccessful.

DIRECTING

Directing involves motivating and leading employees in such a way that the comprehensive goals of the organization can be achieved.

People are usually rational, consistent, and predictable. But, occasionally, their behavior becomes irrational and unpredictable. An effective administrator understands these characteristics, and within this difficult framework, he is able to give guidance and generate motivation toward effective work.

Basic Human Needs

The literature on this subject indicates that social psychologists today generally agree with the hierarchy of needs presented many years ago by A.H. Maslow in one of the classic articles on the needs of employees.[10] Maslow included five needs in hierarchial order: physiologic requirements, safety and security, concern and affection, esteem, and self-actualization. It is believed that a person usually tries to satisfy these needs in order of their ranking, and does not emphasize satisfying a higher need before the lower needs have been reasonably fulfilled. Thus, a person first acts toward physiologic needs, and then he focuses on safety needs, and so on. Each basic need in the hierarchy has several important aspects, and an administrator's understanding of these needs and their effects on behavior is important.

Physiologic needs pertain to the maintenance of the body; examples are food, drink, shelter, and relief from discomfort.

Safety and security needs refer to one's desire for freedom from threatening circumstances. The desire for safety and security encompasses both economic and psychologic aspects. People are especially concerned about such things as continued employment and a flow of adequate income. They also want to be free of potential expenses associated with long-term illness and property losses. Much of the social legislation and employee benefits of recent decades can be traced to the safety and security needs of people: social security, unemployment insurance, health and accident insurance, retirement benefits, and the like.

Concern and affection needs encompass the desire for friendship, compassion, and interactions with others. Man is a social being who is highly desirous of associations with others and feelings of belonging. These needs are met on the job to some extent through belonging to an organization and the personal interactions that take place there.

Esteem needs encompass self-esteem and the esteem of others. Every individual wants to feel self-worth and self-respect, while also having the respect of others in his surroundings. This results in desires for positions and titles and feelings of achievement and approval. Esteem needs also comprise desires for prestige and recognition. The forms these needs take vary considerably among individuals.

Self-actualization needs are the desires one has for fulfillment through the best use of abilities and development of potential. These needs are often less obvious than the other needs, and many people have not moved far towards fulfilling them. If each person's potential could be fully expressed, everyone would have a greatly enhanced quality of life.

It is obviously important for an administrator to be alert to the different kinds of needs that every individual feels and to help fulfill these needs to the extent that is possible on the job. This is a complex and important part of the *directing function* and it is an aspect of management toward which some administrators are insensitive.

The two *lower order needs*—physiologic and safety and security—tend to be fixed or finite, and they are satisfied primarily through economic endeavors. One can actually overindulge in fulfillment of the physiologic needs by too much food or over emphasis on physical comforts. This also appears to be possible with safety and security needs. One can become so concerned about security that he pays too little attention to other important matters. Furthermore, a person can become so safe or feel so secure that he becomes apathetic. Also, when too much security is provided individuals become excessively dependent. The needs for concern and affection, esteem and self-actualization, are not fixed or finite. As one increases fulfillment of these needs, they tend to enlarge or shift upward. Thus, the higher order needs are never fully satisfied.

The employment relationship and the income one earns are used largely to obtain what is necessary to satisfy physiologic and security needs. A relationship can also exist between employment conditions and the satisfaction of higher order needs. People may, for example, use their earnings and free time to participate in private clubs, take on hobbies, buy goods and services for their own satisfaction, further their education, seek positions of status and leadership in private or voluntary organizations, serve society through charitable endeavors, and improve their personal skills and artistic abilities. The higher order needs, however, generally are satisfied by the meanings the individual attaches to personal experiences. They are satisfied in accordance with how a person perceives himself, and his role in life.

Whenever people work together, informal groups develop. The members of these groups are frequently in contact with each other in connection with their work: during lunch, at breaks, before and after work, and off the job at social gatherings. Being part of the group can provide satisfaction and fill certain needs. The group serves as a medium for conversation, socializing, and moral support. Certainly, there is some degree of psychologic security in belonging to such groups. Self-actualization of employees may be enhanced by belonging to the group, depending on the skills, abilities, and desires of the individuals and how well the group can provide avenues for developing these.

It is helpful for an administrator to know as much as possible about the traits of the individual employees with whom he works. With this kind of information and insight, the administrator is better prepared to work effectively with and for the employees in helping to fulfill their needs while working toward accomplishing the goals of the organization. (Related information is contained in Chapter 8, which deals with personnel management, and in the section on motivation in Chapter 6.)

People Emphasis versus Production Emphasis

One of the crucial issues in management is the question of a correct balance in terms of the emphasis on people as opposed to emphasis on production. Some would argue that such a choice is unnecessary because it doesn't have to be one or the other, the emphasis can be placed on both. It is a fact, however, that different administrators seem oriented more in one direction than the other, and circumstances sometimes influence the balance of emphasis. By its very nature, education is people-oriented. Education, however, also has a product (educational results) that is at the focus of the total educational effort. To help in one's analysis of where to place the emphasis, a two-dimensional grid appears in Figure 4-1. Concern for people is represented on the horizontal axis, and concern for production on the vertical axis. Several leadership styles can be identified on the grid. Ideally, it should be the goal of the administrator to achieve style 5-5.

(1-1) Represents a weak administrative leader who shows little concern for either people or production.

Figure 4-1. An example of a two-dimensional grid, pertaining to the relative administrative emphasis on people and production.

(5-1) Represents a production-oriented leader who places high priority on production with little consideration for human factors.

(1-5) Represents a people-oriented leader who is concerned primarily with human factors and gives little emphasis to production.

(3-3) Represents a balanced leader who gives about average attention to both people and production.

(5-5) Represents an ideal administrative leader who shows a high level of concern for both people and production.

CONTROLLING

If we take the adage "a chain is no stronger than its weakest link," the main problem associated with the control function is that management does not always know in advance which link of the operation is the weakest or when it will break. Therefore, a control system must be formulated that will detect potential or actual deviations from the organization's plan, and do so early enough to prevent setbacks. The control function is essentially a monitoring process for the purpose of identifying and handling weaknesses and potential problems. It might also be viewed as an ongoing process of evaluation, involving (1) defining standards, (2) measuring actual results against the standards, and (3) taking appropriate actions to prevent problems and overcome weaknesses.

Measuring Performance

Established standards, no matter how well conceived, are useless unless information on actual performance is obtained, compared with the standards and results, and communicated to those in positions to act. Measurement is essential if the organization is to know whether its work is proceeding according to plan. With this in mind, two considerations stand out: how to measure and when to measure.

The question of how to measure has many answers, depending on the particular nature of the organization. Among the more widely used methods are personal observation, written and oral reports, statistical data, and personal conferences. All of these methods have the same general goal, that is, to supply the administrator with reliable feedback. Each method has its own strengths and weaknesses, so an administrator should not depend on information from any one source. Rather, he should combine information from all of the reliable sources and methods available.

The question of when to measure has no clear-cut answer. The fact is that measurement in the form of observation and informal conversation goes on continuously, whereas the more formal methods occur only when planned, and they can happen as often or as seldom as the situation warrants.

At certain strategic control points, special consideration is given to the effectiveness of the organization and its various processes and personnel. For example, at the end of each school year and each semester or term, certain aspects are critically evaluated to determine what changes would be beneficial. Another kind of strategic control point is at the time a position becomes vacant. It is then convenient to evaluate the effectiveness with which the job has been performed, the strengths and weaknesses of the one who vacated the position, whether the position should continue, whether the job description should be altered, and exactly what qualifications should be required of the one who will assume the position. Major financial and narrative reports also provide strategic opportunities for evaluation. (Related information on this topic is contained in Chapter 18, which pertains to evaluation methods.)

Taking Corrective Action

Although measuring and evaluating can focus attention on deviations from accepted procedures and standards of performance, they are only abstracts without the practical next step—appropriate corrective action. In some cases, only minor adjustments are needed, but occasionally, evaluation results show a need for major changes. Thus, in one case corrective action might involve a minor shift of resources or a realignment of personnel so that the organization can regain its direction, some other case might call for a major reformulation of plans and an adjustment of goals.

Behavior Aspects of Control

The objective of control is to get people to work more effectively toward the organizational goals, and especially to identify and eliminate weaknesses in that process. The administrator, in exercising the control function, must consider how those who are affected by it will react.

Control measures are typically unpopular, especially among those being controlled. Much of people's daily lives is regimented by cultural norms, religious values, safety regulations, and family roles, to name just some of the restraining influences. The thought of additional controls can be distasteful, so the administrator must be prepared to deal effectively with negative responses.

A negative reaction can often be lessened, if not reversed, if the manager is careful about interpreting and implementing control measures. Important in this respect, are the clear interpretation of organizational goals and the education of employees about the goals and about the methods necessary to achieve them. Employees should understand that the goals and the processes used to achieve them make employment possible. If the goals are vague or inapplicable, it will be difficult for employees to generate enthusiasm toward them. It is important for employees to be able to see where their work contributes to the goals of the organization. This will help each one to know that measuring his or her performance is legitimate and necessary. Also, employees will better understand the reasons for adjustments when the evaluation results show a need for corrective action.

The administrator should encourage employees to participate in setting performance standards that are both challenging and obtainable. Management by objective (MBO), discussed previously, is one example of participation by employees in setting goals and evaluating progress. The value of this cannot be overemphasized because it is almost a certain guarantee of personal committment. Standards that are too low fail to motivate employees toward achievement, whereas standards that seem unobtainable or too remote fail to stir enthusiasm and are likely to cause disinterest and discouragement. If the standards are to induce positive results, they must be challenging, realistic, obtainable, and mutually agreed upon.

BIBLIOGRAPHY

1. American Management Association: Workshop Notes on Management Responsibilities and Techniques. New York, NY, 1981.

2. Barnett, M.L.: The administrator as a helper. JOPER, 50(1):42, 1979.

3. Bennis, W.: Organization Development: Its Nature, Origin, and Prospects, 2nd Ed. Reading, Mass., Addison-Wesley, 1977.

4. Blake, R., and Mouton, J.: Corporate Excellence Through GMD Organization Development, 2nd Ed. Houston, Gulf, 1980.

5. Drucker, P.F.: Management, 2nd Ed. New York, Harper and Row, 1981.

6. Ehrle, E.B.: Observations on the nature of deaning. JOPER, *50*(1):44, 1979.

7. Hall, J.: What makes a manager good, bad, or average? Psychology Today, *10*:52, 1976.

8. Haynes, W.W., Massie, J.L., and Wallace, M.J., Jr.: Management: Analysis, Concepts, and Cases, 4th Ed. Englewood Cliffs, NJ: Prentice-Hall, 1981.

9. Herzberg, F., Mausner, B., and Snyderman, B.: The Motivation to Work. New York, John Wiley and Sons, 1959.

10. Maslow, A.H.: The theory of human motivation. Psychological Review, *50*(4):370, 1943.

11. Scott, P.: The new administrator. JOPER, *50*:40, 1979.

12. Thune, S., and House, R.: Where long range planning pays off. Business Horizons *13*:81, 1970.

13. Ziegler, E.F.: The case for management theory and practice. JOPER, *50*:36, 1979.

Chapter 5

MANAGING TIME AND MAKING DECISIONS

Studies show that many administrators are plagued by the frustrating condition of more work to do and more people to see than they can satisfactorily handle. Although many administrators work longer hours than other employees and have above average energy and powers of concentration, they often feel the anxiety of unfinished tasks and unsolved problems. Underlying this is the concern that unfinished administrative work means delayed decisions and disrupted productivity of others in the organization.

TIME MANAGEMENT

Some outstanding examples show that many administrators in demanding positions are able to organize their work in a way that leaves time for solid thinking about basic problems and for outside interests that make for a well-rounded life. Some, however, find it necessary to carry a problem-packed briefcase whenever they leave the office. An administrator who consistently faces this situation ought to consider whether the problem is *real* or only a symptom of something more basic. The basic problem might be *improper time management*.

Unfortunately, the busier a person becomes, the less time he has to analyze his procedures and to plan better. Some administrators allow themselves to get into a situation of always scrambling to keep from being overwhelmed by the mounting tasks of the job. Such a person, more than anyone else, needs sufficient time to identify his weaknesses, and improve his administrative procedures.

Where Does The Time Go?

Budgeting time, like money, is an ongoing challenge, and the allocation should be in accordance with the priorities of one's responsibilities. There is an interesting example of a group of educational administrators who met to analyze their problems associated with time. They decided that each one should prepare a statement of the approximate number of days per year spent with each major area of responsibility. When they had finished, the total some of them came up with exceeded the number of days in the year. One administrator counted 381 days. The group drew three conclusions: (1) They thought they were spending more time on certain responsibilities than was actually being spent. (2) They had failed to delegate enough of their responsibilities to subordinates. (3) They were spending too much time on certain unimportant aspects of administrative work; i.e., their use of time was not in accordance with the real priorities. Reportedly, every one of the administrators went home and immediately delegated certain responsibilities, and then realigned the allocation of time to better fit their priorities.[1]

Periodically, every administrator ought to go through this kind of analysis. It is an exercise that can be done independently or as a member of a group as in the preceding example.

Another valuable exercise is to keep a detailed record for a week of exactly how your time is spent. This can be a real eye opener. Most people have analyzed their financial expenditures by keeping a record of everything that is spent, and many have improved their personal budgeting by this method. It is equally possible to improve the management of time by the same method.

Consider the example of one administrator who had a number of complaints from department heads about understaffing and heavy work loads and about the consequent lack of time for planning and supervision. One morning, each department head was handed a request to keep track on an hour-by-hour basis of how each day was spent, and then write an evaluation at the end of the day of how well the time was used and where improvements could be made. It was requested that each member of the department be required to follow the same procedure. After the evaluations had been completed, there were no more requests for additional staff. Instead, a general tightening up resulted, and the level of production increased. Figure 5-1 provides a sample form for recording and analyzing how a person spends his time.

When the job pressures mount, the inclination of the conscientious person is to press harder and harder to get things done. This process can lead to a vicious circle which results in reduced time for planning. The consequent feelings of frustration and fatigue make working time less and less efficient. If you find yourself in this circumstance, take time at once to analyze your situation in a calm and collected manner. Arrive at a sensible plan for improvement, then apply the solution with confidence and composure.

Maldistribution of Attention. Some administrators spend a disproportionate amount of time on relatively unimportant matters. This is known as the "maldistribution practice." There is a tendency to give attention to matters that are simple and uncomplicated, because with such matters success is easy and immediate. Obviously, a busy administrator cannot afford too much time dealing with $100 matters if $1,000 matters are being neglected.

NAME _____ DATE _____

Hour	Description of Time Use
8:00	_____
9:00	_____
10:00	_____
11:00	_____
12:00	_____
1:00	_____
2:00	_____
3:00	_____
4:00	_____
5:00	_____
Evening	_____

Summary and Analysis of How Time was Used (Hours spent)

Meetings _____

Telephone _____

Paper work (routine) _____

Special problems _____

Reports _____

Teaching _____

Research _____

Luncheons and social _____

Other _____

Figure 5-1. Example of a time analysis form.

It is true that routine items such as parking privileges, janitorial services, and food dispensers must receive attention by someone. But, these matters should be kept in proper perspective. They must not infringe too much on the attention needed for the main objectives of the organization. Maldistribution of administrative time and energy is a potential weakness that needs to be constantly monitored. It involves the challenge of keeping first things first.

Inability to Discriminate. The term discrimination usually carries a negative connotation, but it also has a positive aspect. A person in an administrative position must be highly discriminating relative to (1) the number of people and the particular ones that he permits to use up his time in conferences, interviews, and telephone conversations; (2) the particular reports, surveys, and other written material that he spends time on; and (3) the parts of the administrative job he handles directly as opposed to those responsibilities he delegates. Unfortunately, many administrators are unable or unwilling to discriminate clearly between the more important and the less important matters to become involved with.

Long Conversations. Some people who aspire to administrative work are unsuccessful because they lack the ability to keep routine conversations short and to the point. Most conversations involving the administrator must be adequately thorough, yet relatively short. When the important business has been covered, the conversation should end. Another desirable element of conversation is one's ability to bring up the important points and lead the discussion to a conclusion without wasting time, and yet not cause the conversation to seem rushed. Furthermore, it is important for the administrator to play his proper role in each conversation and permit other people to do the same. One-way conversations are usually uninteresting and often unproductive; each conversation should result in an adequate exchange among those involved. The administrator is usually the one expected to give direction to the conversation and to keep it on track. Remember that a conversation always involves at least one other person, sometimes more. The effective use of the other person's time as well as your own is also an important consideration.

Paper Handling. A certain amount of paper work is associated with administration, but it can easily be carried too far. For example, it is not necessary to make and keep on file a copy of every routine written communication. Neither is it usually desirable for two or more officers in the same organization to file the same kind of information. Furthermore, there is no need to put every kind of communication in written form. In short, an organization can easily become over burdened with too much handling and filing of paperwork. Many highly successful administrators "travel light" in this regard. The key is the ability to discriminate between what is necessary and what is not in terms of producing, handling, and filing written material.

Another important aspect of paperwork is expediency. An efficient administrator will have a consistent and highly structured approach to handling papers. The ideal is to handle each paper only once, but of course, this is not always possible. When you look at a particular written correspondence for the first time try to decide what to do with it. Sometimes the decision is easy—discard it. In other cases it requires no action, but should go to the secretary for filing. Perhaps a telephoned response should be made immediately or maybe a quickly dictated reply would be better. Some papers should be passed on immediately to others in the organization, and a few papers require delayed attention—tomorrow, next week, or next month.

Some administrators can be labeled one-time handlers, some two-time handlers, and some multihandlers of paperwork. If you are a multihandler you need to streamline your approach. Increased expediency of handling paperwork should be one of your immediate objectives.

Excessive Travel. Travel falls into two general categories: daily *travel within the vicinity* of your work, and *out of town trips.* Some people spend 2 to 3 hours per day traveling to and from work and running errands. If you are one of these people, you need to consider what you could accomplish on the job with a portion of this time, and what changes could be made that would help you capture some of it. Often, not much can be done about commuting time unless you are willing to change the location of your residence or your work. Perhaps reducing unnecessary errands has more potential for saving time. Are you spending time delivering items that a secretary or other office employee could do? Or maybe your procrastination in handling matters on time requires too many hand deliveries that could be accomplished by mail if done a day earlier. Keep in mind that time spent traveling or running errands is time away from administrative duties.

Out of town travel has contributed to the downfall of many administrators. Some who enjoy business trips, use various excuses to go when the need is truly doubtful. Or if the need is there, perhaps another member of the staff could fulfill it as well or better than the chief administrator. A few administrators seem to believe that there is a direct relationship between time spent on business trips and job effectiveness. This is not consistently true.

Certainly, an administrator should not resist being away when there is a legitimate need to travel. If this were carried too far, he could easily lose touch with people and events with which he should maintain contact. But it is true that some administrators should carefully evaluate whether less travel and less days away from the office would improve overall effectiveness.

Some Time-Saving Ideas

You might find it useful to make copies of a form such as the one shown in Figure 5-1 on which to *record your activities* of the day and the amount of time involved in each one. Evaluate the results at the end of each day and each week. Be analytic about how you could eliminate certain time-consuming activities, and how you could improve the efficiency of your procedures. At the end of the year, it is valuable to reflect on the amount of time you spent in different categories of your job and to determine whether all aspects were in proper balance. For example, how much time was absorbed in travel? How much was used up with luncheons, receptions, banquets, and other functions? How much time did you spend handling paperwork, preparing or reading reports, and sitting in meetings? How much time was used in solving personality conflicts and dealing with emergency problems that should have been avoided? Did you have adequate time for serious thought and planning and for your own preparation and improvement?

You will probably be surprised to learn how many time-consuming activities in your schedule are unproductive in terms of what really matters. In connection with the analysis of how your time is used, ask what are the things that take time and contribute little; and what would happen if these things were not done at all. Ask whether you are giving the right kind of time for the truly important things. One of the differences between ineffective and truly effective administrators is that the effective person knows the limitations of time. He does not believe that he has 24 hours in a day or even 8 hours. He knows that he has a very small amount of time beyond the basic requirements, and he knows that time is a peculiar resource which cannot be increased. He knows that the really important things he has to do take solid blocks of time, and if he does not give the right amount of time to them, his effectiveness will be greatly reduced. If there is one thing that can make an administrator more effective, it is knowing where his time goes, so that he can better control and direct it toward his truly important responsibilities.

Some administrators advocate the *open door policy*, which means that employees can come in without an appointment. It is true that such a policy can contribute to congenial relationships and a friendly atmosphere; but, in some cases, this is not the best way to improve accessibility to the administrator. Open doors often increase the wrong kind of communication—trivial and unproductive chatter. Interruptions are multiplied, and the administrator is frequently distracted from important matters. For administrators with demanding schedules, the open door is usually a poor policy. Controlled access through a congenial but discrete secretary is usually better.

The *10-minute head start* technique for effective time management is worth considering. This is how it works. Whenever you leave the office, time your schedule so that you can leave 10 minutes earlier than necessary. This will provide a time buffer to cover unforeseen delays or unexpected phone calls. The benefits are that (1) it helps guarantee your promptness, which will have a positive influence on the promptness of others, and (2) it removes excessive tension caused by last minute rushing. Furthermore, it sometimes results in a little "gliding" time, which can be used constructively for thinking about the next important activity.

In order to organize yourself and your work effectively, you must *apply the "talent for perspective"* about yourself and your job and about your co-workers and their jobs. What should your job really entail: what should it include and what should it not include? Perhaps it would be useful to restate the description of your position in terms of duties, responsibilities, authority, and accountability. Ask yourself what are the educational and experience requirements, and what is expected and needed by way of continued professional preparation? This kind of analysis will help clarify whether your job is really the same as the traditional description—the description that might be in the file or in the operational manual. Perhaps your perspective of the job is different than is seen by others in the organization. If so, these inconsistencies must be resolved.

Once your job is seen in perspective, no matter how pressed you have been for time, it is usually safe to say that, with reasonably good organization, adequate delegation, and good relationships, your work will be manageable without an impossible work load or an excessive time requirement. This is a logical assumption because, for most positions, a predecessor was able to handle the job and people in comparable positions are able to handle their jobs. It is safe to rely on the thesis that the problem of insufficient time usually lies within the person more than in the work situation. If the content of the job really is too much, it will become clear by means of perspective analysis, and this will help provide a basis for corrective action. On the other hand, if the job content is reasonable, then proper time management should serve as an effective solution to any time problems that you have.

CONTROLLING STRESS AND TENSION

Some administrators have oversized desks and stuffed briefcases; and they are sometimes thought of as ulcer-ridden bundles of complexities, obsessed with the idea of success and burdened with endless responsibilities. This picture is, of course, a grossly distorted version of an administrator. Yet, it cannot be denied that some administrators do feel the strain of their jobs and often suffer from tensions that rob them of both enjoyment and efficiency. (The problem of stress can also apply to teachers and athletic coaches.)

It is not possible to measure exactly the loss of efficiency emotional tension causes, even though psychologists are able to point to a considerable body of evidence that shows that efficiency suffers when one works under too much stress. Excessive tension can cut drastically into work accomplishments, and in extreme cases, it can disable an administrator. Even a modest reduction in emotional stress can often produce a sharp upswing in imagination, foresight, and judgment, and this can add significantly to the effectiveness of the organization.

Some people are more susceptible to tension than are others. Some, in fact, generate their own private emergencies and remain more or less constantly on guard against their versions of disaster. This is a fatiguing approach to life, and such people do indeed find life an exhausting experience. Some of these people become administrators, and although they may be uncomfortable and perhaps unhappy, they are not always ineffective.

Knowing that too much tension can be destructive, what about too little tension? What happens to efficiency when people are too secure, too comfortable, and too complacent? Efficiency tends to decrease; people have to be motivated if they are to accomplish anything. As it happens, a sense of urgency and the pressures of disapproval or possible failure are pretty good motivators. Most people have to be at least a little bit apprehensive and keyed up to do their best work, and some are never so efficient as when they are half-scared. Emotional tension is not therefore, an altogether undesirable thing. Tension becomes harmful only when it exceeds a reasonable level of tolerance or when it persists too long.

Too much tension can waste one's time in several ways. It can throw judgment out of kilter, so that it takes longer to reach correct decisions; and it may indeed prevent a person from making a decision at all. It can narrow one's perspective to a highly personal viewpoint, and cause the objectives of the organization to become secondary or obscure. It can cause exaggeration of the importance of small problems at the expense of more important matters. It may cause an administrator to be unable to solve or lay aside the problems causing tension long enough to consider other items of importance. It can change a smooth, integrated thought process into a series of broken plays.

Sources of Tension

It is not likely that a person can alleviate tension unless the sources of it are identified and controlled. Following are possible causes of tension among administrators.[1]

1. *Inadequate command of the situation* can be both a cause and a result of tension. Tension can develop if a person senses that he is not holding things together, that problems are developing faster than they are being handled, and that he is gradually becoming more of a problem solver than a forthright leader.
2. *Pressures resulting from lack of delegation* can relate to the situation explained in Item I. If the administrator tries to give direct attention to too many responsibilities, it becomes impossible to cover them adequately. This can cause him to feel that the job is rolling over him.
3. *Waivering confidence* or distrust in one's own ability can cause tension to rise rapidly in pressure situations.
4. *Distrust of subordinates* can cause one to feel nervous about whether the responsibilities of subordinates are being done well.
5. *Insecurity* is a feeling that others in higher positions are not happy with your performance. This may be a product of imagination or caused by a lack of communication.
6. *A guilt feeling about authority.* Some administrators think they are not cut out to be separated from the rank and file, and they feel nervous about the authority and responsibilities they hold.
7. Other potential sources of tension are *problems at home, personal fi-*

nances, and *poor social relationships.* These can have negative influences on job effectiveness.

Controlling Tension

Unfortunately, the person who suffers from stress is in a weak position to control it. Once it develops, he is less able to think clearly, analyze objectively, or command the situation. A good solution is to remain highly sensitive to the development of tension and try to nip the problem early before it becomes hard to handle. A person's supervisor can often be helpful toward figuring out potential solutions, giving encouragement and building self-confidence.

Sometimes a good solution is to withdraw from the situation, separate yourself from the location, and do something that is filled with diversion and enjoyment. This can cause the tension to subside and the mind to clear, and it can help one to see things in proper perspective.

Some people are able to reduce tension by simply adjusting their attitudes toward it. This can be done by taking firm mental command of oneself and mental command of the pressure-causing situation. It can have an immediate result of increased confidence and better control.

DELEGATING RESPONSIBILITIES

The opposite extremes of delegation are well illustrated by a classic story that has often been told about two military situations. The first relates to an officer candidate in the Corps of Engineers who relied extensively upon delegation. He was asked the best way to get a heavy powerline pole upright in a hole. The candidate's response was, "Sergeant, take six men and put that pole up." The story showing the opposite extreme involves a captain who complained that the major who was his superior officer never let him run his company (Company B). When the captain was promoted to major and took the place of his former boss, his first comment was, "From now on Company B will be run my way." Both of these stories make their point by over simplification, because in between the two extremes lies a full range of delegation practices. Each administrator must decide whether he is going to function in the middle ground of delegation or in one of the extremes.

When a person advances up the managerial ladder, he has a tendency to take along portions of the old job. This is illustrated clearly in the following example given by the American Management Association.[1] The chairman of a public transit authority had been elevated from a job where he was a hard-hitting front line administrator. When promoted, he took his old job upstairs with him, including three telephones, through which he could bark orders to numerous employees down the line. Many of his meetings were interrupted by subordinates who had to consult him frequently for solutions to problems. He lived his job around the clock and made colorful copy for the press by taking personal charge of traffic jams or mishaps. But, the long range program of the traffic authority suffered. What was actually a double job of chairman and superintendent, left too little time for reflection of policy decisions, for the fundamentals of statesman-like conduct, and appropriate planning and preparation for the future. This example shows the time-eating effects of poor delegation.

Researchers have found that, in many cases, decision making would be vastly improved if the top administrator made fewer decisions. Often, others have more time to give adequate consideration to the influencing circumstances, and they are sometimes better informed on the specifics that should affect the decisions.[2]

It is a fact that one who cannot delegate effectively is incapable of a high administrative position. This inability forces some people to remain in nonadministrative positions or in positions at lower levels. Delegation involves the following:

1. Selection of competent personnel who can accept and handle delegated duties.
2. Clear definition of the responsibilities that are being delegated.
3. An adequate amount of freedom for the subordinates to handle the assignments their own way within the framework of correct procedures and sound practices.
4. Accountability for the results. A painful aspect of delegation is standing by and watching a subordinate struggle without interfering. One administrator made a wise statement about accountability when he said, "I won't tamper with the fiddle and then hold you responsible for the music."

Confusion sometimes exists about the real meaning of delegation. It is different than simply assigning work to someone else. Delegation means that you pass on to a subordinate a portion of your *responsibilities,* along with the *authority* and the *accountability.* Some responsibilities are delegated with guidelines to define the framework within which they are to be conducted. In other cases, responsibilities are delegated with total freedom as to how to handle them.

In analyzing whether you delegate effectively, the following questions will be especially helpful.

1. Are you unavailable because you are almost always too busy? If so, are there valid reasons for this, or do you spend too much time doing things that someone else ought to do?
2. What would happen if you were suddenly taken out of circulation for a few days? Some administrators take pride in the idea that the place cannot get along without them. Such indispensability, however, (even if true) indicates an organizational weakness.
3. Is the operation slowed down and productivity diminished because others must wait for you to fulfill all your responsibilities? Are others waiting for decisions that should have been made last week?
4. Are communication channels too rigid, requiring subordinates to chan-

nel too much information through you and not permitting them to cut across departmental lines, provided they keep you properly informed?
5. What does an analysis of your homework show? Does your briefcase bulge each night and on weekends with correspondence and reports?
6. Are there certain administrative matters that someone else could handle instead of you, even if not quite as well, or perhaps even better under the circumstances?
7. Are there responsibilities that someone could do at less expense than you, in view of the dollar value of your time?
8. Could a secretary or administrative assistant do many of the things you are doing, and would the additional freedom of your schedule more than compensate for the cost of the extra person through improved management and better results?

Why Some Administrators Fail to Delegate

Usually administrators understand the theory of delegation, but many are unwilling to apply it. Failure to delegate is usually inherent in the individual rather than the situation. Here are some interesting reasons that have been culled from the literature that explain why some administrators resist delegating.[9]
1. *Fear of being found out.* Some administrators are not as well informed as they like others to believe. There is a tendency to defend against this by keeping others detached and uninvolved.
2. *Overdeveloped sense of perfection.* Such an administrator has the attitude that in order to have it done right, he has to do it. So he tries to do it all and the result is an organization that gets "gummed up" at the top level.
3. *A reluctance to admit that others know more about certain aspects of the operation.* If competent personnel are given ample opportunity for development, some will know more about certain responsibilities than the chief administrator. Some administrators find this hard to accept.
4. *Fear of not getting credit.* Here, a fundamental insecurity manifests itself—the desire to get personal credit. This form of pettiness is found in high-ranking administrators as well as in lower level supervisors.
5. *Fear of subordinates progressing too fast.* This can seem like a threat to an administrator who is afraid of "slipping."
6. *Fear of poor relationships.* Some administrators have such a strong desire to be well-liked that they avoid being firm in demanding that subordinates carry their share of the load.

An administrator cannot, of course, solve all his time problems by simply shoving projects off to subordinates. At the same time, he cannot hope to keep close tabs on every activity that occurs in the organization. He must strike a position in between; avoiding, on the one hand, doing too many things himself or, on the other hand, giving away so much control and authority that he finds himself out of touch with matters that he should control.

MAKING DECISIONS

Making decisions is often the most difficult function of an administrator. Decisions involve judgments that are based on a combination of information and reasoning. Teaching an individual to make good judgments is difficult; some say it is impossible. One can learn how to organize the steps in decision making, how to avoid certain mistakes and pitfalls, and how to gather, organize, and utilize facts. But even within the framework of all this, some are much better at making sound judgments than others.

In decision making, there are four possibilities, the first three of which result in error.[9]

1. Making the wrong decision about the wrong problem.
2. Making the right decision about the wrong problem.
3. Making the wrong decision about the right problem.
4. Making the right decision about the right problem.

This points out that identifying the *real problem* is just as important to the solution as figuring out the *best answer* to the problem.

Every difficult decision is, to some degree, a compromise, because it is not possible to arrive at a perfect or ideal solution. Sometimes, however, it is a good idea to start out by defining the ideal solution, because this provides a better chance of arriving at the best compromise. The objective is to make the decision that has the best overall chance for success, and this involves compromising some points in order to strengthen others.

Most written sources about decision-making emphasize: "get the facts." Obviously, this is important, but effective administrators do not rely totally on facts. Actually, a decision starts out with an opinion. Opinion plus important facts lead to understanding. Understanding enables one to identify the alternatives and to evaluate them accurately and select the best one. This process can rightfully be termed "considered judgment," a process that results in a well thought-out conclusion.

In the military, *quick* and *accurate* decisions save lives, and there are other settings where such an approach can be beneficial. In most cases, however, *timely* and *accurate* decisions are more appropriate. It is important to be abreast of situations and have readily available the best information on which to base correct decisions.

Some administrative decisions have little consequence, whereas others have significant and far-reaching effects. It is necessary to clearly recognize the importance of the decision and its potential consequences. This requires a level of understanding and insight that some people lack.

Decisions are often labeled *right* or *wrong;* however, these are extreme labels. More meaningful terms are *strong* or *weak, appropriate* or *inappropriate, sound* or *unsound, good* or *bad* (or poor). In some cases, it is more descriptive to use a five-point scale: *poor, fair, acceptable, good, excellent.*

Many people with a good batting average for making decisions follow a structured approach toward identifying and defining the problem, considering all the important factors, and then arriving at a decision. Sometimes this procedure is not apparent to others; the decision maker may not even be aware of it himself. The following steps, if applied, will improve the probability of good decisions. Study these steps and attempt to build them into your pattern of thought. As with any new skills, the first few attempts might seem awkward, but gradually the process will become more natural.

State the Apparent Problem. When a problem is first recognized, the solution often seems obvious; there is a tendency to plunge ahead to a quick decision. Unless adequate thought is given, you might find that you are only on the fringes of the real problem, and in some cases, you might even be looking at the wrong problem. Also, there is a tendency to deal with only the symptoms and not the underlying cause. To avoid this mistake, put the principle of definition to work. State the problem as it appears. Then think about it, and perhaps discuss it with others. Knowing that the apparent problem might not be the real problem, go on to the second step.

Search Out the Important Facts. In order to clarify the problem, it is important to examine the circumstances that surround it. You will need to judge how thoroughly this should be done, but as a rule, it is better to do too much than too little. In gathering information, remember the following:

The individuals you involve will each see the situation from a different point of view, and their interpretations will be tilted in the directions of their philosophic beliefs, preferences, and personal needs. In light of this, you must have keen insight into what each one's point of view means in relation to the particular problem.

Once a person has taken a stand on a matter, there is a tendency to hold to it, especially if emotions are involved. Therefore, it is a good idea to get people's input without causing them to take a firm stand. Keep the alternatives open.

It is pointless to try to change people's attitudes in the fact-gathering stage. Such an attempt would be premature.

Discovering *why* the problem exists will help immensely in arriving at the best solution.

Define the Real Problem. The most important part of decision making is to correctly define the *real* problem. Often, when all the needed information is gathered, the real problem turns out to be different than the one originally observed. In fact, that which seemed to be the problem sometimes turns out to be a result of the real one.

Obtain Expert Opinion. An important element is to recognize your own limitations and seek assistance from experts when needed; experts who understand your kind of problem. In this regard, remember that the considered judgment of one expert is more useful than the opinions of numerous nonexperts. The former is the application of intelligence, whereas the latter is the pooling of ignorance.

One advantage of consulting with an expert is that the interchange of ideas has a stimulating effect on the thought processes of both people, and this tends to have the influence of a third mind. The exchange often produces ideas that would not have occurred to either person in the absence of the interaction. Conversing with experts is not a means of letting others do your thinking, but rather a means of letting them help you think more clearly.

Sometimes the cost of consulting with an expert from outside the organization seems prohibitive. It should be remembered, however, that an expert brings special training and usually new insights into a situation. Often, not using the expert would be "costly" in time delays or wrong decisions due to improper analysis of the situation.

Two important guidelines are, (1) let your decisions be influenced by new facts and well thought-out judgments of experts, and (2) avoid being influenced too much by self-appointed "specialists," half-baked opinions, and unproven theories. Nonexpert opinions are the cheapest kind of advice, and they are often worth even less than they cost.

Analyze the Alternatives.   Carefully evaluate the strengths and weaknesses of each alternative, considering both the immediate and long-term effects. Sometimes, one alternative will stand out clearly from the others, which makes the solution relatively easy. In other cases, you might have to take the reverse approach and eliminate the alternatives one by one as you decide against them.

Select the Best Solution.   In the final selection, keep the following in mind: (1) Too much haste can lead to an expedient compromise, which is less than the best solution. (2) Conversely, if a decision arrives too slowly it can lose its favorable impact, and in the meantime, the indecision can become a problem. (3) The right solution at the wrong time is often no better than the wrong solution at the right time—*timing* and *accuracy* are both very important. (4) The solution for a particular problem may be different for the short-term than the long-term, and sometimes it is necessary to deal with those two separately.

Implement the Decision.   Laying the groundwork for acceptance of a decision is an important element. The people involved or affected by the decision should be adequately informed through the proper sources. Sometimes the stage is already set for acceptance, and nothing more needs to be done. In other cases, careful preparation is needed. In the absence of adequate attention, implementation can bog down, making the decision ineffective.

Obtain Feedback and Evaluate.   The final step is evaluating the correctness of the decision, the effectiveness of its implementation, and whether some adjustments are needed. This step involves gathering information as to how people feel about the decision, and whether it is living up to its expectations. You might discover the decision is not working well and that certain modifications are needed. Basically sound decisions usually work well when people join together and make them work, whereas seemingly good decisions often fail when the people involved are not unified and supportive.

Remember these important steps toward decision making:

State the Apparent Problem
Search out the Important Facts
Define the Real Problem
Obtain Expert Opinion
Analyze the Alternatives
Select the Best Solution
Implement the Decision
Obtain Feedback and Evaluate

Guard Against Procrastination and Half Measures

Business statisticians have found that among those who have failed in business, one of the most prominent reasons has been indecision: the lack of ability to make timely decisions that would have kept the business moving forward.

Most of us have a tendency to avoid making difficult decisions. It is enticing to wait until more information is available, to think it over longer, or hope a development will occur that would make the decision easier. But too much waiting can be detrimental. Rushing important decisions, however, or making them without adequate investigation and careful thought is also unwise.

Success is associated with people who are able to make accurate decisions quickly, often in the absence of complete information. Once a decision is made, it is important to stick to it, unless ample evidence to the contrary becomes available. In a nutshell, it can be said that highly successful managers make decisions *quickly* and change them *slowly,* whereas making decisions slowly and changing them quickly is a characteristic of unsuccessful administrators. Definite goals make it easier to reach sound decisions.

A related problem is the practice of taking half measures. A half measure is a form of temporary compromise which only postpones a more permanent solution. Those who practice half measures are like the person who writes a promissory note with great flourish and then says, "thank goodness that bill is paid." A bit of this kind of blind spot seems to be in all of us. Some administrators settle on half measures in order to stave off unpleasant action, or to settle on a compromise that will pacify those who resist forthright action.

It is true that a half measure is not always undesirable. Sometimes it can furnish a temporary solution and buy time that is truly needed to work out the best long-range solution. But a half measure is detrimental when used as a hedge against a full measure that is really needed.

Creative Thinking in Decision Making

The process of creative thinking starts with seeing or sensing a problem or clearly analyzing a situation. One of the salient traits of a truly creative person is that he sees problems and potential solutions more clearly than others see them. It has been said of Einstein that a part of his genius, like that of many other creative thinkers, was his inability to readily accept what seemed obvious.[10]

One who is satisfied with situations tends to be blind to shortcoming and oblivious to the need for change. Some measure of dissatisfaction with the present state of affairs is a prerequisite to any attempt at transformation or improvement. The creative person feels what poets have called "divine discontent" and what others call "constructive discontent."

The problem must be properly perceived and correctly defined. When it is, the very statement of the problem carries within it hints or suggestions as to how it may be solved. Improperly defined, the problem may appear insolvable. The task then, for one who is going to solve a problem, is to analyze the total situation and delineate and simplify it until the crucial circumstances are isolated.

After becoming aware of the problem in general, the creative thinker is capable of reorganizing and restructuring the problem in different ways so that all of the possibilities of solution can be seen.

An important factor that may hamper attempts to solve problems creatively is the amount and availability of information pertinent to the solution. Too little information will impede or even make impossible the best solution. On the other hand, it is possible to overwork the information gathering process to a state of "mental dazzle," which makes the problem and the surrounding circumstances seem more complex than they really are.

As a result of training and orientation, administrators are usually disposed to approach a problem with a highly analytic attitude. One would be ill advised to do otherwise, yet in one sense, structured analytic perception is the enemy of creative insight. Analysis disassembles a whole into its parts. At a certain stage, this is necessary if progress is to be made, but in the course of analysis, certain attitudes that pertain to the phenomenon as a whole may be destroyed. What is needed, if there is to be a creative reorganization, is a free, spontaneous look at the whole situation in order to fully appreciate it. Such an approach encourages the use of imagination, which is so crucial in the reorganization of a problem.

People can be influenced to be more creative through "brainstorming" and stimulating discussions with other creative thinkers.

It is generally believed that certain characteristics of thought are possessed by people who think creatively.

1. The creative individual forms concepts more easily and quickly, and the concepts are more clear.
2. The creative person forms concepts that are more diverse and encompass a broader range.

3. The concepts formed by creative individuals are usually more flexible because they are formed in a mental environment that is relatively unstructured and permits free flow of thought.
4. The concepts of the creative individual tend to be more complex and far-reaching.

The Ideation Method

The problem solving technique of "ideation" has been used with some success in physical education and related areas. The setting is an informal session in which suggestions and possible solutions are presented. The following rules are simple, but must be observed so as to reap the maximum benefits for all those participating.[7]
1. Identify in detail the specific problem to be addressed.
2. Present the problem for discussion and limit discussion to only that problem.
3. Keep statements of ideas as short as possible; eliminate details at this point, as discussion will be held later.
4. Keep accurate notes.
5. Record all ideas, regardless of how strange they may seem.
6. Do not permit comments in the form of judgments, ridicule, or praise; however, building on a previous suggestion is permitted.
7. Set an approximate goal for the number of suggestions and stop when all the participants appear to have finished.

After all the suggestions have been recorded, allow a review session where positive and negative responses are permitted. This is a good time to work out details on specific items or combine ideas to come up with several possible solutions

The administrator must now decide how the solution is to be determined. One way is for the administrator to choose the best solution from the five most acceptable to the group. Another approach is to allow the group to choose the solution they like the best and will work the hardest to implement. This is the better method for several reasons, but the administrator must be willing to accept their decision, as it is not a good idea to overrule after the privilege of decision-making has been given.

BIBLIOGRAPHY

1. American Management Association: Workshop Notes on Time Management. New York, 1981.

2. Arnold, J.D.: Make up Your Mind: The Seven Building Blocks to Better Decisions. New York, AMACOM, 1978.

3. Baird, B.: Introduction to Decision Analysis. Massachusetts, Duxbury Press, 1978.

4. Boettinger, H.M.: Is management really an art? Harvard Business Review, 53(1):54, 1975.

5. Braverman, J.D.: Management Decision Making: A Formal/Intuitive Approach. New York, American Management Association, 1980.

6. Bridges, F.: Management Decisions and Organizational Policy. New York, Harper and Row, 1971.

7. Cornell, A.H.: The Decision Maker's Handbook. Englewood Cliffs, NJ, Prentice-Hall, 1980.

8. Davidson, J.: Effective Time Management: A Practical Work Book. New York, Human Sciences Press, 1978.

9. Drucker, P.F.: Management, 2nd Ed. New York, Harper and Row, 1981.

10. Goslin, L.N., and Rethans, A.J.: Basic Systems for Decision Making, 2nd Ed. Dubuque, Iowa, Kendall/Hunt Pub., 1980.

11. Hogarth, R.M.: Judgment and Choice: The Psychology of Decision. Chicester, NY, John Wiley and Sons, 1980.

12. Huber, G.P.: Managerial Decision Making. Glenview, IL, Scott, Foresman, 1980.

13. Knezevich, S.J.: Administration of Public Education, 2nd Ed. New York, Harper and Row, 1981.

14. Massie, J.L., and Douglas, J.: Managing a Contemporary Introduction, 2nd Ed. Englewood Cliffs, NJ, Prentice-Hall, 1977.

15. Northwest Regional Educational Lab.: The computer in educational decision making: an introduction and guide for school administrators. Oregon NWRL, 1978.

16. Patz, A.L.: Strategic Decision Analysis: A General Management Framework. Boston, Little, Brown and Co., 1981.

17. Pearson, R.: An Instructional Guide to Cost Effective Decision Making. New York, McGraw-Hill, 1977.

18. Peters, H.C.: Rational decision making in business organizations. Am Econ Rev, 69:511, 1979.

19. Radford, K.J.: Modern Managerial Decision Making. Reston, VA, Reston Publishing Co., 1981.

20. Reynolds, H., and Tramel, M.E.: Executive Time Management: Getting 12 Hours' Work out of an 8-Hour Day. Englewood Cliffs, NJ, Prentice-Hall, 1979.

21. Richardson, R.C.: Decision making in the 1980s: pragmatists vs. involvers (community college presidents). Jr Educ Digest, 46:41, 1981.

22. Rutherford, R.D.: Just in Time: Immediate Help for the Time Pressured. New York, John Wiley and Sons, 1981.

23. Tversky, A., and Kahneman, D.: Framing of decisions and the psychology of choice. Science, 211:453, 1981.

24. Weisselberg, R.: The Executive Strategist: an Arm Chair Guide to Scientific Decision Making. New York, McGraw-Hill, 1979.

Chapter **6**

ACHIEVING SUCCESS

It is especially useful for an administrator to be well informed about attitudes and methods that accentuate positive results. This chapter deals with that theme, with special emphasis on the topics of Formulas for Success, Traits to Emphasize, and Motivating Oneself and Others.

FORMULAS FOR SUCCESS

Many people, including some school employees and students, attain relatively low levels of success because they do not understand or do not apply the right formulas. It is important to know the ingredients of success, and even more important to apply the ingredients consistently. One of the most prominent factors in success is a positive approach.

Positive Thinking

An interesting psychologic law is known as the *law of attraction*. It means that a person's energy, actions, and achievements are attracted in the direction of his thoughts. We do not always achieve all of our thoughts, but we are at least attracted in that direction. This implies that if you have positive thoughts leading toward worthy goals, your actions will be attracted in the direction of those goals, and you will utilize your energy in their accomplishment. If you think constructively, your actions will be constructive; if you think about the welfare of others as well as yourself, your actions will demonstrate this concern. The law of attraction suggests each of us should purposely guide our thoughts toward well-defined and worthy goals. We should think positive, constructive, and humane thoughts, so that our energy will be used accordingly. This will help us in our efforts toward worthwhile achievements.

Another law known as the *law of positive expectation* means that if you expect good things to happen, it is likely that they will. The very fact that you expect it will cause you to dedicate your efforts in that direction. Others, who know that you expect it, will also help. Positive expectation truly pays off. Conversely, negative expectation has the same kind of attraction. If you expect negative results and psychologically condition yourself for them, and let other people know of your expectations, negative results are more likely to occur. An administrator ought to take advantage of these two laws by thinking positively and expressing positive but realistic expectations to others.

A related concept is the *self-fulfilling prophecy*. Basically, the theory is that if you believe and want badly enough for something to happen, it likely will. Observation, combined with a limited amount of research, has provided some evidence that, if expectations are high and confidence from one's associates is strong and genuine, better results will be achieved through a stronger effort by the student or worker.

The "Add" Concept of Improvement

Norman Vincent Peale explains the *add concept* in his book Enthusiasm Makes the Difference. [9] It simply includes the ingredients of *attitude, direction,* and *discipline* (ADD).

A person's attitude is an outward expression of his inward feelings. To effectively move along any program or idea, you need to have a positive attitude. You must think in terms of success. An administrator with an attitude toward mediocrity will encourage mediocrity. One with an attitude toward enrichment will cause enrichment, and one with an attitude toward excellence will cause excellence. Attitude can truly make the difference.

How is your attitude toward positive progress of your organization or program? Do you think progress is important; do you think it is possible; and do you think that you're capable of giving adequate leadership toward its achievement? Next, how is your attitude toward the people in your organization? Are you really interested in their development and welfare or do you only have interest in yourself? Now would be a good time to clarify in your own mind the fact that one way to improve your organization is to improve the personnel who compose it. The organization will strengthen with the improvement of its people.

How is your attitude toward your work? Do you think of it as a good way to spend your professional life? Are you pleased with what you do and with the label that you carry? Do you radiate a proud attitude that is contagious to others?

The term *direction* in the add concept refers to being goal oriented. Having well defined goals is one of the starting points toward significant achievement. Many people and many programs reach low levels of achievement because there were no goals set, the goals were too meager, or the programs were not managed toward achievement of the goals. Most people (or organizations) who fail to accomplish much, do so because they did not plan to accomplish much.

Many people's professional approach parallels the response given by a businessman when he was asked how he thought his business would do this year. He said, "It will do better than last year." When asked how it did last year he replied, "I don't exactly know."

Without knowing the direction you are headed for the future, how can you possibly know whether you are progressing toward your goals? More importantly, how can you reach your goals if you do not know what they are. People who do a good job are those who plan to do a good job. Clear direction helps to make the difference. Remember, "No goals are bad and meager goals are sad."

The third element of the "add" concept is *discipline*. It has been said, "We are what our habits make us." Habits are acquired slowly. Sometimes we do not realize that a habit is developing until it is already formed. To give some examples, ask yourself these questions. Which cigarette gives the smoker the smoking habit? Which bit of food makes a person 20 pounds overweight? Which drink causes one to become an alcoholic? The chains of a bad habit are too weak to be recognized until they become too strong to break.

Habits are formed through the practices one follows repeatedly. If you adhere to good work practices, you will develop good habits, and this is where discipline comes in. Each of us is actually two people. We are first the person that we know and others know, and second we are a much bigger person—the person that we should and could be. Plan for the kind of person you want to be, then discipline yourself accordingly. Without proper discipline, your plans for yourself and your program can never be achieved. Discipline is molding yourself into the kind of person you ought to be. It is probably the most important ingredient of self-realization.

More About Goals

Chapter 1 includes a discussion about goals and how goals can be structured and applied. The information presented here relates to that section, but the emphasis is on achieving success through the effective implementation of the right goals. It is true that a systematic approach to the application of goals can be a great asset to any administrator. Effective goal setting will help toward accomplishment of both short- and long-term projects, and it will benefit both the organization and the administrator.

Napoleon Hill, in his famous book *Think and Grow Rich,* [7] emphasized the vital importance of these three steps in connection with goals: (1) crystallize your thinking, (2) develop a plan, and (3) follow through with consistency. These elements are important in nonprofit organizations as well as profit-seeking ventures

Crystallize Your Thinking. A person needs to determine which goals should be achieved—short-range, intermediate and long-range—then state the goals in writing, clearly and concisely. Writing crystallizes one's thoughts because it is necessary to clearly understand a concept before it can be written. Once it is written it can be reviewed again and again and crystallized even more.

General and vague statements indicate lack of clear thought and exact purpose. A person must know precisely what he wants to achieve if he is going to be successful in doing it. One should be vivid and crisp in his thoughts about goals.

Goal setting should involve creative and imaginative thinking, tempered by reality. There is no reason to state goals that are lowly, common, uninteresting, unchallenging and unworthy. On the other hand, it is senseless to set goals that are clearly beyond one's reach or which fail to lead in the direction of one's long-range purpose. Setting realistic, intelligent, and challenging goals is one of the administrator's most important single acts toward progress and long-term success. Setting goals helps turn theory into practice, thoughts into action, and energy into desired results. A plan of action based on clearly defined goals discourages procrastination, reduces indecisiveness, and increases efficiency.

Develop a Plan. It would be largely unproductive to state goals without forming a plan to accomplish them. The plan serves as the blueprint or roadmap toward success. It always includes at least two basic elements: the tasks to be accomplished and the desired time schedule. A well-conceived plan will keep you on track and help you meet your timetable toward goal achievement. It will reduce floundering and the dissipation of energy, and make success more likely.

In planning, one should recognize possible roadblocks and obstacles; and have some ideas on how to get around them. The plans should take into consideration the strengths and weaknesses of those who will need to implement them. The planning should also pinpoint the useful talents and skills each person possesses and take into consideration the potential for additional development.

A plan is only a concept of action and the action must be performed by people. This means that the effectiveness of any plan, regardless of how well conceived, is influenced significantly by the ability of the people who have to make it work. Some very good plans have failed because the people involved did not have the expertise to succeed. Conversely, some very able people have failed because the plan they attempted was unsound or ineffective. Although there is no such thing as a perfect plan, the plan for any educational endeavor ought to be relatively faultless.

When planning, it is often important to know the opinions of those affected. An example of a source of expertise from which an administrator can draw is a teacher sitting in consultation with the district supervisor, principal, or department chairman to formulate a plan for completing a particular faculty remodeling project. Another example is a group of instructors from the district getting together, along with the district specialist, to set down in writing a plan of action for the achievement of instructional goals. Each teacher would be able to represent his program or department. In this way, various points of view can be considered, and people are less likely to feel overlooked or isolated from the planning process.

Follow Through With Consistency. It is important to keep in mind the difference between *wish* and *desire*. A wish is a passive thought which may never result in significant action. It only expresses an idea of what you would like to happen. Desire, on the other hand, compels a person toward action, and if the desire is consistent and strong, the action will persist until the desired results are achieved.

In order to help ensure that your plans will remain valid, evaluate them regularly, with an open mind, and adjust them as needed. As long as you are satisfied that your plan is sound, stick with it in spite of the obstacles you meet or what others may say. Dedication involves persistence, and persistence leads to accomplishment. Avoid floundering, vacillating, and procrastinating. Instead, move forward with confidence and determination. With this approach, your emphasis will be toward how things can be accomplished instead of why they cannot.

TRAITS TO EMPHASIZE

Leadership comes from individuals; and each individual has certain traits which are an advantage or disadvantage in the leadership role. Fortunately, the traits of individuals can be changed within certain limits. Part of the formula of success for an administrator is to improve himself through emphasizing valuable traits. The following discussions describe the traits that consistently contribute to an administrator's success. It would be well to give considerable emphasis to the development of these traits in yourself.

Specialized Knowledge. Before a person can expect to accomplish his administrative goals, he must prepare himself with the specialized knowledge and skills that would logically make such accomplishments possible. He must set aside, on a regular basis, the necessary time for self-development. Improvement of specialized knowledge and professional skills is fundamental to long-term administrative success. Sometimes, an administrator finds that more knowledge and skills are required than he or she has the ability to acquire, in which case, the best alternative is to engage other people as consultants or assistants who can help provide the necessary specialization.

Creative Ideas. It is a basic truth that those things that finally become results started as ideas. When combined with clear purpose, desire, and persistence toward achievement, an idea is the origin of success. Creative and ingenious ideas are trademarks of effective administrators.

Imagination. Imagination is the workshop where ideas and plans are created. Some leaders stress that a person can achieve anything he can clearly imagine. Once the mental concept is formed, the accomplishment is primarily a matter of follow-through. Unfortunately, two of our most basic limitations seem to be lack of imagination and lack of willingness to pursue with determination and vigor that which is imagined. As a person thinks of goals, it is important to be imaginative about how to achieve them. The mind needs to be stretched relative to self-improvement, organizational approaches, and effective procedures.

Desire. It has been proven many times that desire is one of the first requisites of success. It is the starting point for action toward all forms of achievement. Yet many people encounter their first stumbling block at this point. Emerson stated it well when he said ". . .the implanting of a desire indicates that its gratification is in the constitution of the creature that feels it." This indicates that a person would not feel a desire unless he were capable of achieving it. It suggests that each of us has a built-in control that causes our desires to be modified by our abilities and aptitudes. To the extent this is true, whatever you sincerely desire can and should be yours to achieve.

It is well known among coaches and athletes that, in order to run faster, you must either lengthen or quicken your stride or both. A similar approach is needed for one who wants to move faster and more steadily toward desired goals. Consistent desire toward worthy goals will cause one to lengthen and quicken his stride in the right directions.

The following are six concepts or guidelines as to how desire can help to achieve your goals.

1. Be both definite and realistic about the level of achievement you desire.
2. Determine clearly what you are willing to sacrifice or the price you are willing to pay in terms of dedication and effort to accomplish your desire.
3. Establish a definite timetable on which to apply your plan and reach your goals.
4. Put in writing a clear plan you intend to follow. Think it through carefully to be sure that the plan is sound. Then implement it with confidence.
5. Read your plan periodically in order to refresh your memory of its content. Crystallize in your mind the procedures involved, and keep yourself motivated toward its achievement.
6. As you study the plan, try to visualize and feel yourself already in possession of your desired accomplishments. Gaining this mental image is important to your success.

Faith. In order to succeed, one must have faith in oneself and faith that the goals that have been set are worthy and will prove beneficial. Faith is a state of mind which may be induced or created, and it is a potentially strong motivational force. Every great enterprise or accomplishment takes its first step toward success on the basis of faith: faith that it is worthwhile and faith that it can be accomplished. Often, the dominance of a person's strong inner faith expresses itself overtly and affirms itself in actual accomplishment.

Enthusiasm. Enthusiasm is the positive, inward drive that is expressed overtly as optimistic approval or the desire for energetic involvement. Enthusiasm is a form of emotional expression; a stimulating sensation for action. Enthusiasm can be influenced by overt circumstances such as potential reward, either tangible or intangible, or encouragement and support by others. It can change would-be drudgery into a pleasant and challenging pursuit. It can make the difference as to whether you feel stimulated to continue, whether you can recover from setbacks, motivate others to assist with your plan, or sustain the necessary effort to ensure success.

Persistence. Persistence is illustrated by the power of one's will. It is to a person what carbon is to steel. When applied to all the aspects of one's aspirations and plans, persistence can make the difference between success and failure. Unfortunately, many people are lacking in this trait, and this keeps them from approaching their potential for achievement. Many have good ideas and formulate sound plans, but when the going gets tough, they falter. Lack of persistence deprives them of a full measure of success.

Persistence is a mark of courage, dedication, and strong will. Persistence is both a state of mind and a personality characteristic. Like other characteristics, it can be cultivated and improved.

Self-Confidence. Confidence is influenced by a combination of adequate preparation and successful experiences. Positive thinking about one's ability to succeed can have a favorable influence on confidence. A person is still limited in self-confidence unless he is thoroughly prepared to accomplish his goals and proves it by having successful experiences along the way. Self-confidence discourages and intimidates those who might oppose your efforts or resist the accomplishment of your goals. The confident and positive approach will help you to be more thorough because you will be more enthusiastic and more dedicated. It will cause you to make fewer mistakes and recover more quickly from the mistakes you make.

Within the framework of reality and good judgment, you should never give serious mental recognition to the possibility of failure. Some setbacks will happen along the way and a person must be able to take these in stride and handle them gracefully, but do not let the temporary setbacks affect your positive thinking. Keep sight of your goals and pursue them with confidence.

Active Mind. The human mind represents one of the most unrealized potentials in our environment. If the wealth of the world were available and you chose to take only a $1000 bill, this would represent the extent of development of the minds of most people as compared with their potential. The human brain, the physical organism within which the mind works, is the most powerful organism the world knows. It has been determined that there are between 10 and 14 billion cells in the brain, and this vast network represents a person's analytic and interpretive power. This is a uniquely human power which ought to be developed and applied effectively.

It is the power of the mind that has given us supersonic airplanes, probes into outer space, complex computers, electricity, power-driven engines and all our other mechanical and technical devices. The power of the mind has enabled us to develop complex social and human aspects of civilization. All the elements of life that are uniquely human are related to the functions of the mind.

A person thinks with his memory—the mental storehouse. Without memories we would have no sources from which to formulate thoughts and draw conclusions. We would be unable to recollect or to analyze and synthesize. Hunches, intuitions, and judgments are all products of the mind's storehouse of knowledge.

Our minds need to be continually developed through useful experiences in order to further load our memories with valuable information. This process results in an expanded supply from which new ideas and better conclusions can be drawn.

Sixth Sense. The information present in one's mind has come from the accumulation of experiences. During these experiences, the five senses have been in operation, serving as receiver sets, which feed information and impressions into the mind. Some information is recorded in the conscious mind, some in the subconscious mind and apparently some is not recorded at all, at least not in reproducible form.

The mind does not simply record and store information, it reproduces it in a different form. This is the formulation of thoughts, judgments, and conclusions, and it is sometimes referred to as the "sixth sense." The sixth sense uses the information stored in the brain, and through the process of analysis and synthesis, it creates ideas. A person with a strong sixth sense can produce ideas that are a far cry from the raw material from which they are created. The ability to create useful ideas is a great advantage to a person, whether his objectives are to make a lot of money, manage an organization, invent and market a new product, improve educational methods, or whatever.

Everybody possesses the sixth sense in some degree, just as everybody possesses some amount of health, fitness, or intelligence. The development of the sixth sense to a high level is an ongoing process of mental self-improvement. This development follows the same principle as the development of strength or endurance: the application of progressive overload. In this case, it can better be termed "progressive mind stretching," a result of regular participation in mentally challenging activities. As the sixth sense develops, the subsequent "mind stretching activities" must be more complex in order to bring about further development.

The unique ability to create and produce ideas is one of the most distinguishing characteristics of humans as compared with other forms of life. It is truly a wonder and a blessing if developed thoroughly and used properly.

MOTIVATING ONESELF AND OTHERS

Some people might have greatness thrust upon them, but no one is able to inherit excellence. It must be achieved. Excellence cannot be achieved unwittingly, and neither can it be stumbled into in the course of amusing oneself. It requires discipline and tenacity of purpose, and these characteristics are dependent on motivation.

It is a fact that some people achieve success with much more ease than others, and there seem to be two important aspects of this condition that are often not apparent. *First,* a person should try to achieve success in areas in which he has a high aptitude; all else being equal, this makes it easier and more likely. *Second,* one's motivation to succeed must be strong and consistent. Perhaps the more important of these factors is motivation.

Motivation is the inner strength that releases itself in the form of energy and propels a person along the track of success. It is expressed in the form of desire and determination to reach one's goals. It provides willpower to resist temptations that would dissipate or misdirect energy; it keeps a person on track and moving forward.

Motivation stems from one's needs and drives. When a person senses an unfulfilled need, he is usually motivated to do something about it.

External sources of motivation—the cheering of a crowd, slaps on the back, handshakes, certificates, medallions, and monetary rewards—are helpful; but these often have only temporary effects. Once their influence has passed, the person once again depends almost totally on internal motivation. This is based on one's inner thoughts, ideals, and aspirations, the sources from which the more permanent motivational energy originates and flows.

For the most part, it is an error to depend too much on others for motivation. Creating and sustaining the necessary level of motivation is largely a "do-it-yourself" project.

Let us consider what some other writers have said about the nature and sources of motivation. Gallon[4] describes motivation as emotional drive to excel; and he listed five important sources.

1. Recognition and praise from peers, parents, and members of the public.
2. Ego reinforcement, which comes from a feeling of conquest or fulfillment.
3. Material gains such as money or material proof of achievement in the form of medals, certificates, trophies, and the like.
4. Emotional fulfillment or sensation derived from the achievement of a goal.
5. Fear of failure; a negative form of motivation which produces positive results.

Wilt[10] wrote that motivation means providing reasons or incentives that cause, or sustain, dedication toward a particular activity. According to him, the three dominant motivators are:

1. The need to feel important and recognized or the need for identity.
2. The need for refreshing change or new stimulation.
3. The need for a feeling of security.

Wilt also emphasized that there are two kinds of motivation: external, provided by circumstances outside oneself; and internal, which comes from an inner drive, wish, or need. He stressed that internal motivation is potentially more powerful and more consistent.

Wilt applies his ideas to athletics by saying that "an athlete can train for months at his sport, go through several trial performances, get the proper rest and food, and have correct technique and knowledge of the activity, and yet if he doesn't have the internal motivation or will to excel he will fall far short of his expectancies."

Tutko and Richards[9] also discussed the phenomenon of external and internal motivation. They explained that praise and punishment were two of the more common forms of motivation, and that praise provides the best results. Praise is better than punishment in giving the athlete an idea of what is correct. Punishment creates doubt and confusion and hinders the athlete's ability to accurately assess himself. They suggested the following approach for criticizing or correcting a problem: open with praise, make the correction or suggestion, end by complimenting.

John Wooden,[11] the legendary basketball coach at UCLA, used the positive-negative-positive approach. Says Wooden, "you will never motivate an athlete by alienating him." Wooden would demonstrate the desired behavior, quickly imitate the player's mistake, then follow with another demonstration of the proper way to do the skill. This seems to be a way of minimizing the alienation of the player by the coach, while being an effective way to constructively criticize and give positive feedback.

Motivational techniques are important points of knowledge for every coach, teacher, and administrator. The more techniques one knows and can effectively utilize, the better the chances of helping individuals reach their potential. The wise administrator understands that rewards are both intrinsic and extrinsic and knows how to motivate in both ways; yet keeps in mind that intrinsic motivation is better. The administrator must become well-acquainted with those he deals with, in order to know which motivational techniques will work best with each individual.

A Motivation Plan

Probably the best assurance of an organization's success is to have successful people. Productivity and achievement by people is what makes the difference. In light of this, the need for an effective plan for motivation becomes apparent.

Herzberg and Mausner[5] did some significant research on how employees feel about administrative techniques and work conditions. They found *motivation factors* and *maintenance factors,* with the motivation factors being those which bring forth initiative in employees and move them to a higher level of personal and organizational effectiveness. They listed the following as important among motivation factors: occupational achievement, deserved recognition, advancement, enjoyment of the work itself, opportunities for personal growth and enrichment, and responsibility.

The specific job conditions Herzberg and Mausner claimed will motivate people to perform better are: (1) personal involvement in challenging tasks, (2) using abilities fully, (3) opportunities for testing one's knowledge, (4) discretionary control over one's own behavior and work conditions, (5) clear performance feedback, and (6) opportunity to interact with high-level administrators.

Herzberg presented another list of job conditions that do not consistently result in better performance, but are necessary for the maintenance of an acceptable work level. When these conditions do not match expectations, employees are dissatisfied and job performance often diminishes. The conditions are: salary, job security, personal lifestyle, general working conditions, occupational status, good company policies and administrative procedures, interpersonal relations with supervisors, peers, and subordinates, and good technical supervision. These factors are necessary for encouragement and maintenance of morale.

Administrative policies and practices relative to *motivational* factors involve the concept of job enrichment.

Job enrichment can take several forms, and some people are more responsive than others to the different forms. This necessitates that job enrichment opportunities be tailor-made to fit the situation and the particular employees.

One of the classic examples of motivation combined with goal setting is illustrated in the athletic achievement of Dr. Roger Bannister when he set out to break the 4-minute mile barrier, a feat that had been approached by several but accomplished by none. This example can serve as an excellent guide for others, including those in administrative positions.

It is generally accepted that Bannister was not the best physical specimen in the world at the time to accomplish this unusual feat, but the right combination of important characteristics resulted in his success. Bannister claimed that the achievement was more dependent on psychologic preparation and self-motivation than on physical ability, although the physical ingredients had to be present. Through long hours of preparation he convinced himself that he could be the first human to ever surpass the 4-minute mile. He reasoned that if he could run the first three quarters in less than 3 minutes, he could certainly add the fourth quarter in 1 minute or less. He prepared himself both physically and mentally to hold that pace. When he hit the three-quarter mark slightly under 3 minutes, he knew almost for certain that he was only a quarter mile away from one of the world's greatest athletic achievements and one of history's great success stories—the mile run at 3:59.4.

Ironically, within the same competitive season, another man, John Landy from Australia, beat Bannister's time by running the distance in 3:58. It is unusual indeed, nowadays, for the mile to be won in a time slower than 4 minutes in a high-level national or international meet, and several athletes each year break this barrier. The world's record is now beneath the 3:48 mark, more than 12 seconds faster than the historic achievement of Bannister only three decades ago, and the present record is threatened often by modern-day superstars.

Both physiologists and psychologists contend that the 4-minute mark was more a psychologic than a physiologic barrier. Once the first person broke it, the barrier tended to dissolve in the minds of others, until now it is viewed more as a stepping stone than a barrier.

An interesting parallel situation has to do with the high jump. World class high jumpers flirted for a decade with the 7-foot mark, and several of them surpassed 6'11". Finally, John Thomas, a 17-year-old high school student who was apparently unimpressed by the 7-foot psychologic barrier, cleared the bar at 7'1". Almost immediately, a handful of other world class jumpers exceeded the 7-foot mark. Since then, high jumpers have surpassed 7'6", and a few are now pointing toward the 8-foot "barrier."

The elimination of barriers such as the two mentioned can serve as a good lesson for administrators as well as people in other walks of life. It points out that in order to accomplish one's goals, the person must define the goals, determine a plan that will lead toward their accomplishment, and implement the plan systematically and with determination. If the goals are realistic in the first place, they can be achieved if approached with an organized plan and with dedication, persistence, and enthusiasm.

One word of caution in connection with all of this is do not try to take steps that are too big. A world record breaker like Bannister reached the pinnacle of success by taking one step at a time. He had won many races at various levels of competition. With each improved performance, he reached a new level of achievement and put himself one step closer to his ultimate goal. By accepting each new challenge and planning toward it, Bannister used the stairstep approach until he finally arrived at the point in his preparation and progress that the 4-minute mile became the next step. By simply following essentially the same procedure that he had followed many times before in achieving lesser goals, he took one more step and crashed the 4-minute barrier.

All of us ought to apply a parallel approach to this in our own lives. First, we should reach levels of achievement that are within reasonable striking distance for us, and then use each new level as a base from which to take the next step. We should remain aware that each succeeding level is more difficult to achieve, and the risk of failure gradually increases.

Motivating others is a complex administrative technique. It seems to happen best when the motivator demonstrates consistency, as opposed to an erratic or moody approach. Methods that are sincere and genuine produce better long-term results than superficial or phony efforts.

It has been explained that the kind of motivation that serves the best and lasts the longest comes from within the individual himself. In view of this, a basic challenge of the administrator is to cultivate the self-motivation mechanisms of those he works with. This is an important element both in day-to-day performance and professional development and improvement of the employees. The ideal would be to cultivate the self-motivation of each individual to the point that only a motivational maintenance approach would be needed, along with the adequate direction of truly inspired employees.

Who Motivates the Motivator?

One of the searching questions in the field of management is how those individuals stay motivated who have responsibilities to motivate others. Unfortunately, some administrators fall prey to the pitfalls of the uninspired. The result is diluted success, at best, and eventual failure.

How many times have you observed a division or department head demonstrate a status quo attitude? How often have you seen people retained in leadership positions whose creative energy has evaporated and whose aspirations for progress have withered? In these cases, the potential motivator has lost his motivation and there is not much chance that he is going to have any inspirational effect on others.

It has been said that most of an administrator's responsibilities fall into two categories: "shedding light on the track" and "putting steam in the boiler." In order to put steam in other peoples' boilers, an administrator must keep his own boiler steamed up. He must retain a high level of self-motivation and communicate this to others. If this process is effective, it is like adding fuel to fire, causing it to produce more heat as well as more light.

What about you in particular? Do you have a burning desire for professional and personal success? Do you see yourself moving up, fulfilling a bigger and better purpose? Do you have enthusiasm for improvement and for opportunities to employ yourself in a larger capacity? Or has your ambition begun to settle; are you gradually becoming complacent and more satisfied with mediocrity? Do you find it harder to approach your responsibilities with zest? Has it become more difficult to express optimism and enthusiasm to others? Are you reminiscing more and producing less? If the answers to these questions are yes, then you should not prepare for an administrative position, and you certainly should not seek one. Your challenge is to improve your own attitude, revitalize your enthusiasm and rededicate yourself. In short, you need to be motivated.

The following four danger signals can warn one whose motivation is on the decline. They are signs of administrative suicide which often develop at an undetectably slow rate.

1. Procrastination: the practice of putting off needed decisions, falling behind on important tasks, hesitating to take considered risks, and hoping the problems will take care of themselves.

2. Devotion to false emblems: too much emphasis on one's title, office, furniture, or other material objects, giving way to egotism or personal pride, and placing too much emphasis on numbers and statistics as opposed to real human values and meaningful results.

3. Complacency: the inner urge to take it easy, the idea that you can glide a little more and think and do a little less, the attitude of being satisfied with good enough instead of excellent or superior. Related to complacency is the tendency to accept lack of initiative and originality among subordinates. As a result, the whole organization begins to settle. Often a subsequent step is to appoint mediocre workers in supervisory po-

sitions to help keep the boat from rocking and to assure one's own security.

4. Loss of purpose: lacking concrete plans or seeing insufficient reasons to develop and implement them. The executive who has lost his sense of purpose has outlived his usefulness as an administrator. There is no way that such a person can furnish adequate leadership to others and cause the programs of the organization to advance satisfactorily toward the goals.

An administrator should not hesitate to face the fact that he needs certain rewards in order to avoid discouragement and to remain enthusiastic. Ideally, the kinds of rewards that he pursues should be highly acceptable and not dilute his relationships or his image among others in the organization or members of the public. In accomplishing this, the administrator needs to be self-analytic in trying to identify the particular circumstances or endeavors that help to keep him motivated and integrate these into his work pattern.

It is sometimes stressed, and rightfully so, that the best source of motivation is a positive attitude toward achievement and service. Albert Schweitzer said, "The only ones among you who will be truly happy are those who have learned to serve." It is highly desirable for service to be the main component of one's motivation; but at the same time, it should be recognized that the majority of people also need other forms of motivation. Those who lean too hard for too long on the reward of service sometimes become discouraged and eventually develop the attitude that they have given too much and received too little. The potential development of such an attitude should be carefully monitored.

One of the recurring problems in education, which is opposite of the "service attitude," is for a person to hang on to an administrative position in the absence of adequate motivation. An administrator ought to hold to the attitude that as long as he occupies the position he will maintain himself as an energetic and effective leader. If he is not motivated to do this, then he should relinquish the administrative job and move to a position where his lack of motivation toward administrative work will not retard the productivity and achievement of others.

In addition to the satisfaction an administrator experiences in connection with his work, there are several self-motivating methods that administrators build into their lifestyles. For example, some read inspirational stories or thoughts written by or about highly successful people. Some listen to meaningful speeches by those who have experienced unusual success or who talk convincingly about the enthusiastic pursuit of achievement. Others find it both satisfying and inspiring to associate with successful colleagues or with individuals who demonstrate zest for life and high regard for achievement.

These methods might seem unreasonably time-consuming, but this need not be the case if you are selective about the motivational experiences you choose and if you use these as special interest pursuits or pleasure breaks from the routine of your work.

In addition, an administrator can be motivated by approval and encouragement from those to whom he accounts and by the approval and support of those within the organization he administers. Regardless of the other sources of motivation, the administrator needs to have a strong inner drive, a clear sense of purpose, and consistent dedication to achievement. He must be a self-starter, a self-motivator, and a self-director. These are marks of professional maturity that many people never attain. It is a form of maturity that keeps one's focus on organizational goals and results, professional development and enrichment, and overall managerial efficiency.

BIBLIOGRAPHY

1. American Management Association: Workshop notes on Employee Motivation. New York, 1981.

2. Ball, S.: Motivation in Education. New York, Academic Press, 1977.

3. Cooper, B.S.: Incentives that work: an administrative innovation in the Dade County schools. Phi Delta Kappan, Boston, 61:523, 1980.

4. Gallon, A.J.: Coaching: Ideas and Ideals. Boston, Houghton Mifflin, 1974.

5. Gellerman, S.: Meaning of morale. Management Today, 53:82, 1976.

6. Herzberg, F., Mausner, B., and Snyderman, B.: The Motivation to Work, 3rd Ed. New York, John Wiley and Sons, 1979.

7. Hill, N.: Think and Grow Rich. Brooklyn, NY, Fawcett Crest Publishers, 1960.

8. LeMaire, W.: Employee Motivation on the Production Line: How to Win Workers and Influence Profits. Boston, Cahners Publishing Co., 1975.

9. Peale, N.M.: Enthusiasm Makes the Difference. Englewood Cliffs, NJ, Prentice Hall, 1967.

10. Tutko, T.A., and Richards, J.W.: Psychology of Coaching. Boston, Allyn and Bacon, 1971.

11. Wilt, F.: Motivation and Coaching Psychology. Los Altos, CA, TAFNEWS Press, 1971.

12. Wooden, J.: They Call Me Coach. New York, Bantam, 1972.

13. Zweger, J.: Increasing productivity: how behavioral scientists can help. Personnel Journal, 42:513, 1976.

Part III
MANAGEMENT TECHNIQUES

Chapter 7

MANAGEMENT SKILLS
AND PROCEDURES

This chapter includes information about clear communication and correct techniques in connection with staff meetings, committees, and private conferences. The application of the guidelines set forth here can contribute significantly to one's effectiveness as an administrator.

COMMUNICATING EFFECTIVELY

For a busy administrator, it is important that all aspects of communication, from highly official to unofficial be performed effectively. Some important considerations that can help the administrator communicate better are as follow:

1. What information should be communicated and to whom and for what reasons?
2. How much explanation should be given?
3. Should the information be labeled confidential or restricted, or should no limits be placed on it?
4. Is it important for certain individuals to receive the information directly from the administrator?
5. Should certain persons receive it before others?
6. Through what sources should the information be passed, and how fast does it need to move?
7. What risk is there that the information will be misstated or misinterpreted?
8. Will certain individuals add their own versions, thus distorting the information?

Some communication can better be accomplished *orally,* whereas other messages should be in *written form*—memos, letters, or directives. Still other information is transmitted by *mood,* expressions and gestures.

Oral Communication

Some important considerations of this form of communication are to speak audibly so those listening do not miss words or phrases, use correct volume and an effective tone to make the words appealing and interesting, and select the right words and use statements that are easily understood. Placing the proper emphasis on words and phrases helps listeners to better understand the true meaning. Keep wordiness, unfamiliar terms, and meaningless jargon to a minimum. Business conversations should be brief and to the point. Oral presentations should be well thought out, carefully organized, and follow a predetermined plan.

The Use of Silence. Many administrators use combinations of silence and facial and body expressions more or less unconsciously. But conscious use of this technique can add a subtle dimension to your communicative abilities, because you can convey an attitude or opinion without making a commitment.

The Power of the Pause. Good communicators blend speech with nonspeech. Fast talkers, on the other hand, avoid the pause, perhaps believing it to be a sign of weakness or lack of authority. As a result, they are more susceptible to repeating themselves, making misstatements, or overworking a point.

Since pauses can be as much a part of communication as words, administrators should strike a balance between the two in order to communicate with maximum effectiveness. A silence can have a cooling effect on an emotional situation. It can help to recapture the attention of those in a meeting or force a response from another person who wants to keep the conversation moving. Following a particular statement, it can give the statement special emphasis.

Written Communication

Good writing should be much like good speaking. Writing, however, should be even better because one has more opportunity to organize and express thoughts clearly.

A written communication should always have a theme, which usually leads to certain conclusions. Some writing experts advocate stating the conclusions first and then developing the points that support those conclusions. Others believe that one should develop the theme and then state the conclusions. Whichever approach is taken, the main aspects are the theme and the conclusions. The theme must be developed logically and in as few words as possible, and the conclusions should be stated concisely and clearly.

Style is as important to writing as is organization. Keep your sentences and paragraphs "clean" and free of useless jargon. Use words and phrases that are clear and precise. Avoid words that might be unfamiliar to the reader or might confuse the meaning of a statement. Be cautious about words that have generalized or relative meanings such as good, large, and inexpensive.

The tone of a memo or letter is influenced by the selection of words and phrases. Attention to tone can make the difference between whether the written message sounds rude or polite, reserved or enthusiastic, personal or impersonal, complimentary or noncomplimentary.[4]

Receiver – – – –┼–►TO: John C. Doe

Sender – – – –┼–►FROM: James R. Peterson

Subject – – – –┼–►RE: Curriculum Changes

Date – – – – –┼–►DATE: 12-14-82

Body – – – – –┼–►The attached curriculum revision forms

             are submitted for your review and approval.

             Please note that . . .

Figure 7-1. Components of a memorandum.

Usually *memos* are used for written communication within the organization. Memos normally contain these elements: name of receiver, name of sender, date, subject, body, and signature (Figure 7-1).

A *business letter* format is normally used to send communications outside your own organization. Only on rare occasion is the letter format used within the organization. A business letter normally has the following elements: return address, date, inside address, salutation, body of the letter, complimentary close, signature, and special notations (if any). In preparing the letter, give special consideration to the theme, conclusions, communication efficiency, and tone (Figure 7-2).

A *proposal,* another form of written communication, is usually based on a substantial amount of thought and study, because acceptance or rejection is often influenced by how well it is prepared. A proposal normally includes a cover letter explaining its purpose and nature, recommendations, and justifications.

The telegram and registered or certified mail are sometimes useful methods of communication. The reason for using one of these methods is to ensure that an important message or material reaches the intended destination. At the destination, the message must be signed for, ensuring that delivery was made.

A *written report* often consists of a combination of primary and secondary information, with primary being original and secondary coming from other written sources. Usually, a report includes a letter of transmittal, an introduction, the main body (presentation of data), a summary, and conclusions.

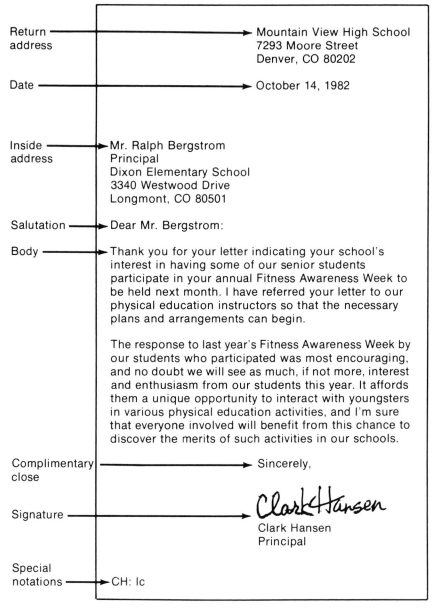

Return address → Mountain View High School
7293 Moore Street
Denver, CO 80202

Date → October 14, 1982

Inside address → Mr. Ralph Bergstrom
Principal
Dixon Elementary School
3340 Westwood Drive
Longmont, CO 80501

Salutation → Dear Mr. Bergstrom:

Body → Thank you for your letter indicating your school's interest in having some of our senior students participate in your annual Fitness Awareness Week to be held next month. I have referred your letter to our physical education instructors so that the necessary plans and arrangements can begin.

The response to last year's Fitness Awareness Week by our students who participated was most encouraging, and no doubt we will see as much, if not more, interest and enthusiasm from our students this year. It affords them a unique opportunity to interact with youngsters in various physical education activities, and I'm sure that everyone involved will benefit from this chance to discover the merits of such activities in our schools.

Complimentary close → Sincerely,

Signature → *Clark Hansen*
Clark Hansen
Principal

Special notations → CH: lc

Figure 7-2. Components of a business letter.

Sometimes the summary and conclusions are placed at the beginning and sometimes at the end. A report must be well thought out, so that it contains the essential information arranged in logical sequence and stated clearly and concisely. It is important that the information be current, accurate, and pertinent. The readability of a report and the impressions it leaves often have a substantial influence on its acceptability and the results it generates.

The written communication format should not be overworked because it becomes cumbersome if done too extensively, and it is a less personal approach than a direct conversation. On the other hand, written communication can be beneficial because the opportunity exists to make sure that it says exactly what is intended, and it can be referred to in the future if need be. The reader also has the advantage of being able to study important communications to make sure he understands their full meaning. Written communication is sometimes more efficient and convenient than oral communication, depending on the accessibility of those involved.

Mood

An administrator communicates either intentionally or unintentionally by the *mood* he conveys. For example, the enthusiasm with which he greets a co-worker the facial expression he shows when a co-worker comes to his office, or the amount of attention he gives sends a clear message.

Some administrators purposely use expression of mood as a form of language, whereas others show mood naturally. The primary danger of using this method of communication is the possibility of being labeled *moody, inconsistent,* and *unpredictable.* Administrators are generally more successful if they portray an even temperament and use a consistent approach.

Emotional Responses

People in administrative positions sometimes feel a need to put somebody in place, set the record straight, discipline a subordinate, or react firmly to a colleague. It is easy to become emotional in situations of tension and stress, and there is a tendency to make sharp and sometimes abrasive statements. Remember that once something has been said it is on the record, and it will never be completely erased. So be sure that you say what ought to be said and what you would want to say when not influenced by emotion. Keep in mind that the administrator is expected to be relatively mature, objective, and composed.

When you feel emotional about a situation and want to lash out, try to hold back until you have had ample time to think it over. If you are going to respond in writing, follow the motto "write now, send later." In other words, after writing the memo or letter, put it in your desk drawer for a day or more while your emotions settle; then read it. If you honestly feel that it should be sent, go ahead; but there is a good chance you will decide to rewrite it or not send it at all. Be very cautious about coming out quickly with statements that you will wish later had not been said.

Listening

Listening is the other side of the communication coin. It is surprising what an administrator can learn about the organization and its people if he just listens. There is an important psychologic aspect to listening; being attentive to what others say is satisfying to them.

Careful listening is especially useful in the case of grievances. Usually, when a person has thoroughly stated his grievance in the presence of the administrator, the problem is more than half solved. The remainder of the solution takes some checking and follow through, and this part is equally important.

There are many mind blocks to careful listening. Unfair prejudgments and stereotyping can prevent a person from effective listening. Anger or other emotional feelings can also get in the way, as can sloppy habits about paying attention. Good listening is more than just letting sounds pass through your ears. It involves concentrating on the meaning of what is being said and recording the important points in your mind (remembering). Here are some common pitfalls to effective listening that should be avoided.

1. Inadequate attention or divided attention.
2. Refusal to concentrate.
3. Over-emphasis on details. Do not try to memorize too many facts and figures; listen for ideas and concepts.

Listening cannot always be casual and relaxed. Serious listening requires precise attention and serious concentration. It is not just hearing words; it is also understanding statements, interpreting concepts, evaluating relative importance, appraising intent, and evaluating usefulness and application of the information. Often, effective listening involves "reading between the lines." Sometimes it involves interpreting what the person is trying to say or wants to say. It also involves watching expressions and gestures, recognizing emphases on words and phrases, and mentally attaching the correct meanings to the statements. It is said that some people listen but do not hear, others both listen and hear but do not understand. Effective listening includes *listening, hearing,* and *understanding.*

Additional Points

A great deal of time can be saved if you learn to *dictate* correspondence instead of writing it in long hand before typing. To use a dictaphone properly, be sure to speak clearly and at a steady pace. If you expect the dictated material to be typed in final form, spell out unusual words and announce new paragraphs. If you wish to break into a letter with instructions, preface your remarks with the name of your secretary in order to separate the instructions from the text of the letter. If enclosures are to be included or a number of copies made, be sure to mention it. Finally, do not allow dictated letters to be sent with your signature without first reading them to check for mistakes, or have someone else do it in whom you have confidence.

To *use the telephone efficiently,* have the secretary screen the calls. You might want to set aside specified times in the day for returning calls. Grouping similar activities such as telephone calls can help you make more efficient use of time. When speaking on the phone, identify yourself immediately, be courteous, get to the point quickly, but not in a hurried or abrupt fashion, and keep a pad and pencil handy to record information.

Using the telephone can help lay the ground work for a future meeting. This mode of communication allows for an *exchange of ideas,* without the travel time of a face-to-face conference. A *conference call* among several people might accomplish as much as getting everyone together, and at a much lower cost in terms of both time and money. It is also possible, with the use of a *telephone speaker,* to link large groups together for a free exchange of ideas, so that everyone has access to the information. Telephone *message recorders* can sometimes be used to good advantage.

Reading

Reading administrative material is another important aspect of communication. Concentrate on what you are reading by avoiding distractions. Underline important statements or write notes in the margin or on a note pad as needed. Remember that some material should be read thoroughly in an effort to get the full meaning, whereas certain other material can be skimmed for broad concepts and high points.

STAFF MEETINGS

Administrators get involved with staff meetings of three different kinds:

1. Meetings with other administrators, such as a dean meeting with department heads; a superintendent, with principals; a department head, with area coordinators; or an athletic director, with members of the administrative staff or with head coaches.

2. Faculty meetings including all or a portion of the teachers in the administrative unit.

3. Meetings with nonteaching personnel.

Too often, staff meetings are viewed by those who attend as ineffective, and rightfully so. Thus, one important challenge of an administrator is the effective handling of staff meetings. This involves several considerations: when and how often to call meetings, who to include in each meeting, how long the meeting should last, and which items should appear on the agenda.

On the wall of a firm, a motto used to hang expressing the sentiments of the president. It said "intelligence is no substitute for accurate information; enthusiasm is no substitute for experience; willingness is no substitute for ability." After a series of meetings someone added, "and meetings are no substitute for progress." [5]

Unfortunately, a high percentage of meetings are semi-failures, and the reasons are usually lack of preparation and poor leadership. A successful meeting usually requires a strong leader who is dedicated to the participative process and knows how to implement it. It is his job to see that the discussion moves toward the purposes of the meeting. The Standard Oil Corporation has in its administrative manual the following description of a meeting chairman. "He must plan, promote, lead, direct, inform, interpret, encourage, stimulate, referee, judge, moderate and conciliate."

Clear meeting objectives and time limits should be established and adhered to. If possible, the discussion leader should have a clock or a watch within view. With a time frame in mind and with a written agenda, the leader is obligated to move the meeting along at the appropriate pace, and to accomplish the purposes of the meeting within a reasonable time. [9]

In the planning stages of a meeting, several important questions must be considered.

1. What are the purposes? This should be answered clearly in the opening remarks. If members begin to digress, restate the purposes of the meeting.

2. What is needed in the way of facts and figures? Should the leader present these or let someone else do it? Who is best prepared to do it?

3. Should certain information be copied and distributed either ahead of time or during the meeting?

4. Will there be any visiting experts? If so, are they fully oriented as to what is expected of them?

5. Would visual aids help? A picture can be worth a thousand words, but only if it is the right one and it is used effectively.

6. Would a demonstration be useful? Sometimes a well planned demonstration can make a point that people otherwise will not grasp.

Be especially cautious about expounding in tedious detail, monopolizing the discussion, or permitting anyone else to do so. A joke about one leader who droned on in a meeting illustrates the point. One of the members finally left the room. In the hallway, he met another sufferer who had escaped early. "Has he finished yet?" the first escapee asked. "Yes" said the other, "long ago, but the meeting is still going on."

President Eisenhower claimed he once received the following good advice from Sherman Adams: "Never neglect an opportunity to keep your mouth shut."

Tactfully silencing others requires gentle diplomacy combined with firmness. It seems to be a maxim that those who have the least to say take the longest to say it. But sooner or later, even the most long-winded person has to take a breath. When he does, the leader must come in promptly and take command of the discussion or pass it to someone else who will keep it moving.

An executive of a successful company stated this useful point:

> Every person on our staff has better ideas than mine, but my job is to get the jury to agree. Most of the decisions made in our meetings are based on compromises, because many of the good ideas are not compatible with each other. But occasionally, a diehard in the group, unwilling to bend, blocks the process of all the others. In such cases, I have to state a reminder that the purpose is *not to win a point but find a solution.* [26]

One wise administrator found that too much time was being wasted in meetings. He made a rule that everyone who wished to present a problem had to prepare and submit a memorandum answering these questions: What is the problem? What is the cause of the problem? What are the possible solutions? Which solution do you recommend? As a result of this procedure, the number of meetings was drastically reduced because the solution usually became apparent.

It is true that meetings are often held too frequently and last too long, but a positive side to meetings was illustrated well by a seasoned administrator. The younger person asked why there were so many meetings. The older man pointed out the window to two cars in the parking lot, one sparkling new and the other very old, and asked "Do you know the difference between those two cars?" The younger elaborated on the numerous differences that were apparent. Then the older man replied, "The difference between those cars is meetings. Through dozens of meetings, administrators, engineers, and factory workers have been able to design and produce a vastly superior product. In the absence of meetings, that never would have happened."

Meetings can be highly useful for training, building group morale, decision making, grievance settling, creative brainstorming, encouraging group action and gathering or disseminating information. Unless a meeting is really needed, however, it should not be held. According to a study made by the 3-M Company, meetings cost American industry over $35 million a year. During the last decade, the number has almost doubled, and the cost has tripled. So before you call your next meeting, ask yourself if it is really the thing to do. If it is, then go ahead; but do it right so that the meeting truly will be worth its time and cost. Be sure your meetings do not support the claim of one meeting critic who said, "You can accomplish work or go to meetings, but you can't do both."

A Written Agenda

Some meetings deserve a written agenda, whereas an agenda would give others too much structure. For example, an agenda should always be considered for a faculty or staff meeting, but often is unnecessary for a committee meeting. A good rule is "if in doubt, prepare an agenda."

An agenda offers several potential advantages. It forces decisions as to what should be included in the meeting; helps guarantee premeeting preparation; permits the arrangement of items into logical groupings and desired sequence; and provides an overview of what is going to be discussed, which gives each person a better opportunity to contribute to the discussion. Time is usually more effectively utilized with a written agenda, because it helps the discussion move systematically from one item to the next.

COMMITTEES AND CONFERENCES

Committees and conferences can be among the greatest consumers of an administrator's time. Yet, guided group thinking is necessary for the proper conduct of any organization larger than a one-man shop. The potential fault lies not in the tool, but in its use or abuse. The ability to conduct an effective conference or give productive leadership to a committee is a necessary administrative skill.

A *business conference* is a meeting with one or more people for the purpose of analyzing a situation and receiving useful input, or mapping out a plan to be enacted. A *committee meeting* between the administrator and a task force or standing committee is for the purpose of receiving information from the committee or giving direction to it.

The administrator should keep in mind that the judgment of a few experts is worth more than the opinions of a large number of nonexperts. The former is the collection of intelligence, while the latter is the pooling of ignorance. Valuable administrative time can be wasted by listening to the opinions of people who are not qualified by background, education, training, or seasoned judgment.

An error that some administrators make is attempting to apply conference and committee techniques where they have little chance of success. Conferences and committees are no substitute for executive action. Using these techniques to rehash old subjects over and over violates the fundamental purpose of conference and committee techniques and retards administrative action. Following are three useful guidelines:

1. Usually it is necessary to involve members of the organization in conferences and committees in order to capitalize on their ideas and expertise and to allow them meaningful input into management.
2. On the other hand, it is important to avoid obtaining judgments and opinions and then failing to give them fair consideration. When this happens, co-workers recognize that they are only being taken through the motions—that the conference or committee procedure is phony.
3. Conferences and committee meetings may be highly formal or relatively informal. If the meeting is formal, an official record should be kept of the proceedings, decisions, and recommendations. In a less formal situation, there may be no need for a written record, although sometimes a brief memorandum of the high points of the discussion serves well as a matter of clarification and record.

In the conduct of a conference or a committee meeting, the leader usually serves as a catalyst who draws out information and gives guidance to formulate a logical plan of action based on the specialized knowledge of those present. The following are important characteristics of the conference or committee leader.

1. An analytic mind to define the problem clearly and break it down into logical parts for analysis.
2. A quick mind to handle a rapid interchange of ideas, and keep them flowing along the right track.
3. Tact in gracefully eliciting or squelching discussion as needed.
4. A sense of humor to smooth things over in a witty manner if differences of opinion get too subjective or emotional.
5. A sense of timing to know when to table a certain topic or when to bring the discussion to a conclusion.
6. An open mind and a sincere interest in the opinions and judgments of others.

Leading the Discussion

The right psychology must be employed by the group leader in order to handle potential difficulties. For example, if the group consists of a mixture of higher and lower ranking employees, the lower ranking personnel may be reluctant to enter the discussion. One or more dominating personalities may intimidate others in the group. Perhaps one member talks too much but has relatively little to offer, or another leads the discussion astray.

It is important to have the members of the conference or committee say as much as they want without having the discussion become exhaustive. In this regard, the leader must exercise the right balance between thoroughness and expediency. It is undesirable to shut off any member's comment by a sarcastic or preemptory remark. This does not mean that a certain line of discussion should not be curbed or ended, but it should be done tactfully.

The leader should discourage two or more group members from having private discussion during the meeting even if the discussion relates to the topic at hand. Such conversations are distracting and usually unproductive.

Unfortunately, some individuals have a tendency to use almost every kind of meeting for gripes and petty complaints. This has a deteriorating effect on the meeting's productivity. Such people are often excluded from important conferences or significant committee assignments because of this characteristic. When they are included, the discussion leader faces the challenge of letting them participate without allowing them to have a disruptive influence.

The leader should avoid stifling a discussion when a disagreement is stated. In a situation in which the differences are so pronounced that the meeting does not seem to be progressing, it is helpful to work toward agreement on some generalities as stepping stones toward the specifics to be accomplished.

If the discussion is to be continued in a subsequent meeting, it is a good idea to end the meeting with a summary of what has been accomplished and where the next meeting will begin. The time and place of the next meeting should be set, and it should be clarified whether anyone is expected to do preparatory work prior to the meeting. If the purposes of the conference or committee have been accomplished, the leader should make this clear and he should summarize the results and conclusions that have been reached.

Some Additional Guidelines

1. Usually, it is awkward to have a leader of a committee whose direct supervisor is a member. Other participants might tend to side with "the boss," thus reducing the effectiveness of the group leader.
2. If the leader is one of high authority, it is important that he not impose his personality or authority on the participants. This tends to squelch the free exchange of information.
3. Each participant in a conference or committee should be qualified to make a contribution. It is a waste of time to include unqualified people

unless their participation is viewed as a developmental experience for them.

4. From the standpoint of economy, the following should be avoided:
   a. duplication of talents.
   b. involvement of those who cannot afford the time.
   c. a larger number than necessary to accomplish the purposes.
5. Simple rules of courtesy or protocol such as the following, are important:
   a. give sufficient advanced notice.
   b. clear with the head of another department if a subordinate in that department is going to be invited.
   c. give proper recognition and introduction to participants from outside your organization.
   d. give prompt notice to all participants, together with an explanation, when a meeting must be cancelled.
6. The leader should make a practice of starting on time so that everyone will learn to expect this and act accordingly.
7. Serious attempts should be made to keep meetings within business hours.
8. At the outset of each meeting, the leader should describe the intent, and the meeting should end with a summary statement that caps the discussion and states what is to happen next.

Divided Attention

Imagine yourself sitting in conference with an administrator for one hour and accomplishing 30 minutes of valuable work, with the other 30 minutes spent by the administrator conversing with everyone who calls on the telephone or sticks his head in for a comment. A co-worker who is in the administrator's office on legitimate business deserves a reasonable level of, if not undivided, attention. This is especially true if the person is there by appointment. Allowing regular interruptions shows inconsideration for the person who has come to the office for a face-to-face meeting. It is inefficient and can be offensive to co-workers.

Another sign of inadequate attention is when the administrator reads paperwork out of the corner of his eye or fills in his schedule book or writes reminder notes not related to the conversation. These practices send a clear message to the other person that the administrator has a low level of interest in the conversation. Usually, an administrator will accomplish more overall if he does only one thing at a time and does it well.

OFFICE MANAGEMENT

Office activities should not be viewed as a separate function. They are integrated aspects of the overall function of the organization. Although a central office is usually needed, not all office work takes place in that location. Often, office work is decentralized in order to best serve the organization. Some of the usual aspects of office work are discussed in this section.

Receiving Visitors

The manner in which people are received when they come to the office has a significant influence on their impressions of the organization. When one considers that the receptionist has contact with many more people than does the administrator, the importance of this function becomes apparent. Consistent application of these guidelines will help assure the effectiveness of the receptionist.

1. A person who comes to the office should receive a pleasant greeting and immediate attention.
2. The receptionist should be knowledgeable about how to deal with routine matters and where to direct matters that can be handled better elsewhere.
3. Every person is important and should be treated with this in mind. Furthermore, every person's problems are important, at least to him.
4. When possible, the receptionist should help utilize waiting time by exchanging information preparatory to the visitor's appointment.
5. The receptionist's function should not include idle conversation or entertaining of visitors. It is a business procedure which deserves the right balance of friendly formality and efficiency.

Organizing

One aspect of organizing is the definition of employee responsibilities and working relationships (Chapters 7 and 16). Another aspect is office space utilization. For example, the placement of furniture and equipment in offices is important from several points of view: attractiveness, efficiency, flow of traffic, and intraoffice relationships. The challenge is to use the available square footage to the optimum to enhance the efficiency of the operation. Intraoffice business relationships and the particular duties of each person should be clearly understood. Overlap or confusion about this will reduce efficiency and detract from the desirable supportive and congenial atmosphere.

Another aspect of organizing is the committment of time. Appointments should be properly spaced to accommodate the necessary business, yet not cause any waste of time. Appointments should be clearly communicated so there is minimal chance of misunderstanding.

Office employees ought to be especially attentive to maintaining the established office hours. Doing otherwise detracts from efficiency and contributes to a poor image.

Paper Handling

Some persons could be labeled *one-time paper handlers,* some are *two-time handlers,* and others are *multiple handlers.* Every employee in the office ought to strive toward being a one-time handler of paper work. This requires that when you first give attention to a task, you bring it to a conclusion and dispose of that particular matter. As you go through your mail, for example, complete as many items as possible at the time. Pass appropriate items to the secretary for handling so as not to occupy your time with matters that she can do. Items that can better be handled by other employees should be sent on to them immediately. Certain items require dictation which can be done at the time, or these items can be grouped together if you have a scheduled time for dictation. Items that must wait for one reason or another should be filed by a method that will bring them to your attention again on the appropriate timetable. Following are some additional procedures that you will find helpful:

1. In the file drawer of your desk have a folder for each month of the year, and use these for filing materials that should come to your attention at a later date. For example, if in June you receive paper work that should be handled in September, place it in the September file.

2. Also, have a folder on your desk labeled *immediate,* one labeled *tomorrow,* and one labeled *next week,* and place papers in the respective folders for timely handling.

3. Keep in the file drawer folders labeled with the names of people with whom you often do business. When an item comes across your desk that should be handled through conversation with a particular person, drop it in that person's file, then make it part of the agenda next time the two of you meet.

4. Certain items of paper work are marginal in terms of whether they should be filed. In order to safeguard against premature disposal and, at the same time, keep the files clear of unnecessary material, have a drawer that you view as a *temporary wastebasket.* Drop the items in the drawer and let them remain there for a safe period of time. After a certain period, say once each month, move these papers to a location that you view as a *semi-permanent disposal* and let them remain there for a longer time—several months. Any item that you have not needed during this time will probably never be needed. This system keeps unnecessary papers from cluttering up the files.

Another aspect of paper work is the processing of forms. Every organization has certain standard forms to expedite management procedures. In most cases, the forms are prepared to furnish duplicate copies as needed. A purchase order is an example of a standard form. It is important to have an adequate supply of current forms, and office employees need to be knowledgeable about completing and processing the forms properly. Recording complete and accurate information on the forms is of obvious importance. It is desirable to keep a copy of each standard form that is processed.

Record Keeping and Filing

Questions as to which records to keep and the methods of keeping them require some discriminating decisions. Some people are guilty of "keeping everything and being able to find nothing" whereas others are too casual about keeping records. The following questions are pertinent to the record keeping of any organization, and the answers will serve as useful guidelines for establishing a simplified, streamlined, and crisp approach.

1. Should typists always prepare a duplicate of correspondence and file it, or should only an original be typed unless a duplicate is specifically requested?
2. How should office copies of standard forms be filed, and how long should they be retained?
3. Should all material kept on record be placed in file folders or should some be placed in loose-leaf binders or bound copy?
4. Which material should be filed in the secretarial office and which should be in a different place in order to provide the right balance of accessibility and confidentiality?
5. How should confidential records be protected, and who should have access to them?
6. How often should the files be cleared of unnecessary and obsolete material, and who should do this?
7. Which kind of filing system should be used?

Certain decisions, responses, policies, and procedures should be in writing. One reason for this is to reduce the chances of miscommunication or misunderstanding about what was said or decided. The written record can be referred to later, if the need arises. Examples that justify written records are financial agreements, contractual agreements, policy statements, and important positions of the organization or attitudes of the administrator.

Usually, the minutes of a meeting furnish an adequate record of the proceedings. Sometimes decisions and agreements that justify a written record are reached outside of formal meetings. In these cases, it is a good idea to follow-up with a letter or memo stating your interpretation of the important elements of the discussion. This helps to ensure that you and the others agree, and it provides a written copy for reference.

Application of Technology

The age of computers has entered into the area of office management. Computer programs are available for almost everything from scheduling teachers, classrooms, and students to keeping student records and helping with financial accounting. Computers are used to assist teachers in scoring tests, printing report cards, and storing grades. Intramural personnel can use a computer for scheduling facilities, teams, and officials as well as for overall record keeping. Some districts use computers to print reports of the AAHPERD Youth Fitness Test for each child, including name, age, grade, raw score, and percentile rank on all test items. The more sophisticated computers are able to store and analyze budget information, as well as compile lists and costs of supply items. It seems that whatever needs to be done where information is printed, stored, retrieved from storage or analyzed, a computer has the potential of doing the job quickly and accurately.

Many time-saving devices have also been developed for secretarial work, such as the memory typewriter, which can reproduce entire letters, and word processors, which allow a letter to be composed and later edited and typed.

Typing and duplicating materials are among the more usual aspects of office work. These materials must be done on time, in correct form, and at the acceptable quality level. Frequent decisions are needed about which materials should be typewritten, photostatically reproduced, dittoed, mimeographed, or printed.

Dictation equipment can be useful if much written correspondence is to be done. A portable dictaphone to go along with the desk set is an added advantage. This combination of equipment makes it possible to dictate almost any time and place. In turn, the use of dictating equipment makes it possible for the typist to fit dictation conveniently into his schedule, because it can remain in the machine until the preferred time.

Office equipment suppliers are developing improved products for the future, and the office of the future is naturally a topic of interest to management experts. In one sense, the office of the future never arrives; although in another sense, yesterday's office of the future is already here. The competent manager will plan for the office of the future and implement it on a timely schedule. It will be more efficient, more economical, and more effective overall.

Applying Controls

An important aspect of office management is keeping a tight rein on matters that must be controlled. For example, the issue of keys requires careful control and accurate record keeping, otherwise the security plan will deteriorate (Figure 7-3). Office supplies should be controlled at just the right level to avoid waste and still allow employees to feel that supplies are adequately available. Forms such as requisitions and budget adjustment forms should be available only to those who have official use for them. The right degree of control on the use of office machines—typewriters, xerox, mimeograph, and calculators—is needed in order to avoid breakage and get optimum use of the machines. It is useful to have a fee schedule per sheet or per hundred sheets when the machines are used by personnel from other departments or for nonofficial purposes. This can help pay for supplies, maintenance, and replacement. Controls are also needed on the availability and flow of official information.

POLICIES AND PROCEDURES

Standard policies and procedures are normally in writing, and the written form contributes toward their standardization. Nonwritten policies and procedures are less standardized. Other terms sometimes used for policies are *regulations* and *practices*.

```
┌─────────────────────────────────────────────────────────────────┐
│                    REQUEST FOR ONE KEY                            │
│                                                                   │
│  Issue one key to _____      Faculty _____      │
│                                            Staff _____       │
│  Home Address _____       Student _____       │
│                                            Other _____       │
│  Phone _____ Date _____          (explain)          │
│                                                                   │
│                                                                   │
│  I will not duplicate this key.            _____  │
│                                                    Position        │
│  I will not loan this key.                                        │
│                                                                   │
│  I will return this key when my need       _____  _____  │
│     or employment terminates.              Office Address Extension│
│                                                                   │
│                                                                   │
│                                         _____  │
│                      Signature of Person to whom Key is Issued     │
│                                                                   │
│  _____                  │
│                                            Do Not Write in         │
│  Key to fit _____     This Space             │
│                                                                   │
│  Building _____     Hook No. _____       │
│                                                                   │
│                                            Date _____       │
│  _____   _____                                          │
│  Supervisor   Signature                    Issued by _____      │
│                                                                   │
│                                            Posted by _____      │
│  _____   _____                                          │
│  Administrator Signature                   Rec. by _____        │
└─────────────────────────────────────────────────────────────────┘
```

Figure 7-3. A key request form. This is one kind of control that deserves exact procedures and accurate records.

Every organization of much size and complexity ought to have a set of written policies and procedures to serve as basic guidelines as to how people should operate within the structure of the organization. Such statements can contribute to streamlining the organization and reducing confusion and misunderstanding. These statements should deal with information of significance. If too much detail is included, the organization becomes over-structured and thereby loses the desirable amount of flexibility.

Ideally, policy and procedure statements should be concise and to the point, easy to understand, and deal only with the matters of the operation that need to be standardized.

Many policies pertaining to a local situation are developed within the framework of higher authority. For example, the Constitution of the United States sets forth certain conditions that affect policy in organizations throughout the country. Within this context, educators must comply with (1) the equal rights legislation as it applies to differences in race, sex, and age, (2) the concept of separation of church and state, and (3) the various conditions inherent in fair or due process. The State Code contains various statements that influence the policies and procedures of the political subdivisions, including school districts, and state colleges and universities. The State Board of Education establishes policies and procedures that apply to the local educational units. These include such items as the number of days school must be in session, teacher certification requirements, subject requirements, salary requirements, salary guidelines, and regulations pertaining to the school tax base.

Within the framework established by higher authority, local school officials establish local policies. As a general rule, the cliche "many hands (or heads) make work easy" is true in developing policies and procedures. Optimum involvement of people has two potential advantages: it results in useful input, and people feel better about adhering to policies and procedures when they participate in developing them.

Various approaches can be used successfully in preparing policy statements. One method is to identify the topics about which written statements are needed, and then assign a committee to formulate the statements in tentative form so that they can become finalized through approval of the administrator and/or employees. Another approach is to have the administrator state policies and procedures based on his own perception and then go through the appropriate steps of having them accepted by others in the organization. In schools, policies are often adopted from other schools or school districts where they have functioned successfully. This is a convenient method.

Policies and procedures should be viewed as guidelines and not absolute rules. The desirable amount of flexibility in connection with each policy might vary, depending on the topic and the related circumstances; but a strong element of consistency should exist. Policies and procedures should be viewed as dynamic in the sense that they should be kept current, undergoing additions, deletions, and changes as the circumstances justify.

Sample Policies and Procedures

Following are two sample policy statements, actually taken from a policy and procedure manual, which pertain to physical education and athletics.[14]

Policy Statement I: Scheduling Facilities. The facilities of the department will be scheduled in accordance with the following priorities: (1) regular daytime classes and athletic practices and contests; (2) other activities sponsored by the department such as intramurals, extramurals, rehearsals, evening classes, and free play; (3) scheduled activities sponsored by other divisions of the school; (4) activities sponsored by student, faculty, and staff groups; (5) activities sponsored by groups not affiliated with the school.

Policy Statement 2: Grading.   Because grades are important to students in several ways, the instructor is obligated to give careful attention to the application of a sound system of grading. The instructor ought to do the following:
1. At the beginning of the course, clearly inform the students of the criteria for grading in that course.
2. Interpret for the students what each grade means in terms of quality and quantity of work or performance.
3. Be sure adequate information is obtained about each student and that accurate records are kept to support the grade.
4. Be especially careful in reporting grades in order to minimize the number of grade changes.

Other Topics for Written Policies and Procedures

Each organization varies in terms of the topics for which standard policies and procedures are needed; therefore, the following list would not apply to any particular situation. However, it provides insight about the topics for which statements are often prepared.

Class Conduct

Attendance records and class make-up procedures.
Student evaluation and grading.
Class attire for teachers and students.
Facilities, equipment and supplies for class use.

Facilities

Priorities.
Procedures for scheduling.
Availability and restrictions for nonschool purposes.
Care of facilities.
Facility security—key acquisition and accountability.

Equipment and Supplies

Procedures relative to purchase.
Maintenance and care.
Checking out and in.
Responsibility and accountability.

Health and Safety

Safety regulations, particularly relative to hazardous areas and activities.
Reporting accidents, injuries, and sickness.
Availability and use of school nurse and physician.
Care and treatment of injured persons.
Student health services and insurance.

Personnel

Handling of contracts.
Tenure and dismissal procedures.
Sick leave, official leave, and vacation time.
Advancements.
Salary schedules and extra pay for extra service.
Retirement.
Definition of work load.
Teacher evaluation procedures.

Professional Development

Time and travel expenses for conferences, conventions, and others.
Advanced study and higher degrees.
Professional development leaves.
Additional remuneration.

In addition to the topics stated above, policy and procedure statements are often prepared on such matters as *committee work, in-house communication, financial administration, nonschool relationships, conflicts of interest, and professional ethics.*

BIBLIOGRAPHY

1. Baskin, O., and Aronoff, C.E.: Interpersonal Communication in Organizations. Santa Monica, CA, Goodyear Publishing Co., 1980.

2. Berko, R.M., Wolvin, A.D., and Curtis, R.: This Business of Communicating. Dubuque, IA, W.C. Brown, 1980.

3. Blicq, R.S.: On the Move: Communication for Employees. Englewood Cliffs, NJ, Prentice-Hall, 1976.

4. Bonner, W.H., and Voyles, J.: Communicating in Business: Keys to Success. Houston, TX, Dame Publications, 1980.

5. Bradford, L.P.: Making Meetings Work: A Guide for Leaders and Group Members. LaJolla, CA, University Associates, 1976.

6. Bradley, P.H., and Baird, J.E., Jr.: Communication for Business and the Professions. Dubuque, IA, W.C. Brown, 1980.

7. Brown, D.: Why executives can't write. Work Press R, 28:52, 1981.

8. Brown, H.M., and Reid, K.K.: Business Writing and Communication: Strategies and Applications. New York, Van Nostrand, 1979.

9. Carnes, W.: Effective Meetings for Busy People: Let's Decide it and Go Home. New York, McGraw Hill, 1980.

10. Charles, K.C.: Communicating more than meets the eye. Nations Bus, 69:72, 1981.

11. Guth, C.K.: How to Put on Dynamic Meetings: Teaming the Oral with the Visual. Reston, VA., Reston Publishing Co., 1980.

12. Hunt, G.T.: Communication Skills in the Organization. Englewood Cliffs, NJ, Prentice-Hall, 1980.

13. Keeling, B.L., Kallaus, N.F., and Neuner, J.J.: Administrative Office Management, 7th Ed. Cincinnati, South-Western Publishing Co., 1978.

14. Jensen, C.R.: Policy and Procedure Manual, College of Physical Education, Brigham Young University, Provo, UT, 1982.

15. Koehler, J.W., Anatol, K.W.E., and Applbaum, R.L.: Organizational Communication: Behavioral Perspectives. NY, Holt, Rinehart & Winston, 1981.

16. Lawson, J.D.: When you Preside, 5th Ed. Danville, IL, Interstate Printers and Publishers, 1980.

17. Leaming, M.P., and Motley, R.J.: Administrative Office Management: A Practical Approach. Dubuque, IA, W.C. Brown, 1979.

18. Murphy, H.A., and Peck, C.E.: Effective Business Communications 3rd Ed. New York, McGraw Hill, 1980.

19. Nolan, R.E., Young, R.T., and DiSylvester, B.C.: Improving Productivity Through Advanced Office Controls. New York, AMACOM, 1980.

20. Preston, P.: Communication for Managers. Englewood Cliffs, NJ, Prentice-Hall, 1979.

21. Quible, Z.K.: Introduction to Administrative Office Management. Cambridge, MA, Winthrop Publishers, 1980.

22. Richardson, M.A., and Caton, I.: Creative communicative designs, JOPER 50:30, 1979.

23. Ryckman, W.G.: What Do You Mean By That? The Art of Speaking and Writing Clearly. Homewood, IL, Dow Jones-Irwin, 1980.

24. Snyder, M.C.: Some correlations of communication roles in organizations, Acad Mgmt J 22:55, 1979.

25. Terry, G.R., and Stallard, J.J.: Office Management and Control: The Administrative Managing of Information. 8th Ed. Homewood, IL, R.D. Irwin, 1980.

26. Tyson, C.H.: Communicating with self and others. (Address September 9, 1980), Vital Speeches 47:16, 1980.

Chapter *8*

PERSONNEL MANAGEMENT

Personnel management is among the most important responsibilities of an administrator, because personnel compose the most important resource of the organization. This is particularly true in an educational organization, where all of the primary objectives have to do with the improvement of people. Underlying personnel management is the concept that if you can keep the right people in the right positions and provide them with an optimum amount of direction and support, they will cause the organization to succeed. Conversely, it is impossible to succeed in the absence of well-qualified personnel.

Aspects of personnel administration include the following: defining positions (job analysis and descriptions), selecting and hiring, employee benefits, orientation, supervision, staff productivity, personnel evaluation, handling of grievances or special problems, termination procedures, personnel files, professional ethics, professional improvement, and the application of equal opportunity laws and guidelines.

JOB ANALYSIS AND DESCRIPTION

Job analysis involves determining the responsibilities that go with each position, the qualifications that are required or desired for the position, and the overall value of the position to the organization. Critical job analysis often results in certain modifications and realignments of job responsibilities.

Written descriptions of the various positions in an organization serve a useful purpose by clarifying the personnel structure. Job descriptions should be written clearly and with enough specificity to cover the subject adequately, without spelling out every detail of the job. Some positions are relatively easy to describe, whereas others are difficult due to the diversification and unusual nature of the responsibilities.

Some of the jobs in educational organizations that need to be described are superintendent, principal, supervisor, specialist, dean, director, depart-

106

ment head, teacher, coach, researcher, athletic trainer, secretary/re-
ceptionist, stenographer, typist, equipment manager, and issue room clerk.
Not all of these positions would exist in any one organization; and in certain
organizations, some jobs might exist that are not named here. In two different organizations, a position with the same title might have a slightly different description; but usually, the descriptions are similar. In order to provide
representative samples, descriptions of two positions are included here:
stenographer and swimming pool manager. In addition, descriptions of the
following administrative positions appear in Chapter 14: school superintendent, school principal, college dean, assistant dean, department chairman,
and athletic director.

Stenographer

1. Takes shorthand; types routine correspondence, minutes, tests, class
   materials, etc.
2. Answers the telephone and assists visitors, students, faculty, and others
   who contact the office.
3. Maintains budget records as assigned.
4. Maintains the office files and keeps complete and accurate records.
5. Proofreads correspondence, reports, etc.
6. Supervises part-time office employees.
7. Determines work priorities.

Swimming Pool Manager

The Pool Manager is directly responsible to the Natatorium Supervisor.
His specific duties are as follows:

1. Coordinates the selection, hiring, training, scheduling, and supervision
   of lifeguards.
2. Coordinates the maintenance and upkeep of all equipment and materials associated with the operation of the pools, with special attention
   given to safety equipment.
3. Coordinates the ordering and replacement of equipment and materials
   as needed.
4. Coordinates the scheduling of all activities in the swimming pools.
5. Coordinates the conduct of all competitive swimming, diving, and
   water polo meets held in the pools.
6. Posts and maintains regular office hours, during which time interested
   persons can discuss activities relating to the pools.

SELECTION AND HIRING

Some of the most important decisions made by an administrator are those
involving the selection of personnel to be employed in the organization. If
these are consistently good decisions, the organization will be staffed with
well-prepared and effective people, which will help to assure its success.

The exact procedures for selecting and hiring personnel vary with different organizations, but certain procedures are basic:

1. Usually files are established and maintained on prospective faculty members so that when a position becomes vacant, these individuals will receive consideration.

2. In most cases, a position vacancy form must be processed. This includes a description of the position, the required qualifications, and eventually, a list of all those who are considered and the one finally selected.

3. An announcement of the vacancy is printed and/or posted in various sources and locations. The announcement includes the necessary information to attract the attention of potential candidates and an explanation of the procedures for applying.

4. Applications are received and handled in accordance with prescribed procedure. In some cases, the decision is made by one person in an administrative position; sometimes two or three administrators are involved; and in other cases, a search committee or selection committee is involved.

5. After reviewing the applications, a small number of applicants are offered interviews, and from this group a final selection is made. The terms of employment are agreed upon and the person becomes officially employed.

The following steps are taken in the selection and employment of faculty members at Brigham Young University.

Procedural Steps for Employment of New Faculty Members [4]

Obtain authorization to fill position, including position vacancy form.

Prepare and distribute official announcement of the position vacancy with the essential information included.

Receive applications and complete files of those who are legitimate prospects.

Submit the files for review by the selection of personnel committee if such committee is utilized.

Arrange for interviews of selected applicants. This involves travel arrangements and appointments with the interviewers.

Submit a "Request for Appointment," including recommended salary and rank.

Obtain authorization to make an official offer.

Send offer letter to the selected candidate.

Send a copy of the candidate's reply to the vice president.

Initiate a letter of appointment (contract) to be sent to the new employee.

After the signed contract is returned, have official notice of employment prepared and sent to the new employee along with information about orientation procedures.

Assessing Applicants

Much useful information can be obtained from a well-prepared job application form. Such a form should include essential information about educational background and degrees earned, previous work experience, special or unusual achievements, and numerous other pertinent facts. The application becomes even more useful if it is accompanied by a personal resume or vita.

Assuming that an applicant's job performance in the future would be consistent with that of the past, recommendations from former employers may be excellent sources of information. One should be cautious about accepting letters of recommendation at their face value because (1) such letters are usually written by individuals of the applicant's choice, and (2) in writing letters of recommendation, people are often more complimentary than is justified. Letters of recommendation from reliable sources, however, can furnish some of the most valuable information in the selection process.

The best indication of potential success is immediate previous success in a similar position. Other indicators are much less reliable, but still useful. Among the other indicators are academic achievement, prediction tests, direct impressions of how well a candidate would perform, and success in other lines of work.

Figures 8-1 and 8-2 show examples of forms that can help to give structure to the selection process.

CONTRACTS

A contract is an official agreement between two or more parties with certain conditions described. It is common practice for teachers and administrators to be employed under contract, whereas other school personnel are normally employed under contractual arrangements, such as by time card at an hourly rate or by the month. A properly prepared and signed contract is a legal document; meaning that both parties are bound and are expected to adhere to the conditions of the contract, unless the parties mutually agree to a contract release or modification. Certain points of information are essential in a teacher contract, such as duration of employment, salary, job title and/or rank, fringe benefits (unless explained elsewhere), and the basic responsibilities.

Figure 8-3 shows an example of a typical contract. Most contracts include an attachment or enclosure that provides additional information about the specific conditions of employment.

BENEFITS

In educational organizations, employee benefits normally cost between 15 and 25% of an individual's salary. It is assumed that the benefits are actually worth this much to the individual. Employees and prospective employees need to know the specifics of the benefits and their monetary value.

PROSPECTIVE EMPLOYEE RECOMMENDATION FORM

The below named applicant has given your name as a reference for a position in our school system. Your evaluation will be kept confidential. Please rate each category: (0) unobserved, (1) below average, (3) average, or (5) above average.

Date _____

To _____   RE: _____
                                      (applicant)
Address _____
                                 For _____
_____   (position)

	0	1	2	3	4	5	Remarks
1. Appropriate model for students							
2. Overall appearance							
3. Scholarship in major teaching areas							
4. Scholarship in minor teaching areas							
5. Rapport with students							
6. Ability to effectively organize							
7. Ability to effectively communicate							
8. Ability to motivate students							
9. Ability to control students							
10. Competency in teaching (coaching)							
11. Acceptance of responsibility							
12. Overall professionalism							
13. Overall ability to succeed							

How long have you known the applicant? _____

In what relation have you known the applicant? _____

Would you hire the applicant for this position? _____

Additional comments _____

_____

Signature _____   Title _____

Figure 8-1. Example of a prospective employee recommendation form.

INTERVIEW FORM

Name of Organization _____

After the applicant has left the room, complete this rating form. The rating categories are: (1) below average, (3) average, and (5) above average.

Date _____

Interviewer _____

Applicant _____   For _____
             (name)   (position)

	1	2	3	4	5	Remarks
1. Personal appearance						
2. Ability to communicate						
3. Personality appeal						
4. Interest in the position						
5. Positive professional outlook						
6. Knowledge of subject area						
7. Knowledge of student characteristics						
8. Attitude toward students						
9. Philosophy of teaching/coaching						
10. Degree of appropriateness for the job						

Strengths: _____

_____

_____

_____

Weaknesses: _____

_____

_____

_____

Comments: _____

_____

_____

Figure 8-2. Example of an interview form for prospective teachers.

Letter of Appointment

Name and address   Date _____

of faculty member _____

_____

     On behalf of the Board of Trustees and the President, I am
pleased to offer you a faculty position for the year beginning

_____ and ending _____. Your

salary will be $_____, to be paid to you in twelve equal

installments, commencing _____, and your rank or

title will be _____.

     This letter is being sent to you in duplicate. If the terms of your
appointment are acceptable, please sign and return one copy within twenty
days of the date of this letter; otherwise this offer will lapse. We are required
to set this time limit in order that we may immediately recruit someone in your
place if we do not receive your acceptance within such period of time.

     We are enclosing a memorandum relating to employment of faculty
members of this institution. Compliance with the terms of this memorandum
is a condition of your employment.

     If you have any questions about this appointment, I suggest that you
confer with your dean, director, or other officer supervising your work.
Questions concerning payroll deductions, group insurance, and other fringe
benefits should be directed to the Benefits Office.

     The Board of Trustees and the Administration are most appreciative of
the loyal service of the faculty of the University. We trust that the continued
spirit of cooperation and devotion to duty will improve even further the
quality of service to our students and our performance in our other duties.

                                      Sincerely,

                                       Academic Vice President

     I hereby accept the appointment stated above this _____ day

of _____, 19__.

                                 _____

Figure 8-3. Typical letter of appointment for a college teacher. A high school teacher contract
would be similar.

Normally, the two major aspects of the benefits program are retirement and insurance. Most professionals in education are enrolled in the state education retirement program, and these benefits are comparable from one state to another, even though they differ in some respects. Well-established private education organizations usually provide retirement benefits that are comparable to the state schools. The insurance program normally includes health and accident coverage and sometimes, life insurance.

When a teacher considers a new position, he should become well-informed about the benefits associated with it. This can be done by a combination of the following approaches.

Information provided in interviews, the orientation sessions, or other conversations.

Information in the written contract, the policy and procedure manual, or other written documents containing such information.

Information obtained directly from the personnel office or from administrative officials.

Personnel benefits help school employees obtain benefits that they could not obtain as well, or as cheaply, on an individual basis. A good benefits program helps in the recruitment and retention of competent personnel and the enhancement of good morale among employees. Following are the kinds of personnel benefits available; however, it is unlikely that any organization would furnish all of these.

Retirement (including participation in social security)

Insurance—group life and medical

Workmen's compensation

Periodic medical examinations

Tenure

Leaves of absence—sick leave, maternity, emergency, professional development (conferences and workshops, travel study, sabbatical)

Credit union benefits

Legal services (under certain conditions)

Parking privileges

Free or reduced admission to special interest and entertainment events

It should be rememebered by both employer and employee that benefits that have true value are the same as money in the bank. Most employees, however, would prefer increases in salary rather than an equivalent amount in benefits. The proportion of resources that go into salary and benefits needs to be kept in proper balance for the overall good of the organization and the individuals.

ORIENTATION

The orientation of a new employee occurs through a combination of several approaches, including the interviewing process, study of the school's policy and procedure manual, and conversations with other school personnel. In addition to these procedures, new employees usually go through a

114 • *Management Techniques*

formal orientation session. This can be viewed as an educational or professional development experience designed specifically to prepare employees to be informed about policies, procedures, regulations, benefits, and restrictions that pertain to their positions. It is especially important that the orientation be well planned and effectively conducted. The manner in which the orientation is accomplished can have a significant influence on the employees' early impressions of the organization and its administrators.

SUPERVISION

Only a small amount of supervision is necessary and appropriate for employees who are highly responsible, dependable, and well prepared. A good employee has little need for a "boss." In such cases, the "boss" needs only to provide general direction and support. This form of supervision is usually pleasant and relatively easy for both the supervisor and those being supervised.

On the other end of the scale are employees who need close and constant supervision. Such people are incompetent in the sense that they are irresponsible and undependable. They violate rules of efficiency and effectiveness and take advantage of the employer. The practical way to deal with such people is either to bring about positive change or else replace them with more competent personnel at the earliest opportunity.

Some guidelines for a supervisor are as follow:

1. The supervisor should view himself as both an educator and a motivator. The *educational* role involves teaching the employees how to better perform their responsibilities. The *motivating* function involves regular encouragement and meaningful challenge.
2. A congenial and business-like relationship is recommended. This contributes to pleasant working conditions and yet prohibits the employee from taking advantage of a relationship that might be too casual or chummy.
3. Either oversupervision or undersupervision can be detrimental.
4. Those who are given limited supervisory responsibilities have a tendency to want to stop their other work and become full-time supervisors. This can contribute to inefficiency.

STAFF PRODUCTIVITY (Figure 8-4)

In the literature on personnel relationships, two opposite views are often compared—the negative precept and the positive precept. The negative precept holds that (1) the average employee dislikes work, tries to avoid it when possible, and must be coerced into performing adequately; (2) is not ambitious, dislikes job responsibilities, and needs to be supervised closely; (3) is naturally self-centered and indifferent or oblivious to organizational goals; (4) consistently resists change; and, (5) desires job security and economic rewards above all else.

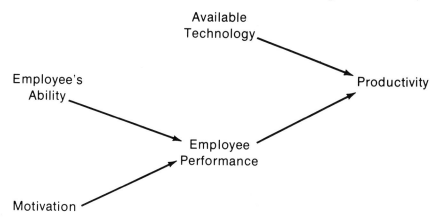

Figure 8-4. Factors contributing to employee productivity.

The positive precept emphasizes that for the average employee, (1) the expenditure of physical and mental effort in work is natural and rewarding; (2) self-directon and self-control can be expected; (3) commitment to specific objectives is a result of the rewards associated with their achievement; (4) it is satisfying to accept rather than avoid responsibility under proper conditions; (5) a substantial capacity exists for imagination, ingenuity, and creativity in solving organizational problems; and, (6) most organizations only partially use the employee's potential.

Both the negative and the positive precepts have elements of truth, and certainly there are individuals and work groups who can be strongly identified with either of these extremes. Most people, however, fall somewhere between the two. Fortunately, professional educators typically tend toward the positive precepts. However, there are some unfortunate exceptions to this, and educational organizations employ numerous nonprofessional individuals, many of whom may be more aligned with the negative precept. Any professional educator who is not strongly oriented toward the positive precepts would be a poor representative of his profession and a bad risk for an educational organization.

An administrator must be alert to the kinds of precepts the individual employees emphasize, and try to utilize that information in the motivating process. Often, positive changes can be brought about by encouraging individuals to emphasize the positive precepts. The selection and hiring process often provides the best opportunity for developing a high level of productivity. Strong decisions relative to personnel selection are crucial.

In addition, the total environment should be conducive to high-level productivity. There ought to be adequate facilities, equipment, and supplies; a climate that is motivating and relatively free of friction, apprehension, and frustrations; challenging assignments; and an atmosphere of encouragement.

Employee morale is another important factor in productivity, and the administrator is usually in a strong position to influence this. If good morale is to be attained, the administrator must have concern for the staff members and their welfare; and he must maintain an atmosphere of trust, honesty, and openness. Clearly stated objectives, consistency of procedures and overall administrative efficiency have positive influences on morale. A further discussion of this topic is included in the section on motivation in Chapter 6.

The crucial factor in education is student progress toward the educational objectives. Teachers are the primary facilitators of student progress. Therefore, teacher effectiveness must be viewed as the primary objective of administration.

Administrative practices and techniques have a direct influence on teacher productivity in several ways.

1. The administration can be either effective or ineffective in providing adequate facilities, equipment, and supplies.
2. Ample compensation is important not only because of the economic factor, but also because it sends a message about how the teacher's worth is perceived.
3. Clearly defined and expedient administrative methods can contribute to the efficiency of everyone in the organization.
4. The administrative climate can be either motivating or demotivating to teachers. Research has indicated that a positive, congenial, and open administrative atmosphere contributes more to motivation and results in less absenteeism and dissatisfaction; whereas the opposite results are associated with an administrative climate that is antagonistic and closed.

Practically all administrative efforts are pointed either directly or indirectly toward staff productivity.

TENURE

The rationale of tenure for teachers is based on the legitimate need to protect teachers from being dismissed for unjustified reasons, such as personal differences with a school administrator; legitimate participation in politics; making room for an administrator's friend or favorite, and practicing reasonable academic freedom, which might not be fully acceptable to a certain administrator. Tenure contributes to stability of the faculty and to peace of mind for the individual employees.

Although most school systems in the United States operate under a tenure law, some do not. Where tenure laws do not apply, a "continuing contract" usually does. This means that a teacher's contract will be automatically renewed the next year unless the teacher is notified to the contrary before a specified date, in which case all aspects of correct due process should be followed.

New teachers are normally on a nontenured, or probationary, status for a period of 2 to 5 years (this time varies in different states) before becoming eligible for tenure. Coaches may receive tenure as teachers, but the coaching assignment is normally not subject to tenure.

The concept of tenure is clearly justified, and the results are generally positive. The tenure system has one glaring weakness, however; it gives a certain amount of job security to some teachers who have become outdated and incompetent. Unfortunately, almost every school system has some teachers who have acquired job security at relatively high salaries, and who could easily be replaced by more competent younger teachers at lower salaries. The control or correction of these situations is an important challenge for school administrators.

According to the records of the National Education Association, states fall into four categories in terms of tenure laws.

Group 1 States with statewide tenure laws.

Alabama	Minnesota
Alaska	Missouri
Arizona	Montana
Arkansas	Nevada
Colorado	New Hampshire
Connecticut	New Jersey
Delaware	New Mexico
District of Columbia	North Carolina
Florida	North Dakota
Hawaii	Ohio
Idaho	Oklahoma
Illinois	Pennsylvania
Indiana	Rhode Island
Iowa	South Dakota
Kentucky	Tennessee
Louisiana	Virginia
Maine	Washington
Maryland	West Virginia
Massachusetts	Wyoming
Michigan	

Group 2 Tenure laws that are less than statewide (exceptions noted).

California: Optional in districts with average daily attendance under 750 pupils.
New York: Certain rural districts not covered.
Texas: Law is permissive; all districts have the option of coming under the tenure provision.
Georgia: DeKalb, Fulton, and Richmond counties only.
Kansas: Kansas City, Topeka, and Wichita only.
Nebraska: Lincoln and Omaha only.
Oregon: Districts with an average daily attendance of 4,500 or more, and districts where tenure was in effect on August 24, 1965.
Wisconsin: County and City of Milwaukee only.

Group 3 Continuing contract laws with notification of termination required by a specified date (except as stated in group 2).

Kansas
Nebraska
Oregon
Wisconsin

Group 4 Annual or long term contracts.

Georgia (exception stated in group 2)
Mississippi

South Carolina
Utah
Vermont

GRIEVANCES

These days it is common practice for an educational system to have a prescribed procedure for the handling of personnel grievances. The procedure should be simple but effective. Ordinarily it involves the following:

1. Discussing the grievance with one's immediate supervisor and attempting to solve it at that level.
2. If this effort is unsuccessful, the grievance is taken to the next higher administrative level.
3. If the grievance remains unresolved, it will sometimes be taken one level higher, but more likely it will be placed in the hands of a grievance committee, composed of three or more staff members. This committee will study the pros and cons of the situation and attempt to bring the matter to a satisfactory solution.

Grievances ought to be kept to a minimum because they use up time and energy that could better be spent on more productive matters. Effective control of grievances is closely related to the administrator's sensitivity and responsiveness to potential tension-causing situations, along with his personality, good judgment, and implementation of sound procedures. However, it is not possible to totally avoid grievances; therefore, an organization must have a fair and effective procedure for dealing with them.

TERMINATIONS

Termination can occur by initiative of the individual or by action of the organization. Termination procedures ought to be spelled out in the policy manual, and they must be enforced in order to ensure that terminations occur in an orderly manner. Regardless of who initiates the termination or what reasons are behind it, the procedures should include the following: (1) sufficient advance notice; (2) written notification placed on file; (3) processing the termination form, which ensures proper checkout and clearances in terms of keys, equipment, library materials, and the like; and (4) final financial settlement.

PERSONNEL FILES

A file is kept on each member of the faculty, and files are also usually kept on other employees. It is important that personnel files contain as much useful information as possible, but not become filled with trivia or nonapplicable material. The files should be available only to those who rightfully have access to them, and be treated with a high level of confidentiality. Most administrators would probably agree that an individual should be able to examine his or her own file upon request; however, this practice is usually governed by an organizational policy that spells out the handling and accessibility of personnel files.

PROFESSIONAL ETHICS

Professions adopt codes of ethics as recommended guidelines for conduct of those in the profession. The education profession has a code of ethics that has been set forth by the National Education Association (NEA) and the American Association of University Professors (AAUP). The American Alliance for Health, Physical Education, Recreation and Dance (AAHPERD) has prepared a code of ethics, which is reprinted here with their permission. All administrators, teachers, and coaches in physical education and athletics should be well informed about the contents of this code.

Preamble

Believing that the strength of our American democracy and its influence upon the course of events everywhere in the world lies in the physical, mental and moral strength of its individual citizens; believing that the schools of America possess the greatest potential for the development of these strengths in our young citizens; believing that the teachers of physical education have a unique opportunity, as well as a responsibility to contribute greatly to the achievement of this potentiality; believing that all teachers of physical education should approach this great responsibility in a spirit of true professional devotion, the AAHPERD proposes for the guidance of its members the following:

PRINCIPLES OF ETHICS

1. Inasmuch as teachers of physical education are members of the teaching profession, the AAHPERD endorses without reservation the Code of Ethics for Teachers, adopted by the National Education Association.

2. The aim of physical education is the optimum development of the individual. To this end teachers of physical education should conduct programs and provide opportunities for experiences which will promote the physical development of youth and contribute to social, emotional, and mental growth.

3. In a democratic society every child has a right to the time of the teacher, to the use of the facilities, and a part in the planned activities. Physical education teachers should resist the temptation to devote an undue amount of time and attention to the activities of students of superior ability to the neglect of the less proficient.

4. The professional relations of a teacher with pupils require that all information of a personal nature shall be held in strict confidence.

5. While a physical education teacher should maintain a friendly interest in the progress of pupils, familiarity should be avoided as inimical to effective teaching and professional dignity.

6. The teacher's personal life should exemplify the highest ethical principles and should motivate children to the practice of good living and wholesome activities.

7. To promote effective teaching, the teacher of physical education should maintain relations with associates which are based on mutual integrity, understanding, and respect.

8. The physical education teacher should cooperate fully and unselfishly in all school endeavors which are within the sphere of education. He should be an integral part of the school faculty, expecting neither privileges nor rewards that are not available to other members of the faculty.

9. It is an obligation of the teacher of physical education to understand and make use of proper administrative channels in approaching the problems encountered in education and in schools.

10. It is the duty of the physical education teacher to strive for progress in personal education and to promote emerging practices and programs in physical education. The teacher should also endeavor to achieve status in the profession of education.

11. Professional ethics imply that altruistic purpose outweighs personal gain. The teacher, therefore, should avoid using personal glory achieved through winning teams for the purpose of self-promotion.

12. It is considered unethical to endorse physical education equipment, materials and other commercial products for personal gain or to support anything of a pseudo-educational nature. Nor should a teacher profit personally through the purchase of materials for physical education by the school.

13. It is the responsibility of the teacher of physical education to acquire a real understanding of children and youth in order that he may contribute to their growth and development. To achieve this understanding, it is essential that an earnest effort be made to foster and strengthen good school-home-community relationships.

14. It is the duty of every teacher of physical education to become acquainted with and to participate in the affairs of the community, particularly those concerned with making the community a better place in which to live. The teacher should take an active interest in the work of the various child- and youth-serving agencies, participating as a citizen, and as a leader of children, youth and adults.

15. Inasmuch as physical education will progress through strong local, state, and national organizations, the teacher of physical education is obligated to membership and active participation in the proceedings of professional organizations, both in general education and in the specialized field of physical education.

16. Institutions preparing teachers of physical education have an ethical responsibility to the profession, to the public and nation for the admission, education, and retention of desirable candidates for teaching. To meet this obligation, curriculum offerings must be in harmony with the highest standards of professional education.

17. Teachers of physical education should render professional service by recruiting qualified men and women for future teachers of America. The physical education teacher also has a professional obligation to assist in the learning, practice and understanding of student teachers in the field.[1]

PROFESSIONAL IMPROVEMENT

One approach to professional improvement involves the earning of a higher degree. There are also other kinds of educational involvement that have practical value, such as attendance and participation at conventions, clinics and workshops; meaningful research and writing; and the reading of professional literature.

In allocating funds for professional development, administrators must be discriminating to make sure that the optimum improvement is gained for the amount of funds expended. In this regard, it is not good enough to simply respond to employees' ideas. It is also important to aggressively generate and implement other professional development opportunities. In connection with each employee, especially the faculty, the concept of the individual development cycle presented in Figure 8-5 ought to be applied.

Figure 8-5. Diagram of an individual development program cycle.

Implementing professional development opportunities has two purposes: (1) to prevent employees from becoming outdated and less competent, and (2) to cause them to become better prepared and more competent. Professional improvement should be viewed as a valuable supplement to an individual's basic preparation and professional experience. It should be approached with enthusiasm and high expectations, and viewed as an opportunity to improve both the individual and the organization.

In order for professional development experiences to be beneficial, they must be well planned (this usually involves a written proposal); approved and funded with enough lead time for adequate planning and preparation; and include an oral or written report of sufficient detail. In the case of professional development leaves, interim reports are also often required.

Retrenching of Personnel

Occasionally, an educational organization finds that the curricular emphases have evolved away from the competencies of certain faculty. Two acceptable solutions to this are either to replace the faculty members who have become outdated or to have outdated faculty members retrench themselves to fit the present and future curricular needs. Retrenching is usually done through the various professional improvement opportunities over a period of time, causing each faculty member to keep up professional competencies. Occasionally, the need for new competencies is so pressing that, in order to meet the need, a person must go through extensive repreparation. Administrators should carefully monitor the need for professional retrenchment and try to provide attractive and timely opportunities to help the employees keep current with the needs of the program.

TEACHER UNIONIZATION

Administrators typically oppose unionization of teachers because it emphasizes the labor versus management concept. This feeling of competition causes a barrier between teachers and administrators which detracts from a congenial working relationship. It contradicts the "happy family" environment that teachers and administrators have traditionally enjoyed. Some believe that unionization tends to damage the public image of the education profession.

In spite of these disadvantages, unionization among teachers has become popular and will probably remain so during the foreseeable future. Through collective bargaining, educators have gained some financial benefits. Whether unionization among teachers continues to be effective will depend largely on the public's attitude toward it and whether the union leaders act wisely.

EQUAL EMPLOYMENT OPPORTUNITIES

No discussion of personnel administration would be complete without reference to the laws pertaining to equal employment opportunities and affirmative action. The original equal employment opportunity act was Title VII of the Civil Rights Act of 1964, amended by the EEC Act of 1972. Educational institutions, at both the public school and university levels, in their role as employer, are under the jurisdiction of this act.

Title VII is the federal statute designed to provide all persons an equal opportunity for meaningful employment, regardless of race, religion, color, sex, or national origin. This law represents the federal effort to eliminate past patterns of discrimination in employment and to ensure that free and open access to employment will exist for all qualified applicants.

The basic concepts of Title VII are found in section 703, which outlines discrimination in employment, and makes an employment practice unlawful when it:

1. results in a failure or refusal to hire any individual because of such person's race, religion, color, sex, or national origin;

2. results in the discharge of any individual because of such person's race, color, religion, sex, or national origin;

3. differentiates between individuals with respect to compensation, terms, conditions, or privileges of employment because of such person's race, color, religion, sex, or national origin;

4. limits, segregates, or classifies employees or applicants for employment in any way which would deprive or tend to deprive any individual of employment opportunities, or otherwise adversely affect such person's employment status, because of such person's race, color, religion, sex, or national origin.

Other federal government programs pertaining to equal employment opportunities include the following:

Affirmative Action

Since January 13, 1973, all educational institutions (both public and private) with one or more federal contract(s) of $50,000 or more and 50 or more employees have been required to maintain a written affirmative action plan. Although the requirement to maintain a written plan does not apply unless an institution has a federal contract of $50,000 or more, federal contracts during any 12-month period that have an aggregate total exceeding $10,000 subject an institution to compliance with the executive orders and Office of Federal Contract Compliance Programs of the Department of Labor.

The basic authority requiring affirmative action is Executive Order 11246, as amended by Executive Order 11375. These orders require each federal contracting agency to include in every contract entered into by that agency, provisions that obligate the individual contractor, in part, as follows:

The Contractor will not discriminate against any employee or applicant for employment because of race, color, religion, sex or national origin. The Contractor will take affirmative action to ensure that applicants are employed, and that employees are treated during employment without regard to their race, color, religion, sex, or national origin. Such action shall include, but not be limited to the following: employment, upgrading, promotion, or transfer; recruitment or recruitment advertising; lay-off or termination; rates of pay or other forms of compensation; and selection for training, including apprenticeship.

WOMEN AS ADMINISTRATORS

Evidence seems to support the idea that women who have equal preparation can be equally effective as men in administrative positions. Furthermore, the legal framework has encouraged equal opportunities for women in the form of the Civil Rights Act of 1964 and the Title IX legislation of 1972. Yet, a proportionately small number of women are in educational administrative positions, particularly in physical education and athletics. It was assumed by many that the strong trend toward the combining of men's and women's programs in the schools would result in a higher proportion of women in key administrative positions. However, the great majority of physical education and athletic programs at all levels of education are presently administered by men. Undoubtedly, this is partly because considerably more men are in the profession, and partly because the men do not need to combine a profession with rearing a family as many women do, and partly due to tradition.

Reif[18] did a study entitled "Exploring some myths about women managers," in which he found that no significant differences exist between men and women that would limit the capacity of women to perform effectively in administrative roles. Lied[12] investigated the attitudes and administration. He concluded that few, if any, significant differences exist between the leadership behavior of women and men, and the same kinds of preparation experiences apply equally well to both. Lied emphasized that with the same preparation for administrative leadership, women and men should be able to function with approximately equal effectiveness. It would appear that the framework is established for women to enter the field of administration more frequently than in the past. Probably the psychology associated with women managers is more positive than ever before, and more women today are interested in managerial positions than in the past. This combination of circumstances will undoubtedly contribute toward a higher proportion of women administrators in physical education and athletics in the future.

SOME SPECIAL PERSONNEL PROBLEMS

An administrator must guard against certain potential personnel problems. If these problems occur and persist, they can have a dragging effect on the organization. If they get out of hand, they can become disruptive.

Law or Regulation

Equal Pay Act of 1963, with Education Amendments added in 1972	It declares that discrimination on the basis of sex is prohibited on pay scales and benefits. Equal skill, effort, responsibility, and similar working conditions are the criteria of determination.
Title VI of the Civil Rights Act of 1964	This section states that no person in the United States shall, on the ground of race, color, or national origin, be excluded from participation in, be denied the benefits of, or be otherwise subjected to discrimination under any program or activity receiving federal financial assistance from the Department of Health, Education and Welfare.
Age discrimination in Employment Act of 1967 Amended in 1978	The Act declares that discrimination on the basis of age is prohibited against those in the age bracket of 40 to 70 in hiring, promotion, discharging, and benefits.
Executive Order 11246 Amended by EO 11375 of 1968	This action prohibits discrimination in all phases of employment on the basis of race, color, religion, national origin, and sex. Nondiscrimination requires the elimination of all existing discriminatory conditions. Requires Affirmative Action, including setting goals in achieving employment mixture.
Title IX of the Education Amendments of 1972 (Public Law 92-318)	This Title is designed to eliminate discrimination on the basis of sex in any education program or activity receiving federal financial assistance.
Rehabilitation Act of 1973— Section 503 and 504	Section 503 requires that organizations shall take affirmative action to employ and advance in employment the qualified handicapped. Section 504 prohibits discrimination against qualified handicapped persons in

employment and in the operation of programs and activities receiving federal financial assistance.

Veterans Readjustment Act of 1974

This Act declares that employment openings are to be listed at Job Service, veterans should be given priority, and veterans are eligible for readjustment points.

Adverse Feelings

An administrator must be sensitive to the potentially adverse feelings of others and be able to cope with these effectively. One such feeling is frustration, which people express in various ways. One common response is either positive or negative aggression. For example, one person might express feelings of frustration through aggressive pursuit of positive goals, whereas another might strike out against a co-worker. Still another might resort to rationalization, such as when one tries to explain away a failure by blaming the boss for playing favorites or blaming "organizational politics." Some react to frustration with child-like behavior, such as an employee who, because he is denied a promotion, withdraws and pouts.

The administrator needs to avoid frustrations himself and help others to do the same. Feelings of frustration are unpleasant and contribute to unproductive uses of energy. When frustrations do occur, an administrator can help others see that rationalization, regression, and negative aggressiveness are undesirable behaviors typical of the relatively immature.

Unacceptable Relationships

Administrative positions are often thought of as lonely in the sense that the administrator cannot afford to be too friendly or appear too close to his co-workers. Chummy friendships with certain co-workers can create problems in the minds of other employees, causing them to feel suspicious or hurt. An administrator must show a strong element of consistency in the relationships he has with the various people in comparable positions within the organization. Yet it is desirable and certainly workable for him to be generally friendly and congenial with all members of the organization.

Personal Neglect

Some people permit themselves to become physically or mentally deteriorated to the point that they are unable to perform their work. A reduction of energy or a loss of productivity due to deterioration or staleness has been the downfall of many administrators. No pat solution to this problem exists because it has various causes. Sometimes the culprit is the natural aging process and sometimes it is a pathologic ailment. Frequently, however, it is deterioration or staleness due to lack of exercise or diversion.

People who maintain a reasonable level of fitness function more effectively in all respects and have greater longevity. Many executives claim that they actually accomplish more in a day when they devote one hour to vigorous physical exercise. This causes the physiologic systems to function more efficiently, thus decreasing the amount of rest required and increasing work output. Many administrators are dedicated to the importance of periodic diversion from the work routine. The need for diversion varies with different individuals, but everyone has some need for it in order to keep interest level high and avoid becoming stale.

Another potential problem is overweight. Most administrative work is passive. At the same time, administrators are often involved in luncheons, dinner meetings, and banquets. Under these circumstances, low resistance to food or lack of dietary discipline can result in overweight. In turn, overweight can be a contributor to a variety of other health problems.

BIBLIOGRAPHY

1. American Management Association: Personnel Management Workbook, New York, 1981.

2. Austin, D.A.: Renewal. JOPER, *51*:57, 1980.

3. Beach, D.S.: Personnel: The Management of People at Work, 4th Ed. New York, Macmillan, 1980.

4. Brigham Young University: Personnel Manual. Provo, UT, BYU Press, 1981.

5. Byars, L.L., and Rue, L.W.: Personnel Management: Concepts and Applications. Philadelphia, W.B. Saunders, 1979.

6. Cayer, N.J.: Managing Human Resources: An Introduction to Public Personnel Administration. New York, St. Martin's Press, 1980.

7. Crase, D.: Development activities: a hedge against complacency. JOPER, *51*:53, 1980.

8. French, W.L., and Hellriegel, D.: Personnel Management and Organization: Fields in Transition, 2nd Ed. Boston, Houghton Mifflin, 1979.

9. Greenlaw, P.S., and Biggs, W.D.: Modern Personnel Management. Philadelphia, W.B. Saunders, 1979.

10. Hackman, J.R., and Oldham, G.R.: Work Redesign. Reading, MA, Addison-Wesley, 1980.

11. King, J.C.: Some requirements for successful in-service education. Education Digest, *43*:14, 1977.

12. Lied, M.: Women as Leaders and Managers. M.A. Thesis, University of Illinois, 1977.

13. Machlowitz, M.: Your coaching committment: how to develop subordinates. Work Wom, *6*:44, 1981.

14. Mann, D.: Politics of in-service. Education Digest, *44*:19, 1979.

15. McGregor, D.: The Human Side of Enterprise. New York, McGraw-Hill, 1960.

16. Miner, M.G., and Miner, J.B.: A Guide to Personnel Management. Washington, D.C., The Bureau of National Affairs, 1978.

17. Porter, J.: In-service education. Education Digest, *43:*42, 1978.

18. Reif, W.E., et al.: Exploding some myths about women managers. California Management Review, *17:*72, 1978.

19. Scheler, J.L.: Why so many workers lie down on the job. U.S. News, *90:*71, 1981.

20. Walker, J.W.: Human Resource Planning. New York, McGraw-Hill, 1980.

21. Wescott, W.: Physical educators and coaches as models of behavior. JOPER, *50:*31, 1979.

22. Wilcox, A.W.: Workers: eager for responsibilities. Nations Bus, *68:*38, 1980.

Chapter 9

FINANCIAL MANAGEMENT

An administrative unit and the programs within it must be managed in a financially sound manner. The administrator and others in the department should hold a high level of respect and credibility with those who control the finances of the larger organization. This means that budget requests should be based on accurate information and sound rationale. Expenditures should be made wisely and in accordance with the budgetary plan. Accurate financial records should be kept, and the program conducted in a manner that is both cost-efficient and makes a substantial educational contribution. If these procedures are applied consistently, they will win financial support.

PRINCIPLES OF FINANCIAL MANAGEMENT

1. Administrators are often judged by their competence in financial management. Meticulous preparation and thorough justification of budget proposals and careful control of the expenditures reflect on an administrator's image.
2. Regardless of who else is involved, the administrator of the given budgetary unit is ultimately responsible for proper financial management. He is accountable for the utilization of all the resources available to the unit.
3. Even though the major responsibility for fiscal management rests with administrators, it involves all employees to some degree. The employees should understand this.
4. Except in unusual cases, those who furnish money for any enterprise have the right to know how it is spent. This is particularly true of the tax-paying public.
5. Funds for athletics should be allocated and accounted for in generally the same way as funds for other aspects of the school program. The revenue should go into the general fund, and the program should operate on an allocated budget.

6. As much return as possible should be realized on any surplus funds that are on deposit either within the organization or in a bank or investment program. The principle of "return on your money" applies to organizational funds as it does to private funds. In some cases, this can be a substantial source of revenue.

7. In financial management, saving money is important but spending money is also important. An important guideline is to obtain and spend the right amount in the right manner for the good of the program and get the most possible for the money spent.

PLANNING THE BUDGET

Budget planning and preparation are more complex processes than many people realize. Budget planning leads into all aspects of program planning, because the budget must be designed to finance the programs. In turn, the program must be administered in accordance with the budget. Some guidelines for budget planning are as follows:

1. The budget should accurately represent the financial needs of the program in relationship to the stated program objectives.

2. Honesty in budget preparation is the recommended approach. Padding the budget will become apparent to alert financial personnel. This often damages the credibility of the administrator and may result in exaggerated budget cuts.

3. Accurate determination of enrollment, student credit hours, or other influencing factors is fundamental to effective budget planning.

4. The planning process should take into account anticipated income from all sources (both appropriated funds and revenue) and balance this with the anticipated expenditures.

5. The possibility of financial emergencies should be recognized and included in the budget. Sometimes funds are placed in contingency to cover unforeseen needs.

6. The budget should have the right balance of rigidity and flexibility— enough rigidity to give adequate structure and enough flexibility to accommodate unforseen changes.

7. The budget should be prepared on a timetable that leaves ample opportunity for thorough analysis, evaluation, and review.

8. The budgeting process ought to involve all those in the organization who should rightfully be consulted.

9. The budget categories and the amount in each category should be correctly aligned to fit the financial needs of the different aspects of the program.

10. Usually, a detailed budget has a cover sheet that summarizes income and expenditures, so that the total budget picture can be seen at a glance.

Budget Preparation

Although the exact steps involved vary with different budgetary approaches, certain steps should be included in all approaches. They include the following: (1) clearly determine the objectives of the program the budget is to finance; (2) determine as accurately as possible the real financial needs of the program; (3) prepare the budget in adequate detail so that it can be clearly understood; (4) present the budget through the prescribed administrative channels; (5) administer the budget in accordance with the approved plan and by the proper financial policies and procedures; (6) carefully evaluate the adequacy and effectiveness of the budget.

Each organization has its own version of budgetary forms. Within any particular organization, however, the forms are similar regardless of the budgetary approach used. Figures 9-1 and 9-2 are examples of budget preparation forms, showing the different categories. Although the forms may be similar, the procedures followed in arriving at the information vary significantly with the budgetary approach. The following section includes descriptions of the various approaches: conventional, PPBES, zero base, and cost analysis.

Conventional Approach

Conventional budgeting is a rather superficial and mechanical method, and yet, due to its simplicity, it is often used. It is also known as "line item," "shopping list," and sometimes, "incremental" budgeting, since each succeeding year usually involves an incremental increase from the previous year (often labeled cost-of-living or inflationary increase). Despite the weakness of this method, it is probably the most widely used approach. It is relatively simple, easily understood, requires minimal work, and helps to preserve the status quo. With this approach, the person preparing the budget might be provided with a guideline figure—say an 8% increase over last year's budget. Last year's budget then becomes the starting point. The additional money is applied and other adjustments are made in accordance with the best judgment of how the money should be used. Under this system, the most mechanical approach is simply to apply the percentage increase to every category. Usually, however, based on changes in circumstances and one's judgment of projected needs, the different categories are increased by various amounts. Some categories may even be decreased so that others can be increased disproportionately.

The main strength of this approach is its simplicity; however, it has one clear weakness. The present status of the budget tends to be perpetuated without thorough analysis of productivity as related to expenditure, i.e., return on the dollar. It is assumed that last year's budget is accurate; and increases are tacked on each year for factors such as inflation, compensation, and new employees and projects. Thus, inefficient functions may be retained year after year. It is conceivable that a budget item that should have

DEPARTMENTAL BUDGET REQUEST SUMMARY SHEET

Department _____   _____
                                            Signature of Dept. Chairman

College/Division _____

Account Code _____   _____
                                              Signature of Dean

Column	A	B		C		D		E	
Object of Expenditure	Cate-gory Code #	Present Budget		Request for Next Year		Program Improvement Request		Total Budget Request (C + D)	
		Amount	FTE	Amount	FTE	Amount	FTE	Amount	FTE*
1. Administrative salaries		$		$		$		$	
2. Full-time Faculty salaries									
3. Full-time Faculty Supplemental Earnings									
4. Part-time Faculty salaries									
5. Full-time Staff salaries									
6. Student Assistant salaries									
7. Student Wages									
8. Non-student part-time or temp. wages									
9. Payroll taxes, insur-ance, and retirement									
10. Equipment repairs and maintenance									
11. Rented–leased equipment									
12. Computer Services									
13. Capital Equipment									
14. Travel									
15. Supplies and other expenses									
16. Miscellaneous									
17. TOTALS		$		$		$		$	

* Full-time equivalent personnel

Figure 9-1. Budget proposal form for an instructional department, showing the different categories of the budget.

ATHLETIC BUDGET REQUEST SUMMARY SHEET

Account Code				(Sport)
Object of Expenditure	Code #	Last Year	Present	Request Next Year
1. Administrative salaries				
2. Faculty salaries (coaches)				
3. Full-time Staff salaries				
4. Student Asst. Salaries				
5. Student Wages				
6. Payroll Taxes, Ins., and Ret.				
7. Telephone				
8. Vehicle Operations				
9. Repairs and Maintenance				
10. Capital Equipment				
11. Travel				
12. Supplies				
13. Postage and shipping				
14. Printing				
15. Programs				
16. Laundry				
17. Advertising				
18. Films				
19. Gear				
20. Award Jackets				
21. Recruiting (off campus)				
22. Coaches Clinic				
23. Scouting				
24. Grant-in-aid				
25. Grant-in-aid—Spring				
26. Books				
27. Training Table				
28. Tutoring				
29. Officials				
30. Guarantees				
31. Game Management				
32. Facilities				
33. Dues and Membership				
34. Insurance				
35. TOTALS				

Approvals:

Administrator   Director

                                            Coach

Figure 9-2. Budget proposal form for an athletic program, showing the different categories.

been eliminated or drastically reduced 3 years ago is still in the budget and has received standard annual increases, while some other item that deserves considerably more emphasis has also received standard increases. This does not necessarily happen, but it can with the conventional approach.

Inherent in the conventional approach is a special need to *control waste*, because it encourages a tendency to make needless purchases toward the end of the fiscal year. Departmental personnel often feel that if the entire budget allotment is not spent, next year's budget will be dropped to match this year's spending. This is a foolish and wasteful approach to budgeting because, as the end of the fiscal year approaches, money is often spent on items that otherwise would not be purchased.

Ways in which this perpetual wasting can be controlled include requiring that purchase orders be approved by the principal and business officer during the last month of the fiscal year. Another method is to establish a reward system referred to as a "percent return rule." It simply means that a certain percentage of the total amount of the original budget (say 3%) can be carried over to next year's budget and placed in the unallocated category. This would mean that for a departmental budget of $30,000, as much as $900 could be carried over. This procedure encourages tight control of funds and provides for some flexibility in next year's budget. Unfortunately, few educational organizations permit this procedure; although a few have implemented it and are benefiting from its success.

Systems Approach (PPBES)

In order to coordinate the various steps involved in budgeting, a systems approach has emerged. It has been labeled PPBES (originally PPBS); which stands for *Planning, Programming, Budgeting,* and *Evaluation System*. Even though this method was first developed through noneducation agencies, the process has been adapted to education and is used extensively. The adapted process has also been referred to as "the Educational Resources Management System."

The most widely known PPBES system was developed by the United States Department of Defense during the 1960s, and in its evolved form, the system is still used by that agency.

By the late 1960s, the merits of this approach had become recognized in other agencies, particularly in the field of education. As demands by the public for accountability increased, many school systems across the country began using the PPBES.[6,7]

The *planning* component of PPBES involves preparing goals (objectives) and defining expectations in terms of student accomplishments. The *programming* phase involves the selection of activities and events that will be included in the program for the purpose of accomplishing the goals. The *budgeting* component involves the preparation of a financial proposal that will enable the sponsorship of the program that has been planned. Of course, this must include all aspects of financial need such as facilities, equipment, and personnel. The *evaluation* aspect of the system involves a careful analysis of how adequately the budget fits the program, how well the program leads toward the goals, and how valuable the accomplishments are as related to costs.[7]

The four phases constitute a complete cycle, with its different aspects having a logical sequence and a close relationship. The final step of the cycle (evaluation) logically lays the groundwork for the first step of the new cycle. One of the main advantages of the systems approach is the fact that it forces one to give adequate attention to all the important aspects of budget preparation and administration.[2]

Sometimes explanations of the PPBES cause it to seem complex and cumbersome, but this need not be the case. It only involves the four steps that have been identified in proper sequence. With a large and comprehensive program each step is more involved, but regardless of the size of the program, the system still uses the same four phases.

Zero Base Budgeting

Zero base budgeting was developed at Texas Instruments Company in 1969 by a management team trying to find a better way to relate input to company objectives. It is a system of budgeting that focuses on the complete justification of all expenditures each time the budgeting exercise takes place. It does this by assuming that every element of the organization starts from zero and must justify its existence by its relative contribution to the organization's objectives. Its rapid increase in popularity can be attributed to three basic characteristics: the participative nature of the method by administrators at different levels, the merging effect it causes between budgeting and planning, and the crisp influence it has on decision making.[5]

In effect, ZBB results in a thorough review of functions from the ground base (zero base) and proceeds in an upward direction. The method was developed to offset some of the undesirable features of the conventional budgeting technique. The most important difference is that ZBB avoids the practice of considering last year's budget as the base; and therefore, avoids the question of how much is required next year to continue with a particular function. Rather, the question is whether funding should be allocated at all. This method denies the assumption that each aspect of the budget should be automatically continued.

Perhaps the foremost feature of ZBB is that it provides an avenue for budgeting and planning to take place at the same time. Often these functions are performed too independently of one another. When program planning and financial planning proceed together from a zero base, relating decisions about programming and financing becomes easier.

The specific steps to be carried out when implementing ZBB vary from one application to another. However, in a general sense, the following are common aspects of ZBB approaches:[5]

Definition and Goals.   Stating the goals (objectives) of the program is one important step. The goals influence the decisions involved in preparing the budget.

Program Planning.   The program must be planned in light of the goals. In the program planning phase, the following questions are important: What is the reason for doing it? What would happen if it were not done? Is there a better and more economical approach? Where does it fit in terms of priority? After the current aspects of the program have been scrutinized in this manner, new activities and approaches can be considered by the same procedure.

Identifying Alternative Decisions.   The previous step should result in a careful analysis of the relative value of the various aspects of the program. The purpose of this step is to identify and evaluate alternative approaches to accomplishing those aspects of the program that are considered important. For example, scheduling team air flights far enough in advance to take advantage of "super saver" rates; having the school cooperate with the city on the construction of new tennis courts, and having them lighted so that they serve both the school and the community; closing certain facilities during low-use periods so that money can be diverted to other aspects of the program; or scheduling more contests in a particular sport at home and fewer, away.

Cost Analysis of the Alternatives.   This step involves cost comparisons of the alternatives. It would involve questions such as the following: What are the relative costs of a team traveling with two vans as opposed to one bus? What would be the relative cost of playing more games at home and fewer games away, taking into consideration all of the financial factors, gate receipts, travel costs, guarantee, and others.

Making the Decisions.   The information from the previous four steps brings the situation to the decision-making point. It is now time to decide two important questions. (1) Which functions should receive funding and which ones should not? (2) For those activities that will be funded, which of the alternative approaches is best? The decisions must be realistic and in accordance with the information from the previous steps. It would be futile to go through the process and then make arbitrary decisions based on preferences that are inconsistent with the facts obtained.

If the ZBB approach is used properly, it will result in funding that fits the best plan for the accomplishment of the stated objectives. With the ZBB method, each aspect of the program has to be justified on a cost-benefit basis and this has to be done each year (or each time the ZBB approach is used). Precedent, tradition, personal preference, and bias have no place in the ZBB method. It is a straightforward calculation of how much money can be justified in support of each function, when the functions are weighed carefully against each other.

The ZBB method has specific advantages. For instance, it allows new programs to compete for funds against established programs. It increases decision flexibility with discretionary funds. It is especially useful in high-growth situations where program expansion is prevalent. Although cost reduction is not a required objective of ZBB, it is oriented toward cost reduction because the process naturally identifies and eliminates areas of the program that are overfunded or relatively ineffective in goal accomplishment.

ZBB is not a simpler method than other approaches; and there is no guarantee that its use will enable budgetary reductions. ZBB should, however, lead to an improved organizational climate as a result of the increased involvement and the direct participation by staff members. It should also result in better utilization of the funds toward accomplishment of the goals due to the careful interrelated analysis of objectives, programs, costs, and alternative approaches.

ZBB as a system is not a panacea, but it can be especially valuable to an organization that needs a "face lifting" in terms of budgetary procedures or one that needs to add rigor to its decision-making process. On the other hand, ZBB should be avoided by any organization whose budgeting approach is adequate and yet simpler and less time-consuming than the ZBB method. In other words, apply the adage that "if it isn't broke don't try to fix it." Also, ZBB ought to be avoided if the organization is involved in major changes in personnel, procedures, or organizational structure.

If zero base budgeting is used, an interesting question is how often the process should be repeated. Valid arguments for and against ZBB as an annual exercise are summarized as follows:[5]

FOR:
1. A different system would have to be used in off-years.
2. ZBB provides alternatives for budget modification during changing circumstances.
3. Administrators will become more proficient at using the system if it is done annually.
4. If the system is effective, then it would seem that annual implementation would be an advantage.

AGAINST:
1. The greatest benefit of the ZBB system accrues the first year and diminishes thereafter.
2. There would be a tendency to repeat the same decisions every year.
3. The process is time-consuming.
4. Good managers review programs critically on a continuous basis without ZBB.
5. ZBB is not needed every year since programs and activities change little from one year to the next.

ZBB does a vast amount of analysis that is not normally a part of the budget exercise. It creates an atmosphere of rethinking, which can have a renewing effect on the organization since it allows the organization no longer to be bound by budgetary precedent. However, many who try ZBB become disenchanted and look for some other "miracle cure" for their organizational problems. Such disenchantment may relate to failure to recognize that a budget system is a tool not a manager. No system can substitute for poor management. No budget approach is any better than the people who operate it.

Cost Analysis

In education, cost analysis is a procedure whereby all expenses of the program are related to the total number of students served. In cost analysis budgeting, projected costs are computed on a per student basis. The total number of students is figured in one of two ways: the average daily *student membership* or the average daily *student attendance*. The membership represents all of the students enrolled in the school; whereas on any given day, the attendance is usually less than the membership. Most experts agree that the membership is the better measure of the two because teacher's salaries must be paid whether 95% or 100% of the pupils are in attendance. Also, school facilities, furnishings, books, and other costs remain approximately constant and do not fluctuate with average attendance.

If cost analysis is employed, a different formula (amount per student applies at the different school levels because the nature of physical education and athletics varies at the different levels. The formula might allow for a certain dollar amount per student to cover the total expenses of physical education and athletics (and related programs), or it might provide specific amounts per student for physical education instruction, athletics, and intramural sports. In some cases, the school as a whole receives a set amount per student, and the principal assigns the amount for each phase of the total school program.

Although some room for variation exists within budgeting methods, the concept is consistent: the amount of allocation is based on the student population (either enrollment or attendance). This concept is based on the idea that there is a close relationship between educational costs and number of students. Under this method of budgeting, the best way to obtain more money in support of a program is to get an upward revision of the formula.

Sometimes, cost analysis is based on the production of student credit hours rather than on the number of students. In such cases, noncredit activities such as athletics and intramurals have to be budgeted on a different basis.

PRESENTING THE BUDGET

Several steps may be involved in presenting a budget, depending on the particular situation. In a high school, the proposal might go from director to the principal, to the superintendent, to the school board. In a university, the budget might pass from the director to the dean, to the financial vice-president, to the president, and the board of trustees. At each step along the way, the budget proposal must be reviewed and approved. At any stage before final adoption, modifications might be required. These guidelines will help in the presentation process:

1. Be sure that the budget proposal is in the recommended format and that it is sound, accurate, and complete.
2. Have available all the information to justify the budget, such as (a) the objectives of the program; (b) evidence of previous success; (c) rate of student participation; (d) statistical data about the program that would be useful to the review personnel.
3. Have sufficient copies of the proposal so that each member of the review team can have one. Sometimes, it is helpful to have copies of the budget delivered to the individuals in advance so they can study it.
4. Consider bringing along other persons who can speak in favor of certain aspects of the proposal. The circumstances of the review indicate whether this would be appropriate.
5. Be thoroughly familiar with the content of the budget proposal and the rationale behind it.
6. Be precise and forthright in your presentation and responses. Avoid being vague or evasive.

SOURCES OF FUNDS

The most reliable source of funds is from *budgetary appropriation*. This method of funding adds stability and consistency, and is clearly the preferred source.

In some situations, athletic *gate receipts* provide a source of revenue. In the public schools, gate receipts are relatively small; but in certain university programs, the gate receipts are substantial. It is strongly recommended that gate receipts go into the general fund, and that budgeted funds be used to finance the athletic program. This puts athletics on the same financial basis as other school programs, and it is a protective measure for the stability of athletics.

Special fees constitute another source of income. Some schools require each student to pay an athletic fee in connection with registration. When this is done, students usually have free admission to athletic contests. Sometimes, a physical education uniform fee or a facility use fee is paid by each student.

Several other sources of income are pursued with varying amounts of success by different educational institutions. These include the following: *donated funds* from foundations, companies, and individuals; *annual giving* by individuals through fund raising clubs, athletic booster clubs, and the like; *government grants* for area and facility development or special projects; *athletic guarantees* paid in connection with contests played away from home; revenue from *concessions, auto parking,* and *program sales* at athletic contests; and *special fund raising* events, such as walkathons, marathons, and novelty athletic contests.

It should be noted that, in some states, the law prohibits the expenditure of tax dollars on athletics. In this situation, the athletic department should have help from athletic boosters (or other sources) to stabilize funding to ensure a healthy program.

EXPENDITURE OF FUNDS

In order to properly control expenditures and ensure accountability, it is necessary to be explicit about who is authorized to expend funds from a particular budget. The use of an authorized signature card such as the one shown in Figure 9-3, gives a clear definition of who can expend funds.

In the case of educational budgets, the great majority of expenditures are for the payment of personnel and the purchase of equipment and supplies. Occasionally, large amounts are paid to contractors in connection with construction projects. Relatively small amounts are expended for travel, leasing of equipment, student awards, and other ongoing expenses.

```
AUTHORIZED SIGNATURE CARD


_____
Account Code

_____ for
Authorized Signature

_____
Account Name


_____ whose signature appears
(Name—Print or Type)

above is authorized to obligate the above account code.

Restriction (if any): _____

_____


Approved by: _____
(Dean or Director)

Date: _____
```

Figure 9-3. A form for providing authorization to sign for expenditures against a particular financial account.

Payment of Personnel

Personnel are hired on *regular contract, special contract,* or *time card* arrangement. Full-time faculty and administrative staff are normally hired on an annual contract. Important elements in the contract are the title, the faculty status, the salary, the conditions of payment (such as monthly, for 12 months), and at least a general description of responsibilities. Some contracts are lengthy and definitive, whereas others cover only the essentials, although the latter sometimes have supplementary information enclosed.

A written contract with the proper signatures is a legal and moral agreement between the individual and the organization. Both sides should be anxious to live up to the conditions of the contract, whether the conditions are explicitly defined, implied, or reasonably assumed. Not all the conditions of employment can be described in a contract, but it should include the more important ones. In addition, it should be understood that the contact represents a "good faith agreement" between the two parties. Breach of contract without justifiable reason is both illegal and unethical. It ought to be strictly avoided. On the other hand, both parties should be open to reasonable negotiation when there is sufficient reason to modify an agreement. An example of a contract (letter of appointment) for a university faculty member is shown in Figure 8-3.

Special contracts are used for the employment of game officials and the accomplishment of special projects. A sample contract for game officials can be found in Figure 16-2.

Clerical and support services personnel are usually hired on a time card arrangement. This involves processing a form that establishes a record of employment and spells out the essential conditions, including hours per week and the hourly pay rate. Once employment is established, time cards are submitted on the prescribed time schedule, and each time card indicates the number of hours for which the person is to be paid. A sample of an employment request form appears in Chapter 8.

Personnel must be hired and paid in accordance with the approved budget. Monthly budget reports are invaluable to the administrator as a method of checking that the amounts being paid each employee correspond with the amounts that were allocated.

Purchases

The normal procedure for making purchases is to complete a requisition form, which is then followed by a purchase order. Sometimes a different form is used if the purchase is to be made from another division on campus or within the school district, as opposed to a purchase from a supplier or vendor. Figure 9-4 shows a campus or district purchase order, and Figure 9-5 is an example of a purchase requisition. The following is a discussion of some guidelines relating to purchasing:

PURCHASE ORDER

Date _____   Ship When _____

Ordered
from   Ship to
Vendor

Bill in Duplicate to: Requested by: _____
                                         Authorized Representative
                                             or Principal

                          Approved by: _____
                                         Program Director

                          Approved by: _____
                                         Purchasing Director

Account Number	Vendor No.	Purchase Order No.	

Invoice Number	Total Amount	Discount	Partial	Full	Net Amount	Approved for Payment

Quantity Ordered	Quantity Received	Description	Unit Cost	Est. Cost

TOTAL AMOUNT

Figure 9-4. Example of a purchase order or requisition. (Courtesy of Alpine School District.)

School ——————

Street ——————

City ——————

Date ——————

A/C No. ——————

Quantity	Units	P.O.#	Index #	Description	Supp. A/C #	Code	Unit Cost	Total Cost

Approved By: ——————

Received By: ——————

Figure 9-5. Example of an intraschool district requisition form. (Courtesy of Alpine School District.)

When completing a purchase form, provide all pertinent information, including a complete and correct description of the item(s), the number desired, color (if this applies), sizes, model number, and the recommended source of purchase, if there is reason to make such recommendation.

Place orders far enough in advance to make sure that the items are going to be available when needed and to allow the purchasing agent ample opportunity to properly investigate the various sources of purchase. Avoid rush orders because they are inefficient.

Order the right amount. Too much of a certain item in stock occupies valuable storage space, costs interest on the money invested in the items, and presents the risk of potential loss through fire, theft, or deterioration. Conversely, with orders that are too small, you sometimes lose the advantage of bulk rates, pay a high price on the next order due to inflation, and cause decreased efficiency because of frequent purchases and deliveries.

As a manager of public funds, you are obligated to search out and accept the best bargain. Of course, the best bargain is not always the cheapest price. Other important considerations are involved, such as quality of the product, quality of service, and convenience. However, when all else is essentially equal, the vendor who can provide the best price is the one that ought to be selected.

Avoid accepting substitutes by vendors unless you feel satisfied with the product and the price. When items arrive, be sure they go through the proper receiving steps and are properly inventoried.

There are two kinds of organizational plans for purchasing, decentralized and centralized. With the decentralized plan, each school or department makes its own purchases directly from the vendors. The disadvantages of this system include the inability to buy in quantity; having too many school personnel dealing directly with vendors, and the lack of control due to numerous people involved in the various aspects of the purchasing process. The greatest advantage is the convenience of quick buying to fill unexpected needs.

With the more commonly used centralized approach, all purchases are made through a central purchasing office. It is economical because it allows quantity buying and involves purchasing specialists who often have more leverage with vendors and experience negotiating with them. For these reasons, the centralized method is usually the better of the two.

Whenever the purchase is large enough to justify it, the normal procedure in purchasing is to obtain bids from different vendors. The purpose in *bid buying* is to obtain the best price possible for the specified product or for some acceptable substitute. In preparing a package for bid, one must provide exact specifications of the materials to be purchased. Incomplete or vague descriptions can contribute to inconsistencies among bids from the different vendors. The description must also indicate whether substitutions will be considered. An organization can consistently save money through the bid buying process because it creates competition among vendors and affords the purchaser the opportunity of accepting the "best deal."

Often, large organizations have *direct buying* sources from which large purchases are made. Direct buying is making purchases from the wholesaler of the product and eliminating the retailer. Normally a substantial price advantage is to be had with this method. Retail suppliers oppose this procedure because it eliminates their opportunity to do business, and through direct buying, an organization loses the advantage of the service and convenience provided by a local retailer. In each situation, the advantages and disadvantages of direct buying must be carefully weighed. If possible, information should be kept current as to which items can be bought from a local retailer at the same price as from the wholesaler. This can help to maintain a good relationship on the local level while saving money on larger items. An organization should not be coerced into doing business with local retailers at a higher cost unless sufficient reasons exist.

COMPUTERIZED BUYING

The computerized budgeting system for acquisition of physical education and athletic supplies is not apt to assist a single school or a small school district. For a large district, however, it can contribute to overall efficiency.

The highly technical aspects of computerized budgeting are handled by the data processing technicians, whereas the nontechnical components of this approach are relatively easy.

In the following explanation, the Beaverton School district in the state of Oregon is used as the model. The Beaverton District athletic director has outlined steps for the computerized system as follows:

1. The school district established a comprehensive physical education and athletic request catalog by developing a master file with item specification and estimated costs. This catalog lists the most often requested supplies and equipment for the physical education and athletic program.
2. The printed request catalog is distributed to physical education teachers and athletic coaches through the school principals.
3. Individual coaches and teachers make requests in the catalog by specifying the quantity of each item by account number. The requests of each coach are then reviewed for accuracy, modified, and totaled by sport and/or P.E. department for each school.
4. Each school's budget is then returned to the central office where the budgets are
    a. Reviewed again for accuracy (particularly new or modified item specifications and cost).
    b. Key punched and verified.
    c. Fed into the computer with all data that processes the program master file and order request file to produce a request report by

location and account, comparing physically tabulated totals with computerized totals by location and account prior to the next step and printing of the bid document.

5. The bid document is reproduced in quantities to supply each vendor with two copies. Vendors indicate bid prices on items as specified. Substitutes must meet original specifications. Bid documents are returned to the central office by bid deadline.
6. Completed bid documents supplied by vendors are key punched to obtain updated vendor file names, addresses, I.D. numbers plus vendor numbers, item numbers, and prices of all submitted items. The completed bid documents are processed to provide a vendor bid report, which lists by vendor each item in ascending bid price.
7. Selection is made of successful bids by product and unit price from the bid report. The selected vendor is indicated by flag for the next key punch. Low bid is automatically selected unless flagged.
8. The flagged items are key punched by vendor number and item number and subsequent processing produces the winning bid report.
9. Itemized purchase orders are produced by processing of master file, order request file, vendor file, and winning bid file. Two different purchase orders are produced.
   a. Each district purchase order contains a breakdown of items in account number, and the total of the purchase order is broken down by account numbers for input into the district's physical accounting system.
   b. Each vendor's purchase order contains a description and quantity of desired items and totals of extensions.
10. Distribution and an inventory control report are arrived at by processing the master file and order request file to produce a report by item, listing unit price, quantity ordered, and school.

BUDGET REPORTS AND ADJUSTMENTS

In order to manage a budget effectively, it is necessary to receive periodic budget reports from the financial services division. Normally, these reports are provided on a monthly basis. The reports should include all of the financial transactions that have occurred during the reporting period.

The report can serve two purposes: as a check to make sure that only the correct entries have been recorded against the budget; and with each report, the administrator can evaluate whether the expenditures are on the proper time schedule or whether the rate of spending is too fast. The budget must fit the approved plan, both in terms of amount and kind of expenditures and the time frame over which the expenditures are made.

Each budget report should be carefully reviewed soon after it is received. Also, the report ought to be kept for a reasonable time for possible future reference.

Fortunately, the great majority of educational organizations have adopted a system of computerized (data process) budgeting. Among the advantages to this approach are the following:

1. Accuracy is increased and errors are more easily detected.
2. The budget report forms are simple and easy to understand.
3. The process is both fast and economical.
4. Numerous copies of a report can be produced, which can be convenient and timesaving.
5. The financial management process can be streamlined by eliminating certain steps.
6. By-products of the process assist in other aspects of administration, such as short cuts in purchasing procedures, improved inventory tracking, and availability of computer on-line budget information.

Sometimes it is necessary to transfer funds from one category to another, although this is not recommended as a common practice. For example, suppose a certain amount of money to pay the salary of a full-time secretary is in the staff salary category. Part way through the year, the secretary leaves, and a decision is made to finish out the year with part-time student secretaries. In this case, the remainder of the money would have to be transferred from the staff salary category to the student wage category. Ordinarily, education organizations have a special form on which to process budget adjustments (Figure 9-6).

AUDITS

Financial audits are part of the normal procedures of almost all organizations. The audit usually involves two aspects of the evaluation, financial *procedures* and financial *expenditures*.

Many people think of audits in a negative sense, but this should not be the case. An audit should be a useful procedure for both the larger organization and the budgetary unit by whom it is performed.

For the larger organization, the audit helps to monitor correct procedures and expenditures, and to identify deviations or irregularities, if any exist. For the budgetary unit, an audit can be an educational experience for both the administrator and the others in the unit. Recommended procedures and guidelines relative to expenditures that might otherwise remain vague can be made clear. An audit usually has a sharpening effect on the financial process, which contributes to overall efficiency.

There are *routine* audits and *special* audits. Routine audits occur periodically for the reasons just explained. They are part of the overall financial procedures of most organizations. A special audit may be initiated by someone higher up in the organization or by the unit administrator. One reason for a special audit is to investigate a suspicion or accusation about misuse of funds or improper procedures. Useful information can be acquired through the audit process that will enhance the financial management of the unit. An audit is often important in preparing for a change of administrative personnel or reorganization of the unit.

From _____ To: Budget Office

_____   _____

BUDGET ADJUSTMENT REQUEST
For School Year 198__-8__

I hereby request a transfer of funds for the following budget accounts:

DEPARTMENT	ACCOUNT NUMBER	INCREASE	DECREASE
_____	_____	$ _____	$ _____
_____	_____	_____	_____
_____	_____	_____	_____
_____	_____	_____	_____
_____	_____	_____	_____
_____	_____	_____	_____
_____	_____	_____	_____
_____	_____	_____	_____
_____	_____	_____	_____
_____	_____	_____	_____

TOTAL $ _____ $ _____

Approvals (authorized signatures):   Date:

_____   _____

_____   _____

Figure 9-6. A form for transferring funds from one budget category to another.

FINANCIAL PITFALLS

Some people get into pitfalls either because of carelessness or dishonesty. The following guidelines for avoiding pitfalls should be helpful:

1. Keep adequate records of financial agreements and transactions. The following paper work must be kept on file: (a) personnel contracts or other employment agreements; (b) purchase requests; (c) a record of the essential information submitted on time cards; (d) contracts for athletic contests; and (e) memos, letters, and other written agreements that explain financial terms. It can be embarrassing and awkward to be unable to produce the necessary paper work in support of financial commitments or transactions.
2. Money can be collected only by designated personnel. This includes the sale of tickets and collection of student fees, among others. Those authorized to collect funds usually have clear instructions on how to handle and process the funds; and if much money is involved, the individual is bonded. Persons unauthorized to collect money ought to avoid doing so except in small amounts and for sufficient reason. A good practice is for unauthorized personnel to direct people to authorized collectors.
3. All collected funds should be deposited in the appropriate account, so that an official record is made and the funds, in turn, are utilized by the approved procedure and subject to financial audit.
4. Avoid having an unauthorized flow of petty cash, and if you have an authorized petty cash account, be sure it is tightly managed in accordance with correct procedures.
5. Avoid having cash in obvious places and never leave cash unsecured where it offers the potential for theft. In cases where much money is collected, deposits should be made frequently.
6. It is especially important to keep accurate financial records in connection with the collection and deposit of money.

BIBLIOGRAPHY

1. American Management Association: Financial Management. New York, 1981.

2. Anthony, R., and Herzlinger, R.: Management Controls in Non-Profit Organizations. Homewood, IL, R.D. Irwin, 1980.

3. Avedisian, C.T.: Planning programming budget systems. JOPER, 43:37, 1972.

4. Brigham, E.: Financial Management: Theory and Practice, 2nd Ed. Hinsdale, IL, Dryden Press, 1979.

5. Dirsmith, M., and Jblonsky, S.: Zero-base budgeting as a management technique and political strategy. The Academy of Management Review, 5:555, 1979.

6. Financial Planning Models: Concepts and Case Studies in Colleges and Universities. August 1978. Edited by J.B. Wyatt, J.C. Emery, and C.P. Landis, Princeton, NJ, EDUCOM, 1979.

7. Hartley, H.J.: Educational Planning–Programming–Budgeting–A Systems Approach. Englewood Cliffs, NJ, Prentice-Hall, 1968.

8. Mann, J.: Harder times bring out a rash of risk taking, U.S. News, 90:61, 1981.

9. Musgrave, R., and Musgrave, P.: Public Finance in Theory and Practice. New York, McGraw-Hill, 1978.

10. Neave, E.H., and Wiginton, J.C.: Financial Management, Theory, and Strategies. Englewood Cliffs, NJ, Prentice-Hall, 1980.

11. Novie, D.: The origin and history of program budget. California Management Review, *11:23*, 1980.

12. Schick, A.: The road to PPB: the stages of budget reform. Public Administration Review, *25:253*, 1966.

13. Seven don'ts for new budgeteers. Changing Times, *34:43*, 1980.

14. Staffo, D.F.: Stretch athletic and physical education budgets. JOPER, *52* (2):56, 1981.

15. VanHorne, J.C.: Financial Management and Policy, 3rd ed. Englewood Cliffs, NJ, Prentice-Hall, 1980.

16. Weston, J.F., and Brigham, E.F.: Managerial Finance. New York, Holt, Rinehart and Winston, 1969.

17. Wildarsky, A.: A budget for all seasons? Why the traditional budget lasts. Public Administrative Review, *37:501*, 1978.

Chapter *10*

PUBLIC RELATIONS

It has been said that two forces are primarily responsible for social change: public opinion and the law, which is dependent on public opinion. This idea can serve as a useful guideline to school personnel in regard to the importance of public relations.

Public relations can be kept at a low or high pitch, can be emphasized or neglected, or can be positive or negative in terms of results; but, it cannot be avoided. Pertinent questions are how extensive the results will be and to what degree they will be favorable or disfavorable.

School personnel spend the public's money, while molding the public's most precious possession (the children) into products that must meet the public's approval. In view of this, members of the public have a right to know what is being done with the money and with their children. If the public feels dissatisfied and nonsupportive regarding the efforts of the schools, then the public has a right to bring about the desired changes. This is one of the basic reasons for the necessity of open and forthright communication between school personnel and the public. Without it, a school cannot serve its purpose well in a democratic society. Public relations should begin with the golden premise that the public has the right to know everything about the school system, and not just what school personnel want the public to know.

Successful business establishments have leaders who have learned to work effectively with the public. Although educational organizations have been generally effective in their public relations, educators have given less attention to it than is needed or justified. Through public relations, educators can improve their effectiveness winning broader and more favorable public support for their programs.

Those school personnel involved with athletics and physical education have greater public relations opportunities and responsibilities than most other school employees. For example, athletic events are of particular interest to the public and attract a relatively large amount of fan support and media coverage. The public invests considerably more in physical education

150

and athletics than in other areas of education by way of facilities, including gymnasiums, swimming pools, playing fields, tennis courts, stadiums, racquetball courts, and the like. If adequate facilities of this nature are to be provided, the programs must be good enough to justify such a large expenditure, and the public has to be convinced of the value of physical education and athletics. They must be willing to pay the bill.

DEFINITION AND SCOPE

People frequently interpret public relations to mean only radio, television, and newspaper coverage. The media is certainly one important aspect of public relations, but an overall public relations effort is much more inclusive. For example, in a school setting, public relations includes at least the following: (1) relations with other school personnel, including both students and employees; (2) relation with parents; and (3) relations with the public in general. The avenues through which an effective public relations program can be launched include (1) the mass media (radio, television, and newspapers), (2) direct conversation (face-to-face or by telephone); (3) written communications (letters, notices, school reports, bulletins, and report cards); (4) the image of the program and the way it is communicated by students and faculty; and (5) the effective conduct of educational demonstrations, athletic contests, and other public events. All of this can be summarized by saying that public relations involves everything that influences the image of the school in the mind of the public.

Organized public relations may range from the "hard-sell" campaigns of business or politics to the "soft" approach of nonprofit organizations and educational institutions.

An effective public relations program can be surprisingly simple. It need not contain "show business," gimmicks, or dramatic events. It can be a well planned, normal, ongoing exchange of useful information between school employees, students, and members of the public. It should be a naturally integrated part of the school's overall efforts. This does not mean that the program should not have special emphases. Sometimes these are needed to inform the public about certain issues or matters of special concern or to convince the public of a new and useful idea or particular need.

Public relations can be thought of as both an attitude and a process. As an attitude, it involves realistic optimism and positive thinking. As a process, it involves open and effective communication, with emphasis on the good and the positive. Public relations seeks to bring about a harmony of understanding between any group and the public it serves and upon whose good will it depends.

PURPOSES AND IMPORTANCE

Public relations in education has two main aspects; sponsoring an excellent program and effectively communicating that fact to the public. Certainly, the first aspect is more important, but both aspects deserve adequate attention. Among the specific purposes of school public relations are the following:

1. To inform the public as to the work and accomplishments of the school.
2. To establish confidence in the schools.
3. To rally adequate support for the educational programs.
4. To develop awareness of the importance of education.
5. To improve the partnership that should exist among the schools, the students, the parents and other members of the public.
6. To correct any misunderstandings that occur as to the aims and activities of the schools.

Public relations is pertinent to all areas of human activity—education, religion, business, politics, military, and government. It can be a powerful force which can sometimes make the difference between the success or failure of an institution. A good public relations program is not haphazard; it must be well planned and wisely implemented.

Although official polls show that the great majority of Americans are basically satisfied with the schools their children attend, they are still unwilling to give the level of support the schools need. Educational programs could be better if the public would channel more support to them. It is a dismal fact that people spend more for tobacco and twice as much for liquor each year as for education. Apparently, the tobacco and liquor industries do a much better job than the schools in terms of public relations.[4]

WHO SHOULD BE INVOLVED?

Some people think that public relations is the responsibility of a specialist who can give overall direction to the public relations effort and assist others in contributing their fair share; but a public relations specialist or even a staff of specialists cannot do the job alone.

Every school employee has a public relations responsibility. Each one, whether a coach, secretary, janitor, administrator, lunch room employee, or whatever, has the potential for presenting a positive image and generating good will or for doing the opposite. Each faculty member has his own public relations opportunities in connection with any particular phase of the program. Each one needs to contribute to the larger public relations effort of the school.

The better the employees are informed about matters of particular interest in public relations, the better prepared they are to give accurate information and to foster a positive image of the school. Well-informed employees can be a great asset.

The idea that "quality builds quality" applies well in education. The first consideration of quality should be personnel. If a discipline is staffed with high quality personnel, they will build quality into other aspects of the program. An administrator should consider the public relations qualifications of each prospective employee, and this should play its rightful role in the selection of those to be hired.

Each individual in the profession has a responsibility to improve the public image of the profession. This can be partly accomplished by each one giving attention to the following:

1. Are you well groomed and attractively dressed or do you belong to the sloppy sweatshirt group?
2. Check your personal habits. Do you smoke in front of your students or anywhere in school? Are you seen in local bars? Do you use profanity? Have you let yourself become flabby and overweight through lack of exercise and self-control?
3. What about the quality of your teaching? Do you have your courses planned in advance for the semester, with carefully planned objectives you want your students to reach, or do you improvise from day to day and on the spur of the moment?
4. Do you treat your students with kindness and understanding, but at the same time maintain discipline?
5. Are you well-read, or do you find the scholarly life a bore? Are you seen at concerts and public meetings in addition to athletic contests and other desirable events?

In addition to the public relations of employees, students can be effective ambassadors of the school. How they represent the school and what they say about it certainly have impact on the school's image. Focus is brought on certain students because of outstanding achievements in academics or athletics or because of popularity or social adeptness. These students have a greater than normal influence on the school's image.

Often, school personnel, programs, and procedures become topics of discussion in the home. The impressions communicated by the students have a significant influence on the minds of the parents. Parents view the attitudes of their children as reliable indicators of the success of the school programs. Parents also become emotionally involved and will, therefore, often accept their child's attitude at face value without seriously questioning the validity of it. For these and other reasons, the first front on which the public relations battle should be fought is the classroom. If the students believe in the program, the personnel, and the procedures, they will be a major factor in maintaining a high image and substantial public support.

The idea that "people listen better when others toot your horn" is an important consideration. Even with the same set of facts, what you say about your own program has less impact than what someone else says. Therefore, it is often useful to involve nonschool personnel in public relations efforts. For example, it could be beneficial to have a news article by a prominent physician about the health instruction program, or the need for encouragement in the home of good health practices, or for emphasis on physical fitness. Sometimes, if a certain prominent citizen says that a facility or program is needed, the majority of others in the community will accept what is said at face value.

A school-community public relations council can be a highly useful instrument if it functions properly. It can be a valuable source of ideas and can help implement them. It can serve as a barometer to measure effectiveness and also provide useful feedback for evaluation of the public relations effort.

The school public relations program depends on many people, including employees, students, and nonschool personnel. It is a complex effort that requires careful planning and continuous attention.

COMMUNICATION

The art or act of communicating is one of our most effective measures for learning and it is of utmost importance in administration. Communication provides the thread that binds an organization together by ensuring common understanding. Effective communication is essential in good public relations; persuasive communication can sway or influence people's opinions.

Chapter 9 contains a major section about communication. Certain aspects of that section apply to the importance of communication in public relations; therefore, that section should be reviewed in connection with the present topic.

Listening is as much a part of good public relations as talking, and for some, listening is much harder. Listening can be highly informative; and it represents a show of respect for another person's point of view. Unfortunately, many people are better talkers than listeners.

Among public relations specialists, the following "Six C's" of communication have become popular. They can be effecively applied in the field of education, as well as in other fields.

Content. Communication should accurately state the intended message as clearly as possible. Correct content is fundamental to effective communication.

Clarity. Communication should be stated in a manner that will be easily understood. This will reduce the chances for misinterpretation, misunderstanding, and confusion.

Credibility. Communication should be based on accurate information from appropriate sources.

Context. Communication should fit the situation or the environment. It must be appropriate in terms of kind, style, and content.

Continuity and Consistency. Communication should flow with consistency and regularity in order to maintain open channels and mutual trust.

Channels. Defined and appropriate channels of communication should be used.

NEWS STORIES AND PUBLICITY

News stories, whether in written or oral form, are generally of four types: pre-event, postevent, feature, or editorial. All these can be used effectively in the school's public relations program, and each one should receive ample consideration.

News stories can often be generated by direct contact with news personnel. Ready access to useful photographs can often result in the publication of pictures along with printed material. Photographs attract special attention to news articles, and they can be highly communicative of themselves.

To establish good working relationships with the news media, consider the application of the following guidelines:

1. School personnel should become acquainted with the newspeople, and the newspeople should be encouraged to see the programs about which they are expected to write.
2. School personnel should become aware that a good story sent to the wrong department may be lost, since distinct differences exist between departments that handle sports news, political news, or social stories.
3. Coaches should have score books and statistics available for ready reference when they talk with news personnel regarding their sports.
4. The newsperson has an obligation to the public to give the news as he sees it. Teachers, coaches, and administrators should expect to get the bitter with the sweet and should not consider it a personal attack.
5. Newspeople should be treated fairly. A story should not be given freely to other newspeople when a particular one has worked hard to obtain it. If both evening and morning news reports are available in the same locale, the big stories should be broken at alternate times so as to ensure fair coverage. Dated releases may be used to achieve this end.
6. The attempt to buy favorable stories with gifts and promises beyond the usual and accepted practice should be avoided.
7. Careless and indiscreet statements to news personnel should be avoided. They often end up causing both embarrassment and damage.

Publicity means attracting public attention or public acclaim. It can be one important aspect of public relations, but it is not synonymous with public relations. Publicity is the dissemination of information about an event, program, or individual. Normally, competitive athletics receives much more publicity than all other school programs combined. Consequently, the publicity about athletic events is of signficance in the school's public relations program.

Publicity can be as unfavorable as it is favorable. It can be either overdone or underemphasized. It can accomplish the intent or, if handled improperly or misinterpreted, can backfire and accomplish the opposite. Publicity can be done in the form of paid advertisements or through the reporting of newsworthy items and events. However publicity is accomplished, it involves the purposeful attraction of public attention toward something such as an event or a program. It is usually done for promotional reasons.

IDENTIFYING A PUBLIC

A public is a group of people who are drawn together by common interests, are located in a specific geographic area, or are characterized by some other common feature, including age, religion, sex, occupation, race, nationality, politics, income, social status, affiliation, or educational background. The more that can be known about a particular public, the easier it is to plan an effective public relations approach.[7]

In order to gather information about a public, various techniques may be used: surveys, questionnaires, opinion polls, interviews, and face-to-face conversations. Prevalent opinions in a particular public are often the result of influence in earlier life, but they are also influenced by peoples' more recent experiences and by the mass media.

Until recently, each neighborhood and/or community had its own school. The neighborhood school concept enhanced parental awareness and support. However, recent trends, including school consolidation, civil rights actions (busing of students to other neighborhoods), and other demographic and sociologic changes have altered the neighborhood school idea in many localities. This makes it difficult for school administrators to identify the public with whom they need to communicate, and it makes their public less accessible.

The several publics that must be considered in the public relations effort include: the present student body, past students (alumni), school employees (teachers, administrators, and others), parents, and other members of the general public. The methods of communicating effectively with these different publics vary both in content and procedure. It is important for the schools to have a sound plan that gives adequate attention to all segments of the population.

Sometimes the target group for certain information constitutes only a portion of the larger public, such as athletic fans, members of the PTA, particular ethnic groups, or parents of children of a certain age. It is important to define the population that the public relations effort should be pointed toward. This "target" approach can greatly improve effectiveness.

METHODS

An effective public relations program must have a strong element of consistency. It should involve an ongoing effort that keeps ahead of potential problems, as opposed to a crisis or "brush fire" approach. In public relations, "an ounce of care is better than a pound of cure."

Straightforward honesty is important, and the consequences of any amount of dishonesty are usually disastrous in terms of public relations.

A well-balanced public relations program includes a variety of approaches, several of which are described in this section. Of course, the total public relations effort extends far beyond these methods. It involves every kind of information and impression given to the public by school personnel, whether intentional or unintentional.

Parent–teacher *conferences* offer one of the best potentials for public relations. The effectiveness of this method depends largely on the nature of the conferences and how well they are conducted.

Another valuable approach is to *take students out* into the community, on field trips, special interest tours, educational visits to museums, historical sites, industial and manufacturing plants, and the like.

One of the most useful means of public relations is through *handouts and notices* to students and parents. These can range all the way from report cards to informational materials and notices of future events.

It is important to publish periodic *reports* relative to the school's well-being (financial and otherwise) or about the personnel, programs, or special achievements. Reports about school deficiencies and special problems that need public assistance also can be helpful.

Report cards sent home to parents that include more description than the simple basics can serve as a good method of communicating important information about student achievement as related to expectations. Sometimes, certain other information can be appropriately enclosed with the report cards. This causes the information to receive more attention than if distributed separately.

Student performances on *youth fitness tests* as compared to state and national norms can be highly meaningful to the public. The awarding of fitness certificates and other forms of special recognition can be helpful.

Exhibits, demonstrations, and *open houses* have been used successfully in physical education programs. Parents like to see their children participate in such events. Whenever demonstrations of this kind are given, they should portray interesting aspects of the school program rather than something "dreamed up" for the entertainment of the public.

Information can be transmitted to parents by use of mimeographed *bulletins* that are carried home by students. Such bulletins should contain pertinent information that is written in an appealing manner, so that they will have a positive image and parents will be motivated to read them.

Well kept *bulletin boards* can serve an excellent purpose. Much interesting and useful information can be communicated through bulletin board displays.

Trophy cases are useful, particularly in connection with athletics. Much interest and pride can be instilled through the proper display of trophies.

Face-to-face *conversation* is one of the most effective implements of public relations. This can take place on the playing field and in the gymnasium with students, and on some occasions, with parents and other members of the public at athletic events, PTA meetings, service clubs, church meetings, and other such events.

In addition to worthy news items that are routinely provided to the media, special *feature stories* can be developed about new programs, outstanding teachers, or unique student achievement.

Valuable information for use by the media can be obtained from various state and national organizations. For example, every state has a Department of Education with one or more *specialists* in the area of health, physical education, school recreation, and athletics. This state agency is capable of providing useful information in the form of news releases, news letters, and information bulletins. Certain national organizations can also be helpful. For example, the AAHPERD has a special public relations program known as PEPI (Physical Education Public Information), which provides a constant flow of information to the state PEPI representatives who in turn, have the responsibility of providing it to the media and/or sending it on to local school personnel. Also, the President's Council on Physical Fitness provides facts and statistics that are of value and interest to the public.

Numerous *films* can be acquired on free loan or at reasonable rental rates from such agencies as the AAHPERD, the President's Council on Physical Fitness, the Athletic Institute, and West Glen Films at 565 Fifth Avenue, New York, NY. To give an example, the AAHPERD has two highly useful films entitled, "All The Self There IS" and "Every Child a Winner." These films illustrate the value of physical education in the total development of children and youth. Films like these can help members of the public better understand the objectives, values, and concepts of physical education. The other organizations mentioned have films on a variety of subjects.

Special opportunities for public relations exist in connection with *athletics*. These include the following:

1. The particular manner with which athletic events are conducted: public address procedures, programs, adequacy of seating, ushering, cheerleading activities, half-time performances, and the conduct of coaches and athletes.
2. Athletic brochures: content, design, distribution.
3. Newspaper, radio, and television coverage—amount, type, and content.
4. Booster club activities: a booster club can be helpful if it has valid and clear objectives and if it is well managed. Conversely, a booster club that is not well managed can become a problem to the athletic program.
5. Promotion and ticket sales, and provision of parking privileges.
6. Public appearances by coaches at banquets, on television shows, radio interviews, and other public settings.
7. Awards presentations.

HANDLING COMPLAINTS

Every organization that deals with the public will receive some complaints. This is especially true with education that involves people's children and is financed by public funds. A complaint involves one of two circumstances: a weakness or fault that justifies the complaint or a miscommunication or misunderstanding. A condition always motivates a complaint. Even agitators and chronic complainers are motivated by some weak or questionable situation. A complaint left unresolved results in a continuing problem; one that is likely to grow and lead to other complaints.

From the public relations point of view, complaints should be handled in an open-minded and gracious manner. The one dealing with the complainer should avoid being defensive and abrupt. Try to understand his point of view and help him to understand yours. If the complaint is justified, then admit it and make the necessary corrections. If it is not justified, help the complainer to recognize that. This kind of objective approach will help soothe feelings and win support.

PRINCIPLES

1. A school system cannot avoid public relations. Relations with the public will exist in some form, good, bad, or indifferent.
2. The public relations program should be clearly defined, including purposes, procedures, responsibilities, and expected results. The better the program is understood, the better chance it has for success.
3. The public has a right to information pertaining to the school and all of its various programs. Educators should try to avoid operating in a world of their own, isolated from the public, to whom they owe their existence. However, it is a fact that the school officials must stay in control of the program, and reserve the right to make the decisions and manage the program in a highly professional manner.
4. A vital function of public relations is to establish an open channel so that the public will be sufficiently informed to properly influence decisions.
5. While good public relations requires a well-conceived plan, flexibility and adaptability are necessary. It is important to adjust to changing circumstances and also to capitalize on unexpected opportunities.
6. The public is entitled to know the truth about school policies, finances, and programs. Hidden weaknesses fester and sooner or later erupt. If granted full knowledge of the facts, the public can often help in the solution of problems.
7. The way something is done is often as important as what is done. The particular approach can make a great deal of difference as to/how a decision or a circumstance is accepted.
8. The most fundamental aspect of good public relations is a superior program, for which there is absolutely no substitute. Educators should not expect public support of programs that produce inferior results.
9. Public education is a form of social institution which is financed and maintained by the total public, not just those with children of school age. Therefore, educational programs must be designed and managed with the benefit of all of the people in mind.
10. One excellent means of public relations is through the students. Parents are especially interested in the attitudes and well-being of their children. Even though a teacher may have 200 students in a day, he is still Jane's coach or Billy's teacher in the minds of the parents.

11. Public relations whitewash wears off sooner or later, and then the facts become embarrassingly obvious.
12. Every well-planned public relations program is pointed toward a defined population. The population often has sub-populations who deserve special attention.
13. News stories and other reported information ought to be factual, relevant, free from bias, and appealing.
14. The public relations program should be a continuous, integrated phase of the overall school effort. Poorly planned, hit-and-miss efforts are only partially successful at best.
15. One of the most effective public relations approaches is person-to-person, teacher to student, student to parent, or teacher to citizen.
16. Some aspects of public relations need funding. If funding is inadequate, the success of the program is jeopardized. Adequate funding is just as necessary for public relations as for other aspects of the program.
17. Effective public relations specialists usually stay in the background instead of seeking the limelight; keeping abreast of the factors that affect the program, developing a wide acquaintance, and making helpful contacts.
18. A highly reputable image can serve several useful purposes, of which one is public relations.
19. A sense of humor, especially with some of it directed at yourself, can be helpful in public relations. Good, wholesome humor is a universal language.
20. Public relations, like other phases of the school program, requires both near and long-term comprehensive planning.
21. School personnel who make sharp or abrasive statements or who criticize frequently or react defensively must gain control of these bad characteristics in order to become positive forces in public relations.

EVALUATION

Regular, critical evalution of the over-all public relations effort is a method by which success is determined and improvements are made. This should include an ongoing process of error detection and correction. It helps to ask yourself searching questions about your public relations approach and give yourself honest answers. Clearly defined public relations goals that are obtainable can serve as measures of success.

The school public relations program must be honest in terms of both intent and implementation. It must be continuous, positive, comprehensive, sensitive to the particular public, and communicate information that is useful and easily understood. The identification of weaknesses in any of these elements is good reason to adjust the public relations approach.

BIBLIOGRAPHY

1. Carter, G.F.: Marketing physical education. JOPER, 50:36, 1979.

2. Clay, W.B.: First class and getting better. JOPER, *52:*19, 1981.

3. Haddock, B.A.: Improving board/staff relations. Phi Delta Kappan, *60:*607, 1979.

4. Jones, J.W.: Building Public Confidence in Your Schools: A Source Book of Proven Public Relations Practices. Arlington, VA, National School Public Relations Association, 1978.

5. Lesly, P.: Public Relations Handbook, 2nd Ed. Englewood Cliffs, NJ, Prentice-Hall, 1978.

6. Marsh, D.B., Smith, J.L., Jenkins, D., and Livingstone, E.: Program promotoion. JOPER, *52:*24, 1981.

7. Marston, J.: Modern Public Relations. New York, McGraw-Hill, 1979.

8. McLaughlin, D.: "Chip-n-block" for parental involvement. JOPER, *52:*22, 1981.

9. Nolte, L.W.: Fundamentals of Public Relations: Professional Guidelines, Concepts, and Integrations 2nd Ed. New York, Pergamon Press, 1979.

10. Peake, J.: Public Relations in Business. New York, Harper & Row, 1980.

11. Reilly, R.: Public Relations in Action. Englewood Cliffs, NJ, Prentice-Hall, 1981.

12. Smith, N.W.: Community involvement through a curriculum study project. JOPER, *52:*16, 1981.

13. Voros, G.J., and P.A., Alvarez, (eds.); What Happens in Public Relations? New York, AMACOM, 1981.

14. Wagenhalls, J.G., III.: Involving parents in after school activity programs. JOPER, *51:*13, 1980.

Chapter 11
LEGAL ASPECTS

Murphy's Law states "anything that can go wrong will go wrong." Some consider this to be a negative point of view, and not the attitude that should prevail. As a safety measure, however, constant awareness of Murphy's Law can help an administrator remain alert to potential pitfalls.

The growing concern for individual rights has taken precedence over the traditional concept of *sovereign immunity*. Teachers, coaches, and administrators are no longer held immune from liability under the law simply because they are employed in an educational system run by the state. As a result, educational personnel are obligated to pay particular attention to the protection, health, and welfare of students. This chapter is designed to help the teacher, coach, and administrator to better understand the legal aspects that pertain particularly to physical education and athletics.

Although physical education and athletics are among the more hazardous of the teaching areas, there is no reason to be apprehensive about providing a well-rounded program of meaningful activities. Generally, the courts are aware of the inherent risks in these activities and acknowledge the fact that the potential values exceed the risk expectancy, thus viewing most risks as being within the parameters of "reasonable risk." It is normally assumed that the programs are based on adequate knowledge of student needs and are conducted by competent and prudent instructors. One must recognize, however, that liability suits against teachers and coaches are definite possibilities. Therefore, the teacher/coach must (1) be well informed about the laws that pertain to educators, (2) use adequate caution and control in all the activities within his responsibility, and (3) always try to act wisely and prudently. The teacher/coach can meet his legal obligations by carrying out the responsibilities of his job in the correct manner.

SELECTED LEGAL TERMS*

The following are definitions of some common legal terms, which may be encountered by educators and administrators in dealing with the legal aspects of managing physical education and athletic programs.

---

* Much of the specialized legal information in this chapter was furnished by Professor Linda Carpenter, Ed.D., J.D., of Brooklyn College.

Act of God	Unavoidable incident due to forces of nature which could not have been foreseen or prevented.
Assault	Unlawful force directed at another person with the obvious intent and capacity to do harm. Assault may cause physical harm (criminal assault) or result in mental or emotional stress and apprehension (civil assault).
Assumption of risk	Participation or involvement in an activity or situation where an element of risk is inherent. Voluntary participation can be interpreted as an acceptance of risk. In physical education and athletics, an element of reasonable risk is normally assumed by the participant and his parents.
Attractive nuisance	A facility or situation that attracts participation and is hazardous. Examples are unsecured gymnastics equipment or trampolines, an unsupervised swimming pool, or playground equipment in poor repair. Whether a situation would be legally declared an attractive nuisance is influenced by the laws of the particular state, the age and competence of the injured person, and the various circumstances surrounding the incident.
Battery	Physical assault, resulting in injury.
Causative factor	The situation or factor that was obviously the main cause of an injury or incident.
Civil law	Civil action implies a noncriminal infringement upon the rights of a person, agency, corporation, or other. Tort and contract disputes are examples of civil suits. Civil law is different from criminal law.
Common law	That body of governing principles and rules of action derived from past practices, customs, and traditions.
Comparative negligence	A situation in which the injured party has contributed to his own injury by some type of negligence. This differs from contributory negligence, because rather than acting as a complete block to legal recovery, the injured party's negligence simply reduces the recovery

by a percentage equal to his comparative negligence.

Contract	A promise or set of promises. Three elements must exist to have a contract: an offer, an acceptance, and consideration (something of value contributed by each side such as money for a service rendered).
Contributory negligence	Applicable when an individual's action was not the primary cause of negligence but a contributing factor to the negligent act. A secondary or indirect cause of negligence.
Criminal law	That portion of the law which involves crime or illegal wickedness. A criminal action involves the breaking of a law, as in theft, battery, perjury or murder. Different than civil law.
Damages	Monetary compensation awarded by the court in payment for loss or injury incurred.
Defendant	The party against whom relief or recovery is sought in a law suit. Opposite of the plaintiff.
Due process of law	The right of notice, the opportunity to be heard and defended in orderly court proceedings, and the right of appeal.
Equal protection of the law	The right of equal treatment by the law and law enforcement agencies for all persons under similar circumstances.
Foreseeability	The individual responsible for the negligent act could have and reasonably should have foreseen the danger that existed.
Immunity	Freedom or protection from legal action. Sovereign immunity refers to the protection of the government or the ruling body against possible suit or blame. It is based on the concept that "the king (or ruler) can do no wrong."
Injunction	A prohibitive ruling issued by a court directing a person or agency to refrain from performing a specific act.
In loco parentis	The purpose of acting in the place of a parent or guardian. It may be complete or partial. Teachers are considered to be in loco parentis

to students, during the time the students are under their supervision. The degree of this condition is influenced by the age of the students and the nature of the school.

Liability — Being responsible for a negligent act or other tort; having legal responsibility that was not fulfilled and resulted in injury.

Liability insurance — Insurance policies that provide protection against financial loss from liability claims.

Litigation — A lawsuit that is in process.

Malfeasance — An act that is illegal or improper and should not have been performed.

Mandatory legislation — Enacted legislation that must be observed. Opposite from *permissive* legislation.

Misfeasance — An act that may be legal, but was done in an improper manner.

Negligence — Not exercising the care or following the procedures a person of ordinary prudence would under similar circumstances. It can take the form of commission or ommission.

Nonfeasance — Failing to perform an act that should have been done.

Permissive legislation — Legislation that legalizes an action but does not require or mandate it. Opposite from mandatory legislation.

Plaintiff — One who seeks to enforce the law by bringing legal action against another party. Opposite of the defendant.

Precedent — The utilization of a previous court decision in judging a similar court action with comparable circumstances.

Proprietary function — As pertaining to schools, a function different from the normal educational process, usually of a profit-making nature. Athletic contests that produce gate receipts are often classified as proprietary functions. Other examples are fund-raising events and renting or leasing out of facilities. It is the opposite of governmental functions.

Proximate cause — A situation or factor that was the cause or contributing cause of an injury or incident.

Prudent person	One who acts in a careful, discreet, and judicious manner in view of the particular circumstances.
Respondent superior	The responsibility of an employer for the negligent acts of his employees.
Statutory law	Law governed by statutes enacted by legislative bodies.
Tort	A civil wrong or injustice independent of a contract, which produces an injury or damage to another person or to property.
Wanton and willful act	An act against another person committed deliberately or with reckless disregard for safety.

TORT LAWS

The term tort is used to classify a group of civil wrongs, as opposed to criminal wrongs, which involve a violation of a specific law for which fines or imprisonment might be imposed. Negligence is a major tort; others are trespass, nuisance, and defamation.[3]

Disputes about contracts, although they fall within the category of civil rather than criminal wrongs, are not classified as torts. A person entering into a contract voluntarily takes upon himself certain duties or responsibilities. In tort law, the existence of a duty or responsibility, the violation of which might make the individual liable for legal action, is not taken voluntarily. Other characteristics of torts are the following: (1) Torts are prosecuted by the injured person rather than by law enforcement officials. (2) An act may be both a tort and a crime, but not all torts are crimes. (3) To prove a tort, the injured party must demonstrate by a preponderance (more than 50%) of the evidence that his claim is justified. This last characteristic differs from a criminal case, in which proof beyond a reasonable doubt is required.

Under tort law, a person who causes injury to another, for which a legal liability exists, is frequently answerable to the injured person in money damages, although other forms of reparation are also used. People are not liable in tort for every accidental injury; a person is only liable for a tort when that person intentionally or negligently causes or contributes to an injury. The injured person (plaintiff) must prove that the injuring person (defendant) was the "proximate cause" of the plaintiff's injury. Proximate cause is an elastic legal term. Sometimes, to be considered the proximate cause, a cause need not be the immediate, or even the primary cause, only a contributing factor in producing the harm.

Tort law is common law or judge-made law. It has its most basic foundation in the concept of *fault*. For a fuller explanation of the concept of tort law, the reader should refer to one of the education law books in the bibliography.

CONDITIONS OF NEGLIGENCE

One of the most important areas of tort law that an administrator should understand is negligence. In the legal sense, negligence is the failure to perform one's duties at the level expected of a responsible person under particular circumstances. Good intentions alone are no safeguard, because negligence denotes an unintentional failure to do what is reasonably expected. The fact that a teacher or coach is certified by the state indicates a level of expected behavior. When one falls short of these expectations and this contributes to damage to another person, the teacher can be declared negligent. Often, negligence is difficult to prove, and many individuals who are inclined to sue become discouraged when the legal grounds are weak or insufficient. In order for a person to be declared negligent, the following elements must exist.[3]

1. The defendant must have a *duty toward the plaintiff.* Teachers, supervisors and administrators clearly have a duty toward the students entrusted to their care. In most states, a person does not have a legal duty toward a stranger, even when the stranger is in dire need of help. To encourage aid when needed, some states have passed "Good Samaritan" laws.

2. The plaintiff must have been *harmed* by the tort or wrong committed by the defendant. This could be in the form of property damage, personal injury, or damage to one's character or reputation.

3. The individual having "duty" must have breached that duty by an *act of omission* (nonfeasance) or an *act of commission* (misfeasance). This means that a person who does nothing when something should have been done is often as liable as one who responds incorrectly.

4. The breach of duty must have been directly related to the damage done by the plaintiff. In other words, the breach of duty was the proximate cause of the damage.

These four elements pertain to legal negligence, and all of them must exist in order to justify legal action. Sometimes nonlegal negligence is committed by a teacher, but if no tort results (due to the lack of one or more of the four elements, such as no "harm") the teacher's behavior might be the rightful subject of administrative action but is not a matter for the courts.

SITUATIONS OF POTENTIAL NEGLIGENCE

Several conditions are frequently found in teaching or coaching situations that, if unattended, could injure a student and cause the teacher to be guilty of negligence. It is important to understand these potential hazards and deal effectively with them.

Faulty Equipment

Acting both as instructor and supervisor, the teacher or coach must prevent students from using defective equipment. For example, requiring or even permitting students to climb a dangerously frayed rope would be grounds for negligence, if the rope should break and cause injury. The same would be true of permitting students to use faulty gymnastic apparatus, a trampoline with a damaged bed, or defective playground equipment.

In addition to the duty to prevent the use of defective equipment, the duty exists to periodically inspect the equipment with the intent of discovering any defects.

Attractive Nuisances

Hazardous equipment that may attract students, such as bows and arrows, climbing ropes, trampolines, and scuba equipment, must be safely secured or made inoperative in order that students not be attracted to use it in the absence of proper supervision. A swimming pool that is unsecured or lacking supervision is an attractive nuisance.

Inadequate Supervision

Negligence could result from permitting people to swim in an outdoor area during a lightning storm, permitting children to play in an area too close to traffic where one might spontaneously dart in front of an automobile, or permitting play on a field where the surface is too hard and rough or otherwise unsuitable for the particular activity.

Poor organization can also constitute negligence. When students are required, encouraged, or even permitted to participate in a school activity, a reasonable amount of organization and supervision is expected.

Other Hazardous Situations

Poor selection of activities can contribute to negligence where there is a likelihood of collisions among participants, or inappropriate rough-and-tumble or tackle activities. Inadequate provision for individual differences, as in a mismatch in a combative activity, can also result in a problem.

Lack of provision for protective equipment and procedures could be declared an act of negligence. Examples would be to permit students to participate in tackle football, fencing, ice hockey, or lacrosse without the proper protective equipment.

THE JURY'S INTERPRETATION

A jury decides whether a teacher in a particular situation, acted reasonably in performing his duty to protect from harm. What a teacher thinks is reasonable might be considered unreasonable, and thus negligent, by a jury of nonteachers.

Reasonable-Man Test

The *duty of care* is the major question decided by the courts. In all states except Illinois, the duty of care required to avoid tort liability is that which a reasonable person of ordinary prudence would exercise for the safety of others, in the circumstances. In Illinois, the standard of the duty owed has been lowered to the imposition of liability only for willful or wanton misconduct.

The test to be applied in most situations is what the particular individual should have reasonably foreseen and done. This standard is often referred to as the *reasonable-man test*.

The reasonable-man test also allows courts and juries to adapt society's views of reasonableness as they change from time to time and place to place. A child is not held to the same degree of "reasonableness" or responsibility as an adult. Therefore, if a child's duty were in question, the test would be whether a reasonable child of the same age, intelligence, and circumstances would have acted in the same way. It is important to recognize that the law does not require that all possible harm be removed, only that which can be done so reasonably.

DEFENSES TO THE CHARGE OF NEGLIGENCE

Some of the factors or conditions that help to keep a person from negligence are considered in the following paragraphs. Each of these defenses should be carefully considered when a liability suit is a possibility.

Lack of Legal Duty or Proximate Cause

Sometimes a plaintiff will try to establish liability against an individual who has no legal duty that is related to the damage. In the absence of legal duty, liability normally does not exist.

Even though an individual breached a duty and was involved in the chain of events associated with damage done to another person, the associated individual might be free of liability due to lack of proximate cause. In other words, a clear and direct linkage must exist between the action of the defendant and the damage done the plaintiff. There has to be evidence that the defendant actually contributed to the cause of damage.

Assumption of Risk

Certain situations, such as physical education activities and competitive athletics, have inherent dangers. Dangers also exist in industrial arts, chemistry, home economics, driver education, and traveling to and from school. In fact, some element of risk exists in many of the activities of life; but in most cases, the potential benefits justify a reasonable risk. Different activities have different levels of risk, and students, with the aid of their parents, have a certain amount of freedom to pick and choose the activities in which they participate. For example, football, rugby, and skiing are high-risk activities, and for this reason, some people avoid them. Damages that result within the limits of a known, reasonable risk do not constitute liability. Participants should be informed of the typical risks involved in an activity. "Consent forms" are often used, and these will be discussed later.

Contributory or Comparative Negligence

In some cases, the person who sustains damage was a party to his own problem. Perhaps on his own initiative, he took more risks than were necessary, disobeyed warnings or safety regulations, or his emotional behavior caused him to act unwisely. In such cases, the injured person contributed to his own damage, and therefore is guilty of either contributory or comparative negligence. Different states deal with this situation differently. In some states, a type of contributory negligence system is used that bars the injured plaintiff from recovery if he contributed in any way or to any degree to his own injury. Other states (increasing in number) have adopted a system of comparative negligence in which the injured person's recovery is diminished by the percentage that he was at fault for his own injuries. Whichever system is used, the defense, if successful, can reduce the size of the judgment.

Act of God (Nature)

Some acts or conditions of nature cannot be foreseen or controlled by humans, and for which no person can be held responsible. Examples are a student being struck by lightning or someone being injured due to an unforeseen cave-in of the earth's surface.

Sovereign Immunity

In its governmental role as an educational agency of the state, a school system is sometimes protected from suit under the concept of sovereign immunity; however, sovereign immunity is decreasing today, and more school systems are susceptible to suit. Under some circumstances, the school serves as a proprietor or profit-making agency, and under these conditions, the sovereign immunity concept does not apply. Included in the proprietary function are activities where admission is charged, such as athletic events, exhibits, and concerts; and properties owned by the school district and rented or leased to companies or individuals. Sometimes, school districts cannot be sued in connection with their governmental education roles, but they can be sued in connection with their proprietary roles.

PREVENTING A LAWSUIT—BEFORE AN ACCIDENT

Waivers and Permissions

Permission forms that involve a parent's consent to a student's participation in athletics or intramural activities often contain a clause that releases the school and its employees from any injury that happens while participating in the activity. Such permission forms have limited, if any, legal effect. In spite of this, such forms may have a psychologic influence on the parents and decrease the likelihood of their bringing tort suits against schools. Some reasons for the waiver and permission being legally invalid are as follow: (1) It is impossible to release a future tort because of the unpredictability of future events. (2) Parents cannot sign away the rights of a minor child. (3) Children, being minors, cannot release the school from possible tort claims. (4) The waiver or form is usually unspecific as to the rights being waived or all risks involved in the activity.

Although the typical permission or waiver form (Figure 11-1) is not legally binding, it is still a good idea to use it. The completion of such a form should bring to the attention of the adults that risk is involved, and that you wish them to understand that they are making a decision as to whether the student should participate. Thus, both parents and child are aware that they are assuming some risks by participation in an activity.

It is also a good idea to obtain other information on the permission form. Data pertaining to the notification of parents and other emergency information ought to be obtained. The severity of a situation may be lessened if the students' needs and parents' wishes as to medical attention are known and followed.

Adequate Supervision

Negligent supervision is the cause of most school-related lawsuits. The major questions are as follows: Did the teacher inspect, report, or correct an unsafe condition? Did the teacher fail to or wrongfully instruct students? Did the teacher arrange students in an unsafe way? Did the teacher aid a student in need by correcting or offering assistance? Underlying the rest are two basic questions: (1) Did the teacher have a duty to supervise the student in the situation that caused the injury? (2) If there was a duty to supervise, did the teacher breach that duty?

As a physical education teacher or athletic coach, you must be careful to observe some simple principles of supervision. First, do not create danger by your own conduct. This type of situation would be created by instructing students to participate in a dangerous and unsafe activity. Second, avoid foreseeable perils that are created by others.

The school has a duty to supervise school grounds during normal operating hours. Such supervision may also be required before and/or after school hours, depending on circumstances surrounding the use by students. If students are known to misuse the equipment, engage in misconduct, or if the conditions are unsafe for unsupervised play, then supervision is necessary.

Transportation

Athletes or other students require transportation, and sometimes the use of private vehicles is the most convenient and economical method. Whenever possible, however, students should be transported by common carrier. A common carrier is insured and bonded, and the drivers are trained to handle large vehicles. Many school buses are owned by private drivers whose route is appointed by the school board. Privately owned school buses are desirable common carriers, because the initial liability rests with the driver/contractor rather than with the school district or teacher.

NAME _____
                    Last   First

I hereby apply for the privilege of trying out for the _____
team, 19___

I recognize my responsibilities if I try out for the above sport. I will make it a point to so govern myself that my connection with the sport will bring honor to it and to the school, and expect to be asked to withdraw from the team in case I do not.

If extended the above privilege I will:

I. Train consistently as advised by the coach.

II. Not smoke during the school year.

III. Make a serious endeavor to keep up my studies.

IV. Do all in my power to help keep athletics desirable.

V. Make it a point to abide by the rules and regulations of the student body.

VI. So conduct myself at other schools that I will bring credit to my team.

I have read the eligibility rules of the Utah High School Association. I am presently eligible according to these regulations.

Signed _____
                                    Student

Figure 11-1. Athletic permission and waiver form. (Courtesy of the Provo School District.)

Coaches have been found negligent for the following reasons: (1) the coach transports athletes in his own automobile, (2) the coach permits student athletes to return home in student-driven automobiles, (3) the coach drives a bus loaded with students when he is unlicensed to do so and unspecialized as a driver of such a vehicle.

Unfortunately, the laws governing the transportation of students are inconsistent from state to state. Every teacher, coach, and administrator should be well informed about the applicable laws of the particular state in which he works, and within the framework of this knowledge, apply caution and good judgment.

SPORT _____

DATE _____

PARENT'S CONSENT

I hereby give my consent for my son or daughter to participate in the athletic program sponsored by the school.

I further release said school from all liability for injuries received by my son or daughter during, or resulting from, participation in this program, whether during practice or in an interschool contest.

In addition, I hereby release the school from all liability for injuries received by the participant while enroute to or from contests which are held at other schools.

My son, or daughter, is covered by adequate insurance.

School Insurance   Yes _____   No _____

Other Insurance _____
                          (Name and Policy Number)

Signed _____ Phone _____
              Parent or Guardian

Address _____

This student was examined _____ and is qualified to participate in interscholastic athletics.

Signed _____
                          Physician

PREVENTING A LAWSUIT—AFTER AN ACCIDENT

Treatment of Injuries

When a student is injured, the teacher or supervisor is placed in a precarious position. A teacher could be liable for not administering first aid when needed or for administering it incorrectly.

In the case of athletic trainers or of coaches who act as athletic trainers, several guidelines are especially important.

1. Confer sufficiently with the team physician relative to the prevention of injuries.
2. Be well prepared to perform emergency care for injuries commonly incurred in athletics.

3. Obtain medical advice and approval for any medically related treatment beyond first aid.
4. Keep accurate records of injuries, treatments given, and authorizations by medical personnel.
5. Have a medical doctor or emergency medical service at all contests that involve contact sports.
6. Have accurate and up-to-date medical records on each athlete and use that information properly.
7. Permit athletes to return to practice and competition following serious illness or injury only after securing medical approval.
8. Be adequately concerned with the provision and use of properly fitted protective equipment for each athlete.
9. In all actions relating to injury or illness, carefully apply the "reasonable person" concept (act prudently).
10. Be especially cautious about assuming responsibilities that officially or logically belong to the team physician.

Accident Reports

An accurate written report should be prepared as soon as possible after an accident, to serve as a record of the facts. Every educational system or institution ought to have a well-designed accident report form, along with the requirement that the form be completed and signed by the supervisor and the victim, or a witness in the place of the victim. In most states, accident reports are available to the plaintiff as well as to the defendant.

CURRENT ISSUES

Athletics: A Right or Privilege?

Athletics are subject to the requirements of the 14th amendment to the Constitution of the United States and federal civil rights statutes. To be in compliance with the law, a school may not discriminate among students; neither may a school district discriminate among schools and leagues.

Although in certain states, athletics have been established and maintained by statute, participation in athletics by any given student has been held by the courts, in most cases, to be a privilege.

The rightful suspension of a student athlete from participation has been held to be valid by the courts. In some cases, where the student athlete might suffer career losses by disciplinary expulsion form varsity sports, the courts have required prior hearings.

Student Records

The Family Education Rights and Privacy Act of 1974 (FERPA) is the federal regulation that governs the release of educational records. Under FERPA, the methods of administration, rather than any requirements concerning content of student records, are stated.

This federal law creates the right of eligible students (over 18 years of age) and parents, in the case of ineligible students, to see, inspect, reproduce, and challenge the accuracy of their education records. It also requires the student's (or parent's) written permission to be obtained before the disclosure of personally identifiable information to nonprivileged parties. This final provision has implications for teachers and coaches. When college coaches and prospective employers request specific information, the coach must be aware of all the restrictions on the release of such information.

Statutes Governing the Handicapped

The Rehabilitation Act of 1973 prohibits discrimination against the handicapped in all federally aided programs. The Education for All Handicapped Children Act of 1975 (PL-94-142) provides federal funding to aid state efforts in providing appropriate education to the handicapped. In addition, each state has specific statutes dealing with the handicapped with regard to participation in physical education, intramurals, and interscholastic or intercollegiate sports. More is said about this in Chapter 15.

CONTRACTS

A contract is a legally binding agreement representing both sides and explaining certain conditions. It is assumed that contracts are entered into voluntarily, in a spirit of agreement and with a legal purpose in mind.

Teachers, coaches, and administrators enter into various kinds of contracts. Among these are employment contracts, supplemental contracts for extra duties, contracts with suppliers and construction personnel, and contracts with other institutions.

When an institution offers an individual an employment contract, the offer remains valid for a reasonable time or until a specified date, or until the offer is withdrawn. If the potential employee signs the contract, he and the institution become legally bound to the conditions of the contract, and neither party has the legal right to violate or change them unless the explicit permission of the other party is obtained. A similar situation exists with a contract involving an institution and a supplier or construction company; or between two educational institutions, such as a contract for an athletic contest.

Although teacher contracts are usually signed annually, the contract has a different meaning if the teacher is on tenure. Tenure is the right to hold a position indefinitely unless just cause exists for termination. Tenure, and the stability it provides, has both strengths and weaknesses. It may bring out better performances in teachers and make teaching a more attractive profession; but in some instances, schools get stuck with teachers who have lost their motivation or whose incompetence went undiscovered during the probationary period.

Most public schools handle coaching assignments with a separate contract, which is supplemental to the basic teaching contract. This permits flexibility in assigning coaches and changing their assignments without altering the basic contract. This practice is also followed in college situations; but, usually, college level coaching assignments are included in the basic annual contract. A few coaches are given multi-year contracts, but this is the exception, not the rule.

GUIDELINES

1. The protection and welfare of the students should be the top priority in conducting all school programs, particularly physical education and athletic activities.
2. Administrators are responsible for giving leadership to the development and implementation of sound policies, procedures, and safety regulations. This includes posting safety regulations in proper places; *a standardized system* of emergency care in the case of accidents; and a standard procedure for reporting accidents.
3. Teachers, coaches, and administrators should have adequate liability insurance, preferably provided through the school system. If no such provision exists, adequate coverage should be obtained from another source.
4. Up-to-date knowledge about emergency medical care is an important aspect of the professional development of school personnel, particularly those in the areas of high risk.
5. Due to the differences in laws of the various states, educators should become well acquainted with the liability laws of the particular locales in which they work.
6. A teacher, coach, or administrator who consistently acts with prudence in his daily procedures on the job and gives special attention to prudent conduct during times of injury or emergency will greatly reduce, if not eliminate, the chances of his legal involvement.

If an accident takes place under your supervision, a few simple procedures will help to strengthen your case if a suit is brought.

1. Follow all procedures established for first aid, transportation, and notification.
2. Make a record and include as much information as possible about the accident, including names of students involved and witnesses.
3. If the student violated a rule, document this, along with a lesson plan of the instruction and the student's attendance in class that day.
4. Discuss the matter only with the parents, official medical personnel, school officials, and school legal counsel.

BIBLIOGRAPHY

1. Arnold, D.E.: Legal aspects of off-campus physical education programs. JOPER, 50(4):21, 1979.

2. Appenzeller, H.: Athletics and the Law. Charlottesville, VA, The Michie Company, 1975.

3. Carpenter, L.J., and Acosta, R.V.: Violence in sport. JOPER, 50(4):18, 1979.

4. Flygare, T.: Legal Rights of Teachers. Bloomington, IN, The Phi Beta Kappa Educational Foundation, 1976.

5. Hofeld, A.: Athletes—their rights and correlative duties. The Trial Lawyers Guide, *19:*388, 1975.

6. Law and Amateur Sports: Issues of the 80's. Proceedings of a Symposium sponsored by the Center for Law and Sports, Indiana University Law School, Bloomington, IN, 1981.

7. Leihee, H.C.: Tort Liability for Injuries to Pupils. Ann Arbor, Campus Publishers, University of Michigan, 1965.

8. Maillos, H.C.: Legal liability of athletic administrators for injury to student athletes. Athletic Administration, *15:*16, 1980.

9. Mills, J.: Legal Rights of College Students and Administrators: A Hand Book. Washington, D.C., Lerner Law Book Pub. Co., 1971.

10. Peterson, L., Rossmiller, R., and Volz, M.: The Law and Public School Operation, 2nd Ed. New York, Harper and Row, 1978.

11. Reutter, E.E., and Hamilton, R.R.: The Law and Public Education, 2nd Ed. Mineola, NY, The Foundation Press, 1975.

12. You and the Law, Special Reports prepared by The Research Institute of America, 589 Fifth Avenue, New York, NY, 10017, 1981.

13. VanDerSmissen, B.: Legal Liability of Cities and Schools for Injuries in Recreation and Parks. Cincinnati, OH, The W.H. Anderson Co., 1968.

14. Zirkel, P.: These court cases shed light on how you must educate the handicapped. The American School Board Journal, Washington, D.C., *167*(5):27, 1980.

Part IV
PROGRAM
ADMINISTRATION

Chapter *12*

ORGANIZATIONAL PATTERNS AND RELATIONSHIPS

The main aspects of organization involve the relationships that exist among administrative units, programs, and personnel. Some elements of organization can be explained with diagrams (organization charts), whereas others are better explained by defining responsibilities associated with positions and the flow of authority and accountability within the organization. In order to help the reader better visualize the full scope of organizational structure, this chapter is separated into three sections: (1) examples of organizational patterns; (2) explanations of selected administrative positions; and (3) the connection between physical education and athletics and related fields.

ORGANIZATIONAL PATTERNS

There is no such thing as an ideal organizational pattern. Different ones have advantages and disadvantages. To some degree, the structure of an organization must be tailored to fit a particular situation, and no two situations are exactly alike. Also, the personnel of an organization have some influence on which pattern will work the best. Management experts emphasize that the main ingredient of an organization is people; therefore, peoples' personalities, interests, competencies, and relationships have a significant influence on which kind of structure is preferred.

The organizational pattern illustrates lines of authority, responsibility, and accountability. It describes the proper administrative channels and the inter-relationships of personnel and programs. Having the organizational pattern clearly defined and well understood can expedite administrative procedures and enhance overall effectiveness.

The sample organization charts presented here are for administrative units that include physical education and athletics. A careful review of these charts will help provide a clearer concept of how different educational organizations can be structured effectively. Each chart represents either an actual or a typical situation.

One of the disadvantages of the traditional "line of command" organizational pattern is that it shows in a general way the line of authority. Some educators feel that the line of authority should be deemphasized and that nonauthoritative relationships should receive more emphasis. Some feel that their positions or the positions of their programs on the chart fail to give a true picture of them in terms of their significance and total contribution to the organization. For these reasons, many educators prefer a circle chart or some other method of defining the organization rather than a line chart.

Line Organization (Figure 12-1)

This form of administration is characterized by a strong superior–subordinate relationship. There is a direct line of authority. The most basic feature is a chain of command to be followed from the top (highest executive) to the bottom (lowest level employee). The simplest way to explain the line of authority is that the employees at the top "make the rules" and those at the bottom "follow the rules."

Line-Staff (Figure 12-2)

This form of administrative organization is much the same as the line organization. It still contains a strong element of the superior–subordinate relationship and a direct line of authority. The added dimension of this pattern is the presence of advisors (staff) who assist the executive. Supposedly, a staff person is an advisor or special assistant to the administrator and is out of the line of authority. Strict observance of the staff role seldom exists, however, because the staff person often is delegated some amount of decision-making power. In the absence of the administrator, staff personnel often have the "authority" to make and implement certain decisions.

Functional (Figure 12-3)

The functional type of organization contains many of the same characteristics as the line-staff organization. The superior–subordinate and administrator–advisory relationships are still evident.

This type of organization has some unique characteristics. First, employees may be subject to the decisions of several superiors. This changes the way in which authority is exercised. There is no direct chain of command, and as a result, employees must work through two or more decision-making channels. Second, the possibility and encouragement for subordinates to communicate on certain occasions with top level executives. The appearance of "going over the head of someone" is commonplace. This pattern encourages the active participation of lower level employees in administrative matters.

Circle (Figure 12-4)

This organizational pattern is employed most often in business or in higher education. Responsibility and authority from the chief administrator flows

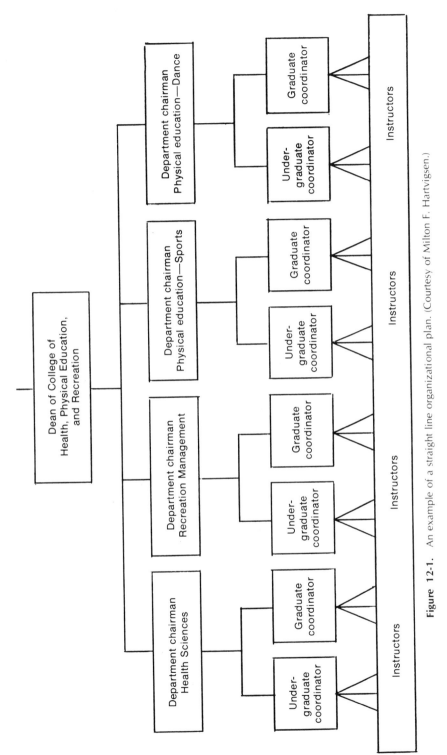

Figure 12-1. An example of a straight line organizational plan. (Courtesy of Milton F. Hartvigsen.)

184 · *Program Administration*

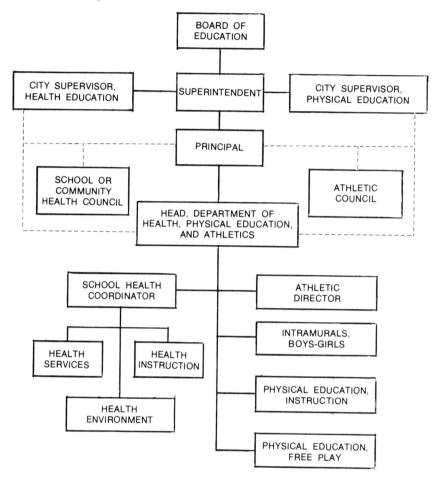

Figure 12-2. A chart showing a line-staff organizational pattern in a secondary school. (Courtesy of Alpine School District.)

outward to the various subdivisions. The vice-presidents (or assistant superintendents) all have the same level of authority, and are all equally accountable to the chief administrator for their assigned responsibilities.

ADMINISTRATIVE POSITIONS

Much insight into organizational relationships can be obtained from knowing the basic responsibilities associated with each administrative position. Following are descriptions of certain administrative positions in the schools.

Superintendent

Typically, local school systems are known as districts, and all of the schools within a district are managed under the administrative leadership of

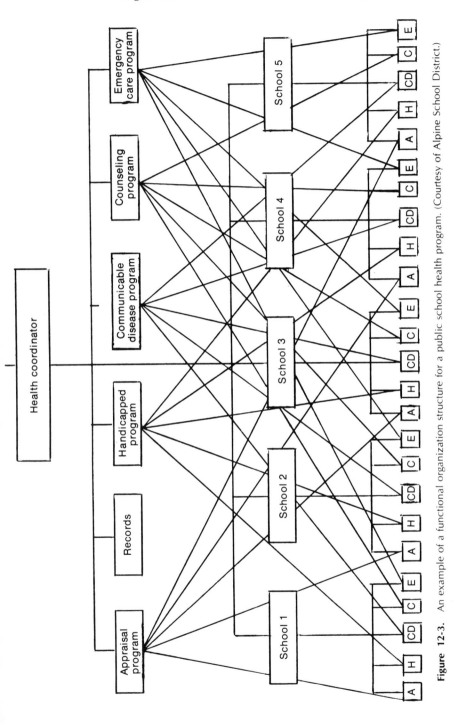

Figure 12-3. An example of a functional organization structure for a public school health program. (Courtesy of Alpine School District.)

Integrated activities include such things as:
1. Curriculum development and management.
2. Student advisement and student records.
3. Cooperative use of personnel, space, and resources.
4. Mutual support and overall cooperation.

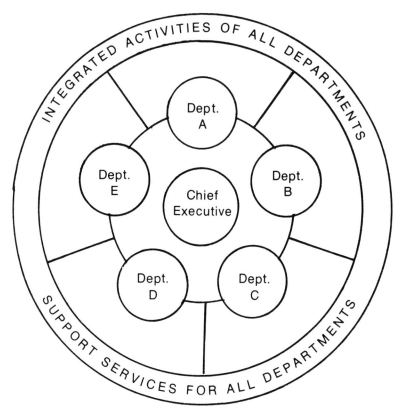

Support services include such matters as:
1. Facility planning and management.
2. Supply and equipment management and issue.
3. Learning resources and support.
4. Computer and media services.
5. Research services.

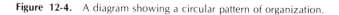

Figure 12-4. A diagram showing a circular pattern of organization.

a superintendent. In general, the superintendent's responsibilities are to give direction to the district educational system in accordance with state laws, regulations, and guidelines, and with the directions and counsel provided by the district school board.

The school board is the local governing authority to which the superintendent is responsible. He works for the school board and manages the educational system in accordance with its actions and wishes. He is the chief administrator for the school district.

The superintendent performs the following specific functions:[10]

1. Prepares the agenda for meetings of the school board and meets with the school board.

2. Recommends the appointment, fosters the development, and provides for the evaluation of all school district employees.

3. Provides leadership to the board of education and the professional staff in defining, clarifying, and modifying educational goals and programs consistent with sound educational practices, democratic ideals, and community expectations.

4. Plans for, manages, and evaluates negotiations with organized employee groups in the district.

5. Maintains and strives to improve communications between the school district and the community and within the school district.

6. Plans and supervises the budget development process to ensure that budget recommendations made to the board reflect prudent planning, efficiency, and sufficient budgetary support of district programs and priorities.

7. Continually assesses the general climate and conditions in the schools through informal visits in schools and in classrooms. Formal and informal conversations with the administrators, teachers, and students, regular administrative staff meetings, meetings with the officers of the district education association, and open agenda meetings with the school faculties.

8. Investigates concerns raised by district residents directly or through members of the board of education.

9. Carries out other responsibilities that are required by law, contractual agreements, and board policies.

A school superintendent should be a well-prepared educational administrator and not a political appointee. The professional requirements of the position vary considerably among school districts. Some districts have small and meager educational systems, while other districts have large and complex school systems. Typically, a small district would require that the superintendent have a master's degree and several years of successful experience. The superintendent of a large system would be expected to hold a doctorate degree and be a highly regarded and reputable educator.

The professional staff of the superintendent's office often includes associate or assistant superintendents, with one in charge of each of the levels of education—elementary, junior high school, and senior high school; and supervisors or specialists of particular areas, such as physical education and athletics, music and art, and special education. A business manager and legal specialist are also important staff positions. The kind of staff and its size vary with the complexity of the school district. Some operations amount to little more than the superintendent and a secretary, whereas others consist of a large and highly specialized staff.

The superintendent's span of control and direct administrative contacts usually involve his assistants (associate or assistant superintendents), supervisors and specialists, and the principals of the various schools within the district.[2]

School Principal

The principal is the chief administrator of a particular school, and he is directly responsible to the superintendent. In general, the principal's responsibilities are to provide effective administrative supervision of all aspects of the school program. Typically, this involves the following:[10]

1. Participation in the selection and hiring of teachers and other personnel in the school.
2. The assignment of teacher loads and the utilization of facilities in connection with the teachers' assignments.
3. Supervision of curriculum development and management of the curriculum for effective results.
4. Administrative leadership of noncurricular activities and programs.
5. Definition of the role of student government in the school, and the administrative supervision of it.
6. Supervision of the school's teaching process.
7. Budgetary planning and management in connection with all aspects of the school.
8. Management of the school—community relations program within the broad framework of the district public relations effort.
9. Professional development and enrichment experiences of school personnel.
10. Administrative leadership toward desirable student values, behavior, and discipline.
11. Supervision of the planning function, both near-term and long-term, with respect to goals, facilities, and programs.

The requirements of a principal's job vary with the size of the school. The job of principal of a school of 200 would be much less demanding than that of a school of 2000, even though the two jobs would include the same elements. The principal is responsible to the superintendent, or in some cases, to an associate or assistant superintendent, as designated.[2]

College Dean

Typically, a university is divided into several colleges or schools, with each college encompassing several departments, related in subject matter. The dean is the chief administrator of a college or school. The chairmen of the several departments report to the dean, and the dean in turn, reports to the academic vice-president or others in the central administration. The

basic administrative responsibilities of a dean require that he perform the following[1]:
1. Coordinate and facilitate personnel matters such as
   a. selecting and appointing new faculty members;
   b. determining faculty and staff salaries;
   c. dealing with rank advancements, leaves of absence; terminations, and retirements; helping determine faculty assignments and evaluating faculty loads and effectiveness;
   d. receiving and evaluating student and faculty suggestions and complaints;
   e. supervising and working effectively with the chairmen of the several departments.
2. Oversee the preparation and management of college and departmental budgets.
3. Review and act on proposals for program and curriculum changes.
4. Review and act on department chairmen's recommendations relative to classified personnel, part-time faculty, and student assistants.
5. Appoint and supervise college committees as needed.
6. Serve as the liaison between the college and other colleges and schools and between the college and the central administration.
7. Serve as the focal point of relationships between the college and nonuniversity organizations and agencies.
8. Supervise nondepartmental functions of the college such as centers, laboratories, and institutes.

Associate or Assistant Dean

A dean may allocate certain responsibilities to associate or assistant deans. The more logical responsibilities to delegate include the following[1]:
1. Review and evaluation of faculty assignments and loads.
2. Supervision of assigned college committees.
3. Supervision of service aspects of the college closely related to academic programs.
4. Management of the college budget and/or portions of it.
5. Coordination of facility scheduling, management of equipment, and ordering of textbooks.
6. Interview and selection of student assistants and part-time faculty.
7. Supervision of nondepartmental units and programs.

Department Chairman

Department chairmen are key members of the administration because they manage programs at the grassroots level. They are the "front line" administrators, who work directly with the faculty and students. The basic responsibilities of a department chairman include the following[1]:
1. Coordinating student advisement and supervising of progress toward completion of student requirements.

2. Determining the need for faculty and formulating recommendations for such to be considered by those in higher administrative positions.
3. Reviewing faculty salaries and participating in recommended salary adjustments.
4. Preparing class schedules and arranging for facilities and equipment in support of classes.
5. Coordinating faculty assignments, generally supervising faculty involvement, and evaluating faculty productivity and performance.
6. Providing recommendations relative to faculty advancement, leaves of absence, terminations, and retirement.
7. Organizing and supervising departmental committees.
8. Supervising departmental staff members in addition to faculty (clerical personnel, student assistants, and others).
9. Preparing and managing the departmental budget.
10. Coordinating curriculum and program planning and modifications.

Athletic Director

The athletic director's responsibilities are similar to those described for department chairmen, except directing athletics does not involve matters relating to class instruction, such as curriculum, scheduling classes, and ordering textbooks. It does involve the following responsibilities not included in the description of department chairmen.

1. Scheduling athletic contests.
2. Implementing and applying rules of athletic eligibility.
3. Providing and managing athletic areas and facilities and acquiring and caring for athletic equipment.
4. Promoting, selling tickets, and conducting athletic events.
5. Coordinating school and public relations in regard to athletics.

The complexity of an athletic director's position varies in proportion to whether he is directing a high school or small college program or a major university program. In the latter case, there is a much greater amount of public interest (and pressure) and, therefore, much more public relations involvement, large crowds to accommodate and control, high-pressure game situations that must be properly managed, and extensive financial involvement. The basic elements of an athletic director's position, however, are essentially the same as described, whether the program is large and complex or small and relatively simple.

RELATED FIELDS

In a general sense, this book pertains to the combined areas of physical education and athletics, and the relationships that exist between these two phases of the school program are apparent. Physical education and athletics are so interrelated that in the majority of schools they are combined into one administrative unit. In many universities and in some large high schools the two areas are separated for administrative convenience; but in most of these cases, there continues to be a close relationship. Physical education is also closely related to other phases of the school program, including *health education, recreation,* and *outdoor education.*

Health Education

Traditionally, health and physical education have been closely associated. In fact, the differences between them have often been too indistinct for the good of either, particularly health education.

In the broad sense, health encompasses the total field of medical science, in addition to some aspects of psychology, sociology, and physical education. Only some aspects of this total field apply to the school setting, and those align closely with physical education.

Even though health and physical education should remain closely associated and strongly supportive of each other, the days are gone when health education can be viewed as part of physical education or supplemental to it. Health should be a separate phase of the curriculum under the leadership of a health education specialist. The American Alliance for Health, Physical Education, Recreation and Dance has published a position statement concerning a comprehensive program of health instruction. It includes the following (reprinted with permission):

1. A program of health education should be unified and organized in such a manner that there is scope and sequence from kindergarten through grade 12.

2. A program of curriculum development should be undertaken that will stress (a) the identification of specific courses with content, learning activities, and evaluation requirements, and (b) coordination and integration with other subject areas.

3. The health curriculum should be jointly developed by school personnel, curriculum specialists, individuals from public and voluntary health agencies, and national and state consultants.

4. Health teachers should be specialists in health education and have a genuine interest in this field.

Within the framework of the above statements, there are several procedures that involve health in the areas of physical education and athletics, including the following:

1. A required medical examination before participation in vigorous sports.
2. Medical services available at school athletic contests where injuries or emergencies are probable.
3. Written permission from a physician after a serious illness or injury before a student can return to physical education or athletic activities.
4. Prescribed procedures for the emergency care of injuries and illnesses in connection with physical education and athletics.
5. The qualification of teachers and coaches to administer emergency care when needed.
6. The provision of adaptive and corrective physical education activities based on health records or medical recommendations.

7. The provision of a healthful and safe environment in locker rooms and physical education facilities.
8. Ample emphasis on physical fitness throughout life as a method of perpetuating optimum health.

In some schools, health education receives little attention beyond that provided by the physical education teachers. In such cases, the physical educators ought to make an honest effort to provide useful health instruction and encourage sound health practices. Health and physical education are too important and too closely related for us to allow either area to be neglected.

In order to help the reader better understand the proper position and role of health education in the schools, the following information has been included. It is an excerpt from the official position statement of the Society of State Directors of Health, Physical Education and Recreation and is printed with the permission of the Society.

Health Program

The Comprehensive School Health Program encompasses School Health Education, School Health Services, and Healthful School Living. Health Education has the purpose of imparting health knowledge and cultivating desirable attitudes, habits and practices. School Health Services undergird the total educational program by identifying and securing correction of, or compensation for, individual health problems. It also provides protection, guidance and opportunities for health learning experiences. Healthful School Living is the provision of a safe and healthful school environment. In addition, this phase provides many opportunities for the reinforcement of school health education and school health services.

The ultimate goal of the Comprehensive School Health Program is to help every young person to achieve his full potential through becoming responsible for his own personal health decisions and practices, through working with others to maintain an ecological balance helpful to man and the environment, and through becoming a discriminating consumer of health information, health services and health products.

ABOUT ADMINISTRATION AND ORGANIZATION

The State Education Agency, in cooperation with appropriate school and health personnel and representatives of official, professional and voluntary health agencies, has the responsibility for establishing goals, objectives, standards and evaluative criteria for the comprehensive school health program.

Every school should formulate and implement health policies, consistent with modern medical and educational concepts and practices, designed to assure each pupil:
—appropriate health education.
—effective school health services.
—safe and healthful living conditions at school and at school-sponsored events.

School health policies should be formulated to facilitate maximum cooperation and coordination within each school and school system, and between the school and the community.

The Comprehensive School Health Education Program should include a planned, sequential series of experiences in health education at each grade level. Time allotments should provide:
—in the elementary school, at least two hours per week of health instruction and other educational activities, which are designed to promote valid health practices.
—in the middle or junior high school, the equivalent of a daily period of direct health education for at least two semesters.

—in the senior high school, the equivalent of a daily period of health education for at least two semesters, one of which may include driver education.

ABOUT CURRICULUM

The Comprehensive Health Education Program should consist of planned learning experiences which will assist students to achieve desirable understandings, attitudes and practices related to critical health issues including, but not limited to, the following: emotional health and a positive self-image; appreciation, respect for, and care of the human body and its vital organs; personal fitness; health issues of alcohol, tobacco and drug use and abuse; health misconceptions and quackery; effects of exercise on the body systems and on general well-being; nutrition and weight control; boy-girl relationships, preparation for marriage, and wholesome family life; the scientific, social and economic aspects of community and ecological health; communicable and degenerative diseases including venereal diseases; disaster preparedness; safety and driver education; choosing professional medical and health services including insurance programs; and health careers and, also, the health aspects implicit in career education. The interrelationships of these topics with one another and with other phases of the school health program make it essential that they be taught and administered as one broad and comprehensive curriculum. Special health problems or emphases should be treated within this comprehensive context and not dealt with in piece-meal fashion.

The curriculum should be directly related to the needs, problems and interests appropriate to the growth, development and maturity level of each student involved.

The scope and sequence of the comprehensive school health education curriculum, grades K-12, should be planned and organized so as to avoid both serious omissions and unnecessary duplication and repetition.

ABOUT SCHOOL HEALTH SERVICES

The State education agency and public health department have a responsibility for cooperative planning between themselves and with other appropriate agencies and professional organizations to develop and implement policies and standards which can be adapted for use in local communities. Similar coordination by community agencies at the local level should be effected.

Careful follow-up procedures are indispensable if school health appraisals are to contribute to the health and education of children and youth. Therefore, the findings of the health appraisals should be used for making adaptations in the school program, interpreting health status to pupils and parents, and motivating and securing correction of remediable defects.

ABOUT HEALTHFUL SCHOOL LIVING

School authorities, in cooperation with health departments and other appropriate agencies, are responsible for providing and maintaining a safe and healthful school environment which will help ensure a wholesome physical, social, emotional, intellectual and moral climate.

Supervisory responsibility for maintenance of school buildings, grounds and equipment should be delineated. Provisions should be made for periodic inspection by qualified personnel. Hazards and defects should be corrected quickly.

In schools where food services are provided, the facilities, time schedules, and menus should contribute to good nutrition, nutrition education, and the development of an appreciation of related social values. The school lunch program should be flexible enough to complement other curricular areas rather than detract from these instructional programs.

A properly equipped health service unit, with separate rest and isolation rooms for boys and girls, as well as adequate personnel to provide supervision and care, should be available.

All school personnel should have periodic health examinations.

ABOUT PERSONNEL

Well-defined, specific standards for certification of teachers and school health personnel (consistent with standards developed by national professional organizations) should be established by the respective state certification agencies.

Every elementary and secondary school should have a school health coordinator, appointed from the faculty or staff and responsible to the principal. This coordinator should receive special training and should facilitate coordination and communication among those who are involved in the Comprehensive School Health Program.

Elementary teachers should have specific preparation which will equip them with the competencies and understandings essential for effective health education, including special abilities in observing the health status of children and in using appropriate referral and follow-up techniques.

Teachers of health education in the secondary schools should be certificated in health education.

The elementary teacher and the teacher of health education in secondary schools should receive assistance from a health education specialist or supervisor who is an outstanding instructional leader. The supervisor should also provide the liaison with health agencies and other community groups that will tie school and community health education together in a consistent fashion.

All teachers and administrators should seriously recognize their unquestionable role as an exemplar before their students. For a teacher or an administrator to teach one thing and be a living example of a conflicting way of life, practice, or point of view is to negate such instruction in the eyes and minds of many students. In this day, when hypocrisy and communication gaps are widely discussed, all school leaders should exemplify the healthy, active, quality life which they promote for their students.

Recreation

Physical educators should recognize the tremendous contribution of organized recreation in providing opportunities for participation in physical education activities. At the same time, those concerned primarily with recreation programs should feel highly supportive of physical education because it teaches skills and develops interests that are useful in recreational pursuits.

Schools become involved in recreation in three ways: (1) education for the worthy use of leisure time; (2) the provision of recreational activities, such as intramurals, club sports, and free play, as part of the school program; and (3) involvement in supporting, co-sponsoring, or sponsoring public recreation programs.

The worthy use of leisure has been recognized as an important function of education for a long time. This is evident by the fact that in 1917 it was stated as one of the seven cardinal principles of education. Several aspects of the school curriculum contribute to this objective, such as photography, art, music, drama, literature, and industrial arts, but a good physical education program can be one of the main contributors. One of the primary common interests of physical educators and recreation leaders is the development of physical skills and positive attitudes toward active participation throughout life. The present emphasis placed on lifetime sports is especially important in the worthy use of leisure time.

The out-of-class *school recreation* program includes special interest clubs, hobby pursuits, and special events, which relate to several aspects of the curriculum. But the noninstructional physical education activities make an important contribution in the form of intramural sports, club sports, and free play.

As part of the enabling legislation of almost all states, school districts are permitted to sponsor and manage public recreation programs over and above their normal educational responsibilities. Few school districts function as the sponsoring agency for the public recreation program (only about 2%; but, many are involved as co-sponsors or cooperative sponsors of public recreation.

School systems have a large amount of both indoor and outdoor facilities. By putting these facilities to effective use, they need not be duplicated in the form of community centers, playgrounds, or athletic fields. School personnel represent a valuable source of leadership that sometimes can be available in recreation programs during the summer and on a limited basis during the school year. School districts are usually not able to adequately manage a balanced recreation and park system, however, because in addition to the recreational facilities and activities that are closely related to the school program, a complete recreation program must involve nonschool facilities, such as golf courses, aquatic facilities, and picnic areas, and sometimes such specialized facilities as cultural art centers, boat launching areas and marinas, winter sports areas, zoos, aquariums, and museums. In other words, even though many aspects of recreation are closely aligned with school programs and facilities, some aspects of them are not. A school district dedicated to doing a good job in sponsoring recreation can make a significant contribution, so long as the school's recreation efforts are supplemented by other local agencies to round out the complete scope of recreational opportunities.

Professional recreation and park planners have strongly encouraged recreational use of school facilities and school use of recreation facilities. This approach has been advanced under the "park–school" and "community school" concepts. The *park–school* is a facility that consists of one or more school buildings constructed on or adjacent to a park site. The *community school* is a modern concept in which the school is conceived as an agency that makes maximum use of its facilities and other resources to serve both the educational and recreational needs of the community, serving people of all ages. It is a "lighted schoolhouse" concept.

Effective implementation of cooperative school and community use of facilities must involve joint planning. This means that each recreation and education facility or area is originally planned and constructed for joint use by the two agencies. Even though this approach is a valuable one, not all recreation and park needs can be satisfied by this method. Opportunities for golf, boating, hiking, picnicking, biologic and zoologic gardens, usually must be provided through other community agencies. Following is a portion of the position statement of the Society of State Directors of Health, Physical Education and Recreation. This information will help to explain how recreation opportunities should fit into education. It is printed with the permission of the Society.

The Recreation Program

Social, economic, and other developments taking place in this final quarter of 20th Century American life highlight recreation as a major cultural force. The school must help prepare each individual to use his free time in constructive, creative and satisfying ways. Furthermore, schools must accept a major responsibility for providing personnel and for making maximum use of their facilities and equipment in a broad, coordinated school-community program of recreation for students, parents and other community members.

ABOUT ADMINSTRATION AND ORGANIZATION

Schools have a basic responsibility to help the community develop awareness and understanding of the recreational needs of its children, youth and adults.

The "community school" concept recognizes the school, augmented by other community resources, as a center of the community's civic, cultural and recreational activities. Elementary schools are natural neighborhood centers. Secondary schools may serve a larger area of the community. This concept should be interpreted, supported and strengthened in and for the community by school personnel.

All government agencies having a vital role in recreation, including the State department of education, should give direct attention to cooperative planning and action through an inter-agency council. The State director of health, physical education and recreation and staff, working with and through the chief state school officer and the state board of education, should provide leadership in the development of the recreation program by:
- —establishing and maintaining cooperative working relationships with other state and local agencies, colleges and universities, professional and voluntary agencies, and other interested individuals and groups.
- —cooperating with state and local leaders in studying pertinent recreation problems and developing recommendations that may be widely disseminated for implementation and evaluation.
- —becoming informed on trends, problems and successful practices and maintaining communication with and providing consultation services to school districts, other agencies, and organizations.

ABOUT PROGRAM

The school curriculum should offer many opportunities for developing attitudes, understandings, knowledge and skills that will lead to the wise use of off-the-job hours.

Schools should provide planned experiences beyond the classroom, including outdoor education, in order to ensure maximum articulation between learning and recreational activities.

Opportunities for children, youth and adults to participate in a variety of the physical, aesthetic, cultural and social aspects of recreation should be provided under school auspices.

ABOUT RECREATION PERSONNEL

State departments of education should provide leadership to help increase the supply of qualified recreation personnel and should work closely with colleges, universities, and professional recreation associations in helping upgrade opportunities for pre-service and in-service education of persons working in recreation programs—professionals, paraprofessionals, aides and volunteers.

Policies and procedures relating to the qualifications of recreation personnel employed by schools should be established by State departments of education.

General areas of professional preparation should include:
—the recreation major who has selected the field of recreation as a career.
—education majors who have selected recreation as a minor to prepare themselves for part-time work in recreation in addition to other education responsibilities.
—other majors who have selected recreation as a minor in order to prepare themselves with a better understanding of the impact of leisure on modern society.

Outdoor Education

Physical education contributes to the skills and attitudes involved in outdoor education. In turn, outdoor education relates to outdoor recreation, because much of what is learned in the educational process is subsequently applied in recreational pursuits. Outdoor education, or at least some aspects of it, is often administered as part of the physical education program. Some examples are camping, hiking, mountain climbing, skiing, archery, marksmanship, and orienteering.

Outdoor education includes *two* major categories: education *in* the outdoors, and education *for* the outdoors. The two categories are closely related and they complement each other. The former category occurs in an outdoor

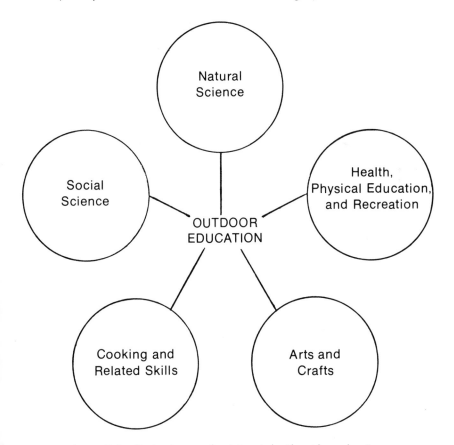

Figure 12-5. Topics that are often integrated with outdoor education.

environment, whereas much of that included in the latter category may take place in an indoor setting. The following will give additional insight into the two categories.

Education In the Outdoors. This entails direct outdoor experiences, involving observation, study, and research in outdoor settings such as school sites; park and recreation areas; camps; school or community owned forests, farms, gardens, zoos, sanctuaries, and preserves; state and federal land and water; and private outdoor resources.

Education For the Outdoors. This entails the learning of skills and the development of appreciation for activities such as the following: camp and survival skills; casting and angling; shooting and hunting techniques; boating and small craft techniques; aquatics—swimming, water sking, skin and scuba diving; archery; winter sports; mountain climbing; hiking and bicycling; use of compass—mapping and orienting; outdoor photography; and outdoor cooking.

Outdoor education should not be separated from other subjects, but should integrate them as much as possible. Figure 12-5 shows the relationship between outdoor education and other school topics.

BIBLIOGRAPHY

1. Brigham Young University: Personnel Manual. BYU, Provo, UT, 1981.

2. Castetter, W.: The Personnel Function in Educational Administration. New York, Macmillan, 1971.

3. Clegg, S.: The Theory of Power and Organization. London, Routledge & Kegan Paul, 1979.

4. Connor, P.E.: Organizations, Theory and Design. Chicago, Science Research Association, 1980.

5. Cunningham, M.E.: Productivity and the corporate culture, (address, February 27, 1981). Vital Speeches, 47:363, 1981.

6. Denhardt, R.B.: In the Shadow of Organizations. Lawrence, KS, Regents Press of Kansas, 1981.

7. Eden, C., Jones, S., and Sims, D.: Thinking in Organizations. NY, Macmillan, 1979.

8. Galbraith, J., and Nathanson, D.A.: Strategy Implementations: The Role of Structure and Process. St. Paul, MN, West Publishing, 1978.

9. Heddinger, F.: Do school principles have enough decision making power? The American School Board Journal, 165(2):30, 1978.

10. Provo School District: Job descriptions of school administrators. Provo, UT, 1982.

11. Yehle, L.: A pro-management plan can help keep employees loyal and happy. The American School Board Journal, 46:27, 1980.

Chapter 13

THE INSTRUCTIONAL PROGRAM

A superior physical education program will involve adequate concern about what students do in tennis, football, swimming, and gymnastics; but, in addition, it will involve much greater concern about what these activities do to the students. Figure 13-1 shows the fundamental importance of the instructional program.

Any program ought to be tailored for the situation and the particular student body. The modifications of the instructional program that are made from time to time should be based on the principle of retaining those practices and educational experiences that have proven valuable and modifying those that are judged deficient. Both change for the sake of change, and blind worship of the old and traditional should be avoided.

Care should be taken to avoid a program that attempts to do some of everything, with nothing done well; repeats the same experiences year after year without regard for progression or expansion into new areas; and treats all students alike, with no serious attempt to meet students' individual needs.

In the design and management of the program, the following considerations should receive serious attention: (1) appropriate class size to enhance effective instruction; (2) appropriate length of class periods and adequate instructional time per week; (3) the use of competent teachers, assigned in accordance with their strengths; (4) provision of adequate facilities, equipment, and supplies; (5) adequate variety to meet the students' needs and interests; and (6) involvement of the right sequence of progressions to lead effectively toward educational goals.

CLASS SCHEDULING

The introduction of computers into education has vastly increased scheduling possibilities. The extensive development of loop films, video tapes, recordings, and programmed learning modules makes it possible for certain instruction to occur separately from teaching stations and faculty.

199

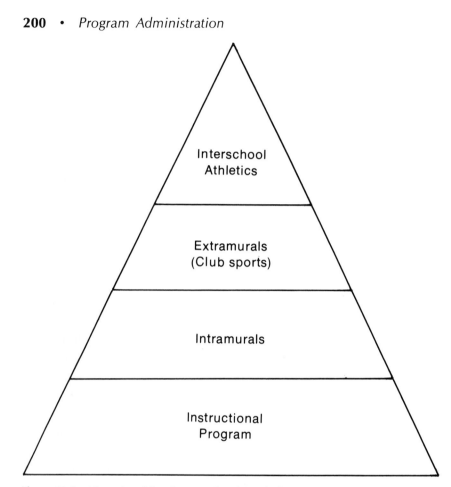

Figure 13-1. Hierarchy of the elements of a physical education/athletic program based on skill level and the usual number of participants. The instructional program forms a base on which other elements of the total program can be built.

The trend toward combining men's and women's programs and emphasizing coeducational classes has also had an influence on class scheduling.*

Traditional vs. Modular

Traditional scheduling is the assignment of a given number of students to an instructor for a certain time slot (class period). Each class period occupies an equal amount of time. Typically, one teacher instructs the class for the entire semester.

Traditional scheduling has certain benefits. It enhances the opportunity for developing close teacher–student rapport, and it is the simplest method of

---

* Much of the specialized information about programs and curriculum in this chapter and chapter 14 was furnished by Professor Joyce Harrison, who is a recognized curriculum specialist and author of the forthcoming textbook on Curriculum Design in Physical Education.

scheduling. It also has some disadvantages. The number of students in the class remains constant regardless of the subject matter that needs to be covered at various times during the semester. The time period remains constant, when in some cases a longer or shorter period would be beneficial. Traditional scheduling does not contribute toward homogeneous groupings of students. Figure 13-2 is a simple example of traditional scheduling.

Time	Monday Tuesday Wednesday Thursday Friday
8:00- 8:55	Biological Science --⊣
9:00- 9:55	Social Studies ---⊣
10:00-10:55	Study --⊣
11:00-11:55	Industrial Arts ---⊣
12:00-12:55	Lunch ---⊣
1:00- 1:55	Physical Education ---⊣
2:00- 2:55	Geometry --⊣
3:00- 3:55	Chemistry --⊣

Figure 13-2. A student's class schedule, using the traditional scheduling method.

Some variations of traditional scheduling are as follows:

Physical education can be scheduled less frequently (two or three times a week), with each session of instruction lasting two class periods. This results in proportionately more instructional time, because less time is utilized in dressing, showering, taking attendance, and other nonteaching activities.

Within the framework of traditional scheduling, *team teaching* can capitalize on the expertise of different teachers.

With *modular or flexible scheduling*, the school day is divided into short periods of time called modules (mods). Each module is the same length, usually 15 to 30 minutes. Modules can be combined into combinations to provide the desired length of time for different instructional units. The instructional periods for a particular subject may vary in length from one day to the next, meaning that a student or a teacher may have a different schedule each day of the week. Once established, the weekly cycle usually remains the same throughout the term. In a highly flexible system, however, an instructor can request class length and frequency on a weekly basis. In such cases, students and teachers pick up new schedules prior to the beginning of each week (or other time cycle). This kind of scheduling requires the use of a computer along with careful planning and coordination among teachers. It is not a frequently used method, but it does function effectively in certain situations. An example of a student's class schedule using a modular or flexible system appears in Figure 13-3.

TIME	M	T	W	Th	F
8:00	English	Indep. Study	English	Social Studies	English
8:30				Indep. Study	
9:00	Indep. Study	Math	Guidance	Math	Social Studies
9:30			Social Studies		
10:00	Math	English	Math	English	
10:30	Indust. Arts		Indust. Arts	Typing	
11:00	Boys' Chorus	Typing	Boys' Chorus	Physical	Math
11:30	Indep. Study		English	Education	
12:00	L	U	N	C	H
12:30	Social Studies	Social	Indep.	Indep.	Guidance
1:00		Studies	Study	Study	
1:30	Physical Education	Indust.		Indust.	Physical Education
2:00			Physical Education		
2:30		Arts			English
3:00					Boys' Chorus

Figure 13-3. A student's class schedule for one week, using flexible scheduling with 30-minute modules. (From Organizational Patterns for Instruction in Physical Education. Copyright 1971 by AAHPERD. Reprinted by permission of the American Alliance for Health, Physical Education, Recreation and Dance, 1900 Association Drive, Reston, VA 22091.)

CLASS SIZE

Class size is influenced by several factors: regulations and policies issued by higher authority, the size of each teaching station, the nature of the subject or activity, and the amount of students that must be accommodated with the facilities and teachers available. A tennis class with only four courts available would have to be smaller (maximum of 16 students) than a soccer class, which would have the use of two regulation soccer fields.

A modern dance class in a studio 30 × 40 feet would have to be restricted in size as compared with one taught in a studio 40 × 50 feet.

Class size is also influenced by the nature of the activity. For example, a class of 25 in modern dance or ballet would be large for one teacher to handle effectively; whereas in ballroom or folk dance, one teacher can handle 40 or more students. In beginning swimming, an optimum ratio is one teacher for 10 to 15 students; whereas, in certain field games, a teacher can manage as many as 30 students effectively.

Another factor is that some teachers handle larger groups better than others. In fact, some prefer relatively large classes because their teaching methods involve pairing or grouping of students and then assisting the students as they teach each other. Conversely, other teachers dislike this method and prefer individual coaching. A few small classes can be justified, provided there are oversized classes to compensate. The important point is to strive for an optimum average class size, with each particular class adjusted in accordance with the influencing circumstances. The average class size recommended by the AAHPERD, the LaPort Study, and the President's Council on Physical Fitness is 35. Adaptive physical education classes should have no more than 20.

TIME ALLOTMENT

Individual states prescribe minimum instructional time. For elementary schools, the AAHPERD recommends that pupils should participate in an instructional program of physical education for at least 150 minutes per week, in addition to time allotted for free play during recess and noon hour. The instruction should occur on a daily basis. The Society of State Directors of HPER recommends a daily instructional period of at least 30 minutes, exclusive of time for dressing, showering, and free-play periods.

For junior high school and high school students, the President's Council on Physical Fitness recommends physical education for one standard class period per day, 5 days per week. The Society of State Directors of HPER recommends at least 300 minutes per week spread over 3 or more days.

Whatever the arrangement, the use of time is more important than the amount. As little time as possible should be spent in dressing, showering, roll call, and other matters that relate to instruction and exercise, but do not produce the intended results. The important question is what is accomplished toward the educational goals rather than how much time is spent.

TEACHING STATIONS

A teaching station is the area assigned to a teacher for a class. One method of calculating the number of teaching stations needed for a *secondary school* is illustrated in Table 13-1.[24] The table is based on a school of 1000 pupils with each pupil having 30 periods per week, five of which are for physical education (one period daily). The result is seven teaching stations needed for physical education. In addition to the method illustrated in Table 13-1, the following formulas are useful:

$$\text{Number of sections to be offered} = \frac{\text{total number of students}}{\text{anticipated class size}}$$

$$\text{Number of teaching stations needed (classes per class period)} = \frac{\text{total number of students}}{\text{class size} \times \text{number of periods/day}}$$

$$\text{Number of teachers needed} = \frac{\text{number of sections}}{\text{number of periods taught/day by each teacher}}$$

TABLE 13-1. Plan for calculating the number of physical education teaching stations needed for 1000 pupils in a secondary school. (Willgoose, C.E.: The Curriculum in Physical Education, 3rd Ed. Englewood Cliffs, NJ, Prentice-Hall, 1979, p. 170. Reprinted by permission of the publisher.)

Plan	Example
1. Divide the anticipated enrollment by the desired average class size. This will give the number of sections needed.	$\dfrac{1000 \text{ students}}{30 \text{ pupils per class}} = 34 \text{ sections}$
2. Multiply the number of sections by the number of periods per week physical education is offered.	$34 \times 5 \text{ periods} = 170$
3. Multiply the resulting number by 1.25 to allow for a utilization factor.	$170 \times 1.25 = 203$
4. Divide the resulting figure by the number of teaching periods available in the school week (30 periods).	$\dfrac{203}{30} = 6.7 = 7 \text{ teaching stations}$

Figure 13-4 is a chart that shows teacher assignments correlated with teaching stations and class periods. In order to assure efficient use of staff and facilities, a two-way chart such as this should be constructed. In the chart, the teaching stations appear horizontally across the top, and the time periods are shown in the vertical left hand column.

To calculate the number of teaching stations required for an *elementary school,* proceed as illustrated in Table 13-2.[24]

In this example, an elementary school of approximately 500 boys and girls would require two teachers of physical education. Each would teach 25 30-minute periods a week, aside from any intramural supervision or program planning.

Few schools have all of the teaching stations they need to conduct a complete program. When necessary, certain activities can be taught in multipurpose rooms, little-used hallways, unoccupied classrooms, or on theatre or auditorium stages.

CLASS PERIODS	GYMNAS-IUM #1	GYMNAS-IUM #2	WRESTLING ROOM	OUTSIDE FIELD	SWIM. POOL
1	Smith	Hansen	Shaw	Jones	Black
2	Smith	Black		Jones	Moss
3	Black	Hansen	Shaw	Jones	Moss
4	Smith	Black	Shaw		Moss
5		Hansen		Jones	
6	Smith	Hansen	Shaw	Black	Moss
7	Smith	Hansen	Shaw	Jones	Moss

(LUNCH between periods 4 and 5)

Figure 13-4. A scheduling form for coordinating periods with the assignment of teachers and facilities (teacher and station assignments).

TABLE 13-2. Plan for calculating the number of physical education teaching stations needed in an elementary school. (Willgoose, C.E.: The Curriculum in Physical Education, 3rd Ed. Englewood Cliffs, NJ, Prentice-Hall, 1979, p. 171. Reprinted by permission of the publisher.)

Plan	Example
1. Estimate the enrollment by counting the number of grades and number of classes in each grade.	A school with 6 grades of 3 classes per grade = 18 classroom groups
2. Decide on length and number of class periods.	A total of ten 30-minute periods per day, or 50 periods per week
3. Decide on the number of periods per week for pupils.	5 periods per week
4. Calculate number of teaching stations:	

$$\text{Teaching stations} = 18 \text{ classroom groups} \times \frac{5 \text{ periods per week}}{50 \text{ periods per week}} = \frac{90}{50} = 1.8$$

STUDENT GROUPING

Placement of students into classes should reflect more than administrative expedience. Classes are learning groups, and students should be assigned to these groups according to their learning needs. Scheduling students into classes can be accomplished in a variety of ways. Among the more prominent reasons for logical student grouping are the following:

1. To safeguard the health of the participant.
2. To group pupils for effective learning.
3. To equalize competitive conditions.
4. To facilitate progress and achievement.

Being in a group with persons of similar physical characteristics and skills ensures some success, a chance to excel and to be recognized, a feeling of belonging, and security. Consequently, this helps the social and personality development of the individual.

The following information from the American Alliance for Health, Physical Education, Recreation and Dance (reprinted by permission) is appropriate when considering the best method of grouping:[2]

1. The need for grouping students homogeneously for instruction and competition has long been recognized, but the inability to scientifically measure such important factors as ability, maturity, interest, and capacity has served as a deterrent from accomplishing this goal.

2. The most common procedure for grouping today is by grade or class.

3. The ideal grouping organization would take into consideration all factors that affect performance—intelligence, capacity, interest, knowledge, age, height, weight, and so on. To utilize all these factors, however, is not administratively feasible at the present time.

4. Some form of grouping is essential to provide the type of program that will promote educational objectives and protect the student.

5. On the secondary and college levels, the most feasible procedure appears to be to organize subgroups within the regular physical education class proper.

6. Classification within the physical education class should be based on such factors as age, height, and weight statistics and other factors, such as interest and skill that are developed as a result of observation of the activity.

7. For those individuals who desire greater refinement in respect to grouping, utilization of motor capacity, motor ability, attitude, appreciation, and sports-skills tests may be used.

Eight different methods for grouping students are presented here. Sometimes grouping is based on a combination of two or more of these methods.

Grade Level—The most common method; the general age characteristics are similar, but maturity and skill level may vary widely.

Height-Weight or Age-Height-Weight Exponent System—Useful in athletics, especially contact sports, and in junior high where physical maturity varies considerably.

Ability or Skill Level—May be determined by skill in a specific sport or by general motor ability; provides for instruction on the student's skill level. Highly skilled students can move quickly to advanced skill development.

Physical Fitness—This is especially beneficial for students with low fitness because they can benefit from a different kind of program geared to their individual needs.

Interest—It increases students' motivation to be in groups where others share their interests; and adds an important social dimension.

Competency—Based on previous competencies passed in a given activity or in a sequence of activities.

Instructional Method—Students can choose the teaching method they prefer.

Sex—Preferred for some vigorous and contact sports or activities of primary interest to one sex or the other.

FACULTY UTILIZATION

The *traditional* method is to assign a teacher to a class, for which he is to be responsible during the term. This is the simplest pattern, and offers the advantage of the teacher becoming well acquainted and establishing a good rapport with the students. The main disadvantage is the lack of flexibility in utilizing the strongest attributes of several teachers.

The *team teaching* method is one in which two or more teachers share the responsibility for a particular class. The purpose is to capitalize on the strengths of each teacher. The two basic styles of team teaching are *topical* and *differentiated*. With the topical approach, each member of the teaching team provides instruction on a particular topic or activity in which he is highly specialized. For example, during a term, the wrestling coach might teach a 4-week course on wrestling, then a gymnastics specialist would teach gymnastics for 4 weeks, then a tennis specialist would teach a 4-week course of tennis. The *differentiated* method involves a master teacher and two or more supporting teachers. The master teacher is "the expert" who directs the class. He gives overall leadership to the learning process and supervises the supporting teachers. The supporting teachers work with subgroups in specialized phases of instruction.

Assignment of Teachers

The main element in a successful educational environment is a competent and concerned teacher. Teachers should be assigned to classes on the basis of their qualifications and proven success and not on preference or convenience. Teachers of potentially hazardous activities, such as swimming, gymnastics, and skiing, should have the specialized knowledge necessary to conduct the activities at a reasonably safe level. In such cases, certification by national agencies associated with the sport is highly desirable.

The several methods of staffing for physical education in *elementary schools*, with each method having advantages and disadvantages, are as follow:

Physical Education Specialist.   One or more specialists in the school teach all of the physical education classes. Advantages are (a) expertise in physical education subject matter and methods; and (b) knowledge about motor learning at the various stages of development. Disadvantages are (a) the specialist does not know the students as well as the classroom teacher; and (b) teaching the same subject all day can become monotonous.

Rotating Specialist.   A specialist assists classroom teachers by team teaching with them at least once a week and providing leadership and program ideas for the instructional periods when the specialist is not there. Advantages include (a) specialist is knowledgeable about physical education subject matter and methods; (b) he is knowledgeable about motor learning; and (c) through in-service workshops, master lessons, and coaching, a specialist can improve the classroom teacher's physical education techniques. Disadvantages include (a) specialists often must travel to two or more schools; (b) some classroom teachers do not work effectively with the specialist; and (c) the specialist is unable to become well acquainted with the pupils, due to limited contact.

Classroom Teachers Trade Assignments.   One teacher instructs physical education for another, who in turn teaches something else for the first teacher. The main advantage is that teachers can teach in areas of preference and expertise. The main disadvantage is the problem of having teachers who are prepared and willing to do the trading that is needed.

Classroom Teacher Teaches Physical Education.   The advantages include (a) the teacher can integrate physical education with other subject matter; and (b) the teacher is familiar with the students and knows their personalities and abilities. The disadvantages include (a) lack of expertise in teaching physical education; and (b) no opportunity for a break from the routine of supervising the same students every period of the day.

Several important considerations exist relative to staffing classes in *secondary schools.*

1. Is it better for a physical education instructor to teach only physical education, or is it better to teach some classroom subjects? Most teachers and administrators would agree that a combination of classroom and physical education subjects is better.

2. Is it desirable for a teacher to instruct in the physical education program several hours during the school day and then have a heavy coaching assignment after school? It is generally agreed that this is too much. A better combination is some classroom teaching along with physical education instruction and coaching.

3. Is it appropriate to perpetuate the belief that a successful classroom teacher or a successful athletic coach can get by with an inferior job of physical education instruction? This attitude should be unacceptable. The idea should be enforced that teaching 30 students in physical education is just as important as teaching 30 students in English or mathematics or coaching 30 students on the athletic field. Any teacher who views it differently, ought to be prohibited from teaching physical education.

4. Secondary school physical educators should be generally informed about the instructional programs in physical education that precede the secondary schools in order that the subject matter and teaching methods fall into sequence and build progressively onto what the students have already learned. In the absence of this kind of preparation, the idea of graduated levels of instruction fails.

Teaching Loads

In *colleges and universities,* it is generally accepted that a teaching load should not exceed 12 class hours per week of lecture courses, 15 class hours of teaching techniques courses, or 18 class hours of activity courses.

In *secondary schools,* it is recommended that class instruction per teacher not exceed 5 clock hours per day, or 1500 minutes per week. Six clock hours per day or 1800 minutes per week should be considered an absolute maximum, and this should include any after-school responsibilities. A daily load of 200 students per teacher is recommended, with an absolute maximum of 250 students. Finally, each teacher should have at least one free period daily for consultation and conferences with students.[7]

The number of hours per day or week is not an absolute measure of teaching load, because other factors must be considered. If a person teaches a different kind of class each hour, more preparation is required as compared with teaching multiple sections of the same class. The correct balance between these two extremes is important, because too much preparation contributes to inefficient use of the teacher's time; whereas, teaching too much of the same subject can make the material routine and dull.

Another consideration is the length of the class periods. A large number of short class periods are more difficult to teach than a smaller number of longer class periods, because more classes require more preparation and contact with more students. For example, six 40-minute classes would be more demanding than four 60-minute classes, even though the total minutes of instruction are the same.

In addition to the time spent in class, a teacher needs time for planning and preparation, student consultation, and consultation with administrators and parents.

Another factor is that many physical educators have extra duties after hours: coaching athletics, conducting intramurals, coaching cheerleaders and marching groups, and serving as advisors for activity clubs. Two prevalent methods are used by schools to compensate teachers for performing extra duties. One method is *extra pay* for extra work, and the other is to give the teacher *released time* from the normal school day. Whichever method is used, the arrangement should be fair and equitable both for the school and the individual. (Extra duties are also discussed in Chapter 15).

SPECIAL INSTRUCTIONAL METHODS

Learning packages, independent study, and learning contracts can work effectively with individual and dual activities and physical fitness programs. These approaches work better with mature students and students who are highly motivated.

In the *learning package* approach, a description is provided of the procedures that must be followed and the achievement levels that are expected. The student then takes an individualized approach to completing the requirements, at which point, credit for the learning package is given.

The *independent study* approach involves a tailor-made program for a particular individual. Once the individual has accomplished all aspects of the prescribed program, credit is received.

With the *learning contract* approach, the student and teacher agree upon the objectives the student will accomplish and the time frame (which is sometimes flexible) within which the accomplishments will occur. The conditions of agreement are described in writing, and this becomes a *contract*. When the student completes the conditions of the contract, credit is given.

All the individualized study approaches must involve the following to some degree: (1) stated behavior objectives (expected outcomes); (2) preassessment and postassessment (and sometimes, intermediate assessments); (3) a clear understanding by both teacher and student of the requirements, the methods of evaluation, and the system for awarding credit and grades.[12]

HANDICAPPED STUDENTS

The Rehabilitation Act of 1973 prohibits discrimination against the handicapped in any federally aided program. Furthermore, the Education for All

Handicapped Children Act of 1975 provides federal funding to aid state efforts in providing an appropriate education for the handicapped.

This second law, commonly known as Public Law 94-142, is intended to ensure an appropriate public education for all handicapped students. In part, the law enables ". . . specifically designed instruction, at no cost to parents or guardians, to meet the unique needs of a handicapped child, including classroom instruction, *instruction in physical education* (emphasis added), home instruction and instruction in hospitals and institutions." The portions of the law that apply the most to physical education are Sections 2, 3, and 4. The provisions that apply directly to physical education are the following:

1. Advertise and search out potential handicapped students.

2. Identify the population that needs service.

3. Provide the least restrictive educational environment.

4. Prepare an *individualized education program* for each handicapped child identified as having special needs.

5. Do an evaluation of the progress of each student at least annually.

6. Conduct a fair hearing for students, or parents on behalf of their children, to establish the needs of the student if there are any questions (grievances) regarding the Individualized Education Program.

Components of an Individualized Education Program

In order to develop the individualized education program in compliance with the requirements of Public Law 94-142, the following components must be included for every handicapped child requiring special education and related services.[17]

A statement of the child's present levels of educational performance, including academic achievement, social adaptation, prevocational and vocational skills, psychomotor skills, and self-help skills.

A specific statement describing the child's learning style.

A statement of annual goals that describes the educational performance to be achieved by the end of the school year under the child's individualized education program.

A statement of short-term instructional objectives, which must be measurable intermediate steps between the present level of educational performance and the annual goals.

A statement of specific educational services needed by the child (determined without regard to the availability of those services), including a description of:

    a. All special education and related services that are needed to meet the unique needs of the child, including the type of physical education program in which the child will participate.

    b. Any special instructional media and materials that are needed to implement the individualized education program.

The date when those services will begin and length of time the services will be given.

A description of the extent to which the child will participate in regular education programs.

A justification for the type of educational placement that the child will have.

A list of the individuals who are responsible for implementation of the individualized education program.

Objective criteria, evaluation procedures, and schedules for determining, on at least an annual basis, whether the short-term instructional objectives are being achieved.

Least Restrictive Environment

The continuum of physical education placement is represented by Figure 13-5. As one of the basic principles (indicated on the diagram), students should be placed in the environment that will allow them to function best—

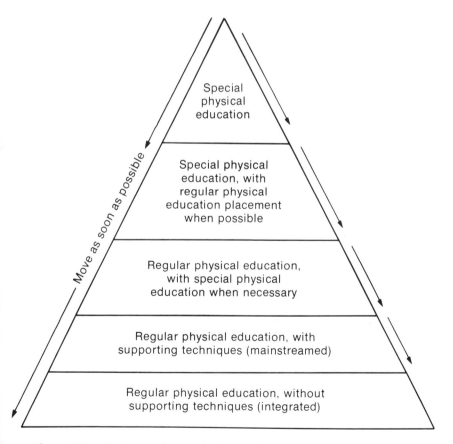

Figure 13-5. Continuum of physical education placement of handicapped students.

the least restrictive environment. The physical education teacher is the person best equipped to make the judgment as to what kind of physical education setting the student belongs.

The concept of least restrictive means that each handicapped child should be placed in as normal a situation as possible. The physical education administrator should be knowledgeable about each situation, so that if called upon, he can provide an accurate report on the status of the individual in question. The administrator must also be aware of how effectively teachers in the department are working with the handicapped students.

As can be seen on the continuum of physical education placement, there are five levels. Four of these involve the assistance of a teacher other than a physical education teacher in a regular class. Public Law 94-142, if applied correctly, might enable a school to hire a specialized staff member to assist those handicapped students requiring special attention.

MARKING (GRADING) STUDENTS

Every teacher should develop effective methods of marking students (the term marking is preferred over the term grading). A student's marks determine to some extent whether he will secure a good position of employment, be admitted into college, win a scholarship, be eligible for lower automobile insurance rates, or gain prestige among classmates. Marks represent to the student and the parents an indication of success in school. Because of the importance placed on them, an accurate system for determining and reporting marks is imperative.[14]

Purposes of Marking

Marks serve different purposes for students, teachers and guidance counselors, parents, and school administrators. A mark should inform the student how nearly he has met the standards on which the mark is based. It should clearly indicate how well he performed as contrasted with how well he might be expected to perform. A mark must be accurate and justifiable and have a strong basis, or it loses its value to the student. It may even destroy the student's interest and incentive and result in a negative attitude toward the subject and the teacher.

Teachers and guidance personnel may use marks for guidance and counseling. If accurately determined, marks can help the teacher predict how successful a student might be in certain pursuits, and may also help the teacher evaluate the effectiveness of his teaching.

Parents are usually eager to learn of their children's success in school and desire to know the reason for the lack of success. Marks that are properly obtained, reported, and interpreted will furnish desired facts. As a result, guidance from home may help overcome deficiencies.

In the present school system, marks are essential to administrators, who interpret them as symbols of progress and indicators of achievement levels. Since marks become permanent records of achievement, they are also used as a basis for promotion and scholastic honor awards. It is essential, then, that marks be established on a solid, equally fair basis, and that they be accurately reported and interpreted.

Criteria for Useful Marks

Marks should be *valid*. They must truly represent the quality and quantity of pupil achievement for which they purportedly stand.

Marks should be *reliable*. They must accurately and consistently represent the same results for each student.

Marks should be highly *objective*. Different teachers, given the same data on a student, should arrive at the same mark. This quality is dependent on a clearly defined marking system.

Marks should be assigned on the basis of *definite standards*. The standards should not differ for each pupil nor should they fluctuate widely from one year to the next.

Marks should be capable of *clear interpretation* with regard to what they signify. If the significance of an A is not evident in terms of quality and quantity of achievement, then the grade lacks meaning.

Marking should involve an element of economy of the teacher's time and effort. Since marking is only one of the teacher's many tasks, only a reasonable amount of time can be justified for it.

Marks should be *timely*. Final marks are recorded only at the end of semesters; but for purposes of incentive, students should be frequently informed of their progress and present standing.

Methods of Reporting Marks

Some of the several methods of reporting student achievement are as follow:

Five-Letter. This is the most frequently used method. The teacher determines the criteria for each grade: A, B, C, D, E (F). Each student is given a letter grade based on his performance in the class. The grade is reported, and sometimes, an interpretation accompanies the grade telling what each means in terms of level of performance.

Pass or Fail. In this system, a standard of acceptability is established. If the student performs up to the standard, he passes; if performance is below the standard, the student fails. Sometimes satisfactory or unsatisfactory are terms used in place of pass or fail.

Percent. With this method the student is given a percentage score as a mark, with 100 percent representing excellent performance. Percentages can then be converted to letter marks in order to make them more meaningful in the school system. Usually it is assumed that 90 to 100% = A; 80 to 89% = B; 70 to 79% = C; 60 to 69% = D; below 60% = F.

Accumulative Points. In this method, the student is awarded points for performing the various activities throughout the unit of instruction. Each student's class standing is determined and reported on the basis of accumulated points.

Contract. Through agreement between the student and the teacher, it is decided which projects the student will complete, and this agreement becomes a contract. The particular conditions of the contract define a predetermined grade that will be received if the student completes all the conditions.

Descriptive Statement. This method consists of a short paragraph explaining the student's status and stating the student's strengths and weaknesses in the subject. The statement is reviewed by the teacher, student, and parent in reaching understanding of the student's progress. Some schools include with the regular report card a sheet showing comparative physical fitness test scores. An example of such a form is shown in Figure 13-6. Items and columns can be altered from this model to fit any specific situation.

COMPARATIVE PHYSICAL FITNESS TEST SCORES

Student's Name _____ Grade _____

School _____ Teacher _____ Date _____

Physical Fitness Test	Student Score	Class Avg.	School Avg.	District Avg.	Natl. Avg.
Sit-ups					
Pull-ups					
Shuttle run					
Standing Long Jump					
50 yd. dash					
Softball Throw					
600 yd. run/walk					
Push-ups					
Set-ups					
Rope Climbing					
Trunk Flexion Standing					
Trunk Extension					
Forward Roll 40 feet					
Backward Roll (Pass or Fail)					
Vertical Jump					
Agility Jump					

Note: Any column left blank indicates that there are no average scores available.

Figure 13-6. A report card for selected physical fitness skills.

A POSITION STATEMENT

The author firmly believes that every student is a unique individual with differing physical, mental, emotional, and social needs. Students have varying abilities, aptitudes for performance, and rates at which motor skills are perfected. Regardless of the differences, however, *every student, including the handicapped*, has the need and the right to benefit from well-planned physical education experiences.

Physical education is an important part of the development of the whole person. Even though the emphasis is on the development of physical fitness and motor characteristics, good physical education experiences also contribute to social, psychologic and mental development. Without an effective physical education program in conjunction with the academic subjects, it is impossible for students to achieve the well-rounded development they need and deserve. An effective program

1. Enhances growth and development, including physical fitness, motor skills, and desirable physique and postural characteristics.
2. Contributes to one's health and well-being.
3. Has potential for enhancing self-image, psychologic adjustment, and social adeptness.
4. Develops desirable lifelong recreational interests and skills.

In a statement of beliefs, the Society of State Directors of Health, Physical Education and Recreation added clarity as to the conditions that should exist relative to the physical education instructional program. The author concurs with this statement, and thinks that every physical educator ought to be familiar with these beliefs. It is printed with the permission of the Society.

Class Instruction

ABOUT ADMINISTRATION

Physical education is essential for all students, boys and girls, from pre-kindergarten through grade twelve. The daily instructional period for elementary school pupils (Pre-K, K-6) should be at least 30 minutes in length, exclusive of time allotted for dressing, showering, recess, free and/or supervised play periods, and noon hour activities.

The minimum instructional class period for pupils in secondary schools should be a standard class period daily, except where the length and frequency of the class periods are altered to offer students a more comprehensive program. Where modular or flexible scheduling is used care should be taken to involve students in some combination of at least 300 minutes of physical education per week spread over three or more days.

All pupils, including those participating in varsity athletics, sports clubs, dance clubs, and the like, should be involved each year in the instructional phase of the physical education program.

Physical education should be adapted for those pupils who have special needs. To the extent feasible, such pupils should take part in regular classes. Special classes should be scheduled for pupils who are severely handicapped or who are otherwise unable to participate successfully in the regular program.

—A physician's recommendation in consultation with teachers, parents and the student should be the basis for assignment to special classes. The physician should work with the physical education teacher in determining the activities which should be prescribed for each child who requires adaptive physical education.

—Students may need adaptive physical education because of poor coordination, lack of strength or similar deficiencies.

—The services of teachers with special preparation in adaptive physical education should be available to every school.

All pupils, from pre-kindergarten through twelfth grade, should be scheduled for physical education according to their physiological development, ability, interests and individual needs.

Credit in physical education should be required for graduation from high school. Standards should ensure satisfactory achievement based upon reasonable objectives for each individual student.

Class size in physical education should be consistent with the activity being taught. Effective physical education instruction requires both large and small groups.

All students should wear physical education clothing which permits freedom of movement and safe participation. Showering should be encouraged whenever class activities are sufficiently vigorous to cause perspiration. Appropriate instruction and supervision should be provided to ensure safe, healthful practices in dressing and showering.

Differences in abilities and interests will create at times separation or grouping within a coeducational physical education class in elementary and secondary schools. In addition to the social values gained, coeducational physical education classes provide instructional flexibility, make maximum use of the talents of instructors and offer students a wider variety of activities.

Physical educators should be alert to changing patterns of school organization, methodology, and educational technology so that the educational potential of new practices and innovations may enhance the physical education program.

ABOUT PROGRAM

Class instruction in physical education should provide a planned, balanced, varied progression of activities based upon needs, abilities and interests of boys and girls at all developmental levels.

The elementary school physical education program should provide instruction in sequential experiences including basic and creative movement, rhythms and dance, relays, games, sports skills, stunts, tumbling, apparatus, swimming, outdoor activities, and other activities which meet the objectives.

The middle school and junior high school program should include rhythms, various types of dancing, aquatics, gymnastics, stunts, tumbling, individual and dual sports, team games, special conditioning activities and outdoor recreation.

The senior high school program should emphasize lifetime sports and carryover activities as well as the involvement, knowledge and understandings necessary to provide insight and motivation for a lifetime of vigorous physical activity. The achievement of personal physical fitness during the school years and the maintenance of fitness throughout adult life should become the goal of every student. Every effort should be made to allow senior high school students the opportunity to select activities appropriate to their own needs and interests.

In addition to the necessary space, indoor and outdoor facilities, equipment and supplies for conducting the instructional program in physical education, good teaching requires an adequate collection and proper use of books, periodicals, audiovisual materials and other teaching aids. Innovative use of modern technology is encouraged whenever it can contribute to improved instruction.

Evaluation of the curriculum by both students and teachers should be continuous. Evaluation should be used to assess student progress toward stated goals, to provide guidelines for adjusting current programs and planning new ones, and to indicate needs for instructional improvement.

Evaluation is an important means of interpreting the program to students and adults in order to improve community understanding of the values and outcomes of physical education.

ABOUT PERSONNEL

Certification standards for physical education personnel, consistent with general certification requirements, should be established and periodically reviewed by each State department of education. Increased interest and involvement in certification on the part of professional associations and teacher preparation institutions should be encouraged and welcomed.

Elementary classroom teachers should have a clear understanding of the contribution good physical education makes to the education of boys and girls, including the relationships of physical growth and development to the general educational progress of all pupils.

Elementary classroom teachers should have sufficient preparation and laboratory experiences in the basic skills, methods, and content of physical education to enable them to conduct an effective program under the guidance of a physical education specialist or supervisor, and to relate the experiences in physical education to ongoing classroom instruction.

Whenever possible, elementary pupils should receive the major part of their physical education instruction from a specialist in elementary school physical education having a major in physical education with strong emphasis in movement education and elementary school physical education. The elementary school physical education specialist should work directly with classroom teachers to coordinate the physical education program with other classroom activities and to foster mutual reinforcement in assessing and helping individual pupils.

Secondary school physical education teachers—both men and women—should have a major in physical education and should be able to demonstrate leadership and teaching skills in the wide variety of activities outlined in the preceding section on Program.

Teachers who work with students who have special needs or characteristics, e.g., inner city, disadvantaged, pre-school, handicapped, ethnic or non-English speaking, should be specially selected and prepared. The tremendous personal and social benefits of physical education for such students should be maximized through the program.

All teachers of physical education should be provided with assistance from supervisors or resource persons who are qualified by education and experience to provide professional leadership and guidance in physical education. In addition, clinics, workshops, and other in-service opportunities should be provided for both classroom teachers and specialists.

Teacher aides, when utilized, should work under the direct supervision of a certificated physical education teacher and only in a supportive and supplementary capacity.

LICENSING

As the educational programs related to physical education and athletics become more refined and more specialized, the trend toward "licensing" continues to grow. Licensing includes both accreditation of programs and certification of specialists.

Teacher certification within each state is already established. Recently there has been a strong push to have athletic trainers certified by the National Athletic Training Association (NATA). Some institutions have established athletic coaching certification procedures, wherein an individual who completes certain requirements at the institution is provided a certificate verifying that he is professionally qualified to coach athletics in the schools. Others offer specialized programs in commercial physical education, and some have established a certification procedure in connection with this specialty. Accreditation of various professional preparation programs has been gaining ground in colleges and universities; and although program accreditation specific to professional education is still infrequent, it seems unlikely that it will escape the growing trend. Program accreditation can serve a worthwhile purpose provided the criteria and procedures are carefully worked out and properly applied.

IMPACT OF TITLE IX

Title IX of the Education Amendment Act of 1972 has had a major impact on the various aspects of physical education. This law is based on the principle that all activities in educational programs have equal value for both sexes. Therefore, the governing regulations state that physical education classes may not be conducted separately on the basis of sex, nor may participation in physical education programs be required or refused on the basis of sex. This concept has caused dismay in the minds of many administrators and teachers, because for many years, separate instruction in physical education skills has been offered, beginning sometimes as early as mid-elementary school. (See also the section on Title IX in Chapter 15.)

With respect to *physical education courses*, Section 86-34 of the law states that an institution or agency may not ". . . provide any course or otherwise carry out any of its education program or activities separately on the basis of sex, or require or refuse participation therein by any of its students on such basis, including health, physical education, industrial business, vocational technical, home economics, music, and adult education courses." The following conditions apply:

1. The law does not prohibit grouping of students in physical education classes and activities by ability as assessed by objective standards of individual performance, developed and applied without regard to sex.
2. The law does not prohibit separation of students by sex within physical education classes or activities during participation in wrestling, boxing, rugby, ice hockey, football, basketball, and other sports the purpose or major activity of which involves bodily contact.
3. Where use of a single standard of measuring skill or progress in a physical education class has an adverse effect on members of one sex, the recipient shall use appropriate standards that do not have such effect.
4. Portions of classes in elementary and secondary schools that deal exclusively with human sexuality may be conducted in separate sessions for boys and girls.

SAFETY CONSIDERATIONS

The teacher or supervisor of a class or activity is fully responsible for seeing that the activity is conducted with optimum safety and in a prudent manner. This involves providing a safe environment in terms of facilities and equipment, adequate supervision, and the proper selection of activities for the particular group or individual. It means especially that a student should not be allowed to engage in activities against a physician's recommendation. Sometimes, because of health reasons, a physician will prescribe modified activity or excused absence for a student. Such a recommendation should always be honored. Figure 13-7 shows an example of a physician's recommendation form.

Another important consideration is the possibility of an accident. In case of an accident to a student in a class or other supervised activity, the person in charge should follow these procedures:

1. Administer appropriate first aid (all physical education teachers and athletic coaches should know correct first aid procedures).
2. If additional care is needed, see that the student is properly escorted to the student health center or the hospital or doctor's office. Call an ambulance if such service is needed.
3. As soon as possible after the accident, complete an accident report form in detail, with the appropriate signatures and have the copies distributed as directed on the form. Figure 13-8 shows an example of an accident report form.

Hazardous Activities

Because of the equipment involved and the nature of the activities, weight training, gymnastics, skiing, swimming, and certain others, present more than a normal amount of hazard. Teachers of these activities are expected to have thorough knowledge of the hazards, teach safe procedures, and provide the supervision that is necessary to ensure safe practices.

Swimming Pool Safety and Sanitation

Since swimming areas require more attention to safety and sanitation than most other areas, specific regulations are described. These are examples, and therefore, may not exactly fit a particular situation or suit everyone's preference. They can, however, serve as useful guidelines for swimming areas in general. Also, these particular regulations provide additional insight into the kinds of safety rules needed with other hazardous activities.

General Regulations[13]

A thorough soap shower must be taken before putting on the suit and entering the pool.

Running, tag, and other forms of dangerous play on the decks are prohibited.

Physician's Recommendation

This is to certify that I have examined _____

from _____school and have found the following

abnormal condition _____

_____

Therefore, I **recommend that** participation in physical education be **as** checked below:

_____ **Normal program—all activities**

MODIFIED PROGRAM

_____ **Relaxation and rest**

_____ **Mild exercises, done** lying or sitting on mat

_____ **Nonvigorous games** or dance

_____ **Body building exercises modified as to need**

_____ **Other (specify)** _____

Duration: for _____ weeks, for _____months, until next examination

Date: _____ Signature _____M.D.

Telephone _____ Address _____

COMMENTS: _____

_____

_____

_____

_____

Figure 13-7. Example of a physician's recommendation for modified physical education or excused absence.

Street shoes may not be worn in the pool area.

Instructors and lifeguards should teach and encourage people to use the most sanitary practices while in the pool or on the deck.

Only one person at a time is permitted to be on a diving board.

A diver is required to be certain that the water area is clear of swimmers before diving from the deck or the board. Swimmers should stay clear of the water in the vicinity of the diving boards.

REPORT OF ACCIDENT

NAME_____ ACCIDENT DATE_____

HOME ADDRESS_____ TIME_____ A.M._____ P.M._____

PUPIL; PARENT; OTHER (Specify)_____

SEX: M F GRADE_____ AGE_____ SCHOOL_____

☐AUDITORIUM	☐CORRIDOR	☐LABORATORIES	☐SHOWERS
☐GROUNDS	☐DRESSING ROOM	☐POOL	☐STAIRS
☐CAFETERIA	☐GYMNASIUM	☐REST ROOM	OTHER (Specify)_____
☐CLASSROOM	☐HOME ECONOMICS	☐SHOP	

NON-SCHOOL:☐HOME ☐TO AND FROM ☐BICYCLE ☐TRAFFIC _____

NATURE OF INJURY

☐ABRASION	☐BURN	☐LACERATION	☐SHOCK (E1)
☐AMPUTATION	☐CONCUSSION	☐POISONING	☐SPRAIN
☐ASPHYXIATION	☐CUT	☐PUNCTURE	OTHER (Specify)_____
☐BITE	☐DISLOCATION	☐SCALD	
☐BRUISE	☐FRACTURE	☐SCRATCH	

PART OF BODY INJURED

☐ABDOMEN	☐BACK	☐ELBOW	☐FINGER	☐HEAD	☐MOUTH	☐TOOTH
☐ANKLE	☐CHEST	☐EYE	☐FOOT	☐KNEE	☐NOSE	☐WRIST
☐ARM	☐EAR	☐FACE	☐HAND	☐LEG	☐SCALP	OTHER (Specify)_____

DESCRIPTION OF THE ACCIDENT

_____

_____

_____

_____

Teacher or supervisor in charge:_____

Present at scene of accident: Yes_____ No_____

Witnesses: Name_____ Address_____

Name_____ Address_____

IMMEDIATE ACTION TAKEN

First aid treatment by_____ Sent home by_____

Sent to school nurse by_____ Sent to physician: Dr._____

Sent to hospital: Name_____

Name and relationship of person notified_____

Number of school days missed_____

Signed: Principal_____ Teacher_____ Supervisor_____

Figure 13-8. Example of a student accident report form. (Courtesy of Milton F. Hartivigsen.)

Double bouncing is prohibited on the boards, except under the supervision of a lifeguard or instructor.

Wrestling and throwing or pushing people in the pool is not permitted.

Admission to the pool will be refused to any person having a contagious disease, infectious condition, or any other condition that in the judgment of the lifeguard or instructor should prohibit participation in swimming activities, either for his own protection or the protection of other participants.

Food and drinks should not be allowed in the swimming pool area.

Participants should be discouraged from calling for help except when help is really needed.

No one (including faculty members) is allowed to enter the pool except when an authorized lifeguard is on duty.

Nonswimmers and weak swimmers are required to remain in shallow water where they can touch the bottom of the pool.

Lifeguard Requirements[13]

In order to qualify for employment, a lifeguard must hold a current American Red Cross, YMCA, or Canadian Senior Lifesaving Certificate.

Preference will be given to those who hold current Water Safety Instructor cards or YWCA Leader Examiner Certificates.

Successful experience in lifeguarding is highly desirable, but not required in all cases.

Official lifeguard uniforms must be worn at all times by lifeguards on duty. Such uniforms may not be worn under any conditions by other people in the swimming pool area.

A lifeguard must remain on duty at his station until a replacement arrives.

Lifeguards are required to be on the job 100%; meaning that they are not permitted to read books, talk on the telephone, carry on nonbusiness conversations or participate in other activities that detract from their effectiveness as lifeguards.

One lifeguard must be on duty at all times when the pool is open; and there must be one lifeguard for every 50 participants in the pool area.

Lifeguards must never leave the pool unguarded even for a few seconds. If a guard needs to leave the pool, he must contact another guard to be sure that the area is covered during his absence.

Each lifeguard will situate himself in a position that is most advantageous to cover his assigned area of the pool.

Whistles will be used sparingly to attract attention, so they will not become commonplace. Whistles may be used by lifeguards only.

When a lifeguard is in doubt in terms of a person's danger, he should assume that the person is in serious trouble and act accordingly.

Lifeguards should be on the watch for weak swimmers, swimmers who are tired, or other persons who may find themselves in difficulty, and should control the activities of these people in order to prevent them from getting into danger.

Lifeguards are responsible for being thoroughly familiar with emergency procedures, know how to use the available emergency equipment without hesitation or fault, and should assist the Pool Manager in making certain that the equipment is in position and operable at all times.

Lifeguards should stress that the best procedure for safety is prevention. It is a duty of lifeguards to help educate people in safe practices and to make sure they follow such practices.

Emergency Procedures[13]

In the case of a potential drowning, begin resuscitation *immediately*. Do not stop until relieved by a competent person. Treat for shock.

Have someone call the emergency number immediately. The nature of the emergency should be explained, so that the emergency personnel will come fully prepared to handle the situation.

Have the pool cleared of people (because lifeguards will be occupied with the victim) and keep people away from the victim.

After the emergency procedures have been handled, have the proper authority (administrator) notified of the situation.

As soon as the more urgent matters have been handled, but within no more than 12 hours following the accident, complete an Accident Report and be sure that *all* pertinent information is included.

BIBLIOGRAPHY

1. AAHPERD: College Physical Education—The General Program. Washington, D.C., 1973.

2. AAHPERD: Organization Patterns for Instruction in Physical Education, Washington, D.C., 1981.

3. Annarino, A.A.: Accountability: an instructional model for secondary physical education. JOPER 52(3): 55, 1981.

4. Austin, D.: A developmental physical education program. JOPER, 49:36, 1978.

5. Bain, L.: Implementing Title IX: concerns of undergraduate physical education majors. JOPER, 50:77, 1979.

6. Bucher, C.A., and Koenig C.R.: Methods and Materials for Secondary School Physical Education. The C.V. Mosby Company, 1978.

7. Camaione, D.N.: A method for determining instructional load credit. JOPER, 50 (5): 58, 1979.

8. Corbin, C.B.: Becoming Physically Educated in the Elementary School, 2nd Ed. Philadelphia, Lea & Febiger, 1976.

9. Daughtrey, G., and Woods, J.: Physical Education and Intramural Programs: Organization and Administration, 2nd Ed. Philadelphia, W.B. Saunders, 1980.

10. Davis, H.: State requirements in physical education for teachers and students. Washington, D.C., AAHPERD, 1973.

11. Fordham, S., and Leaf, C.A.: Physical Education and Sports. New York, New York, John Wiley & Sons, 1978.

12. Heitman, Helen M. and Marian E. Kneer. Physical Education Instructional Techniques: An Individualized Humanistic Approach. Englewood Cliffs, NJ, Prentice-Hall, 1976.

13. Jensen C.R.: Policy and Procedure Manual College of Physical Education, Brigham Young University Press, Provo, UT, 1981.

14. Jensen, C.R., and Hirst, C.: Measurement and Evaluation in Physical Education and Athletics. New York, Macmillan, 1980.

15. Lindeburg, F.A.: Teaching Physical Education in the Secondary School. New York, John Wiley & Sons, 1978.

16. Olson, G.: Physical education for the small school system. JOPER, *51*:24, 1980.

17. Perez, F.V., and Gutierrez, T.: Participation for the handicapped. JOPER, *50* (8): 81, 1979.

18. Rupnow, A.: Eliminating sex role stereotyping in elementary physical education. JOPER, *49*:38, 1978.

19. Stewart, C. C.: Integrating the physically handicapped child into the physical education classroom. JOPER, *51* (4): 17, 1980.

20. Swanson, J.: Developing and implementing objectives in physical education. JOPER, *50*:68, 1979.

21. Thaxton, A.B.: Dealing with unprepared students and large classes. JOPER, *50* (6): 68, 1979.

22. Torres, S.: A Primer on Individualized Education Programs for Handicapped Children. The Foundation for Exceptional Children, Reston, VA, 1977.

23. Weiss, R.A., and Karper, W.B.: Teaching the handicapped child in the regular physical education class. JOPER, *51* (2):32, 1980.

24. Willgoose, C.E.: The Curriculum in Physical Education, 3rd Ed. Englewood Cliffs, NJ, Prentice-Hall, 1979.

Chapter *14*

CURRICULUM DEVELOPMENT AND MANAGEMENT

The school curriculum must be based on sound values that are in harmony with the philosophy of the particular school system. The curriculum should be efficient in leading students toward educational goals. A review of Chapter 1 will help in understanding the importance of goals and working toward them, and a review of Chapters 2 and 3 will help in understanding the importance of sound values on which to base the curriculum.

In order to develop an effective curriculum in physical education, it is necessary to understand the nature and basic purposes of physical education. This has been outlined in the following statement from the American Alliance for Health, Physical Education, Recreation and Dance.

> Physical education is the study and practice of the science and art of human movement. It is concerned with why man moves; how he moves; the physiological, sociological and psychological consequences of his movement; and the skills and motor patterns which comprise his movement repertoire. Through physical education, an individual has the opportunity to learn to perform efficiently the motor skills he needs in everyday living and in recreational activities. He can develop and maintain sound physiological functions through vigorous muscular activity. He may increase the awareness of his physical self. Through expressive and creative activities, he may enhance his aesthetic appreciations. Physical education provides situations for learning to compete as well as to cooperate with others in striving for the achievement of common goals. Within the media of physical activity, concepts underlying effective human movement can be demonstrated and the influences these have on the individual can be better understood. Satisfying and successful experiences in physical education should develop in the individual a desire to regularly participate in activity throughout life. Only through enjoyable and persistent participation will the optimum benefits of physical activity be derived.[2]

ELECTIVE VS. REQUIRED PHYSICAL EDUCATION

Part of the philosophy of a given institution of school system is whether to have required or elective physical education. Physical education has long been a required subject. A strong case can be made for maintaining this status at the elementary and junior high school levels. However, the case weakens slightly at the high school and college levels, where the students are better prepared to make sound judgments relative to electives. At any level, an effective physical education program can be easily justified whether required or elective.

Changing from a required to an elective program does not necessarily mean lesser status or a reduction in faculty or student enrollment. It does, however, change the nature of the program. An elective program defines the activities to be offered and students select those in which they desire instruction. Following are some pros and cons of required and elective physical education.

For Required

1. Mandatory enrollment facilitates scheduling.
2. Physical education might not be emphasized by the administration or might deteriorate if not required.
3. Students take so many required courses, they would not have time for physical education as an elective.
4. All students need daily vigorous activity for emotional release, physical fitness, and total development.
5. Students look at required subjects as being more important than electives.

Against Required

1. A required program does not motivate teachers to meet student needs and interests.
2. Physical education classes may become irrelevant and time-wasters.
3. Students resent requirements and so do parents.
4. Required classes are counter to the principle of individualized education.
5. Many students lack motivation toward required participation.
6. Some students learn to dislike physical education when it is required and want nothing to do with it in later life.

For Elective

1. Student choice of activities increases enthusiasm for participation.
2. Elective programs increase possibilities for meeting individual differences among students.
3. Elective programs increase student freedom and responsibility for making their own decisions and increase the possibility of carry-over into later life.
4. The drive for activity will cause students to enroll voluntarily.
5. Elective programs often better utilize community facilities, thus reducing expenses to school districts.
6. An elective program motivates teachers to do a better job because students will enroll only if the classes are interesting and useful.

Against Elective

1. Those who need physical education the most will not take it.
2. Elective physical education is harder to schedule and tends to result in less efficient use of facilities.

Each state and territory of the United States has legislation that describes the educational requirements. A district or institution may enact requirements beyond those of the state, but a district may not require less. Table 14-1 is a summary of the time and grade requirements for physical education in the various states and territories.[6]

TABLE 14-1. Physical education requirements in the states and territories of the United States.

States that Require Physical Education in the Public Schools Grades 1 Through 12 (the amount of the requirement per week varies with the different states).

Alabama	New York
Alaska	North Dakota
Arkansas	Ohio
California	Pennsylvania
Colorado	Rhode Island
District of Columbia	Tennessee
Illinois	Texas
Iowa	Vermont
Louisiana	Virginia
Massachusetts	Washington
Missouri	West Virginia
New Hampshire	Wisconsin
New Jersey	Canal Zone

States and Territories that Require Physical Education at Least 8 out of 12 Years

Connecticut	New Mexico
Delaware	North Carolina
Florida	Oregon
Georgia	South Carolina
Hawaii	South Dakota
Kansas	Wyoming
Kentucky	Guam
Maine	Puerto Rico
Minnesota	Virgin Islands
Montana	

States and Territories with a Physical Education Requirement of Less Than 8 Years

Idaho	Mississippi
Indiana	Nevada
Michigan	Utah

States and Territories that have no Physical Education Requirement

Arizona
Nebraska
Oklahoma

CURRICULAR GOALS

In order to clarify the discussion, let us first look at some commonly used definitions of what a curriculum is.

1. All of the planned experiences a student undergoes through his participation in a school's instructional program or a particular area of it.
2. An orderly sequence of courses and/or experiences offered by an educational institution to create an environment in which the objectives of the program can be achieved.
3. A systematic set of educational experiences designed to efficiently produce the most important learning and behavior needed for successful living.
4. All of the instructional and extra-instructional activities sponsored by a school. (This is a broader definition than normally accepted, because it includes both instructional/and noninstructional programs.)

The goals (purposes, aims, objectives, and outcomes) with which the curriculum is aligned must be sound and easily understood. The Board of Education in Calgary, Canada,[12] provided a useful concept of purpose when it described physical education as "an integral part of the total education program which contributes to the physical, mental, social and emotional development of the child through the medium of carefully selected physical activities carried on under skilled leadership and in adequate facilities." Additional direction was provided from the same source with five specific statements of purpose. The goals of physical education stress the development of the following[11]:

1. Physical skills which will enable participation in a wide variety of activities;

2. Physical fitness and soundly functioning body systems for an active life in his/her environment.

3. Knowledge and understanding of physical and social skills, physical fitness, scientific principles of movement, and the relationship of exercise to personal well being;

4. Social skills which promote acceptable standards of behavior and positive relationships with others;

5. Attitudes and appreciations that will encourage participation in and enjoyment of physical activity, fitness, quality performance, a positive self concept, and respect for others.

The AAHPERD gave its version of the goals of physical education with the following statement[3]:

Physical Education is that integral part of total education which contributes to the development of the individual through the natural medium of physical activity—human movement. It is a carefully planned sequence of learning experiences designed to fulfill the growth, development, and behavior needs of each student. It encourages and assists each student to:

Develop the skills of movement, the knowledge of how and why one moves, and the ways in which movement may be organized.

Learn to move skillfully and effectively through exercise, games, sports, dance, and aquatics.

Enrich his understanding of the concepts of space, time, and force related to movement.

Express culturally approved patterns of personal behavior and interpersonal relationships in and through games, sports, and dance.

Condition the heart, lungs, muscles, and other organic systems of the body to meet daily and emergency demands.

Acquire an appreciation of and a respect for good physical condition (fitness), a functional posture, and a sense of personal well-being.

Develop an interest and a desire to participate in lifetime recreational sports.

Additional insight into the goals of physical education can be obtained by reviewing the position statement of the Society of State Directors of Health, Physical Education and Recreation, which appears in Chapter 21.

A carefully planned curriculum indicates that those responsible know where they are going, and it helps the students understand where they are going in their educational programs and how to get there. In today's complex and rapidly changing society, the casual or nonchalant approach to curriculum planning just is not good enough. The approach must be thorough, timely, and precise. It requires educators who are truly experts and who are dedicated to providing effective educational experiences.

FRAMEWORK FOR THE CURRICULUM

Among the most important purposes of education in a democratic society are (1) to ensure the development of the type of personality required to perpetuate and maintain the desirable features of a society; (2) to teach the individual to constructively evaluate issues and to influence the social order by contributing to useful changes; and (3) to develop individuals to their fullest potential so they can function effectively within society, both currently and in the future, through intelligent self-direction and group deliberation and action.

In the past, meaningful statements have been set forth that have served as guidelines for the direction of education and for the placement of emphases. For example, in 1918, the Commission on the Reorganization of Secondary Education stated the seven cardinal principles of education.[13]

1. Health.
2. Command of the fundamental processes.
3. Worthy home membership.
4. Vocational preparation.
5. Civic education.
6. Worthy use of leisure.
7. Ethical character.

These principles have been looked upon in the past as guidelines toward sound education. They are still often referred to by professional educators.

In 1938, the Educational Policies Commission[16] set forth four comprehensive educational aims: (1) self-realization, (2) human relationships, (3) economic efficiency, and (4) civic responsibility. Like the cardinal principles, these aims have had significant impact, and they are still considered by educators to be meaningful goals of education in America.

In 1966, the American Association of School Administrators stated the imperatives in education. These are guidelines that should be at the forefront as curricula are developed and modified, instructional methods revised, and organizational patterns reshaped to meet current educational needs.[8]

1. To make urban life rewarding and satisfying.
2. To prepare people for the world of work.
3. To discover and nurture creative talent.
4. To stengthen the moral fabric of society.
5. To deal constructively with psychological tensions.
6. To keep democracy working.
7. To make intelligent use of natural resources.
8. To make the best use of leisure time.
9. To work with other peoples of the world for human betterment.

More recently, the Institute for Educational Management at the United States International University at San Diego, California, was asked to study the most pressing needs of youth for the 1980s. The institute prepared a set of guidelines, which state the following.[19] All youth need to

1. Develop saleable skills.
2. Develop and maintain good health and physical fitness.
3. Understand the rights and duties of the citizen of a multicultural democratic society.
4. Understand the significance of the family for the individual and society.
5. Know how to purchase and use goods and services intelligently.
6. Understand the influence of science on human life.
7. Develop an appreciation of literature, art, music, and nature.
8. Be able to use their leisure time well and to budget it wisely.
9. Develop respect for other persons.
10. Grow in their ability to think rationally.
11. Learn how to make urban life rewarding and satisfying.
12. Discover and nurture their creative talent.
13. Be able to deal constructively with psychological tensions.
14. Learn how to make intelligent use of natural resources.
15. Know how to work with other peoples of the world for human betterment.

STEPS IN CURRICULUM PLANNING

Accomplishments in curriculum design and revision almost always occur as a result of careful planning. In the long run, changes left to chance seldom succeed.

The logical steps in curriculum development begin with establishing a curriculum committee with well-defined purposes and clear direction to do the following:

1. Study the local conditions and attitudes that should influence the curriculum.
2. Study and clarify the philosophy and goals of physical education in the particular school system.

3. Become well informed about opportunities and limitations relative to resources—facilities and potential facilities, teachers, and equipment.
4. Thoroughly evaluate the present curriculum in terms of both strengths and weaknesses.
5. Recommend curriculum changes along with the justification for them.
6. Assist with the implementation of approved changes, including dissemination of information to teachers, students, and public, and inservice training of the staff as needed.

Those responsible for curriculum development should be well aware of the expertise available through national, state, and local organizations and institutions. Curriculum personnel should be diligent about keeping abreast of useful research and curricular trends and innovations. Sources of valuable information include the AAHPERD (publications, staff specialists, position statements, conferences, conventions, and workshops), the state association of HPERD (conferences, workshops, and publications), the President's Council on Physical Fitness and Sports, specialists from the State Department of Education, and college professors who are curriculum specialists.

Curriculum committees take different forms in different situations. For example, a large high school might have a curriculum coordinating committee and several subcommittees representing different areas of the school program. In such a situation, each subcommittee would study the curriculum content in its particular area of responsibility and recommend revisions. The coordinating committee would consider recommendations from the subcommittees, help the subcommittees identify weaknesses and possible solutions, watch for curricular conflict, duplications and voids, and give broad leadership to curriculum development for the school.

In addition to the curriculum committee and/or subcommittees in a particular school, the school district often has a curriculum coordinating committee with two important functions: (1) to serve as a resource body for the curriculum committees in the various schools of the district, and (2) to coordinate the curricular content of the different schools.

The curriculum coordinating committee ought to have representation from the administration, faculty, student body, and community (perhaps through the PTA or the school board). An administrator can provide insight into such matters as budget, potential facilities, faculty resources, and the like. Teachers can represent the grassroots professional level because they work daily with students and are in close touch with what will and will not work. Students can provide information regarding their interests and relevance of learning experiences. A representative of the public can help interpret the usefulness of curricular content in a practical sense as viewed from outside the school.

The local educational system must be compatible with the basic philosophic values that exist in the locale and comply with the needs and interests of the residents. The curriculum must be consistent also with government legislation and regulations.

CURRICULUM TRENDS AND PATTERNS

A curriculum must have a strong element of stability, and yet it should be gradually improved and updated based on changing circumstances and new information. Some of the current trends in curriculum development are the following:

1. Greater emphasis on physical education at the elementary school level, with concentration on perceptual motor learning and movement education.

2. Increased attention to the individual needs and interests of students, resulting in (a) more student involvement in learning methods, (b) student's choice of activities rather than school-imposed activities, (c) equal opportunities for both sexes, (d) emphasis on physical fitness activities and lifetime sports, and (e) increased use of media for instruction.

3. More flexibility in scheduling in terms of time, space, student grouping patterns, and staff utilization; made possible by the utilization of computers.

4. Increased accountability for the effectiveness of the curriculum and instructional methods. Failure of students to attain minimal proficiency in basic skills—reading, mathematics, sports—has resulted in lawsuits by parents and students. Some states have already passed laws requiring teachers and educational institutions to be accountable for their teaching effectiveness. The use of appropriate performance objectives and effective evaluation are becoming more common as a result of this trend.

Physical educators should be aware of the various curriculum patterns that are common in the schools, and the characteristics of each. Some of the more prevalent patterns are as follow:

1. The *separate subjects* pattern.

   The traditional pattern of curriculum organization.

   Teaching of separate subjects—history, English, physics, physical education—for a set amount of time each day.

   Little attempt made to relate one subject with another.

   Tendency for students to learn isolated facts and skills without perceiving them as being related.

   Physical education sometimes left out due to lack of time.

2. The *broad-fields* pattern.

   Seeks to eliminate sharp lines between subjects: physical science, rather than physics, chemistry, and geology, or fine arts rather than music, art, and drama.

   Helps students see relationships between specific subjects.

   Provides for less subject-matter areas and, therefore, longer time periods for each of the broader areas.

Physical education can be combined with health, safety, and recreation, although health is often combined with the biologic sciences. Experience indicates that both health instruction and physical education are more successful when taught as separate subjects; however, the two subjects logically belong in the same curriculum group.

Requires administrative flexibility in scheduling.

3. The *correlated* (integrated) curriculum.

   Seeks to utilize relationships among subjects without destroying the identity of any one subject, i.e., science, English, and physical education can be combined in the following way:

   Students go on bike, canoe, or pack trips involving physical fitness and the study of geology, astronomy, physics, and photography. Students write reports on their findings. All activities are cooperatively planned by teachers and students.

   More common at the elementary school level.

4. The *experience* (problem-solving) curriculum.

   Seeks to organize learning experiences around situations and problems that confront students in everyday life.

   Based on a humanistic approach to teaching: respect for the individual and his needs.

   Has advantage of being highly relevant to youth.

   Results are doubtful because of large time blocks involved and *lack of continuity* in learning basic skills, which in this method are taught as they are needed.

   More common at the elementary school level.

   Movement education in physical education seems to be a way of relating this philosophy to physical education.

   Interests, needs, and purposes of children determine the educational experience.

   Activities are planned cooperatively by students and teacher. Problem solving is the dominant method.

   Teachers need a broad background in order to serve as resource persons. Administrative efforts must be flexible to meet facility, transportation, scheduling, equipment, and budgetary needs.

SELECTING CONTENT

Determining the content of the curriculum from kindergarten through twelfth grade (and through college), is a complex task. The curriculum must have (1) the proper sequence of learning experiences, (2) the proper breadth and scope, (3) the right kind and amount of emphasis at the different stages of child development, and (4) be practical in terms of weather conditions, facilities, equipment, and faculty resources. Sources of information that can be useful in selecting curriculum content include the following:

1. Teachers' opinions based on their own orientation, their professional preparation, and their evaluation of the students' needs and interests within the framework of what is feasible under the circumstances.
2. Information from questionnaires completed by parents and/or students.
3. Consultation, oral or written, with known experts in the field, whose information and judgment on curriculum matters is respected.
4. Information produced and judgments made by a curriculum committee composed of representation from the administration, faculty, student body and public.
5. Curriculum content recommended in curriculum guides and textbooks on curriculum.

Since the amount of school time that can be allotted to any particular topic is limited, those determining curricular content should be highly selective. Well-defined criteria such as the following, can aid in the selection process.

1. Is the activity consistent with the stated goals of physical education for the school? Will it contribute significantly and consistently to the goals?
2. What are the strengths of the activity, be it physical fitness, lifetime sports skills, social interaction, character development, or the development of useful knowledge, attitudes, and appreciations?
3. Is the activity suitable for the particular student level (state of development), and does it fit properly at this point in the overall curriculum sequence?
4. Is the activity relevant, meaningful, and interesting to students, and do students relate to it, have an interest in it, and see a need for it?
5. Does the activity contribute to a logical sequence of curricular content?
6. Is the activity safe, or under what conditions can it be made safe at an acceptable level?
7. Does the school have the resources—faculty, facilities, equipment, or budget, to sponsor the activity?
8. Is the activity compatible with the local situation; is it within the limits of what the public would perceive as acceptable, useful, important and appropriate?

Other criteria could be listed for any particular situation. If they are relatively complete and sound; then proposed curricular content must measure up when compared to this criteria in order to be justified. It should *not* be assumed that each criterion has the same value in the selection process. It is often a good idea to weight the criteria so that each one carries the influence that it logically deserves. Table 14-2 provides an example of how certain activities were evaluated against selected weighted criteria.

SEQUENCE OF CONTENT

Programs are often planned so that every student experiences at least a minimum of exposure to (1) team sports, (2) individual and dual activities,

TABLE 14-2.

Autumn Program		
Grade 7	Grade 8	Grade 9
Power volleyball skills	Soccer skills and team play	Power volleyball
Soccer skills	Indoor racquet skills	Speedball
Field hockey skills		Football (flag)
	Early Winter Program	
Stunts and tumbling	Basketball team play	Advanced outdoor
Basketball skills	Folk dance	challenges
		Social dance
		Concepts of physical
		education
	Late Winter Program I	
Wrestling skills or	Wrestling skills or	Circuit training
Aerobic dance	Self defense	Floor hockey
	Late Winter Program II	
Gymnastics	Gymnastics	Gymnastics
	Spring Program	
	Computerized AAHPER test administered—2 weeks	
Track and field	Track and field	Paddleball
Outdoor racquet skills	Team handball	Climbing
		Softball

(3) rhythms, and (4) aquatics. Although a minimal exposure may be required, students are usually encouraged to explore activities beyond the minimal level, particularly in areas of the students' primary interests.

Curriculum sequence is the order in which the learning experiences occur. The sequence should be logical and related. One of the weaknesses of physical educators has been a failure to provide a graduated sequence of instruction. Too often, the same basketball unit, for example, has been taught repeatedly without offering new learning experiences. The content of the physical education program should be organized into a continuous flow of experiences through a carefully planned, graduated sequence of skills, knowledge, and fitness levels from preschool through high school and into college. The sequence should be developed in light of the students' needs and interests and built progressively toward the attainment of challenging physical education goals. The following discussion is an overview of recommended program emphasis at the different school levels.

Preschool and Kindergarten

The *emphasis* should be on freedom of movement and basic skills, with attention centered on gross motor patterns (running, walking, crawling, climbing, pushing, pulling, and dodging), balance and stability, gross hand/eye coordination, and the development of selfawareness and expression through movement. The *orientation* should be toward the child as a unique individual with his own physical, mental, emotional, and social needs. The *activities* should emphasize spontaneous movement in an environment that provides opportunities and freedom to explore and create movement patterns. There should be an abundance of vigorous large-muscle activity.

Primary Grades (K-3)

The *emphasis* should still be on fundamental or basic movement patterns, but they should be more continuous and unified. Attention should be given to (1) movement and performance awareness, (2) simple, organized activity concepts, (3) basic rules of safety, and (4) the development of flexibility, agility, balance, and coordination. The *orientation* should still emphasize the child as a unique individual. The *activities* would concentrate on large-muscle development, movement exploration (stunts, tumbling, and creative movements), rhythmic activities (singing games and simple creative and folk dance patterns), and games of low organization or student initiation.[9]

The following activities are recommended for students in the *first* grade:
Throwi   and catching with medium and large balls
Informa. bail handling
Relays
Catching and fleeing
Tag games
Jumping and hopping games
Tumbling skills
Dodging and darting games
Balancing skills
Rope jumping
Playground equipment activities
Body flexibility exercises
Rope climbing and swinging (within safe limits)
Basic rhythmic games and simple dances
Basic soccer-type skills

Intermediate Level (4-6)

The *emphasis* should be on the development and refinement of motor skills, physical fitness, the use of correct body mechanics in basic skills, and the development of activity related concepts, such as rules and basic strategy. The *orientation* should be on a combination of individual development and the individual as a member of the group (social interaction). The *activities* should include a logical sequence of experiences in movement education: basic and creative movements, rhythmic and dance activities of a basic nature, vigorous sports and games of low organization, basic aquatic and gymnastic skills, physical fitness activities and tests, and motor skills.[9]

Some of the specific activities recommended for students in the *fifth* grade are listed:

Dodgeball games
Kickball games
Relays and races
Strength and flexibility exercises
Physical fitness activities and tests
Track and field skills
Gymnastics skills
Tumbling activities
Soccer
Basketball
Volleyball
Softball
Note: In all of the above, the proper progression is especially important.

Junior High School

The *emphasis* should be on (1) the development and maintenance of physical fitness, (2) the development of a wide variety of specific activity skills, (3) a basic knowledge and appreciation of a variety of activities to serve as a base for intelligent choices relative to out-of-class participation, and (4) the development of self-awareness and self-confidence. The *orientation* should be on the individual as an emerging adult in society who needs broad exposure and significant challenges. The *activities* should emphasize the development of a diverse range of human talents and interests, which would form a base for choices and contribute toward a feeling of fulfillment and success. The student's frequent awkwardness should be de-emphasized and the need for social interaction, group involvement, and vigorous participation should receive ample emphasis. Team sports are of obvious importance. The program should also include challenging aquatic activities, graduated stunt, tumbling, and gymnastics skills, combative activities for boys, intermediate level dance activities, outdoor education skills and graduated fitness activities and tests.[21]

Table 14-2 shows a sample program covering the different seasons of the year for grades 7, 8, and 9. It is similar to actual junior high school situations. Even though it may not be an ideal program for any particular situation, it will furnish some useful ideas.

Senior High School (Table 14-3)

The *emphasis* here should be shifted more toward lifetime activities, some vigorous and some less so. Also important is the development of knowledge, understanding, insight, and motivation toward "the active life." Emphasis should continue on graduated physical fitness activities and tests. A reasonable amount of group activities should be included with emphasis on the development of self-confidence, individual initiative, character, and respon-

TABLE 14-3. An example of a structured approach to the evaluation of different sports that could be included in the curriculum. (Courtesy of Professor Jacqueline W. Asbury, Lynchburg College.)

Activity (Girls)	Safety 1–5	Safety 29%	Basic Skills 1–5	Basic Skills 21%	Physical Fitness 1–5	Physical Fitness 18'	Total Involvement 1–5	Total Involvement 15%	Social Interaction 1–5	Social Interaction 9%	Leisure Time Skills, Development 1–5	Leisure Time Skills, Development 8%	Total
Senior High Girls													
Tennis	4.3	124.7	3.7	77.7	3.8	68.4	4.3	64.5	3.1	27.9	3.5	28.0	391.2
Basketball	3.2	92.8	4.0	84.0	4.3	77.4	3.9	58.5	4.6	41.4	4.2	33.6	387.7
Folk Dance	4.6	133.4	3.2	67.2	2.8	50.4	3.1	46.5	4.3	38.7	4.3	34.4	370.6
Square Dance	4.6	133.4	3.1	65.1	2.5	45.0	3.4	51.0	4.3	38.7	4.3	34.4	367.6
Modern Dance	4.6	133.4	3.2	67.2	2.6	46.8	3.4	51.0	3.8	34.2	4.3	34.4	367.0
Soccer	3.1	89.9	4.0	84.0	4.7	84.6	3.9	58.5	3.6	32.4	1.8	14.4	363.8
Floor Exercise	4.1	118.9	4.6	96.6	3.5	63.0	3.1	46.5	2.3	20.7	1.8	14.4	360.1
Volleyball	4.6	133.4	3.8	79.8	2.7	48.6	3.7	55.5	3.3	29.7	1.4	11.2	358.2
Swimming	3.4	98.6	3.2	67.2	3.1	55.8	4.2	63.0	4.7	42.3	3.7	29.6	356.5
Softball	3.6	104.4	3.8	79.8	3.8	68.4	3.6	54.0	2.9	26.1	2.6	20.8	353.5
Badminton	4.3	124.7	3.6	75.6	2.8	50.4	2.7	40.5	2.9	26.1	3.9	31.2	348.5
Tap Dance	4.6	133.4	3.0	63.0	2.7	48.6	2.9	43.5	2.7	24.3	4.3	34.4	347.2
Activity (Boys)													
Senior High Boys													
Basketball	3.5	101.5	4.3	90.3	4.5	81.0	4.0	60.0	4.0	36.0	4.1	32.8	401.6
Speedball	3.9	113.1	3.7	77.7	4.0	72.0	3.8	57.0	3.6	32.4	2.1	16.8	369.0
Soccer	2.9	84.1	4.2	88.2	4.1	73.8	4.0	60.0	3.9	35.1	2.8	22.4	363.6
Volleyball	4.0	116.0	3.4	71.4	3.0	54.0	3.9	58.5	3.7	33.3	3.6	28.8	362.0
Flag Football	3.0	87.0	4.0	84.0	3.7	66.6	4.0	60.0	3.9	35.1	2.7	21.6	354.3
Softball	3.5	101.5	3.9	81.9	3.0	54.0	3.4	51.0	3.6	32.4	3.8	30.4	351.2
Calisthenics	4.2	121.8	2.3	48.3	4.1	73.8	3.8	57.0	2.2	19.8	2.8	22.4	343.1
Square Dance	4.5	130.5	2.6	54.6	2.0	36.0	3.9	58.5	3.9	35.1	3.0	24.0	338.7
Running	4.2	121.8	1.9	39.9	4.2	75.6	3.9	58.5	1.7	15.3	3.4	27.2	338.3
Modern Dance	4.5	130.5	2.7	56.7	2.8	50.4	3.3	49.5	3.3	29.7	2.6	20.8	337.6
Wrestling	2.7	78.3	4.2	88.2	4.5	81.0	3.1	46.5	2.4	21.6	2.0	16.0	331.6
Badminton	4.2	121.8	3.1	65.1	2.8	50.4	3.0	45.0	2.5	22.5	3.3	26.4	331.2

sibility to one's self and to others. The *orientation* should be toward the individual as a capable pursuer of activities appropriate for his own needs and interests when given options to choose. The *activities* should include a wide range of graduated participation opportunities in lifetime sports, physical fitness, combatives and self-defense, aquatics, gymnastics, creative and social type dance, vigorous team sports, and challenging outdoor activities.[21]

College

The *emphasis* in college should be much the same as in high school except with more orientation toward lifetime activities in all of the different aspects of the program (team sports, individual sports, aquatics, dance and outdoor skills); and physical fitness, with concentration on the underlying concepts and the ability to design and follow through with a lifetime individualized fitness program. The orientation should be toward the students' needs to gain insight into their future as nonstudents in terms of (1) physical fitness needs, (2) the aging process, (3) potential participation opportunities outside of the school, and (4) the scientific and social concepts that should serve as a basis for selecting from the available activity options. During the course of all this, the selected *activities* should promote the idea of active participation for the pure joy of it. The "enrichment of life" concept should be carefully interwoven into the whole program.

PROFESSIONAL EMPHASIS

During the last few years, there has been a strong upsurge in the emphasis on *athletic training*. This has resulted largely from a combination of two trends: (a) pressure from outside the schools (including lawsuits and threatened lawsuits) to have more and better athletic training offered in the schools, and (b) the significant expansion of athletic competition for girls and women. To accommodate the increased need for athletic trainers, many universities have added athletic training certification programs.

The concept of *movement education* has become well established as the core of the physical education program at the elementary school level. Much information has been gained about the need for physical education at this level, and there have been vast improvements in elementary programs; however, physical education at the elementary level is still lagging.

The two relatively new subject areas, *motor learning* and *biomechanics*, are already well developed, which has had a strengthening influence on professional preparation programs. Further development of these subjects will undoubtedly occur during the foreseeable future.

Some universities have instituted an *athletic coaching* emphasis or a coaching major, which is separate from the physical education teaching major. Typically, the coaching major is designed for one who desires to coach athletics and teach subjects other than physical education. Many school administrators have encouraged this—they need a pool of athletic coaches that extends beyond the physical education staff. Some physical educators do not want to coach and some are not successful at it. Some athletic coaches do not take physical education seriously, whereas they would be serious about teaching a classroom subject.

Commercial physical education is another area in which some universities are offering majors. This has been encouraged by the upsurge of employment opportunities at spas, racquet clubs, golf courses, and the like.

SUBSTITUTES FOR PHYSICAL EDUCATION

Practically every educational system has requests for substitutions for participation in the physical education instructional program, including athletic teams, ROTC, and marching band. These requests should always be evaluated on the basis of the following questions: (1) Does the proposed substitute contribute satisfactorily to the objectives of physical education? (2) If not, what special contribution does it make toward student development that would justify this substitution? Unless the answers to these questions are acceptable, the substitute should be denied.

BIBLIOGRAPHY

1. AAHPERD: Curriculum design: purposes and processes in physical education teaching-learning, Washington, D.C., 1977.

2. AAHPERD: Guide to excellence for physical education in colleges and universities, Washington, D.C., 1970.

3. AAHPERD: Guidelines for secondary school physical education. Washington, D.C., 1970.

4. AAHPERD: Ideas for secondary school physical education, Washington, D.C., 1976.

5. AAHPERD: Personalized learning in physical education., Washington, D.C., 1976.

6. AAHPERD: State legal requirements for physical education, Washington, D.C., (Update by Clayne Jensen, 1980).

7. Abercrombie, E.: Curriculum innovation. JOPER, *50* (7):66, 1979.

8. American Association of School Administrators: Imperatives in Education. Washington, D.C., 1966, Foreword.

9. Annarino, A.A., Cowell, C. C., and Hazelton, H. W.: Curriculum Theory and Design in Physical Education. St. Louis, The C. V. Mosby Company, 1980.

10. Annarino, A. A., and Otto, S.: Curriculum development. Physical Educator, *34*:51, 1977.

11. Bain, L: Description of the hidden curriculum in secondary physical education. Research Quarterly, Washington, D.C., AAHPER, *47*:154, 1976.

12. Calgary Board of Education (Canada): Physical Education Curriculum Action Project, 1978.

13. Commission on Reorganization of Secondary Education: Cardinal Principles of Secondary Education. Washington, D.C.: U.S. Government Printing Office, 1918.

14. Crase, D.: Development activities: a hedge against complaceny. JOPER, *51* (9):53, 1980.

15. Daquila, E., Lubowicki, D., and Ritzie, S.: Celebrating adapted physical education and therapeutic recreation. JOPER, *51* (8):65, 1980.

16. Educational Policies Commission: The Purposes of Education in American Democracy. Washington, D.C., National Education Association, 1938, pp. 9, 24.

17. Gallahue, D.L.: Aims of physical education. Physical Educator, *33:*170, 1976.

18. Gaudiano, M.: High risk activities in physical education. Physical Educator, *37:*128, 1980.

19. Institute for Educational Management: Imperative needs of secondary youth, International University, San Diego, CA., 1980.

20. Knowles, C.J.: Concerns of teachers about implementing individualized instruction in the physical education setting. Research Quarterly for Exercise and Sport, *52* (1):48, 1981.

21. Melograno, V.: Designing Curriculum and Learning: A Physical Education Approach, IA, Dubuque, Kendall/Hunt Publishing Company, 1979.

22. Mikkelson, M.D.: Coed gym—it's a whole new ballgame. JOPER, *50* (8):63, 1979.

23. Olson, G.M.: Physical education for the small school system. JOPER, *51* (5):24, 1980.

24. Sanborn, M.A., and Hartman, B.G.: Issues in Physical Education, 3rd Ed. Philadelphia, Lea & Febiger, 1982.

25. Sanborn, M.A., and Meyer, C.L.: Curricular constructs and parameters for today's physical education. JOPER, *51* (7):42, 1980.

26. Siedentop, D.: Physical education curriculum: an analysis of the past. JOPER, *51* (7):40, 1980.

27. Swanson, J.: Developing and implementing objectives in physical education. JOPER, *50:*68, 1979.

28. Ward, D., and McClenaghan, R.C.: Special programs for special people: ideas for extending the physical education program. Physical Educator, *37:*48, 1980.

Chapter *15*

THE SCHOOL
ATHLETIC PROGRAM

It has been said about *work* that what one receives for doing it is less important than what the work causes the person to become. This concept also applies to athletics. Fortunately, most educators recognize that what is achieved in the win-loss column is of only transitory importance, whereas the experiences that contribute to the development of the individual have long-term significance for both the person and society. In spite of the validity of this concept, however, it must be tempered by the idea that most of the deeper values accrued from athletics can be achieved just as well or better while winning than while losing. After all, one of the obvious reasons for athletics is to achieve excellence, and winning is a natural product of excellence.

Some of the ingredients of a successful athletic program are obvious, but much is relatively unapparent. The obvious portion of a successful program, and the most important part in the minds of the fans, is made up of the competitors and coaches. Forming the base and providing the support for these obvious benefits are such things as (1) school pride and tradition, (2) the philosophy that underlies the program and is integrated through it, and (3) administrative support from various levels of the larger organization.

VALUE OF ATHLETICS

Educators have supported competitive athletics for many reasons. Some concentrate on the entertainment value, and who would deny that athletics can have this effect. Some sight the goodwill of the alumni, and a prominent athletic program surely builds alumni loyalty. Others refer to the importance of successful athletics in promoting a fund-raising program, and there is evidence of a direct correlation between the success of many fund-raising efforts and the success enjoyed on the athletic field. All of these reasons are persuasive, but they are not the most important.

The principal reason that educators ought to support competitive athletics is that athletics can be among the most effective ways we have of teaching some profound principles of life. Following are several examples.

242

Conditioning and the Law of the Harvest

We have all heard of the law of the harvest: "whatsoever ye sow, that shall ye also reap.[11]

This principle is illustrated in the conditioning of athletes. Imagine, for example, a photograph of a highly conditioned athlete racing to victory in a distance event. The caption might well read, "victor paid price." Successful athletes do "pay the price" through the hard work of conditioning, both physically and mentally. This is nowhere more evident than in individual sports, such as swimming, wrestling, gymnastics, golf, and track.

Teamwork

Team sports teach teamwork more effectively than practically any other medium. Team sports such as basketball, football, baseball, and soccer have the greatest attraction for the athletic spectator because these sports move fast and are particularly entertaining. Team sports are, however, a means of teaching some useful lessons.

For many, teamwork means the thrill of the well-executed play, with each member of the team performing his assigned task with diligence and precision. Can anything compare with the excitement we experience when what started out to be a run up the middle for short yardage turns into a game-winning 80-yard touchdown due to teamwork, where every player carried out his assignment to perfection? The same lesson is taught by a precisely executed pass by a wingman in soccer for a quick goal or by a stunning assist on the basketball court.

Teamwork by definition requires a united effort; and sometimes, a majority willing to perform quietly and effectively in the background, as for example the linemen in football. The names of the quarterback, running backs, and receivers are well known, but the hard-working linemen who provide pass protection and blocking are less known. Careful watchers of the game realize how important they are and when even one of them lets down, the total effort is frustrated. A group of players who fails to learn the importance of team play will never be successful.

Preparation

Even a person unfamiliar with athletics can sense the importance of training and preparation. An individual or team who has failed to train—to practice and prepare—will be a witness to their own shortcoming. Imagine, for example, the negative effect of lack of preparation in a wrestler whose skill is good enough to carry him through to victory, but in the third period his muscle and sinew become unable to respond due to insufficient conditioning. The opponent, who is less deserving in terms of skill and potential, becomes the victor. It is not uncommon to see a young athlete in the quarter-mile run who has less speed and less potential for that event emerge as the champion in the final stretch due to dedicated preparation.

Opportunities occur in life on which we can capitalize if we are prepared. We must be ready to pick up the ball and run with it all the way to the goal line. Such opportunities sometimes come with bewildering speed at unexpected times and places. The variations are endless, but the question is the same. Will you be prepared?

Extra-Effort Determination

One of the most exciting characteristics of an athletic contest is the opportunity it affords the players to demonstrate the significance of extra effort. Who has not thrilled at the gymnast or golfer who refuses to crack under extreme pressure; the tennis player who is in his fifth set of a close match, when even the mildest lack of determination can result in a loss; the cross country runner who consistently grinds out 5 to 10 miles a day in a training program; or the powerful and determined running back who can carry tacklers with him by force and determination for an extra yard.

This kind of extra effort applies to almost all activities of life. Many people fail to amount to much because of their half-hearted efforts, and many others, less talented, achieve success and distinction because of their extraordinary determination. There is more of everything for the man or woman who makes the extra effort, and that includes more success, more achievement, and more satisfaction.

Playing By the Rules

Athletic participation teaches us the importance of playing by the rules. A maximum effort is hoped for, but the effort must be within the area marked out for the play of the game. A brilliant defensive effort by a basketball player is of no value if he commits a foul in the process. A swimmer can put in an excellent performance but end up being disqualified if he does an illegal turn. The football player who tackles improperly or blocks from the wrong angle, can incur a severe penalty that will nullify any gain the team has made.

In all activities of life, if we fail to observe the rules, we bring a penalty of some kind upon ourselves and our team.

Defenses Against Discouragement

Another important lesson that athletics can teach is how to withstand stress and potential discouragement. We have all seen teams that slowed down or stopped when things went wrong. Crowds headed for the door mid-way through the fourth quarter, acting on their judgment that the team had stopped trying, that it was discouraged and so were they. We have also thrilled at the opposite—the team that never stops trying, never concedes defeat until the last second has expired.

Competitive athletics have great entertainment value, build loyalty in the alumni, promote fund-raising programs, and contribute to the morale of the student body. The most important contribution of athletics, however, is teaching the essential lessons of life—the lessons that make the difference between failure and success.

GOALS FOR THE PROGRAM

Interschool athletics is generally considered an integral part of the total educational process, which has as its aim the development of physically, mentally, socially, and morally fit individuals. Athletics can serve as a vital educational training ground, incorporating the following worthy goals[4]:

1. To nurture and properly channel the competitive urge that is inherent in all of us.
2. To engender in youth the will to win, by fair and honest means.
3. To promote pride in successful effort for the sake of accomplishment.
4. To build team spirit and desire on the part of those who engage in sports, to work with each other in a cooperative effort.
5. To teach self-discipline and self-control.
6. To develop morale and mold character.
7. To build sound minds and bodies through mental and physical preparation for competition.
8. To encourage spectators and nonparticipants to take an interest in and appreciate the values of competitive sports.
9. To stimulate a continuing institutional interest and loyalty among students, alumni, and friends.

The program should be designed to develop:

Loyalty to purpose
Respect for discipline
Capacity to lead and direct
Respect for rules and authority
Ability to act effectively under stress
Capacity for self-discipline in the interests of accomplishment
Determination to overcome obstacles
Sportsmanship—the "Golden Rule" in practice
Enduring relationships with teammates
Health, strength, and bodily vigor

AREAS OF RESPONSIBILITY

Coaches provide the direct leadership for the athletic teams, but certain school administrators also have important responsibilities.

School Superintendent (Or College President)

The school superintendent has the following important duties in connection with athletics (in an institution of higher education, the president would have essentially the same responsibilities): to (1) clarify and communicate the role of athletics in the particular school system; (2) establish and communicate the athletic responsibilities of the various personnel; (3) evaluate the accomplishments of athletics in terms of its contributions to the educational goals and the welfare of the educational system; (4) maintain a high level of leadership in the athletic program; (5) establish a framework of policies for the provision and use of athletic facilities; (6) make sure that an effective program of public relations in connection with athletics is maintained; (7) give leadership to the basic aspects of the budget, and determine methods by which the program should be financed; (8) establish policies in connection with such matters as the safety of athletic participants, the balance of athletic opportunities for boys and girls, and the scope of the total program; and (9) be accountable to the governing board for all aspects of athletics within the school system.

School Principal

The principal shares with the superintendent some of the responsibilities indicated; however, through cooperation with the school athletic council (if one exists) and the athletic staff, the principal is concerned with more specific problems and procedures than is the superintendent. These include: (1) certifying the eligibility of players; (2) defining responsibilities of athletic personnel; (3) supervising the faculty members involved; (4) giving administrative leadership in terms of crowd control and ethical behavior; (5) making and enforcing policies relative to the use and care of facilities and equipment; and (6) involvement with the selection and hiring of athletic staff members. At the college or university level, these responsibilities are performed by designated middle level administrators.

Athletic Director (and Assistants)

The athletic director is the one responsible for the direct administration and close supervision of the athletic program. Among the director's major responsibilities are (1) scheduling and contracting contests; (2) arranging for officials in accordance with the correct procedures; (3) establishing travel schedules and enforcing travel policies; (4) maintaining athletic eligibility lists; (5) making certain that the program is conducted in full compliance with the rules; (6) preparing for athletic contests and providing administrative supervision of them; (7) providing adequate athletic training and medical services; (8) preparing and administering the budget; (9) properly reporting accidents; (10) providing leadership to an effective public relations effort; (11) supervising coaches in their various responsibilities; (12) evaluating the coaches and trying to help them improve their procedures and effectiveness.

Often an *associate* or *assistant athletic director* carries a portion of the administrative load as delegated by the director. Also, large programs, particularly at the university level, include a business manager, who is responsible primarily for financial matters; a *sports information director*, whose responsibilities include working with the news media; and sometimes, a special events director, who has the responsibility for promotion and management of the athletic contests, the sale of tickets, and the supervision of facilities.

Some of those in administrative positions also have coaching assignments. When the athletic director is also a coach, he must be objective and fair in providing balanced administrative support for the total program. Too often the administrator/coach has used the administrative position to provide disproportionate support for his particular sport at the expense of other sports. Whether or not the athletic administrator should have a coaching assignment cannot be clearly answered. Often, that person's coaching expertise is needed. It is a matter that should be handled with discretion and good judgment in each situation.

Typically, administrators of athletics are former coaches who decided to become administrators when the opportunity arose. An athletic director's job requires many of the same skills and competencies as other administrative positions. Experience as a coach may give an administrator added insight; but a successful coaching career does not guarantee a successful administrative one.

Athletic Coach

Coaching involves a unique combination of teaching and managing. Unfortunately, some people have the idea that a coach is not a teacher. In fact, some of the most sophisticated and individualized teaching methods are applied in athletics. If athletics is to be justified in the educational system, it must be conducted in an educational manner and contribute toward educational goals. Athletics are co-curricular in nature, and they tend to have broad appeal beyond the confines of the school; but at the core of the program is a professional educator (the coach), working with students in a school setting for the purpose of accomplishing the objectives of the educational system. Normally, the coach is required to have the same kind of professional preparation as other members of the faculty, and he holds faculty status. The coach is responsible for (1) maintaining a wholesome educational environment; (2) establishing effective teacher/student relationships; and (3) producing acceptable educational results.

Sometimes a coaching assignment is given to a person who is not competent in the particular sport. This diluted approach, which may be the only alternative to not offering the program at all, results in the supervision of students in a self-teaching exercise without the benefit of a subject specialist to guide effective learning experiences. Students would learn little about English in a class that was simply supervised by a nonspecialist. The same is true of athletics. If a sport is to flourish and if the students are to develop a high level of competency in it, the coach must be a well-prepared specialist.

The professional preparation of athletic coaches is just as important as the preparation of biology teachers, English teachers, or counselors. All else being equal, the best coach is the one who has had the best preparation. Generally, a coach needs three basic kinds of information: (1) thorough knowledge about the nature of the sport, its rules, skills, techniques, and strategy; (2) adequate understanding of people, particularly the age group being coached; and (3) knowledge about the physiologic and psychologic preparation for athletic competition. The coach's success depends to a large extent on the amount of knowledge he has acquired and on how well he is able to apply it. In athletics, as in other phases of education, leadership is the key element in success.

Athletic Council Members

Athletic councils (or committees) are prevalent in colleges and universities, and many exist in the secondary schools. Generally, they are advisory in nature, with their advice flowing to the chief administrator of the educational system. For example, a university athletic council is typically advisory to the university vice-president, dean, athletic director, and coaches; whereas a school district athletic council is advisory to the superintendent, principals, athletic directors, and coaches. In some cases, the council is more than advisory. It gets involved in making and enforcing policies. Whatever the case, it is important that the role and perimeters of the council be clearly defined.

An athletic council is composed primarily of nonathletic personnel. It is designed to give others in the school system (and sometimes representatives from the community) an opportunity to exert influence on the athletic program. This helps to keep athletics in proper perspective and integrated with other aspects of education.

At a university, the council normally includes representatives from the administration, the athletic department, and booster group, the alumni, the student body, and the faculty/staff at large. At the secondary school level, the council includes selected members from the administration, the board of education, the athletic program, the faculty, the student body, and the public (or boosters).

GOVERNING ORGANIZATIONS

Descriptions of selected organizations involved in coordinating and regulating athletics at various levels are given in the Appendices. It is recommended that, in connection with this section, the reader review especially Appendix A.

High School Leagues

For high school athletics, local leagues are formed to enhance scheduling, provide league championship competition and implement useful policies and procedures. In some cases, a district or regional organization encompasses several leagues. Such organizations serve essentially the same purpose as local leagues except on a broader scale. They are the next step of competition.

High schools are classified for purposes of athletic competition on the basis of selected criteria, with size of student body being the most influential factor. In a state with four classifications, the divisions might be I-A, 2-A, 3-A, and 4-A, with 4-A designating the larger schools. The divisions are aligned in various ways and given different labels, depending on the state. Divisions are determined primarily by school population, with geographic location also being a consideration.

State championships are sponsored in a variety of sports in most states. In a few of the larger states, it is not practical to complete all of the competition necessary to determine the state champions, therefore, regional championships are the highest level of competition.

Championships beyond the local league are sponsored under the auspices of the State High School Athletic Association. The three kinds of high school athletic associations are (1) those affiliated with the State Department of Education; (2) those affiliated with a state university (few of these); and (3) those that are unaffiliated (volunteer and not established by law). Most of the state associations are of the third kind—voluntary in nature.

In cases where the state association is affiliated with the Department of Education or with a university, membership in the association is automatic for all public schools, with private and parochial schools having the option of joining. In a voluntary state association, each school or at least each school district has a choice of whether to belong. In practically all cases, schools choose to belong because of the advantages among which are the following:

1. Eligibility for participation in state championship athletic events.
2. Enforcement of regulations for the conduct of athletics.
3. Sponsorship of a classification plan for high schools.
4. Certification and assignment of athletic officials.
5. Enforcement of athletic standards.
6. Published bulletins and newsletters.
7. A final authority for the resolution of questions, controversies, and appeals.

Member schools have some obligations in return, which include compliance with all regulations of the association, cooperation, support, and loyalty.

College Athletic Conferences

Colleges and universities (including junior colleges) are organized into athletic leagues (usually called conferences), through mutual agreement of the member institutions. The conference is governed in accordance with a written constitution and a regulatory code.

The conference is administered under the jurisdiction of one or more governing boards known as a Conference Council and/or President's Council (some conferences have both). If the conference is large enough to employ an administrator, this person is known as the Conference Commissioner. The Commissioner administers the business of the conference. The larger university conferences have a conference staff of six or more people.

Some institutions do not belong to conferences. They remain disaffiliated or unattached, and are known as independents. Teams such as Army, Boston College, Florida State, Marquette, Navy, Notre Dame, Penn State, Pittsburg, Rutgers, and Tulane are just a few that feel it is better to remain independent.

In addition to belonging to athletic conferences, colleges and universities are affiliated with the appropriate national governing organization. For intercollegiate athletics, this means affiliation with one of the following. National Junior College Athletic Association (NJCAA); National Intercollegiate Athletic Association (NIAA); or the National Collegiate Athletic Association (NCAA). Within certain of these national organizations, the member institutions are classified into divisions according to their athletic prominence or to their emphasis on athletics. These national organizations are made up of colleges and universities, not of athletic conferences; but conferences become affiliates of the national organization.

Advantages of Leagues

When a high school or college acquires membership in an athletic league (or conference), the school is obligated to fulfill all requirements of the particular league.

Most athletic personnel agree that the ideal size of a high school league is six to eight schools. College leagues function especially well with eight schools. This size permits a complete round of competition in football and certain other sports, and it permits a home and home arrangement in sports like basketball. In addition, this size of league enhances championship meets in individual sports such as track, swimming, and wrestling.

League schedules are usually prepared by an individual or a committee, and are subject to approval by the appropriate representatives of the various schools. Nonleague contests are arranged by the officials of the two schools involved. Important considerations in selecting nonleague opponents include (1) schools of approximately the same size and with similar athletic programs and facilities; (2) schools that provide natural rivalries; (3) schools that have positive relationships with each other; and (4) schools that are in locations that afford interesting trips without excessive travel.

REGULATIONS AND RULES

The athletic governing organizations establish and enforce regulations for member schools. This was one of the reasons for establishing governing organizations at the different levels. Among the purposes of the regulations are (1) to standardize athletic programs and procedures; (2) to protect student athletes and school personnel against possible abuses of athletics; and (3) to help keep athletics in the proper perspective in the educational setting. The regulations are especially valuable in protecting students, coaches, and administrators against exploitation.

Some of the regulations apply to individuals whereas others apply to schools. Regulations that apply to individuals often deal with the following: (1) age of the athlete; (2) completion of a minimum number of units with an acceptable grade point average; (3) current registration for a specified number of units (minimum full-time student status); (4) parental permission to participate; (5) amateur status; (6) disaffiliation with nonschool teams during the athletic season; and, (7) adherence to transfer rules.

Regulations that pertain to schools typically relate to the following: (1) conditions governing athletic events; (2) limitation of the number and value of athletic awards; (3) use of official athletic contracts; (4) exchange of eligibility lists; (5) control (of prohibition) of postseason games; (6) limitation of the number of contests and the length of season; and (7) specified number of practices prior to the opening contest.

Eligibility

The standards or requirements for athletic eligibility are defined by the particular governing organizations. For example, a university affiliated with an athletic conference and with the NCAA must make sure that the eligibility requirements of both the Conference and the NCAA are strictly enforced. At the high school level, the local league might have certain eligibility regulations in addition to those of the State High School Athletic Association.

The eligibility standards should be reasonable and functional; but once they are established, they must be lived by impeccably. Individuals and institutions are expected to police themselves, although each governing organization has a penalty system for those who violate eligibility rules.

Athletic coaches and administrators must be well informed about the eligibility rules and in total compliance with them. Athletes and their parents must be provided with information on eligibility pertinent to them.

Recruiting

Recruiting is not (or should not be) an element in high school athletics, but at the college and university level, recruiting has become an important aspect of athletic success. Many, including some athletic directors and coaches, feel that recruiting has become both dominant and distasteful. They would like to deemphasize its importance, but do not know how to do so.

Precise regulations are associated with recruiting about which athletic personnel need to be well informed. Administrators beyond the athletic department level must also show serious concern about adherence to recruiting regulations (and all other regulations) to make certain that the athletic program is conducted in accordance with the rules.

WOMEN IN COMPETITIVE SPORTS

Competitive athletics for women has developed slowly. Different leaders and different segments of society have had difficulty agreeing on the involvement of women in athletics. Early advocates of athletics for women experienced a long and hard struggle, and met with little success. During recent times, however, athletic competition for women has escalated rapidly and that trend is continuing.

Women first entered international Olympic competition in 1900 with 12 entries in two events. This milestone turned out to be an exception rather than a rule, because during the several subsequent decades, there was little expansion in opportunities for women. Some momentum was gained following World War II, but still not much happened.

Around 1970, controversy arose about the tremendous differences between athletic opportunities for men and women. The mode of the time emphasized equal rights and equal opportunities regardless of race, creed, or sex. A strong base was laid during the early 1970s, and during the last half of the decade, athletics for women entered a new era. There were several forces behind the movement; probably the most prominent of which was the passage of Title IX of the Educational Act of 1975. Subsequent interpretations of the Title IX regulations have had unusual significance in the athletic world (see the last section of this chapter)

ATHLETICS IN JUNIOR HIGH SCHOOLS

The question of whether junior high schools should sponsor interschool athletic programs and if so, to what extent and under what conditions, has received much attention and is still controversial.

Athletic programs in junior high schools should be conducted under essentially the same sound principles and procedures that are expected at the senior high school level. The main differences ought to relate to the fact that the younger students are generally less prepared physiologically and psychologically for intense competition, and there is less justification to emphasize specialization in athletics at this early age. Therefore, the junior high school program ought to be less intense (more fun oriented), less restricting in terms of specilization, and less demanding physiologically, mentally, and emotionally.

SOURCES OF FUNDING

For the majority of athletic programs, the main source of funding is from appropriated budgetary funds. Supplemental sources, which vary in significance in different situations, include (1) gate receipts; (2) donations; (3) concessions; (4) parking fees; and (5) revenue from special projects sponsored by the booster club, student body, or members of athletic teams. It is usually preferable to have all forms of revenue associated with athletics deposited in the school's general fund and, in turn, have the athletic program managed exclusively on a planned and approved budget. The alternate approach is filled with potential hazard, because if the program depends directly on a variety of nonbudgeted sources, large variations can result in the amount of funding from year to year. Obviously, this would be disruptive in terms of planning and continuity. Also, if the program depends heavily on nonappropriated sources, it is easy for athletic personnel to become obsessed with producing revenue instead of providing the high quality educational leadership that is needed and expected. Outside interests that help with nonappropriated funding sometimes become too involved in athletic policies and procedures. More information about funding is provided in Chapter 9.

Within the basic philosophy described, sponsoring certain fund-raising events can be desirable for two reasons: (1) they can provide funds for some *extras* in the program that otherwise would not be possible; and (2) special fund-raising events can have a *rallying effect* for the program. Here are some ideas that have proven effective in both high school and college programs:

1. *Jog-a-thons (mini-marathons) or swim-a-thons.* Funds can be raised either from the participants paying entry fees or having the participants solicit sponsors who pay a specified amount per mile covered by the participant (or per lap in the case of swimming). Certain events of this kind produce several thousand dollars profit.
2. *Athletic youth camps.* These have become common at colleges and universities, and often a portion of the revenue goes to athletics. Some high schools have also become involved.
3. *Celebrity golf tournaments.* Two potential sources of income exist here: (a) golf enthusiasts pay a specified fee to play in a foursome with a celebrity; and (b) if the field of participants justifies it, admission tickets can be charged.
4. *Special food events* such as ox roasts, chicken frys and hot dog dinners are often sponsored. The tickets are priced to produce a profit. Arrangements can usually be made to have the food contributed by local merchants.
5. Raffles are sometimes held in conjunction with the events described in number 4. The items given away are usually donated by local sporting goods vendors and other merchants. Sometimes a large item like an automobile is given as the grand prize.
6. *Novelty athletic events* such as the Harlem Globetrotters, donkey softball, or varsity vs. alumni games are often successful.
7. *Concession stands* are sometimes manned at university events by high school students or members of the high school's booster club. Sales of printed programs, souvenirs, and folding chair seats offer possibilities.

ATHLETIC AWARDS

We like to think that the joy and satisfaction of participation in school athletics is sufficient reward for the time and effort spent. An athletic letter or other similar award is highly meaningful, however, because it is a symbol of achievement and represents a standard of excellence. In spite of the desirability of a well-managed awards program, some problems are associated with it, especially the following: (1) having clearly defined criteria, which allow the awards program to serve its purpose well and which are fair and just for the student athletes; and (2) the question of how much the awards program costs the school and whether this money could be better spent in other ways. Fortunately, the National Federation of State High School Athletic Associations and its counterparts at the intercollegiate athletic level place an upper limit on the monetary value of athletic awards. The rationale is to preserve amateurism; however, such organizations are also concerned about budgetary and other problems that would surface if desirable limits were not imposed on athletic awards.

Some Guiding Principles

1. Awards should serve as symbols of achievement and have little monetary value.
2. The primary goal of student athletes should be the joy and satisfaction derived from participation and achievement, of which an athletic award is no more than a symbol.
3. Opportunities should be provided for an ample number of students to earn awards, yet the criteria should not be diluted to the extent that the awards become meaningless.
4. Good citizenship should be considered along with athletic participation and achievement.
5. No distinction should be made between awards for different sports or for different levels of achievement, because the lesser awards, then become meaningless, perhaps even unwanted.
6. An award should be given for recognized academic achievement, such as academic-all-conference and academic all-Americans.

Specific Requirements (Criteria)

The requirements for earning an award should be specific but simple. The following are suggested, and they apply equally well to boys and girls in the appropriate sports. The criteria are skeletal, and not all sports are included, but the list provides a sampling of the kind of criteria recommended.

Football. Participation in at least one third of the quarters played by the team in the total schedule.

Basketball. Participation in at least one third of the quarters played by the team in the total schedule, or participation in the state tournament.

Baseball. Participation in at least one fourth of the innings or one third of the games played by the team in the total schedule, or participation in state final. Exception: Pitchers may be recommended for letters without an established requirement of participation. No more than two base coaches may be recommended for letters without an established requirement of participation.

Track. Score an average of two points for the dual meets in the total schedule of the team or qualify in the district or league meet.

Swimming. Score an average of two points for the dual meets in the total schedule of the team or qualify in the state meet.

Tennis. Participation in at least one half of the matches played by the team in the total schedule.

Cross Country. Participation in at least one half of the meets run by the team in the total schedule and finishing among the first seven of his or her school in one half the meets.

Soccer. Participation in at least one half of the halves played by the team in the total schedule.

Wrestling. (a) Score points in each match according to the rules—2 for draw, 3 for decision, 5 for pin; (b) if no points are scored, one point per match will be awarded for participation; (c) a letter will be awarded for averaging one point per match in the total schedule of the team or for scoring two or more points in the district meet.

Service Letter. May be awarded to a student who has been faithful in practice and participation for at least 2 years and has completed the sport season during the senior year without having reached the required standards, either because of injury or lack of skill.

Manager's Letter. May be awarded for a minimum of one season of service as team manager and such letters shall be limited to not more than two per year.

ADDITIONAL REMUNERATION FOR COACHES

Athletic coaches in the public schools put in many after-school hours. They should have some reasonable trade-off for the extra time or a sound formula for additional compensation.

In some cases, coaches are allowed free periods to compensate for the after school hours. Sometimes the plan involves a combination of free periods and extra compensation. The most common is to provide extra compensation in addition to the regular teaching salary. Whatever plan is used, it must be equitable in view of the professional preparation and experience of the individual and the amount and kind of extra services he performs.

A relatively unsophisticated method is to offer the coach a flat salary for his services. This figure is usually arrived at on the basis of merit and is increased based on the quality of the prior years' work. Using a multiplier, which relates to base salary and also includes steps for years of service is a better approach. Such a method is based on the concept that the teacher should be fairly compensated for the fractional amount of time spent and in accordance with his base salary schedule. As the teacher's base salary increases, the extra compensation increases a proportional amount.

The following formula provides a recommended method of calculating extra compensation for extra work. This method can be used with other subjects besides athletics; such as for a language teacher who works extra hours with the language club, or the forensics teacher who coaches the debate team.

Number of hours per day in the extra activity / Number of hours in the school day × Length of the extra activity per year (weeks or months) / Length of the normal school year = Time Index

$$\frac{\text{Number of hours}}{\text{Number of hours}} \times \frac{\text{Length of the extra}}{\text{Length of the normal}} = \frac{\text{Time}}{\text{Index}}$$

For example, the wrestling coach spends 2 hours per day with his team; the work day is 8 hours. The wrestling season lasts 4.5 months, and the school year lasts 9 months.

$$\frac{2}{8} \times \frac{4.5}{9} = \text{Time Index} = .125$$

If the coach's base salary were $18,000, his extra compensation would amount to $2,250. ($18,000 × .125 = $2,250).

PRINCIPLES PERTAINING TO ATHLETICS

1. In terms of relative importance, the "person" should come first, then the "student," and then the "athlete."
2. Interschool athletics should be based on the spirit of nonprofessionalism, so that participation is regarded as important for its own sake and for the personal development and enjoyment that it brings.
3. In order to help avoid undesirable exploitation of school athletics, the program should be confined to events that are sponsored and supervised by the appropriate school authorities.
4. The program should be planned so that it will provide opportunities for many individuals in a variety of sports, with reasonable season limits placed on each sport.
5. Integrated throughout the athletic program should be the important concepts of fair play, ethical conduct, and good citizenship.
6. The cost per student for athletic facilities is considerably higher than for other areas of the school program. Administrators and athletic personnel ought to take this into consideration and make sure the public gets a good educational return on the financial investment.
7. Interschool athletics should be viewed as part of the broad program of physical education. Ideally, the total program should constitute a pyramid of four phases with interschool athletics at the apex. Other elements of the pyramid include club and extramural sports, intramural sports, and the sports instructional and fitness program.
8. Under high-quality leadership, athletics has potential for favorable influence on both participants and fans, more potent than most of us realize.
9. A distinct difference exists in the basic purposes of amateur and professional athletics. The main purpose of amateur athletics is development of the individual, and the main purpose of professional athletics is the production of a profit. This does not mean that amateur events should

not produce a profit when possible, and neither does it mean that professional athletics should not emphasize development of the individual. Both forms of athletics should be enjoyable both for participants and spectators. In spite of the similarities, however, the basic purposes are different.

10. School athletics should be viewed as an integral part of the total educational program and conducted in a manner that can be justified on an educational basis.

11. Athletics should always be conducted in accordance with both the letter and the spirit of the rules and regulations under which the program is sponsored.

12. The athletic program should be as broad-based as possible, so that it will meet the needs and interests of a large spectrum of the student body. The emphasis placed on the various sports in the program should be appropriately balanced and kept in the proper perspective, and the emphasis should relate closely to the program objectives.

13. All around physical fitness, lifetime skill development, and recreational participation are important aspects of the broad program of physical education. Members of competitive teams should not be deprived of these important educational opportunities.

14. Efficiency and effectiveness are important in order to provide the best program for the greatest number with the amount of resources available.

PRECAUTIONS

Athletic leaders and school administrators must constantly safeguard against certain bad practices and false values. Among these are (1) overemphasis on winning at the expense of other important values; (2) overglorification of star athletes; (3) disparagement of nonathletes; (4) presenting school athletic contests as public spectacles instead of education-related events; (5) distortions in the educational program, such as lowering standards to meet eligibility requirements; (6) putting coaches under undue pressure to produce winning teams; (7) improper balance of opportunities for male and female athletes; (8) yielding to community pressures in ways that are inconsistent with sound educational practices; (9) selecting coaches because they were outstanding performers and not because they have desirable leadership traits and are competent educators. The school athletic program is part of an educational institution; it should not become an athletic foundry.

A POSITION STATEMENT

Chapter 13 contains a position statement from the Society of State Directors of Health, Physical Education and Recreation on the physical education instructional program. The Society has also stated its beliefs regarding interschool athletics, and the statement is printed here with permission of the

Society. It would be advantageous for a potential school administrator to be familiar with these beliefs.

Interscholastic Athletics

A well-directed interscholastic athletic program should be made available to all boys and girls who are interested and sufficiently skilled. This area of physical education allows students to participate in competition characterized by varsity teams, leagues, conferences, regular season schedules, specialized coaching, and high quality of performance.

ABOUT ADMINISTRATION

The interscholastic athletic programs should be provided for and financed by boards of education with funds accountable through the general school budget. The program should be administered by school officials.

Interscholastic athletic leagues or conferences should be confined to pupils in grades 9-12.

If elementary school, middle school or junior high interscholastic sports programs are deemed necessary, AAHPER guidelines for such programs should be followed closely.

The rules and regulations of the National Federation of State High School Associations should be used as guidelines in administering the interscholastic athletic program.

The standards and guidelines of the National Association for Girls and Women in Sport, AAHPER, may be used in administering the interscholastic sports program for girls, where considered appropriate.

State Departments of Education should be represented on the boards of control of all state high school athletic associations.

The health and welfare of pupils should be the first consideration in planning an interscholastic athletic program. To protect and promote the health and welfare of competing athletes, the following conditions should be met:
—Policies for the protection of athletes should be based on the best medical knowledge available.
—Policies should include procedures to assure adequate medical examination plus ongoing medical supervision of all athletes. A minimum of one medical examination should be required each year. Preferably this should be given immediately prior to the sport season. Re-examination should be required after any serious injury or illness before the pupil returns to participation.
—Coaches should understand and recognize the physical capacities of individual players. Coaches should be ever alert to note signs of undue fatigue or injury, thereby guarding the health and well-being of all participants both in practice sessions and in contests.
—High quality protective equipment should be provided and carefully fitted for every participant.
—Equitable competition between teams or individuals should be assured by the use of standardized classifications and eligibility requirements.
—Playing seasons should be of reasonable length and should be preceded by an adequate period of conditioning and instruction in fundamentals. No post-season or all-star games should be permitted.
—Contests should be confined to small geographic areas with no interstate competition except between schools located near state borders.
—Practice periods should be of reasonable length and geared to the physical condition of participants.
Awards should be simple, of little monetary value, and provided by schools rather than outside agencies.

ABOUT PROGRAM

The interscholastic athletic program in all high schools should provide maximum opportunity for both boys and girls to participate in a variety of individual, dual and team activities and should provide for differing levels of size and ability.

The high school athletic program should provide full opportunities for girls to compete in interscholastic athletics in accordance with their needs, abilities and interests. The girls' athletic program should be under the general supervision of a woman physical education teacher.

Interschool games and contests should be administered and conducted so as to enhance wholesome social relationships among community members and students, rather than to foster conflicts or extreme behavior based on unreasonable rivalries.

Interscholastic boxing should not be permitted.

ABOUT PERSONNEL

Coaches should be certificated teachers, members of the school staff and well prepared for assuming their coaching responsibilities. Certification of coaches is highly recommended.

Athletic directors should be competent administrators and educators with a rich background in interscholastic athletics. It is recommended that athletic directors acquire specific preparation for their position through formal courses or regular in-service work.

Games and contests should be officiated by qualified personnel who are certified by the appropriate governing body or officials association.

IMPACT OF TITLE IX

Information was provided in Chapter 13 about the application of the Title IX regulations on the physical education instructional program. This section contains parallel information about interschool athletics and intramural activities.

Section 86.41 of the law pertains to interschool and intraschool athletics. It states "that an institution or a district must develop and operate athletic programs according to the following specifications."

1. *General.* No person shall, on the basis of sex, be excluded from participation in, be denied the benefits of, be treated differently from another person or otherwise be discriminated against in any interscholastic, intercollegiate, club or intramural athletics offered by a recipient, and no recipient shall provide any such athletics separately on such basis.

2. *Separate Teams.* Notwithstanding the requirements of paragraph (1) of this section, a recipient may operate or sponsor separate teams for members of each sex where selection for such teams is based upon competitive skill or the activity involved is a contact sport. However, where a recipient operates or sponsors a team in a particular sport for members of one sex but operates or sponsors no such team for members of the other sex, members of that sex must be allowed to try out for the team offered unless the sport involved is a contact sport. For the purposes of this Part, contact sports include boxing, wrestling, rugby, ice hockey, football, basketball, and other sports the purpose or major activity of which involves bodily contact.

3. *Equal Opportunity.* A recipient which operates or sponsors interscholastic, intercollegiate, club, or intramural athletics shall provide equal athletic opportunity for members of both sexes. In determining whether equal opportunities are available the Director will consider, among other factors:

   (i) whether the selection of sports and levels of competition effectively accommodate the interests and abilities of members of both sexes

   (ii) the provision of equipment and supplies

   (iii) scheduling of games and practice time

   (iv) travel and per diem allowance

(v) opportunity to receive coaching and academic tutoring

(vi) assignment and compensation of coaches and tutors

(vii) provision of locker rooms, practice, and competitive facilities

(viii) provision of medical and training facilities and services

(ix) provision of housing and dining facilities and services

(x) publicity

Unequal aggregate expenditures for members of each sex or unequal expenditures for male and female teams if a recipient operates or sponsors separate teams will not constitute noncompliance with this section, but the Director may consider the failure to provide necessary funds for teams for one sex in assessing equality of opportunity for members of each sex.

BIBLIOGRAPHY

1. AAHPERD. Evaluating the high school athletic program. Washington, D.C., 1973.

2. Austin, D.: Administrative competencies for athletic directors. Athletic Administration, *14*:18, 1979.

3. Beck-Rex, M.: Women lose jobs to men. In the Running *2* (4):1, 1979.

4. Brigham Young University: Athletic Policy and Procedure Manual. Provo, UT, BYU, 1982, p. 4.

5. Carpenter, L.J., and Acosta, R.V.: Violence in sport, JOPER, *51*:18, 1980.

6. Deatherage, D. and Reid, C.P.: Administration of Women's Competitive Sports. Dubuque, IA, William C. Brown 1977.

7. Evans, V. and Evans, A.: Certification of coaches —a paradox in the principle. JOPER, *50*, 18, 1980.

8. Forsythe, C.E., and Keller, I.A.: Administration of High School Athletics, 6th Ed. Englewood Cliffs, NJ, Prentice-Hall, 1977.

9. Geadelmann, P., Grant, C., Slatton, Y., and Burke, N.P.: Equality in sport for women. Washington, D.C., and AAHPER, 1977.

10. Henry, R.: Motivation of the non-scholarship athlete. JOPER, *52*:83, 1981.

11. Holmen, M.G., and Parkhouse, B.L.: Trends in the selection for female athletic coaches: a demographic inquiry. Research Quarterly for Exercise and Sport, *52*:9, 1981.

12. Jeter, J.M.: Extramural sports club and varsity athletics. JOPER, *50*:42, 1979.

13. Maillos, H.C.: Legal liability of athletic administrators for injury to student athletes. Athletic Administration, *16*:16, 1980.

14. Maetozo, M. G.: Athletic coaching: its future in a changing society. JOPER, *52*:40, 1981.

15. Mudra, D.: A humanist looks at coaching. JOPER *51*:22 1980.

16. Ness, R.G.: Problems in interscholastic athletics: questioned assumptions. JOPER, *52*:23, 1981.

17. Noble, L. and Corbin, C: Certification for coaches. JOPER *49*:52, 1980.

18. Noble, L. and Sigle, G.: Minimum requirements for interscholastic coaches. JOPER, *51:*32, 1980.

19. Palmeteer, D.: The dollars and sense approach to sports club funding. JOPER, *50:*46, 1979.

20. Parkhouse, B.: To win what do you have to lose? JOPER, *50:*15, 1979.

21. Resick, M., and Erickson, C.: Intercollegiate and Interscholastic Athletics for Men and Women, 2nd Ed. Reading, MA, Addison-Wesley, 1981.

22. Richardson, H.D.: Academic preparation of athletic coaches in higher education. JOPER, *52:*44, 1981.

Chapter ***16***

CONDUCTING ATHLETIC EVENTS

School athletic contests today attract more attention from educators, students, alumni, and members of the public than ever before. Because education is the only business that schools should be involved in, athletic programs must be conducted in accordance with sound educational objectives and procedures.

Athletic competition has tremendous potential for individual development; but, the extent to which the potential is actually achieved depends greatly on the quality of leadership. Athletic competition is neither innately good nor bad. It is only a highly potent medium that can produce positive results when conducted under high quality leadership; however, under poor or improper leadership, negative results are more likely to occur. Leadership is clearly the key toward achieving worthy goals through athletic participation.

School athletics often generates public enthusiasm and sometimes controversy because (1) athletic competition is dramatic in nature, and therefore, stimulates the emotions among both participants and spectators; and (2) athletic contests attract the attention of a relatively large segment of the public, and some members of the public become almost obsessed by athletics. Because of the public's interest, athletic events have a potentially significant influence on the school's public relations.

SCHEDULING

Athletic events, especially those that attract a large number of fans, should be scheduled and announced well in advance. This can be beneficial in scheduling facilities, promoting the events, and avoiding competition or conflict with other activities. Also, scheduling well in advance affords an advantage in the selection of preferred opponents.

Usually the contests that involve many fans and have financial implications are scheduled by written agreement, with all of the important elements specified and with the appropriate signatures affixed. Such an agreement is

---

ATHLETIC CONTRACT

THIS AGREEMENT, Made and entered into this _____day of
_____, 19 ____, stipulates:

FIRST: That the _____ teams representing
the below named institutions shall play a game of _____
at _____ on _____, 19 ____ at
_____ p.m.

SECOND: That in consideration of playing the above named game, the
administrator of the _____ program shall pay
the administrator of the _____ program the
sum of _____

_____

THIRD: That the officials for games shall be settled at least _____
_____ before the contest and the expenses of the same
shall be _____

FOURTH: If either institution refuses to play except for some breach of
this contract, the administrator of the program of the institution refusing to play shall forfeit to the administrator of the other program the
sum of _____

FIFTH: That this game shall be played under the rules of the _____
_____ Conference, and the _____
(national governing organization).

For _____ (institution)   For _____ (institution)

_____   _____
Faculty Representative   Faculty Representative

_____   _____
Director Athletics   Director Athletics

Figure 16-1. Example of a contract form for an athletic contest between two schools. This model contains useful elements from actual contracts, but it does not duplicate any particular one.

referred to as an *athletic contract.* Written agreements are strongly recommended because they reduce the possibility of misunderstandings, and protect against default or unwarranted changes. Contracts are usually not used in connection with nonrevenue sports because many coaches feel that they can work just as well by "gentlemen's agreement." Even in these cases a simple contractual arrangement would be better because it is clearly a good business approach.

Figure 16-1 is a sample athletic contract. Contracts range from less complex to more complex than the one illustrated, depending on the significance of the event and the particular conditions associated with it.

In scheduling events, realistic limits should be placed on their number and the length of the season. There is a tendency for the competitive seasons to become longer and longer and include more and more contests. Reasonable limits must be enforced for the good of the participants and the school program.

Following are some guidelines for scheduling athletic events:

1. Maintain membership in a reputable athletic league made up of schools similar to yours which sponsor similar athletic programs.
2. Scheduling is facilitated if the men's and women's programs are aligned with the same athletic league.
3. Maintain membership in appropriate state, regional, and national athletic organizations. These organizations facilitate scheduling by the classification of schools according to the nature of their athletic programs and by setting appropriate standards and regulations.
4. Carefully select nonleague opponents to give the athletic schedule additional variety and interest. Contests should be scheduled within a reasonable distance due to the time, expense, and hazard of travel.
5. Involve coaches in the scheduling process. The advantages are that (a) it is a morale factor for them; (b) their contacts with other coaches can often facilitate scheduling; and (c) the events must fit in with their practice sessions and other phases of preparation. Coaches should be involved in determining the caliber and location of the competition.

MANAGEMENT

Efficient management of athletic events does not depend on the size of the school. Those events, however, that involve a large number of participants and/or spectators have a potential impact on more people; therefore, their management takes on special significance.

A host of duties must be handled in connection with an athletic event. The best way for the athletic administrator to identify and keep track of all these duties is to prepare a checklist and then review it periodically to make sure that all the duties are handled effectively and on the proper timetable. In some cases, it is desirable to identify the particular person responsible for each duty; however, since this varies from one situation to another, such identification does not appear on the sample checklist that follows.

Some athletic administrators prefer to have a separate checklist that is specific to each kind of athletic event, such as a checklist for basketball games, and a different one for football or track. If this method is preferred, the checklist presented here can serve as a useful guide in preparing the specific checklists.

Normally, the athletic director does not perform all the functions on the checklist; but, he is responsible for seeing that they are handled properly by responsible personnel.

Before Game Preparations

*Check When
Completed*   *Responsible Person
(Optional information)*

_____ Contract completed

_____ Facilities officially scheduled

_____ Eligibility records checked

_____ Medical examinations completed

_____ Permission slips obtained

_____ Game officials scheduled and contracted

_____ Equipment available and in good repair

_____ Facility prepared (lined, cleaned, etc.)

_____ Media coverage arranged

_____ Courtesy arrangements made for visiting team

_____ Tickets printed and ready for distribution

_____ Programs printed and ready for distribution

_____ Arrangements made for concessions

_____ Ushers assigned

_____ Game statisticians assigned

_____ Police arrangements made

_____ Parking areas available and properly prepared

_____ Parking area personnel assigned

_____ Scoreboard in working order

_____ Public address system ready

_____ Spectator area properly prepared

_____ Half-time arrangements made

_____ Decorations completed

_____ Scorers, timers, judges, and announcer selected and scheduled

_____ Physician's presence arranged (game format)

_____ Written time schedule and contest procedures distributed to those who need them.

Game Responsibilities

_____ Supplies and equipment on hand

_____ Tickets and ticket takers available

_____ Ushers present

_____ Contest programs on hand

_____ Officials' quarters ready

_____ Visiting team's quarters checked and courtesies provided

_____ Flag-raising ceremonies arranged

_____ Intermission (half-time) program set

_____ Players' benches in position

_____ Physician present

_____ Scoreboard working

_____ Guards for dressing rooms on duty

_____ Concessions open

_____ Cheerleaders and pep band ready

_____ Police personnel on duty

_____ Rest rooms open, clean, and policed as necessary

_____ Extra equipment guarded

_____ Media personnel arrangements completed

_____ Game statistician ready

_____ Game management personnel prepared—announcers, timers, scorer, etc.

After-Game Responsibilities

_____ Payment of officials

_____ Payment to visiting school

_____ Equipment repair and maintenance

_____ Storage of equipment

_____ Deposit of ticket receipts and concession income

_____ Financial statement prepared

_____ Proper use of game statistics

_____ Proper attention to any lingering problems

CONDUCT OF SPECTATORS AND PARTICIPANTS

In the highly competitive environment of athletics, sportsmanship and proper conduct require special monitoring both of participants (including coaches) and fans. In the educational system, this responsibility lies in the hands of those in leadership positions—the coaches and administrators. The coaches have the primary responsibility for the conduct of the athletes and themselves, whereas the conduct of spectators is primarily a responsibility of the administrators. Coaches and administrators would be well advised to hold a hard line against misconduct of both participants and fans. This problem can escalate rapidly if not strictly controlled, and there is no justification for it.

The AAHPERD has stated some highly useful guidelines for crowd control. They include the following:

> (1) Provide separate seating areas for the supporters of the two teams; (2) have uniformed police officers inside and outside the facility when needed and appropriate; (3) ban alcoholic beverages, mechanical noise makers, and undesirable signs; (4) provide free faculty passes to encourage faculty to attend athletic events; and have the faculty interspersed throughout the spectators; (5) place continuous emphasis on sportsmanship and proper self-control among both athletes and coaches; (6) provide adequate lighting of parking lots and areas adjacent to the athletic facilities; (7) carefully plan spectator flow in and out of the seating areas; (8) have an adequate number of ushers or supervisors located throughout the facility; (9) provide adequate divisions or barriers between spectators and playing area; (10) play restful music over the public address system after the contest. [1]

In addition to these suggestions, Hardy[5] has stated some useful ideas that interested readers might want to pursue.

Sometimes, some brief remarks by a school administrator, athletic representative, or student body officer can be helpful, in which the idea is clearly communicated that athletic events will be permitted only under desirable circumstances of participant and crowd behavior. Those unwilling to accept and support this should refrain from attendance.

GAME OFFICIALS

Poor officiating can be one of the primary sources of negative behavior of athletics fans and unethical conduct by coaches and players. Good officiating, therefore, should be viewed as not only important in itself but also as an effective method of controlling related problems. Of course, no official is capable of doing a perfect job, at least not in the eyes of partisan fans, coaches, and participants. A strong effort should be made to obtain highly competent officials, and get the players, coaches, and fans to recognize that the officials deserve their understanding and support. Game officials should be selected and assigned by the appropriate representative of the athletic association, conference, or league, not by a representative of either of the schools in the contest. A sample contract for game officials is shown in Figure 16-2. A prospective official usually is required to pass written and practical certification tests. To gain experience, the new official often starts with high school junior varsity games. This practice must be carefully scrutinized, however, because often the new players need the best officials. Another starting place for officials is preseason practice games. This provides varsity game experience with less pressure than in league games.

Contract For Athletic Officials

Date _____ 19 ___

This is an agreement to officiate as _____ by

_____ at the _____school
(name)

on _____ 19 ___. The _____
(date)   (sport)

contest between _____and

_____ will begin at _____.
(time)

The fee for this activity will be _____. Mileage will pe paid at

_____ ¢ per mile both ways. Other officials who will be working with

you are:

_____   _____
(name)   (position)

_____   _____

_____   _____

You will be expected to report _____minutes prior to

the contest. In case of postponement, you will be informed of such by

_____.
(time)

_____   _____
(Director of Athletics)   (Official)

_____   _____
(Address)   (Address)

_____   _____
(Telephone number)   (Telephone number)

Return one copy and keep one for your records.

Figure 16-2. A sample form for contracting game officials.

CHEERLEADERS

Cheerleaders, like players, are representatives of the student body, chosen as a result of their skills and general ability to lead. By nature of their positions, they have an excellent opportunity and important responsibility to promote good will and sportsmanship. By setting a proper example, cheerleaders can exert a significant positive influence on other students and on fans in general at athletic contests.

Good sportsmanship is conduct that imposes appropriate self-control, relating to honest rivalry, courteous relations, and graceful acceptance of results. Sportsmanship can be shown in athletic contests, pep rallies, student assemblies, and many other school settings. Good school spirit is a reflection of sportsmanlike attitudes and behavior. If a school is to succeed in one of its prime functions—good citizenship—student groups must radiate proper sportsmanlike attitudes. Sportsmanship is one form of good citizenship in action.

The World Cheerleaders Council has the slogan "You never get a second chance to make a good first impression." Following are some important guidelines for cheerleaders:

1. Stimulate and control crowd response.
2. Choose the right cheers at the right time.
3. Be certain that words used in a cheer are not suggestive in a negative sense, and do not inflame an audience.
4. Use gestures that are synchronized, pleasing to watch, and easy to follow.
5. When booing develops, divert the crowd's attention by starting a popular yell.
6. Do not conduct a cheer that competes with or disrupts the visiting cheerleading squad.
7. Select positive cheers.
8. Develop a large repertoire of desirable and timely cheers, which may be used at appropriate moments.
9. Always maintain enthusiasm and composure especially in trying circumstances, remembering your responsibilities for leadership.
10. Give encouragement to injured players and recognition to outstanding performances regardless of team affiliation.
11. Always show friendliness to rival cheerleaders.

Cheerleaders should have these following important objectives:

1. To develop a wholesome and enthusiastic school spirit.
2. To develop loyalty to the school and team regardless of the outcome of the game.
3. To promote a cooperative spirit between the student body, faculty, and school administration.
4. To promote the kind of sportsmanship that will help students to acquire the basic attributes of good citizenship.

ATHLETIC TRIPS

In scheduling athletic trips, the following considerations should be taken into account. A trip should not involve excessive distance or time; transportation arrangements should be adequate and safe; an adequate amount of responsible leadership should be provided on the trip. The mode of transportation to use—vans, school bus, or commercial carrier—has both safety and legal implications with respect to the choice of vehicle and driver. Occasionally, sufficient reasons exist to cancel an athletic event, such as adverse weather or prevelant illness among team members. The leagues should establish clear guidelines as to what justifies cancellation and the procedures that should be followed.

The best approach to thorough planning and effective arrangements for an athletic trip is the utilization of a checklist, such as the example that follows:

Check When
Completed

_____ Confirm game details with the host school by letter or telephone.

_____ Make travel arrangements by common carrier or other approved mode.

_____ Plan travel itinerary, including food and lodging arrangements for the total trip.

_____ Draw check from school fund to cover the expenses and cash the check.

_____ Secure and distribute or sell the tickets provided for the visiting school.

_____ Send itinerary to parents and secure the signed permission slips for all athletes, as required by the school's policy.

_____ Inform the athletic groups, student groups (band, cheerleaders), and adult groups (athletic booster club, parents of players) of itinerary.

_____ Pack game equipment and assign student manager to guard the baggage. Include athletic training supplies.

_____ Load equipment, inventory the items.

_____ Load athletic team personnel, check roster.

_____ Check team personnel before leaving each stop.

_____ Unload personnel and equipment at contest site.

_____ Contact host staff immediately on arrival.

_____ Assign student manager to guard clothing and equipment during the contest.

_____ Have travel vehicle prepared to leave immediately after the contest.

_____ Secure the contract payment.

_____ Account for equipment and personnel before departing.

_____ Account for equipment and personnel on arrival.

_____ Write courtesy follow-up letter to the host school.

_____ Confirm all matters that apply relative to insurance.

USE OF FACILITIES

Facilities used for athletic practices and competition are also used for other aspects of the physical education and athletic program, such as classes, intramurals, free play, and sometimes other varsity and junior varsity teams. In view of this, at least three important guidelines pertain to facilities:

1. Enter requests for facilities for both contests and practices well in advance, and make certain that the requests are complete and clearly communicated. Early requests are especially important in connection with interschool athletic contests because the contests also involve arrangements with other schools.
2. Be reasonable and considerate in terms of others' needs for the facilities. Unfortunately, some athletic coaches become greedy and inflexible about facility use. Practically all school sports facilities should be multipurpose in nature, and each of the different uses should be held in proper perspective and correct priority.
3. Every teacher or coach has a responsibility to make sure the facilities are used appropriately (and not abused). Also, each one has a responsibility for leaving the facility in as good a condition as possible for subsequent users.

The best way to avoid serious conflicts in scheduling facilities is to have a well-defined priority system and clearly described scheduling procedures, which are strictly enforced. In addition, each teacher or coach should be encouraged to avoid infringing on the scheduled time of others and to consistently contribute to a congenial and mutually supportive relationship in terms of facility use. It is a good practice to prepare a schedule form for each teaching station prior to the beginning of each term.

ATHLETIC ELIGIBILITY

It is extremely important for all schools to honor and respect the eligibility regulations of the athletic league and the state and national athletic associations to which they belong. Some schools have other regulations in addition to those of the league and the associations. It is generally agreed that a student who is not making normal progress toward a degree or a diploma should not be allowed to participate. Figure 16-3 is a sample of a high school eligibility certificate.

SAFEGUARDING THE HEALTH OF ATHLETES

Several years ago, the National Federation of State High School Athletic Associations and the American Medical Association's Committee on the Medical Aspects of Sports issued a joint statement. The statement points out that the athlete has the right to optimal protection against injury to the extent that this can be assured through proper conditioning, careful coaching, good officiating, proper equipment and facilities, and adequate medical care. Periodic evaluation of each of these factors should help to provide a safe and

---

ATHLETIC ELIGIBILITY CERTIFICATION

This is to certify that the students listed below are eligible to represent

the _____ High School in the following

athletic contest _____

to be played at _____ on the

_____ day of _____.

FACULTY REPRESENTATIVE _____

PRINCIPAL _____
                         (Signature)

COACH _____
                   (Signature)

Names of Contestants			Uniform Number		Birth Date	Class
Last Name	First	Initial	Home	Away	Mo. Day Yr.	
1.						
2.						
3.						
4.						
5.						
6.						
7.						
8.						
9.						
10.						
11.						
12.						
13.						
14.						
15.						
16.						

Figure 16-3. Sample form for certifying eligibility of student athletes.

healthy experience for players. The five major areas are explained as follows:

1. *Proper Conditioning.* This helps to prevent injuries by hardening the body and increasing resistance to fatigue. Coaches and athletic administrators should:

   —Give prospective players directions to follow and activities to perform for preseason conditioning.

   —See that there is a minimum of three weeks of practice before the first game or contest.

   —Take precautions to prevent heat exhaustion and heat stroke. This is particularly important in preseason practice for football, soccer, cross-country, and field hockey.

   —Require players to warm up and stretch thoroughly before participating in rigorous activity.

   —Make substitutions without hesitation when players show signs of disability, injury, or fatigue.

2. *Careful Coaching.* Athletes who are well coached are more skilled, which reduces the chance of injury. Coaches and other athletic department personnel should:

   —Stress safety in performance techniques and elements of play.

   —Analyze injuries to determine their cause and suggest ways to prevent them.

   —Discourage the use of tactics and techniques that increase hazards on the field of play.

   —Plan practice sessions carefully and see that they are neither too long nor too short.

3. *Good Officiating.* Qualified officials who know exactly what they are doing promote enjoyment of the game and protection for players. In this respect:

   —Players and coaches should be thoroughly schooled in the rules of the game.

   —Rules and regulations should be strictly enforced in practice sessions as well as in games. If they are not, the risk of injury will increase in practice and players will get into bad habits which will carry over into games.

   —Officials should be qualified both emotionally and technically for their responsibilities on the field or court.

   —Players and coaches should respect the decisions and ruling of officials. If they don't, tempers will flare and the game may get out of control.

4. *Proper Equipment and Facilities.* Student athletes should not be expected to participate in athletic programs unless they are protected by safe equipment and play on safe fields and courts. Specifically, schools should see that:

   —The best protective equipment is provided for contact sports.

   —Careful attention is given to the proper fitting and adjustment of equipment.

   —Equipment is properly maintained; worn and outmoded items should be discarded. The temptation to try and make equipment last one more year should be resisted when the safety of student athletes is at stake.

   —Proper and safe areas of play should be provided and these areas should be carefully and continuously maintained.

5. *Adequate Medical Care.* (Figures 16-4 and 16-5.) Proper medical care is a necessity in the prevention and control of injuries. Athletic educators and school administrators should:

   —See that a thorough preseason medical examination is provided for each athlete and that a detailed health history is taken.

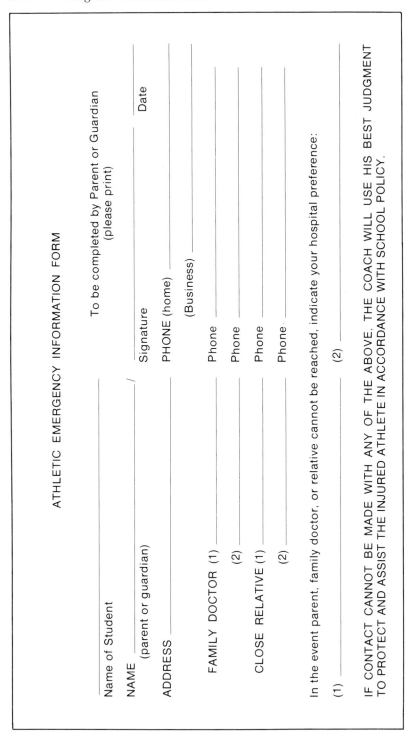

ATHLETIC EMERGENCY INFORMATION FORM

To be completed by Parent or Guardian
(please print)

Name of Student _____

NAME _____ / Signature _____ Date
(parent or guardian)

ADDRESS _____ PHONE (home) _____

(Business) _____

FAMILY DOCTOR (1) _____ Phone _____

(2) _____ Phone _____

CLOSE RELATIVE (1) _____ Phone _____

(2) _____ Phone _____

In the event parent, family doctor, or relative cannot be reached, indicate your hospital preference:

(1) _____ (2) _____

IF CONTACT CANNOT BE MADE WITH ANY OF THE ABOVE, THE COACH WILL USE HIS BEST JUDGMENT
TO PROTECT AND ASSIST THE INJURED ATHLETE IN ACCORDANCE WITH SCHOOL POLICY.

Figure 16-4. Form for placing on record at the school information useful in case of emergency.

SUGGESTED HEALTH EXAMINATION FORM

(Cooperatively prepared by the National Federation of State High School Athletic Associations and the Committee on Medical Aspects of Sports of the American Medical Association.) Health examination for athletes should be rendered after August 1 preceding school year concerned.

| (Please Print) | Name of Student | City and School |

Grade _____ Age _____ Height _____ Weight _____ Blood Pressure _____

Significant Past Illness or Injury _____

Eyes _____ R 20/ ; L 20/ ; Ears _____ Hearing R /15; L /15

Respiratory _____

Cardiovascular _____

Liver _____ Spleen _____ Hernia _____

Musculoskeletal _____ Skin _____

Neurological _____ Genitalia _____

Laboratory: Urinalysis _____ Other: _____

Comments _____

Completed Immunizations: Polio _____ Tetanus _____
                                     Date   Date

Instructions for use of card   Other _____

"I certify that I have on this date examined this student and that, on the basis of the examination requested by the school authorities and the student's medical history as furnished to me, I have found no reason which would make it medically inadvisable for this student to compete in supervised athletic activities, EXCEPT THOSE CROSSED OUT BELOW."

BASEBALL	FOOTBALL	ROWING	SOFTBALL	TRACK
BASKETBALL	HOCKEY	SKATING	SPEEDBALL	VOLLEYBALL
CROSS COUNTRY	GOLF	SKIING	SWIMMING	*WRESTLING
FIELD HOCKEY	GYMNASTICS	SOCCER	TENNIS	OTHERS _____

* Estimated desirable weight level: _____ pounds.

Date of Examination: _____ Signed: _____
                                                        Examining Physician

Physician's Address _____ Telephone _____

Figure 16-5. Health examination form for athletic participation. (Printed by permission of the National Federation of State High School Athletic Associations and the American Medical Association.)

—Arrange to have a physician present at games, and see that a doctor is available during practice sessions.

—Adopt a policy to the effect that the physician will make all decisions as to when an athlete should resume participation following an injury. This applies to both competition and practice.

—Adopt policies on exactly how much medical attention a trainer can perform without a doctor present.

Procedures in the Absence of a Physician

When an athlete is injured and no physician is present, the following procedures should be carried out by the trainer, or coach if a trainer is not available. All athletics employees should be familiar with these important procedures.

1. Make an immediate preliminary examination of the injury.
2. Send for a physician and/or ambulance immediately if the injury is beyond the realm of your ability.
3. Give first aid as needed.
4. Notify the parents, or if they are not available, a designated relative or friend, and inform them of the athlete's condition, what treatment you have administered, or what action you suggest.
5. Determine whether the athlete's condition is such that he should be removed from the area. First, ascertain whether such removal would be sanctioned by a physician. Unconscious players or players who are unable to move comfortably should be moved only if necessary and then only with adequate assistance and by proper stretcher techniques.
6. Have an ambulance available for all games involving contact sports. Keep it out of view of both spectators and players. Have the attendants inconspicuously seated but readily available.
7. Use a standard accident report form on which all important information can be recorded. This form can be used for future reference, especially when the details of certain injuries become hazy memories. Copies should be kept on file in the coach's office, trainer's office, and school nurse's office for reference and for possible use in a legal action.

Duties of the Athletic Trainer

The three basic categories into which the trainers' duties fall are prevention of injury, treatment of injuries, and rehabilitation of the athlete after injury. Within these basic categories, the trainer has numerous specific duties; the more prominent ones are included in the following list:

1. Require a periodic medical examination for each athlete, and help the physician with the arrangements and record keeping involved.
2. Work cooperatively with the coaches in setting up and carrying out a program of conditioning for athletes, especially those aspects that help in the prevention of injury.
3. Administer appropriate emergency treatment to injured athletes on the field, in the gymnasium, or in the training room.
4. Apply protective or injury-preventive devices, such as strapping, bandaging, or bracing.
5. Work cooperatively with and under the direction of the physician in respect to
   a. Reconditioning procedures following injury.
   b. Use of therapeutic devices and equipment.

   c. Fitting of special braces, guards, and other protective devices.

   d. Referrals to the physician, health service, or hospital.

6. Work cooperatively with the coaches and the physician in selecting athletic safety equipment and checking it for effectiveness.

7. Supervise the training room, which includes requisitioning and storage of supplies and equipment, keeping records, maintaining an accurate inventory, and managing the training budget.

8. Supervise, and when necessary, instruct assistant trainers.

9. Counsel and advise athletes and coaches on matters pertaining to conditioning and training, such as diet, rest, and reconditioning.

10. Conduct oneself at all times as a responsible professional.

Insurance for Athletes

Student insurance for team members is extremely important today. An athletic insurance rider can usually be added at a nominal cost to the basic student insurance policy offered through the school. Athletic insurance costs might be paid by the parents, the school, or the local booster club, but the athlete must be covered by insurance.

Student insurance with athletic riders usually includes (1) payment of all hospital costs and some physician's fees or (2) payment of medical expenses after a standard deductible amount is paid by the insured (this kind is less expensive). Insurance for student athletes should contain a major medical clause whereby a high percentage of expenses would be paid for extensive medical care.

STUDENT MANAGERS

Defining the role of a student manager is difficult because it can vary considerably among different sports and with the preference of the coaches. Probably the most accurate definition is that a student manager is an assistant to the coach, who carries certain responsibilities in accordance with the agreement between the coach and the manager.

Many responsibilities of the student manager could correctly be labeled as errands, but certain responsibilities involve much more. For example, the manager's duties often include caring for athletic equipment, keeping inventory, compiling, analyzing and reporting game statistics, and preparing equipment and supplies for team practices and games.

A coach should be careful to add a reasonable amount of dignity to the team manager's position by including some significant duties and treating the manager in a dignified manner. In this way, being a student manager can be a rewarding experience, and the manager can make a useful contribution and enhance the program.

METRICS IN SPORTS

The Congress of the United States passed the Metric Conversion Act in 1975, which—while voluntary—clearly means that the metric system will eventually be put into full-scale use in this country. It is already being taught in many school systems, and science and industry are adopting it. As international athletic competition has increased in scope, intensity, and importance, the need for a common set of standards has also increased.

In college athletics, the NCAA Track and Field Committee is using the metric system for all future championships scheduled to be conducted. The NCAA rule books for the various sports include metric conversions for the traditional imperial measurements. Similar progress toward the use of metric measurements has been made in other levels of athletic competition not regulated by the NCAA; namely, high school, junior college, and open competition.

Detailed conversion charts from the imperial (English) system to the metric system are available from various sources, including the NCAA and other athletic regulatory organizations. Until the metric system becomes universally used in American life, conversions will often be necessary. Most are simple, but some can be a bit confusing. For example, a high jump bar set at 7 feet would be at 2.13 meters. However, the metric system is the simpler of the two, once it is adopted and conversions become unnecessary, because metrics are established on the "base ten," whereas the imperial system lacks this element of consistency. To give a working knowledge of the process of converting imperial measurements to metric measurements, the following conversion table is included:

If you know	Multiply by	To get
inches	×25.4	=millimeters
feet	×0.3048	=meters
yards	×0.9144	=meters
miles	×0.60934	=kilometers
ounces	×28.3495	=grams
pounds	×0.453592	=kilograms

Equivalents	
1 millimeter	=0.0394 inch
1 centimeter	=0.3937 inch
1 meter	=39.3708 inches
1 kilometer	=1093.63 yards
1 inch	=25.4 millimeters
1 foot	=0.3048 meter
1 yard	=0.9144 meter
1 mile	=1.6093 kilometers

SELECTED REFERENCES

1. AAHPERD: Evaluating the High School Athletic Program. Washington, D.C., 1973.

2. Congdon, P.: The mixed varsity: coping positively with cutbacks. Athletic Administration, *15*(1):13, 1980.

3. Deatheraye, D., and Reid, P.: Administration of Women's Competitive Sports. Dubuque, IA, W.C. Brown, 1977.

4. Freischlag, J., and Schmidtke, C.: Violence in sports: its causes and some solutions. The Physical Educator, *36*:182, 1979.

5. Hardy, R.: Checklist for better crowd control. JOPER, *52*:70, 1981.

Chapter *17*

INTRAMURALS AND RELATED ACTIVITIES

The purpose of intramurals is to provide a variety of recreational activities, selected on the basis of their contribution to the development of the individual. Intramurals should be designed to serve the recreational needs of the majority of the student body and not just the athletic elite.

Intramurals are one of the oldest forms of organized sports in American education. The early programs were the result of student leaders' wishes to participate in leisure-time athletic activities of their own choosing. These programs were student led, student financed, and student administered and were present on campuses before required physical education and intercollegiate programs appeared.

Traditionally, intramurals meant all sports activities conducted within the walls of a school. The term intramural is derived from two Latin words: intra (within) and murus (walls). Originally the two words were separate, (intra murals) then hyphenated, and finally evolved into one word.

The present concept of intramurals is that of a comprehensive program of recreational activities conducted within the institution. Institutions differ with respect to the functions of their intramural programs. Some programs provide a wide range of team sports, individual and dual activities, and recreational pursuits, whereas other programs include only a few competitive sports. The scope of intramurals is often related to the size of the institution, with the large schools usually having more comprehensive programs.

Activities that might be involved in an intramural division are included in the following list. The first two are typically associated with the intramural division, whereas the other three are seen less frequently.

1. Organized competitive leagues for both women and men.
2. Special events such as tournaments and meets.
3. Recreational free play.
4. Sports clubs, which may include both competitive and noncompetitive events.
5. Extramurals, which involve competition with teams from outside the school.

The selection of programs and the establishment of participation units should be in keeping with sound educational objectives. Following are 11 guidelines to help ensure this aim. (1) The program should be based on the local needs of the students at their own level and on a sound philosophy of education and sports participation. (2) A wide range of activities should be available that offer opportunities for each boy and girl, regardless of physical ability, race, economic status, or handicaps. (3) Appropriate representatives of the school population, both students and staff, should be involved in planning and administering the program. (4) The same equipment and facilities should be used for physical education and intramurals to avoid duplication of costs. (5) Awards should be relatively numerous and inexpensive. (6) The program should be free to participants; financed from school funds. (7) The program should not serve as a substitute for physical education instruction or interschool athletics. (8) Activities should be modified to suit the needs and abilities of the participants. (9) Participation should be not only an end in itself, but also the means to teach rules, sportsmanship, and values. (10) The decision-making process in the program should be student-centered with guidance from the directors. (11) Students should be offered both leadership and followership roles, and they should learn how to both win and lose properly.

INTRAMURALS AT VARIOUS SCHOOL LEVELS

There is a place for intramurals in school programs at all levels, from elementary school through college; however, the purposes, approaches, and program content are different at each stage of the educational program.

Elementary School

The need of elementary school students to be active, their desire to play, their willingness to accept challenges, and their desire to belong to a group create justification for a certain kind of intramural program at the elementary school level.

Some objectives of intramurals in the elementary school are (1) to develop movement and basic sports skills; (2) to provide moderate competition in a game setting; (3) to provide opportunities for cooperative play; (4) to foster fun; (5) to provide involvement in democratic processes, and (6) to introduce students to play opportunities in a variety of activities.

Simple skills, low organization games, lead-up activities, and modified games should be included. To sponsor a particular activity in the school, the club approach may be used, as well as interest groups or a special theme. Likewise, special events, field days, and mass activities for students are vital parts of the program.[13]

Junior High or Middle School

Excellent opportunities exist for intramural programs at this level, due to the unique needs and interests of this age group. Following are some important objectives of junior high school intramural programs:

1. To provide team activities for the enhancement of esprit de corps and group closeness.
2. To present a wide range of activities to satisfy the various levels of ability and the broad range of interests.
3. To provide corecreational opportunities to aid in socialization.
4. To offer vigorous activities to dissipate nervous energy and contribute to fitness.
5. To give opportunities for individual achievement and recognition.
6. To offer some interesting special events so that students can have fun, meet new friends, and enjoy both competition and cooperation.

Ideally, intramural personnel or other faculty members should serve as officials, and student helpers secure the equipment and prepare for the contests. Supervision by adults is important at this level.

Usually, the activities are conducted after school, but some successful programs also utilize hours before school, during lunch, and on weekends. To some degree, transportation problems can be reduced through careful analysis of this problem.

Units of competition may be based on homerooms, neighborhood units, physical education classes, clubs, or pickup teams. A few schools may use a classification index or skill test results for assignment to intramural teams; but normally, administrative limitations of time and personnel prohibit this approach. Students in junior high school ought to have an opportunity to participate at least once each week

In regard to eligibility, all students except varsity players of the particular sport should be eligible to play in intramural activities. Students should play for only one team at a time, so as not to reduce participation opportunities for other students. But this does not mean that varsity players could not serve as timers, scorers, and even officials as necessary. An interesting use of varsity players is to allow them to work with the elementary students as coaches or instructors.[21]

Senior High School

The general objective of intramurals at the senior high level is to provide a wide variety of activities, in order to encourage regular participation in team and individual sports and special events. Skill development, a positive self-image, fun, friendly competition, and the development of interest in life-time sports are all valid reasons for a high school program.

Through intramural sports, students can be reached who are inclined to drop out of school or who may be turned off by other school activities. The improvement of self-esteem and the breaking down of social barriers can result through sports participation.

At the high school level, intramural activities can be conducted before school, at noontime, during activity periods, after school, or in the evening. The ideal time is after school, except that conflicts with varsity sports often arise. To some extent, facility problems can be overcome by playing the sports out of season, and through cooperative use of community facilities.[12]

Colleges and Universities

The reasons for and the benefits of intramurals are the same in college as in high school, and the kinds of activities included in the program are generally the same. There are some distinct differences, however, that need to be carefully considered. (1) College and university programs are often much larger than public school programs due to the size of the institutions. (2) Often, the facilities are more extensive and more available for intramurals. (3) A large portion of the student body may live in residence halls or apartments, in close proximity to the campus, thus reducing the transportation problem that often exists with public school students. (4) College students have more flexible schedules. (5) A greater variety of circumstances must be considered in light of the eligibility question. (6) Many students at a university live away from home and this creates an increased need for involvement in intramurals and other school activities. (7) The fact that college intramural programs are relatively large affords the opportunity for a greater variety of program offerings.

ORGANIZATIONAL PATTERNS

An intramural program can be organized in several ways. Three different patterns are shown in Figures 17-1, 17-2, and 17-3. The educational level, size of the program, and administrative philosophy are all influencing factors. Usually, the intramural program is associated with physical education. In some schools, however, especially in colleges and universities, it is attached to the Dean of Students office, the Student Union, the Interschool Athletic Department, or the Department of Recreation Administration.[8]

ADMINISTRATIVE AND PROGRAM GUIDELINES

The danger always exists of intramurals becoming caught up in the administrative process and becoming more organized and process oriented than people oriented. Intramural administration exists to provide a sound, wholesome program for participants, utilizing the resources of the school to meet their needs. The following administrative practices can enhance the intramural program:

1. Student leadership and its development should be a major responsibility of those in charge. This can be accomplished through students participating on the intramural council, serving as assistant directors or supervisors, and qualifying and serving as game officials.
2. The policies and procedures applied should serve the needs and interests of the students.
3. The intramural program should be available to students, faculty, and staff, but the major emphasis should be on the students.

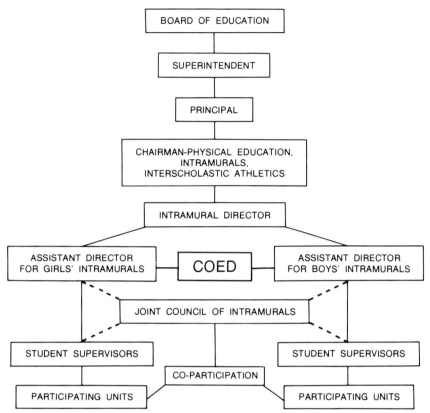

Figure 17-1. Example of a desirable intramural organizational pattern for a secondary school. (Courtesy of Bruce Holley.)

4. The program should foster fair play, sportsmanship, and the will to compete well.
5. The health and safety of the participants is of vital importance; therefore, adequate precautionary measures are necessary.
6. Competition should be equalized as much as possible so that all participants may enjoy rewarding experiences.
7. The program should involve sufficient variety.
8. Novelty and special events may be used for enhancement, but the heart of the program should be sports, both team and individual, that are planned and conducted well.
9. Well-qualified officials should be provided, because poor officiating is both unfair and troublesome.

Effective *units of competition* are essential to a successful intramural program regardless of the scholastic level involved. The competitive units form the basis for effective organization and administration.

Individual, team, league, and all-campus are the units usually found within intramural programs. In *individual* (including dual) sports competi-

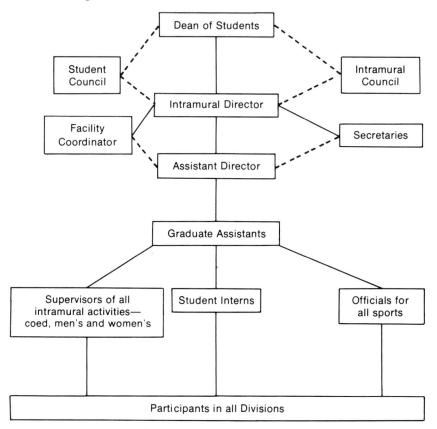

Figure 17-2. An example of an intramural organization for a college, with the program administered under student government. (Courtesy of Bruce Holley.)

tion, the individual is considered a unit because other players are not needed to form a team. *Teams* are developed by groups of interested players, and a team constitutes a unit. A *league* is composed of a logical grouping of teams, such as those representing residence halls. *All-campus* is a tournament or special event (or league) that is open to all who would qualify under the definition of the particular event.

Following are suggested events that could be offered during the year. Included are individual, dual, and team activities. Certain of the activities would be conducted separately for men and women, and others would be coed.[9]

Fall	*Winter*	*Spring*
Individual fitness	Individual fitness	Softball
Football (touch)	Basketball	Racquetball
Tennis	Racquetball	Basketball
Horseshoes	Water polo	Volleyball

Fall	Winter	Spring
Bicycle race	Badminton	Tennis
Soccer	Arm wrestling	Mini marathon
Volleyball	Volleyball	
Racquetball	Bowling	*Summer*
Basketball	Wrestling	Softball
Handball	Water basketball	Tennis
Table tennis	Tennis	Basketball
Badminton	Road rally	Racquetball
Swim meet	Mini marathon	Golf
		Mini marathon

TOURNAMENT ORGANIZATION AND MANAGEMENT

A tournament is organized competition in an activity, usually for a relatively short period of time, which finally results in determining a champion.

The purposes of tournament play include the following:
1. To stimulate interest and develop excellence in the particular activity.
2. To provide challenging competition in wholesome activities.
3. To prepare players for higher-level competition.
4. To determine a champion.

Tournament Terminology

Bracket: The lines used in a tournament chart to show opposing players or teams.

Bye: When a player or team advances to the next bracket without opposition, and a win is credited.

Challenge: An invitation to engage in a match or contest.

Default: Failure of one of the contenders to begin or complete a scheduled match

Division: Normally, a large component of a program, containing one or more leagues gruped under a logical classification, i.e., fraternity, residence hall, graduate, or independent.

Handicap: An advantage given a contender as a means of equalizing competition.

League: The grouping of teams (or organizations) of like characteristics into units for competition.

Match: A contest to declare a winner between two or more opponents.

Qualifying Round: A contest that allows the winners to advance.

Round: The first round in the tournament is completed when all the teams have played one match.

Seeding: The placement of teams or individuals in different brackets so that those with superior records do not meet in the early rounds of a tournament.

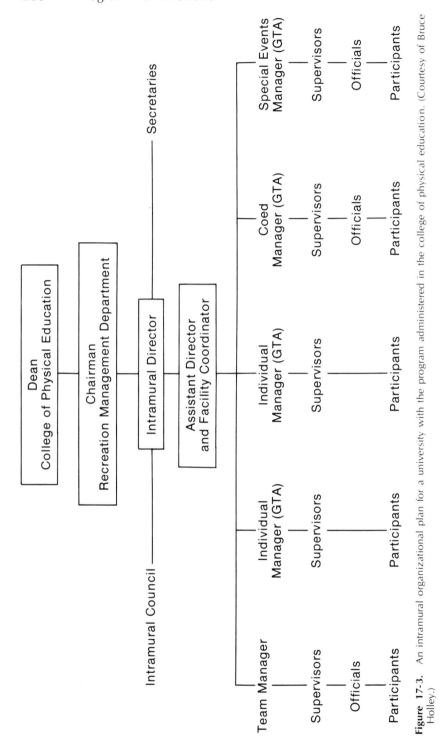

Figure 17-3. An intramural organizational plan for a university with the program administered in the college of physical education. (Courtesy of Bruce Holley.)

Tie Breaker: (overtime or sudden death) A means of declaring a champion after the regular event has ended in a tie, based on points, a period of time, distance, or numbers, depending on the activity. This process ensures an immediate champion.

Types of Tournaments

The particular tournaments described in this section are the round robin, Lombard, challenge tournaments (ladder, pyramid, and funnel), and elimination tournaments (single, consolation, and double). These are the more frequently used tournaments in intramural programs.[9]

Several other kinds of tournaments, which are used infrequently, sometimes fit a situation better than the tournaments mentioned. Among them are the following: Ringer tournament (improvement tournament), Olympic meet tournament, Bagnall-wild elimination tournament (a modification of the single elimination), combination elimination and round robin, and tombstone tournament. Descriptions of these tournaments can be found in textbooks on intramurals.

Tournaments that are selected for use in intramural programs ought to (1) provide a near equal amount of involvement for all participants (avoid early elimination); (2) provide well matched competition; (3) be neither too short nor too long; and (4) select a champion with a few other subsequent places also determined.

The five basic criteria for selecting the best tournament are the number of participants, available facilities and equipment, participants' interest, availability of qualified officials, and the sport or activity.

Leaders should select the tournament offering the most opportunity for participation in the allotted time.

Round Robin.[9] If sufficient time and adequate facilities exist, the round robin tournament is a good choice. It is superior to other tournaments because it produces a true winner, ranks other contestants, and allows all contestants to play without interruption until the end. Each entry plays every other entry at least once; in a double round robin, each contestant plays all others twice. The winner is the contestant who wins the most games.

In scheduling a round robin tournament, the entries are arranged in two columns, as shown in Figure 17-4 under "Rd 1." This provides the pairings for the first round of play. If the number of entries is uneven, a bye is added.

Rd 1	Rd 2	Rd 3	Rd 4	Rd 5	Rd 6	Rd 7	Check
A vs H	A vs G	A vs F	A vs E	A vs D	A vs C	A vs B	A - H
B vs G	H vs F	G vs E	F vs D	E vs C	D vs B	C vs H	B - G
C vs F	B vs E	H vs D	G vs C	F vs B	E vs H	D vs G	C - F
D vs E	C vs D	B vs C	H vs B	G vs H	F vs G	E vs F	D - E

Figure 17-4. Round Robin tournament involving eight teams.

(Bye indicates that the entry paired with the bye does not play during that round.) For the remaining rounds of play, the entry in the top left column remains stationary and the other contestants rotate one position each round. If a bye is necessary, it may be placed in the stationary position. Entries rotate either clockwise or couterclockwise. Counterclockwise rotation is used in the example below. The check round is not scheduled for play. Its only purpose is to check for errors. If it is the same as round one, each round is probably correct. Team names may be substituted for letters.

It is usually best to schedule rounds of play at the same time on the same day each week. This makes the schedule easy to remember. The total number of tournament games required is given by this formula: Total games $= \dfrac{N\,(N-1)}{2}$, where N represents the number of entries. (N must be an even number. If not, add bye to the list of participants.)

Example:

$$7 \text{ teams} + \text{Bye} = 8 \text{ teams} \quad \frac{8\,(8-1)}{2} = \frac{8 \times 7}{2} = 28$$

28 games for a single
round robin tournament.

When the schedule is printed, it should include the date, time, and place for each game, as shown in the following example.

	January 15—Round 1			January 22—Round 2	
	Bye vs. Hotshots			Bye vs. Snappers	
8:00	Snappers vs. Topnotch	Court I	8:00	Bombers vs. Hotshots	Court I
8:00	Bombers vs. Sliders	Court II	8:00	Panthers vs. Topnotch	Court II
9:00	Panthers vs. Flash	Court I	9:00	Flash vs. Sliders	Court I

A win-loss chart such as shown in Figure 17-5 may be posted to report the scores and keep the team records.

If time permits, a double round robin provides an interesting modification. It is even more valid than the single round robin because it results in each entry playing each other entry twice.

Lombard. The Lombard tournament is a round robin played in one day of competition. The number of games to be played is divided into the available time to give the length of each game. As in the regular round robin, each entry plays all other entries. Winners may be determined by adding total points scored by a team and subtracting points scored against it. The entry with the most points left is the winner. More simply, win-loss records may also be used to declare the winner.

Example: Six teams want to play a basketball tournament in which each team plays every other team. They have two courts for 3 hours (6 hours total playing time) to play 15 games. Dividing 15 games into 6 hours (360 minutes) gives 24 minutes per game. Each game could be 20 minutes, with 4 minutes between games.

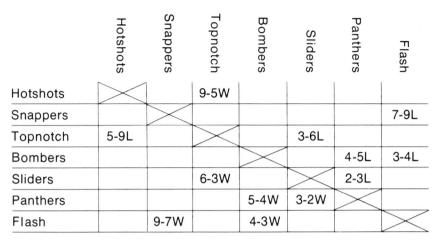

	Hotshots	Snappers	Topnotch	Bombers	Sliders	Panthers	Flash
Hotshots	✕		9-5W				
Snappers		✕					7-9L
Topnotch	5-9L		✕		3-6L		
Bombers				✕		4-5L	3-4L
Sliders			6-3W		✕	2-3L	
Panthers				5-4W	3-2W	✕	
Flash			9-7W	4-3W			✕

Figure 17-5. A win-loss chart.

Challenge.[9]   A challenge tournament is one in which the several contestants are placed in a particular order, and then each entry has the opportunity of improving its position (or standing) by challenging and defeating one of the entries above it. The general procedures are as follow:
1. Announce and describe the tournament, including the rules and the starting date.
2. Make a signup sheet available.
3. Place contestants on the schedule as they signed up, or by drawing or seeding.
4. Challenges begin. If the challenger wins, it exchanges places with the defeated entry. Otherwise, no change in placement is made.

Once a challenge is placed, the challenged entry must agree to play within a certain period of time or forfeit. This keeps the tournament moving. Usually, a player or team is required to play a contestant from below if a challenge has been made, before challenging another player or team above. In this type of tournament, each contestant's objective should be to get to the top by challenging and defeating the contestants above.

There are three kinds of challenge tournaments—ladder, pyramid, and funnel (upside down funnel). These are illustrated in Figure 17-6. In the *ladder* tournament, the entries are arranged in vertical sequence like the rungs on a ladder, then the challenges begin. As a general rule, contestants are limited to challenging only one or two places above. This number should be decided before competition starts.

The *pyramid* tournament offers a greater possible number of games because a contestant may challenge not only any player on the same line but also either of the players on the immediate left or right in the line above. For example, in the diagram in Figure 17-6, Player 9 may challenge Players 7 or 8 on the same line or 5 or 6 on the line above.

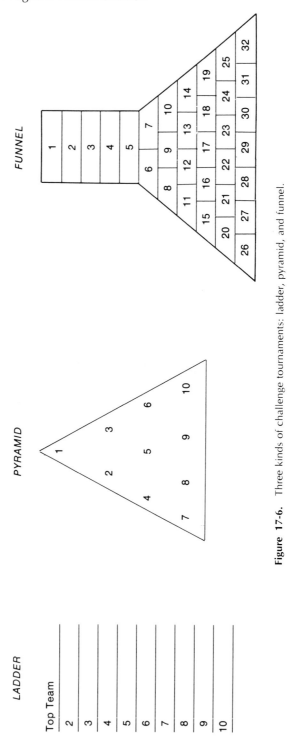

Figure 17-6. Three kinds of challenge tournaments: ladder, pyramid, and funnel.

In the case of an unusually large number of entries, the *funnel* tournament may be a good choice. It combines certain features of the ladder and pyramid tournaments. In the lower portion of the funnel, play is governed by the rules for the pyramid tournament, while in the upper portion play is governed by the rules for the ladder tournament.

Elimination.[9] In elimination tournaments, all competitors except the winner become eliminated. Each entry is eliminated after either one or two losses, depending on whether the tournament is single or double elimination. The bracketing for an elimination tournament is done as follows:

1. Brackets are set up to provide positions for the teams entered if the number of teams is 2, 4, 8, 16, 32, or any other power of 2.
2. If the number of teams is *not* equal to a power of 2, the brackets are set up to the next larger power of 2.
3. Byes are awarded to teams without opponents, making the schedule even. (Example: Use a 16-player bracket for 12 players. Award four byes, two in the upper bracket and two in the lower bracket).
4. To determine the number of byes, subtract the number of teams or players from the next larger power of 2.
5. Place byes as far apart as possible so that they are eliminated in the first round of play.

The seeding process places the strongest teams in separate brackets so that they will not meet in early tournament rounds. Sometimes there is no seeding, but often between one fourth and one half of the entries are seeded. Any necessary byes should be awarded to seeded teams.

In the *single elimination* tournament, the losing contestants are dropped from the tournament and play continues until only one entry remains. The advantages and disadvantages of this kind of tournament are that

1. The tournament is short and expedient, since one half of the entries are eliminated in the first round and half of those remaining are eliminated in each succeeding round.
2. Even though the winner is determined quickly, the best entry may not win, due to the fact that injuries or "off game" may cause upsets.
3. Each team is assured of playing only one game.

The formula for determining the number of games in a single elimination tournament is $N-1$ (N is the number of entries). For example, 25 entries will require 24 games ($25-1=24$). Figure 17-7 shows examples of elimination tournaments for 6 entries and 13 entries. Six entries require a tournament with 8 positions, thus having 2 byes. Thirteen entries require a tournament with 16 positions, thus having 3 byes. The seeded teams are placed in the tournaments so that there is no chance that they will meet each other in the early rounds.

In a consolation elimination tournament, the teams are arranged in brackets in the same fashion as in the single elimination tournament. Actually, the consolation tournament is a single elimination tournament moving

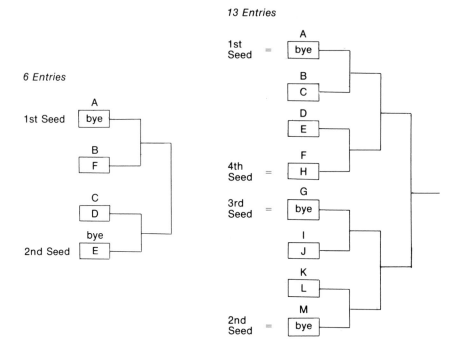

Figure 17-7. Example of two single-elimination tournaments, involving 6 and 13 entries.

to the right with a consolation tournament added which moves to the left. After the first round of competition, the winners go right and the losers go left. From there on, both tournaments are single elimination. The ultimate winner on the winner's side (right) is the tournament champion, while the runner-up on the winner's side finishes in second place. The winner on the consolation side (left) wins third place. Figure 17-8 shows three consolation tournaments involving 4 teams, 8 teams, and 16 teams. Seeding can be done in the same way as in the single elimination tournament.

In the *double elimination* tournament, each entry is assured of playing at least two contests; however, after losing twice a contestant is eliminated. The brackets are established in the same manner as in the single elimination tournament and seeding is also done in the same way. In the double elimination tournament, the formula for determining the number of contests is $2N-1$ or 2 (with N meaning the number of entries). Example: with 12 entries, the formula would be $2 \times 12 = 24 - 1$ or 2×23 or 22 games.

The contestants who lose in the first round move to the left, while the winners move to the right. Subsequently, as a team on the left loses again, it is eliminated because it has two losses, while a team on the right that loses moves over to the loser's side (left). If that entry loses again, it is eliminated. Because an entry is not eliminated until it loses twice, the winner of the

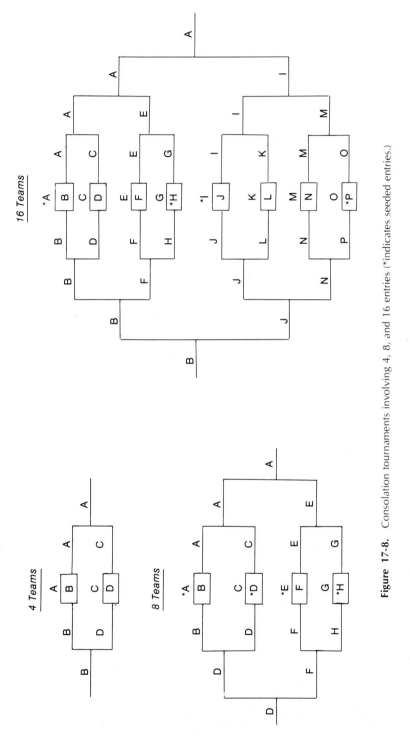

Figure 17-8. Consolation tournaments involving 4, 8, and 16 entries. (*indicates seeded entries.)

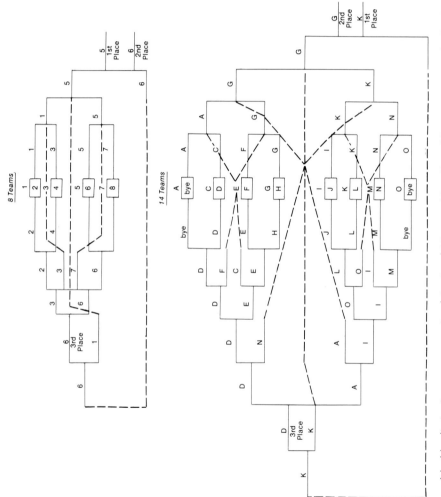

Figure 17-9. Examples of double-elimination tournaments, involving 8 and 14 teams. (Note: Dotted lines may cross each other to different brackets to reduce chances of playing the same team twice).

losers bracket plays the winner of the winners bracket for the championship. Refer to the 8-team tournament in Figure 17-9 and follow these instructions:

1. After the first round, the winners move to the right and the losers to the left.
2. Subsequently, when an entry on the winner's side loses, it moves over to the loser's side.
3. Team 1 plays Team 2, Team 3 plays Team 4, Team 5 plays Team 6, and Team 7 plays Team 8. Teams 1, 3, 5, and 7 are winners, while Teams 2, 4, 6, and 8 are losers.
4. On the winner's side, 1 plays 3 and 5 plays 7. Teams 1 and 5 are winners, Teams 3 and 7 are losers, and therefore, they move to the unattached lines on the left side of the tournament (follow the dotted lines). Team 2 plays 4 and 6 plays 8. Teams 2 and 6 are winners, Teams 4 and 8 are losers and are therefore eliminated because they have each lost twice.
5. Team 2 plays 3 and 7 plays 6. Teams 3 and 6 are winners. Teams 2 and 7 are eliminated because they have each lost twice.
6. Team 3 plays 6, Team 6 wins, therefore, Team 3 is eliminated.
7. Team 1 plays 5, and Team 5 is the winner. The loser, Team 1, moves to the left side.
8. Team 1 plays 6 and Team 6 wins; therefore, Team 1 is eliminated because it has lost twice, but it wins third place in the tournament.
9. Two teams remain—5 and 6. They play each other and Team 5 wins; therefore, it wins the championship, and Team 6 places second.

Tournament Classification System[9]

Sometimes in intramural programs, equalization pretournament rounds are played. All participants end up in one of four classifications: AAAA, AAA, AA, A. AAAA constitutes the top division (best entries).

Participants first play two or more classification games. If an entry wins both games, it will be in class AAAA. If it wins the first and loses the second, it will be in class AAA. If it loses the first and wins the second, it will be in class AA. If it loses both, it will be in class A. This classification procedure does not always have to be followed exactly, however. If you can tell that an entry is sandbagging or not playing to its full ability, you have the option of placing the entry in the class that it ought to be.

Participants then enter tournament play in their respective classes. Some general guidelines follow:

1. Always protect the A class. If there is any doubt of an entry belonging in a higher or lower class, always put it in the higher.
2. Emphasize that it is considered unethical to lose on purpose to get a lower classification.
3. If a contestant wants to be in a higher class, let him.
4. All late entries not participating in the classification rounds should be classified AAAA (no exceptions).

With this classification system, some of the most exciting events occur in the A class. Many participants have been relatively unsuccessful in open or unclassified competition. This system gives all entries a chance to compete against others with a similar skill level; therefore, everyone has a reasonable chance to experience some success and enjoy the benefits of equalized competition. Figure 17-10 shows how the pretournament rounds are arranged to determine the participants in the four classes.

Seeding

The ultimate objective of seeding is to have the best two contestants meet for the final match. Seeding is important to contestants for tactical and morale purposes. The main problem with seeding is the prospect of human error in evaluating the contestants based on available information.

A general principle of seeding is to place the best contestant in the upper half of the draw, the second best in the bottom half, the third best in the upper half and the fourth best in the lower half and to continue this pattern throughout. This distributes the best ranked contestants in a uniform manner.

Seeding for 4 and 8 teams can be readily understood, but seedings for 16- and 32-team tournaments are more complex. The detailed aspects of seeding are covered adequately in other sources, particularly in books on intramural programs.

Supremacy Point System

The supremacy point system can sometimes serve a useful purpose if the same units (such as fraternities, sororities, and housing units) compete in various sports throughout the intramural season. Each unit enters a team in each activity, and points are awarded to relative standing so that at the end of the year, the team with the most accumulated points is the winner. This system can stimulate interest in full participation and increase the excitement and competitive spirit among the various organizations involved in the program.

Opponents of the point system claim that it is not philosophically sound, because it causes students to play for points instead of the satisfaction of participation. Opponents also stress that point programs are expensive to maintain in terms of record keeping and personnel requirements.

A point system does have many benefits. It stimulates interest, may increase participation, allows individuals to examine their standings relative to other players, and rewards not only winning but also participation.

AWARDS

Awards are used to generate student interest, increase participation, and recognize outstanding accomplishments or service. Some leaders consider the awarding of pins, plaques, medals, certificates, and trophies undesirable, saying that it causes students to seek the awards and not the true value received from the experience itself. Awards are sometimes called "bribes"

Figure 17-10. Pretournament for arranging the participants into four classes for league or tournament play.

that lead students to participate more for the extrinsic rewards than for the intrinsic values of participation.

Intramurals probably have a place for an awards program, provided it is on the conservative side and carefully managed. Consistency is important, because an awards program creates expectations among students, and inconsistency results in disappointments.

ELIGIBILITY

The question of who is eligible to participate is one that must be approached with precision and consistency. In intramurals, since participation is encouraged, the general guideline should be that a person is eligible unless sufficient reason exists to deny eligibility.

Intramurals should not be used as a disciplinary measure for students who fail to meet requirements or expectations in other school programs. If the student performs poorly in mathematics, he is not prohibited from attending English or school lunch or assemblies. Likewise, a student should not be prohibited from participating in intramurals due to poor performance in other areas. In fact, the opposite ought to be encouraged, because intramurals have their own potential for development of the participants and can be an integrating and socializing force, which can help certain students remain interested and want to continue in school.

The main questions that pertain to eligibility are the following: (1) Should a current member of a varsity team be permitted to participate on an intramural team in that particular sport? Usually the answer to this question is no; (2) Should a former member of a varsity team be permitted to participate on an intramural team in that particular sport? The answer to this is less definite and varies with different programs. (3) Should an athlete who is trying out for a varsity team but has not yet made it be permitted to participate on an intramural team? (4) Should members of junior varsity teams be eligible for intramurals? (5) Should members of the faculty and staff participate in the same league with students, and if so, should they be on separate teams or play on teams with students? (6) Should a girl be able to participate on a boys' team under any circumstances, and should a boy, on a girls' team? (7) Should part-time students and adjunct teachers participate? (8) Should any limit be placed on the number of intramural activities a person can enter in a given year? (9) Should a participant be able to play on more than one team at a time in a particular sport?

All of the above questions are of concern in determining who can and cannot participate. Other questions would pertain to eligibility, depending on the particular situation.

FINANCES

The financial considerations of any program involve two broad aspects: obtaining a constant and adequate amount of funding, and administering the funds wisely toward meeting the objectives of the program. Although an ample intramural budget is important, many effective programs are sponsored with limited funds, especially in the public schools. Shortage of funds should not be used as an excuse for not having a program. The ideal is a secure source of income that is granted on the basis of actual need. Intramural programs are funded in a variety of ways: appropriated funds, student fees, entry fees, equipment or locker rentals, forfeit fees, gifts, and fund-raising projects. Appropriated funds would have to be considered the best source.

RULES AND REGULATIONS

Rules and regulations are used in intramural programs to equalize competition, provide safe playing conditions, and establish standards of conduct. The following guidelines apply here.

1. Develop and state the rules and regulations in a positive manner, carrying out suggestions from the intramural council and the players.
2. Establish only those rules and regulations that are reasonable, beneficial, and enforceable. The staff may be too small to act as lawyer, judge, and jury.
3. Coordinate the rules and regulations with the total philosophy of the school and its relationship to serving the students.
4. State the rules in simple language.
5. Standardize the administrative procedures for handling violations.
6. Review and update the rules on an annual basis. As the needs of the students and program change, the rules and regulations should be modified.

PRECAUTIONARY MEASURES

The same precautionary measures must be taken with intramurals as with participation in vigorous activity in other aspects of the physical education program. These considerations are discussed elsewhere and they include (1) adequate safety measures for protection of the participants, (2) evidence of fitness to participate, (3) adequate opportunity for student insurance coverage, (4) measures to guard against potential law suits and (5) providing the best qualified officials that can be made available. A form for evaluating intramural officials is shown in Figure 17-11.

COMPUTER COORDINATION
OF INTRAMURALS

Where does one start when looking into the possibility of computerizing a comprehensive program? Brigham Young University went to their Computer Department for a thorough feasibility study, which turned out to be highly positive. After careful consideration of the University's resources, the budget requirements, and the potential for such a program, it was determined that the following benefits would result: overall increased efficiency, better service to the students' needs, a superior evaluation device, and more consist-

Official's Name _____

	Poor	Fair	Average	Good	Superior
Knowledge of the Rules					
Displays accurate knowledge of the rules	1	2	3	4	5
Renders proper interpretation of the rules	1	2	3	4	5
Competency in Mechanics of Officiating					
Assumes proper positioning	1	2	3	4	5
Makes calls and signals in proper fashion	1	2	3	4	5
Alert to total scene of contest and cooperates with other officials	1	2	3	4	5
Physical Attributes					
Satisfactory physical condition and appearance	1	2	3	4	5
Attendance and getting equipment ready for start of game	1	2	3	4	5
Desirable Personal Qualities					
Exerts positive control of responsibilities for supervising the contest	1	2	3	4	5
Displays consistency and sound judgment in decisions	1	2	3	4	5
Reflects confidence and poise, self-control and calmness	1	2	3	4	5

Evaluated by _____

Figure 17-11. Intramural officials' evaluation form.

ency year in and year out, even though student personnel turned over rapidly. This would help eliminate hundreds of hours of scheduling conflicts, mistakes, and problems that occurred with the old program. The following is an overview of the computerization of the BYU program, a result of over 2 years of study and development.[8]

Overview: Computerized Program

When a team enters an activity, the coach fills out an entry form. This includes all team statistics, names, student numbers, telephone numbers, and the like. Each team is assigned a division (e.g., competitive or noncompetitive) and league. The team information is then entered into the computer via the CRT (computer terminal) screen in the intramural office. This is the master record from which all other programs will function. The master record will track individuals and teams, keeping vital statistics on all they do in intramurals.

By using the CRT screen, any of the following information can be obtained:

1. An instantaneous check of students' status to tell whether they are eligible to participate in intramurals (e.g., full-time or part-time).
2. The win/loss record, what teams they have played, and what their team power rating and sportsmanship was for each game played.
3. Who played in each game and who, if any, was suspended.
4. Identification of officials and evaluation of their performance throughout the program.
5. A complete history for each team (can be brought up for review, additions, or deletions).

The graduate assistant in charge of this program schedules the teams for play each week. He does this by entering into the computer the facilities and times given by the facility coordinator. Once this is done, the computer schedules each team to a facility, time, and day, taking into consideration some of the following features:

1. The computer checks eligibility. If the team is eligible, it will be scheduled.
2. If a team fails to show up (forfeit), the computer will drop the team from further play.
3. Two fair or one poor sportsmanship rating or two excused losses will automatically drop the team from further play.
4. The computer prioritizes teams according to the number of games they have played and schedules first those teams with the fewest games played.
5. If, when scheduling a league, the computer runs out of facilities, it will assign byes to all other unscheduled teams and put them on priority for the next schedule.
6. Print-outs are produced for posting on campus; they have the following information: One team versus another team; each team's win/loss record; the facility in which they have been scheduled; the time and day they will play.
7. The print-outs list teams in alphabetic order.
8. The scheduling program has a variety of capabilities. It can schedule on a weekly, biweekly, or an entire semester basis.
9. The computer recognizes a team's identity and will not schedule any two teams to play each other more than once, as in a round robin tournament.

After the computer schedules the teams, it will produce a team sheet with the following information: team statistics, names of players, opposing team name, and the facility, date, and time scheduled. The game sheet is a universal form that is used for all team activities, e.g., basketball, football, softball, water polo.

The intramural computer program at BYU has an inventory of or access to

1. An IBM 360 computer, or one of similar capabilities.
2. A CRT screen with on-line tie in to the admissions and registration data base.
3. An on-line printer.

The entire program has been written in COBAL with the core developed around the teleprocessing system. All programs can be manipulated, adjusted, and revised through the CRT (computer terminal). All of these computer programs can be adapted to similar units, even minicomputers that do not have on-line capabilities.

At the end of the year, the computer is used for program evaluation, statistical analysis, and a final report. Every activity administered through the Intramural Department is analyzed by the computer for participation, money spent, and other criteria to determine program effectiveness. Many questions can be answered that few universities with a large program could answer without such assistance. Some of these questions are as follows: "How many freshmen, sophomores, juniors, seniors, graduates, and faculty participate in the program?" "What are the percentages of each?" "Is the program serving the needs of the students?" "What is the ratio between male and female participants?"

One problem with the large numbers of teams playing each week (500 to 700) was being able to schedule, run, and oversee the program. With the computer doing the work, time is freed for the leaders, allowing them to deal personally with the students. This is essential for quality programs.

BYU's intramural program is a large, diversified one, lending itself to computer support. Other universities on the same scale may find this type of computer program to their liking. In smaller schools, an adaptation of all or portions of the program may better suit their needs.

The computer program has not eliminated any personnel. It has, however, improved the ability to serve the students, and has eliminated many hours of scheduling and other book work. The graduate assistants operate in the best of both worlds—they are exposed to advanced techniques of computerization and to traditional ways of administering programs by hand when the task is considered too small for computer application. Some might say that even though many problems are eliminated, the computer will create more. This may be true to a certain extent, but once understood and developed, the computerization of intramural departments across the country will be the way of the future.

A POSITION STATEMENT

Chapters 13 and 15 contained statements of beliefs from the Society of State Directors of Health, Physical Education and Recreation, with which the author concurs and with which all physical education teachers, coaches, and administrators ought to be familiar. The following are statements of belief from the Society about intramurals and other extraclass programs.

These beliefs help to give clarity to this aspect of the school program. They are printed with the permission of the Society.

EXTRA-CLASS ACTIVITIES
(Intramurals, Extramurals, Sports Clubs and Recreation Activities)

Every school should provide ample opportunity for participation in intramural, extramural and recreational activities for all students. These programs not only supplement physical education instruction but also afford opportunities for social exchange, enrichment of individual personal resources, and wholesome competition below the varsity level of excellence. Extra-class activities should be consistent with the content and philosophy of the physical education program of instruction. Such activities, if handled properly, can be particularly helpful in promoting good human relationships and community involvement, and in minimizing problems of racial integration, student unrest, and the like.

ABOUT ADMINISTRATION

Extra-class activities should be provided for and financed by boards of education.

School administrators should ensure ample opportunity for all students to participate in individual, dual and team sports, and other suitable physical activities. School transportation should be provided when needed.

Extra-class activities should be administered by school officials, but community facilities and resource persons should be utilized whenever the program can be improved through such use.

Extra-class competition should be equalized, in terms of the age, skill, size and strength of participants.

Policies should be established to protect pupils from injury or over-participation.
   —Health examinations should be a prerequisite for participation in vigorous activity.
   —Protective, well-fitting equipment for participants, good facilities and equipment, and capable personnel are essential to participants in intramurals and other extra-class activities.
   —Boxing should not be included at any grade level.
   —Sponsoring of body contact sports below the ninth grade places the school on tenuous grounds, unless the school accepts full responsibility for providing excellent leadership, facilities, equipment, and policies for promoting and protecting the health and welfare of participants.

Awards for extra-class activities are unnecessary. If given at all, they should be simple and of little monetary value, providing only token recognition of an activity satisfactorily completed. Students should be motivated to participate through school-wide emphasis on the values and opportunities inherent in such participation and through the joy afforded by well-planned and well-administered programs.

ABOUT PROGRAM

Education and development of the individual through satisfying and enjoyable participation in selected activities should be the program.

Opportunity to participate in a wide variety of extra-class activities should be provided for both boys and girls of all grades. Activities should be based on the interests, needs, capacities, and level of maturity of the pupils. The program should be broad enough to help meet the needs of pupils who are mentally or physically handicapped or who have social or emotional problems.

Leadership opportunities should be made available to pupils regardless of their sex and skill level.

ABOUT PERSONNEL

Since extra-class program participation is voluntary, the program should be staffed with enthusiastic teachers who possess high-level leadership skills and organizational competencies.

BIBLIOGRAPHY

1. Baren, Donald E.: Improving response and participation in intramural programs. JOPER, *51* (3):51, 1980.

2. Colgate, J.A.: Administration of Intramurals and Recreational Activities. New York, John Wiley and Sons, 1978.

3. Cooney, L.: Sports clubs: their place within the total intramural-recreational sports program. JOPER, 50 (3):40, 1979.

4. Fabian, L., Ross, M., and Harwick, B.: Every player wins in recreational sports. JOPER, *51* (9):29, 1980.

5. Gerou, N.E.: Complete Guide to Administering the Intramural Program. West Nyack, NY, Parker Publishing Company, 1976.

6. Haniford, G.W.: Recreational sports: a component of the campus leisure system. JOPER, *51* (4):48, 1980.

7. Hatcher, P.G., and Shields, S.L.: Recreational sports on a limited budget. JOPER, *52*:29, 1981.

8. Holley, B.: Computer coordination of campus intramurals. JOPER, 51 (4):50, 1980.

9. Holley, B.: Unpublished materials on intramural activities. Brigham Young University, Provo, UT, 1981.

10. Hosberry, W., Marciani, L., and Vos Strache, C.: Intramural-Recreational Sports: New Direction and Ideas. Corvallis, OR, Benton Printers, 1980.

11. Hyatt, R.: Intramural Sports: Organization and Administration. St. Louis: The C.V. Mosby, Co., 1977.

12. Jandris, T.: Possibilities and potentials—high school intramurals. JOPER, *51* (3):49, 1980.

13. Kidd, E., and Pankay, M.: Extension of the elementary physical education class through an intramural program. JOPER, March *51* (3):46, 1980.

14. Kidd, T.R., and Mendell, R.: Organized athletics as a leisure delivery system. JOPER, *51* (4):59, 1980.

15. Maas, G.: High school intramurals—an endangered species. JOPER, *51* (3):52, 1980.

16. Mendell, R.: Campus recreation. JOPER, *51* (4):32, 1980.

17. Mirel, P., and Barrett, P.: The disabled and recreational opportunities on campus. JOPER, *51* (4):43, 1980.

18. Nesbitt, J.A., Snider, W.C., and Van Meter, S.: Recreation services for those with handicapping conditions. JOPER, *51* (4):41, 1980.

19. Peterson, J.A.: Intramural Administration Theory and Practice. Englewood Cliffs, NJ, Prentice-Hall, 1976.

20. Sheilds, E.W.: Intramurals: an avenue for developing leisure values. JOPER, 50 (4):75, 1979.

21. Stineman, G.: The Newton plan—an intramural program for the middle school. JOPER, 50 (8):83, 1979.

22. Tenoschok, M.: Intramurals, above and beyond. JOPER, *52:*32, 1981.

23. Thelen, B.: Points for intramurals. JOPER, *52:*20, 1981.

24. Vannoy, W.: Intramurals for the handicapped students of Kent State University. JOPER, *52:*22, 1981.

25. Woods, J.B., and Daughtrey, G.: Physical Education and Intramural Programs. Philadelphia, W.B. Saunders, 1976.

Chapter *18*

EVALUATION METHODS AND PROCEDURES

Evaluation has numerous facets and various applications. This chapter deals with three important areas of evaluation, that of *students, personnel,* and *programs*. In addition to these major aspects of education, evaluation is also necessary in connection with such items as educational goals, adequacy of facilities, efficiency of procedures, allocation of resources, discipline, and other control factors. Evaluation of the various aspects of the total operation is the process by which weaknesses are identified; however, evaluation for the purpose of detecting weaknesses serves little purpose unless the information is utilized to correct the weaknesses and improve the results.

The term evaluation is inclusive of exact measurements, subjective measurements, and considered judgments. It involves assessment against defined standards, criteria, or goals. The result is the determination of the relative status or worth of that which is being evaluated.

WHY EVALUATE

Evaluation should be approached with a constructive and positive attitude and with a sincere desire to accurately appraise and constructively change. The end product of evaluation should be improvement. Without the honest intent to accurately appraise and improve, evaluation has little purpose and, therefore, little justification.

The three steps in evaluation are collection of useful information about the present status; objective comparison of the information against the desired status or condition; and an effective plan to close the gap between the present status and that which is desired.

The two basic forms of evaluation are known as formative and summative. *Formative* evaluation is the kind that is done along the way to identify weaknesses and problems in order that the best solutions can be determined and implemented. *Summative* evaluation is for the purpose of making a final decision as to whether the person or program being evaluated will be permitted to continue. Formative evaluation carries with it no risk because its

306

end is simply to bring about positive change. Summative evaluation, on the other hand, carries with it the risk of elimination. Its final objective is to answer the question of whether to accept or continue with the person, program, or situation that is under consideration.

EVALUATION OF STUDENTS

In connection with student evaluation, tests, measurements, and evaluations are commonly used terms which have certain similarities and certain differences.

A *test* requires a performance by the individual being tested. The performer receives a score representing how well he performed. The quality or quantity of an individual's strength, speed, jumping ability, knowledge, and so on are determined by the use of tests.

The term *measurement* includes all tests, but is not confined to them. Some measurements do not require a performance by the person. For instance, measurements of body height, weight, and percent of body fat are not tests.

Evaluation is broader and more inclusive than either of the other terms. It is a process of determining the status of something and of relating that status to some standard in order to make a value judgment. For example, evaluations are made of teaching methods, program content, teacher effectiveness, and student performance and progress. Evaluation is often based on test results in addition to information secured from observations, interviews, questionnaires, and other measures.

Reasons for Measuring

Educators are vitally concerned with the kind and amount of student development and adjustment resulting from participation in school programs. They are specifically concerned with the development of knowledge, concepts, and judgments; interests, attitudes, and ideals; strength and skill; and the development of the organic system.

If a teacher is to design a high-quality instructional program and teach students effectively, he must obtain considerable information about the students. The more information a teacher has about students' interests, abilities, and needs, the better an effective program can be designed and conducted. Much of the necessary information can be gathered with the use of tests and measurements.

The basic purposes for measurement in education are to increase knowledge about the students and to improve instruction.

The six specific purposes or uses of measurement in physical education are the following[13]:

Diagnostic. Measurement is necessary to diagnose the differences in abilities, interests, and needs of students in order to plan and conduct effective programs. Objective knowledge about specific student deficiencies is essential to provide both remedial and accelerated programs.

Classification. Sometimes it is an advantage to classify students into homogeneous or heterogeneous groups, whichever is desired for a particular type of instruction, competition, or experience. Such classification is often based on the results of appropriate measurements.

Achievement. Objective measures and accurate records of student achievement and progress form the basis for the selection of program content, for the assignment of grades or marks, and for the advancement of students.

Administration. Objective information obtained from measurements serves as a basis for determining the best methods of instruction and for guiding students into appropriate experiences. Accurate measurements help to determine the success of students and to learn whether students are ready to progress to the next higher level.

Supervisory. Objective test results are often valuable in the evaluation of teachers and teaching efficiency.

Research. The field of physical education is rich with opportunities for valuable research. Most scientific research can be performed effectively only with the use of appropriate tests.

Selection of Measurements

Measurements range from highly *subjective* to highly *objective*. Objective measures are based largely on facts, while subjective measures are primarily a result of judgment. Subjective measurement, such as a teacher's evaluation of a student's character, includes some degree of objectivity, but also involves a large amount of subjective judgment. Objective measurement is based on more precise information. A measure is objective to the extent that it will produce the same results when conducted by different people under similar conditions; in other words, when the subjectivity of the test administrator is eliminated. Teachers should strive for a high degree of objectivity in measurement, but still realize that not all important traits can be measured objectively.

In order for a measurement to be highly objective it must have a high degree of validity and reliability. *Validity* is the extent to which the test actually measures what it is claimed to measure.

Reliability is the degree to which all persons using the procedure will achieve comparable results consistently.

It is difficult to say how much time and money should be devoted to the administration of any measurement; but in every case, the value of the results should be weighed in comparison with the expenditure of money, time, and effort. This is *administrative economy*.

Educational application is the degree to which the testing experience in itself is educational or motivational. Measurements should be harmonious with and supplemental to course content.

Many *kinds of measurements* are applicable in physical education programs. They fall into the following categories.

Fitness

Muscular strength and endurance tests
Tests of circulorespiratory endurance
Measures of flexibility
Fitness test batteries

Motor Performance

Measures of Power
Agility
Reaction time and speed
Balance and kinesthetic perception
Neuromuscular skills (sports skills)

Nonphysical Performance

Measures of the body structure and body mechanisms
Measures of personality traits such as interests, attitudes, behavior, and
character
Tests of knowledge about sports rules and strategies and techniques

Administration of Measurements

Careful attention should be given to the *administration of tests*. Poorly administered tests can produce results that are misleading and useless to both the teacher and the students. The following are some guides for administering tests.[13]

1. Select and administer a test for a specific purpose; and be certain that it is administered in such a way as to accomplish that purpose.
2. Become familiar with the test and the procedures involved before attempting to administer it.
3. Make proper arrangements for all necessary facilities and equipment and be sure the equipment is in usable condition.
4. Determine the layout of testing stations and have needed equipment in place at the required time.
5. Be sure those being tested appear in appropriate clothing, especially in appropriate footwear.
6. Make early arrangements for necessary assistant leaders to help administer the test. In some cases, a short period of training for the assistants may be desirable.
7. Conduct the test in exact accordance with correct procedures.
8. Have the necessary score sheets, pencils, and scoring scales available.

The test results should be interpreted and used to the advantage of the students and the program. Teachers should constantly be aware that the exactness and correctness with which they administer a test influences its reliability. Test results that might have been valuable become useless when they are improperly administered and incorrectly interpreted.

Application of Results

Among the uses of measurement results are (1) the motivation of students toward achievement; (2) evaluation of the effectiveness of the educational program; and (3) evaluation of student progress. In turn, the results are useful in establishing student marks (grades).

Students generally want to be more knowledgeable, more fit, and more skillful. They are motivated by goals and want to demonstrate their achievements and be recognized for them. Furthermore, they want to see evidence that they are progressing, and they become stimulated by such evidence.

Both written and motor performance tests can assess achievement levels. The results of such tests provide students with evidence of progress or lack of progress in attaining these goals. The lack of this kind of information detracts from motivation.

Student progress is the best indication of a successful program. To determine progress, the goals toward which the students ought to strive should be clearly defined, and sound methods for evaluating progress should be employed.

One means a teacher has for determining progress is periodic measurement of student achievement. Measures of achievement in gymnastics, swimming, basketball, tennis, and other sports help to measure the success of these phases of the program. When achievement is low and progress is slow, the teacher should look seriously at the program content and the methods of instruction.

AAHPERD Fitness Tests

The AAHPERD has two fitness tests that are especially useful and that every physical educator and school administrator ought to know about. They are the AAHPERD Youth Fitness Test and the AAHPERD Health Related Fitness Test.

The *Youth Fitness Test* was first developed in 1957. It was revised in 1965 and again in 1976. This six-item test battery is designed to measure the more important elements of physical fitness. It has updated national norms for boys and girls ages 9 through 17 +. The test should be administered in accordance with the instructions included in the AAHPERD Youth Fitness Test Manual. The six items in the test are as follows:

Boys	*Girls*
Pull-up	Flexed-arm hang
Sit-up	Sit-up
Shuttle run	Shuttle run
Standing long jump	Standing long jump
50-yard dash	50-yard dash
600-yard run or 12-minute run	600-yard run or 12-minute run
or 1.5-mile run	or 1.5-mile run

Some school districts have *computerized* the Youth Fitness Test and have thereby made it much more convenient and economical to administer periodically to large numbers of students. It has also made it possible to acquire a computerized printout sheet for each student. A copy of the sheet can be furnished to the parents and the students to serve as a basis for discussion with the instructor. The computerized information can be conveniently stored for long-term use for making comparisons, observing trends, and establishing norms. The computer can also be used to list the winners of both the AAHPERD Fitness Award and the Presidential Fitness Award. It can identify and list those who score low in selected items, and remedial activities can be prescribed for those students. The AAHPERD office can furnish information about computer programs for the Youth Fitness Test.

The *AAHPERD Health Related Fitness Test* was first completed in 1980. It consists of four health related fitness test items especially selected to screen for degenerative-type conditions, such as coronary heart disease, obesity, and musculo-skeletal disorders. The test was especially designed for youth ages 6 to 17+. Of course, it should be administered in accordance with the instructions in the test manual which can be obtained from the AAHPERD. The manual also contains national norms. The four items included in the test are as follows[1]:

Distance run—cardiovascular function
Skinfold test—body composition
Sit up test—strength
Sit and reach test—flexibility

The Youth Fitness Test and the Health Related Test were not intended to supplant each other. Instead, they should supplement each other whenever there seems to be a need for both kinds of test.

EVALUATION OF PERSONNEL

School administrators become involved in the evaluation of both teaching and nonteaching personnel. The evaluation of teaching effectiveness deserves the lion's share of attention; therefore, the emphasis in this section is on teachers. In essence, the measure of good teaching is effective learning, and some important aspects of learning are difficult to identify and even more difficult to measure. Because of this, in order to evaluate accurately, several methods or approaches should be applied. Methods to consider are (1) evaluation by students, (2) self-evaluation, (3) evaluation by the supervisor or administrator, (4) evaluation by colleagues, (5) evaluation of student progress, and (6) comments (solicited or unsolicited) about the teacher's positive and negative aspects.

In the evaluation of teachers one should apply insight and wisdom relative to the source of information, its reliability, and how well the information applies.

Following are five basic principles that should be applied in the evaluation of teachers: (1) it should enhance the growth and development of the teacher as an individual; (2) its main focus should be on teaching effective-ness; (3) evaluation should include a discussion of goals for the future and how they can be achieved; (4) it should involve the person himself in pene-trating self-analysis; (5) some aspects of evaluation should be formalized with pre- and postconferences scheduled, and this should be carried on in a nonthreatening environment.

By Students

When teachers are evaluated by students, two influencing factors should be kept in mind: (1) subjective evaluation by students might portray teacher popularity as opposed to real effectiveness; and (2) it is easier to receive high student ratings in certain subjects. For example, a subject that is enjoyable has better potential for high ratings. This is also true for elective subjects, because students enter them voluntarily and usually with positive attitudes because they were not coerced or required to enroll.

Evaluation by students is a method used more frequently at the college level than at lower educational levels, because college students are more likely to approach the matter seriously and are better prepared to make accurate and fair judgments. If conducted properly, however, evaluations by students can be useful at the secondary level as well. Figures 18-1 and 18-2 are sample evaluation forms which allow students to rate their instructors.

Self-Evaluation

Self-analysis is potentially a great tool for helping teachers improve. The administrator's role is to help the teacher structure the right questions and pursue them with objectivity and thoroughness. The administrator can stimulate and encourage and even suggest penetrating questions that will help generate self-analysis, but the teacher himself must shoulder the main responsibility for making the process effective and for applying the results in a constructive manner. Figure 18-3 is a sample form that can be used in self-evaluation. It can also be used by a colleague or administrator.

One technique that is particularly useful in self-evaluation is instant video replay. This method enables the teacher to see himself in action. It is espe-cially applicable in the evaluation of appearance, gestures, mannerisms, and the effectiveness of delivery in the teaching process.

By Supervisor or Administrator

When the supervisor or administrator approaches the evaluation process, he ought to do so as a resource person and a facilitator. This approach will help to reduce the apprehensions and tension of the person being evaluated. Consequently, the teacher will tend to talk freely and seek help and so-lutions, which he probably will not do if authority is displayed and threaten-ing impressions are conveyed. A communication of the power to do harm if expectations are not met creates a barrier between the evaluator and the one being evaluated. This condition will usually reduce the exchange of informa-

TEACHER'S NAME _____ DATE _____

COURSE NUMBER AND SECTION _____

INSTRUCTOR EVALUATION

1 2 3 4 5 6 7

1. Has an excellent knowledge of the subject matter.
2. Is enthusiastic about the subject.
3. Is well prepared for each class.
4. Makes good use of class time.
5. Gives clear examples and explanations.
6. Makes helpful evaluations of my work (e.g., papers, exams).
7. Clearly explains difficult concepts, ideas, or theories.
8. Responds respectfully to student questions and viewpoints.
9. Is genuinely interested in helping me understand the subject.
10. Is available to students during regular and reasonable office hours.
11. Motivates me by his/her example to want to learn about the subject.
12. Has produced new knowledge, skills, and awareness in me.
13. Starts/dismisses classes at scheduled times.
14. Seldom misses class.
15. Overall rating: _____ Poor _____ Fair _____ Good _____ Excellent

Code: (Place an X in the appropriate square)

1 = Strongly disagree   5 = Agree
2 = Disagree   6 = Strongly agree
3 = Somewhat disagree   7 = Very strongly agree
4 = Somewhat agree

Figure 18-1. A concise but well designed teacher evaluation form to be completed by students. (Courtesy of Brigham Young University.)

TEACHER'S NAME _____ DATE _____

COURSE NUMBER AND SECTION _____

<u>STUDENT EVALUATION OF TEACHER*</u>

Do you feel that the course objectives were clearly stated? Yes____ No____

Do you feel that the course objectives were within your abilities? Yes____ No____

Were the tests and evaluations directed toward the course objectives? Yes____ No____

How well do you feel the instructor demonstrates those skills he teaches?

Very Well					Needs improvement				
1	2	3	4	5	6	7	8	9	10

How well were you able to learn those skills which the instructor taught?

Very well					Needs improvement				
1	2	3	4	5	6	7	8	9	10

How well do you feel the instructor evaluates your skills?

Very well					Needs improvement				
1	2	3	4	5	6	7	8	9	10

Do you have the necessary equipment to do an effective job of learning?

(comment)

Which of the following is expected of you?

____Memorization and recall.

____Making a judgment about something,using given information.

____Understanding the meaning of ideas or concepts.

____Putting information together in an unusual way to solve problems.

____Examining a complexity and breaking it down into parts.

____Using or applying information in a new situation.

Does the instructor show an interest in you? ____ALWAYS ____USUALLY ____SELDOM

Does the instructor encourage you to ask questions and to state your views?

____ALWAYS ____USUALLY ____SELDOM

Which of the following, if any, needs improvement?

____Speech.   ____Sense of humor,

____Planning for class sessions.   ____Tolerance for students' ideas & views,

____Willingness to help students,   ____Ability to inspire students,

____Enthusiasm,   Other:_____

STUDENT EVALUATION Continued.

Does the instructor encourage new ideas and concepts? YES____ NO____

How would you rate your instructor's communications skills—questioning, answering, discussing?

____OUTSTANDING   ____VERY GOOD   ____GOOD   ____ADEQUATE   ____POOR

	Exciting								Boring
Rank the presentations...............	1	2	3	4	5	6	7	8	9	10

	Outstanding								Poor
Rank the instructional planning and organization.....................	1	2	3	4	5	6	7	8	9	10

	Outstanding								Poor
Rank the effectiveness of the instructional methods...............	1	2	3	4	5	6	7	8	9	10

Does the instructor make appropriate use of instructional materials such as text book, films, magazines, manuals, etc.?
                                        YES____   NO____
(comment)

Does the instructor possess an adequate knowledge of course content? YES____ NO____
(comment)

Overall, do you feel the course was good?   YES____   NO____
(comment)

What aspects of the course do you feel were of most value to you?

_____

	Super							Rotten	
Rank the instructor..........	1	2	3	4	5	6	7	8	9	10

Is the instructor available to help you? ` `____ALWAYS ____USUALLY ____SELDOM

What do other students enrolled in this course think of it?

____LIKE   ____DON'T TALK ABOUT IT

____DISLIKE   ____AFRAID TO SAY

____DON'T CARE   ____DON'T CARE EITHER WAY

Figure 18-2. An extensive form with which students can evaluate teachers. (Courtesy of Laramie County Community College, Cheyenne, Wyoming.)

tion, sometimes distort or conceal the facts, and almost always delete the potential for positive outcome. Figure 18-4 provides an example of a form that can be used or adapted for use by the administrator or supervisor in evaluating a teacher's effectiveness.

PERSONNEL EVALUATION

Name _____ School _____ Date _____

Years of Teaching Experience _____ Years in Alpine School District _____

Grade or Subject Area _____

Conference Held: Date- _____ Date- _____ Date- _____

This checklist is used for the purpose of improving instruction and/or evaluation for future employment. This basic set of criteria is the official reference for observation and evaluation. Teachers are encouraged to use this form as a self-evaluation and to discuss these criteria with their administrators.

Final evaluation is to be completed by the principal and reviewed by the teacher. Teacher's signature is only an acknowledgment of having reviewed the final report.

I. TEACHING TECHNIQUES	Superior	Satisfactory	Needs Improve.
Is fair and impartial			
Demonstrates creativity in planning, preparation and implementation			
Varies materials and techniques			
Demonstrates a knowledge of subject matter			
Meets the individual needs of students			
Develops critical thinking			
Uses good English oral and written			
Demonstrates skill in motivating students			

III. PERSONAL ATTRIBUTES	Superior	Satisfactory	Needs Improve.
Shows poise, self-control, tact			
Demonstrates a wholesome sense of humor			
Maintains a professional appearance			
Maintains regular attendance, health, and vitality			
Demonstrates positive attitude toward teaching			
Demonstrates leadership			
Has a good self-concept			
Shows dependability			

Helps students understand and appraise their own work

II. SCHOOL MANAGEMENT

Maintains classroom control

Shows concern for care and appearance of room and equipment

Completes all school assignments

Uses and maintains appropriate school records

Establishes a positive learning environment

Shows evidence of daily planning and development of long range objectives

IV. PROFESSIONAL AND SOCIAL ATTITUDES

Observes professional ethics

Adheres to school and district regulations

Accepts suggestions for improvement

Shows evidence of professional growth

Demonstrates genuine liking for teaching and students

Views own assignment in relation to total school program

Develops positive parental relationships

V. TOTAL FINAL EVALUATION

Teacher's Summary Comment: _____

Teacher's Signature _____

Principal's Summary Comment: _____

Principal's Signature _____

Figure 18-3. Example of a form to be used by a teacher to rate his own effectiveness. The form can also be used by another person, peer, supervisor, or administrator. (Courtesy of Alpine School District.)

TEACHER EVALUATION FORM

Please evaluate the teacher by placing an 'X' in the appropriate square for each item. It is hoped that your comments will be frank, realistic and to the point.

Teacher _____ School _____

Period of employment from _____ 19___ to _____ 19___ Date _____

Secondary-Elementary: _____ Subject or Grade _____

Description of Ratings: P-Poor; F-Fair; G-Good; VG-Very Good; O-Outstanding. Example: P F G VG O — Major and Minor

PERSONAL TRAITS:	P	F	G	VG	O
1. Dependability					
2. Responsiveness to suggestions					
3. Judgment and tact					
4. Industry					
5. Sense of humor					
6. Voice: quality and articulation					
7. Health					
8. Personal appearance					
9. Initiative					
10. Poise					
11. Ethical qualities					
12. Genuine liking for boys and girls					

Analytical Statement:

SCHOLARSHIP:	P	F	G	VG	O
1. Mastery of subject					
2. Knowledge of source materials					
3. General educational background					
4. Correct and fluent English					

CLASS MANAGEMENT:	P	F	G	VG	O
1. Organization of routine details					
2. Control of classroom situation					
3. Maint. of good "emotional climate"					
4. Adaptability					
5. Attention to physical conditions and appearance of classroom.					

Analytical Statement:

OUT-OF-CLASSROOM ACTIVITIES:	P	F	G	VG	O
1. Participation in sponsorship of student activities and in the supervision of out-of-classroom situations					
2. Supervision hallways or playgrounds as required.					
3. Prompt and accurate in filing reports					
4. Prompt in arrival at school and classes					

TEACHING METHODS:	P	F	G	VG	O
1. General skill in planning					
2. Motivation of student interest					
3. Provision for individual differences					
4. Creativity					
5. Awareness and use of life situations					
6. Stimulation of critical thinking					
7. Use of resources and instruction aids					
8. Evaluation of student progress					
9. Use of pupil personnel information					

Analytical Statement:

PROFESSIONAL ATTITUDE:	P	F	G	VG	O
1. Cooperation with staff					
2. Attitude toward teaching profession					
3. Parent-relationships					
4. Membership in professional organization:					

Local: Yes ☐ No ☐
State: Yes ☐ No ☐
National: Yes ☐ No ☐

Analytical Statement:

Signature _____ Title _____

Figure 18-4. Evaluation form for an administrator, supervisor, or colleague to rate a teacher's effectiveness. This form could also be used by a teacher in the self-evaluation process. (Courtesy of the Provo School District.)

ADMINISTRATOR EVALUATION FORM

Please evaluate the administrator by placing an 'X' in the appropriate square for each item. It is hoped that your comments will be frank, realistic, and to the point.

Description of ratings: P-Poor; F-Fair; G-Good; E-Excellent; O-Outstanding

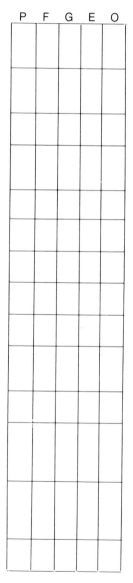

Support

	P	F	G	E	O
1. Administrator has been successful in gaining a high level of respect from other members of the organization.					
2. He has been successful in securing a reasonable level of budget and other kinds of support for the programs.					
3. He is instrumental in maintaining a high level of morale among the faculty and staff.					
4. He helps the organization toward a high level of respect within the larger educational system.					

Personnel Matters

	P	F	G	E	O
1. The administrator is fair and impartial in dealing with other employees.					
2. The administrator communicates effectively with other employees.					
3. He is sensitive and responsive to the feelings, needs, and interests of others.					
4. His own model and his expectations of others stimulates them to higher performance.					
5. The administrator demonstrates desirable ethical and professional behavior and encourages others to do the same.					
6. He causes employees to feel both comfortable and challenged in their positions.					
7. He keeps the faculty and staff free of unnecessary difficulty, stumbling blocks, and disruptions that might detract from their productivity.					
8. He adequately controls conflicts, disputes, controversies, and frustrating circumstances from diluting the efforts of the faculty and staff.					
9. The administrator relates well to other people and is respected by them.					

Figure 18-5. An example of an administrator evaluation form.

Management

	P	F	G	E	O
1. He provides clear direction and adequate insight toward well-established goals.					
2. He is energetic and productive and utilizes his time and energy in a desirable manner for the benefit of the organization.					
3. He permits and encourages ample participation by others in decision making.					
4. The administrative decisions are consistent, timely, and accurate.					
5. He is efficient and effective in performing his various administrative duties.					
6. He follows correct administrative procedures in his work with both the staff and higher administrative levels.					
7. He is a recognized expert in the field of his administration and contributes professionally to the overall good of that discipline.					
8. The administrator is an effective manager in all aspects of administration, especially in the management of people and financial resources.					
9. He is consistent, predictable, and forthright in his administrative duties.					
10. He is both objective and fair in his dealings with other people.					

Figure 18-5 (cont.). An example of an administrator evaluation form.

By Colleagues

Often, colleagues have a better perspective of how well an individual functions under given circumstances. Colleagues are generally mature and responsible individuals who have a basis for making sound judgments and are generally vitally concerned about the welfare of both the individual teacher and the students. For these reasons, evaluation by colleagues has high potential for productive results; however, this procedure often causes apprehension among both the evaluators and those being evaluated because colleagues usually do not like to evaluate each other. Also, the process has some inherent hazards. For example, the relationship between two colleagues is sometimes too positive or too negative to allow the evaluator to be adequately objective. Sometimes the evaluator, either consciously or unconsciously, desires to do the other person undue good or undue harm. This possibility must be carefully monitored by the administrator who will apply the results of colleague evaluations. When the circumstances are acceptable, however, evaluation by colleagues provides an additional valuable dimension to the total process. Figure 18-4 provides an illustration of a form that can be used or adapted for evaluation by a colleague.

Student Progress

There is a sound argument for the idea that student progress is the only meaningful measure of teacher effectiveness. If all forms of student progress could be measured with sufficient accuracy and consistency, perhaps there would be little use for other forms of teacher evaluation. The first portion of this chapter was devoted to information pertaining to measuring and evaluating student achievement. Additional information on this subject can be found in Jensen and Hirst: Measurement and Evaluation in Physical Education and Athletics.[13]

Unsolicited Information

People who work closely with each other have a good feel for how well the other person is performing. The day-to-day observations and impressions mount up to a large amount of information and clear indications as to a person's effectiveness. The unsolicited comments that are passed on from other people, students, parents, and colleagues provide additional information about the effectiveness of each member of the teaching force. These sources of information can serve a useful purpose when combined with the information obtained through the more structured methods.

Evaluation of the Administrator

Many administrators fail to recognize the importance of evaluating their own leadership. They recognize the need to evaluate everyone else in the organization, yet from the standpoint of overall success there is no one whose performance is more important. Therefore, it is vital that administrative effectiveness be accurately appraised and the results applied toward improvement. Some of the same sources of information as for the evaluation of teachers can be used in evaluating the administrator. In addition, Figure 18-5 illustrates a structured procedure that can be used for self-evaluation and colleague evaluation of those in administrative positions.

EVALUATION OF THE CURRICULUM OR PROGRAM

It is not possible to evaluate curriculum effectiveness totally separately from teaching effectiveness. A school could have a superb curriculum and still not achieve superior results, due to teacher ineffectiveness. Conversely, much can be accomplished through expert teaching even if the curriculum is basically weak. The ideal is a superb curriculum combined with superior teaching.

The purpose of curriculum evaluation is to determine how well the curriculum contributes to the educational goals, and especially how it could be modified to contribute better. The methods of curriculum evaluation can

COURSE TITLE _____ DATE _____

PERIOD (TIME) _____ INSTRUCTOR _____

COURSE EVALUATION

1 2 3 4 5 6 7

1. Course objectives are clear.
2. Course is well organized.
3. Student responsibilities are clearly defined.
4. Course content is relevant and useful.
5. Assigned workload is appropriate for credit hours.
6. Assigned homework is *not* just busywork.
7. Text(s) and other materials have helped me understand the course topics.
8. Exams concentrate on important points of the course.
9. Exams are clearly worded.
10. Exams are good measures of my knowledge, understanding, ability to perform.
11. Grading procedure is fair and impartial.
12. Assignments are appropriately distributed throughout the semester.
13. Course as a whole has produced new knowledge, skills, and awareness in me.
14. Overall rating: _____ Poor _____ Fair _____ Good _____ Excellent

CODE: (Place an X in the appropriate square)

1 = Strongly disagree   5 = Agree
2 = Disagree   6 = Strongly agree
3 = Somewhat disagree   7 = Very strongly agree
4 = Somewhat agree

Figure 18-6. Example of a simple but useful course evaluation form to be completed by the students. (Courtesy of Brigham Young University.)

include the following: (1) a determination of the instructional validity—are students learning what is intended as indicated by written tests, skills tests, fitness tests, posture appraisals, information about attitude changes, and character development; (2) student opinions about the curriculum—do they find it interesting, motivating, and appealing; (3) evaluation by teachers and administrators; (4) accreditation committee evaluations (or a committee of

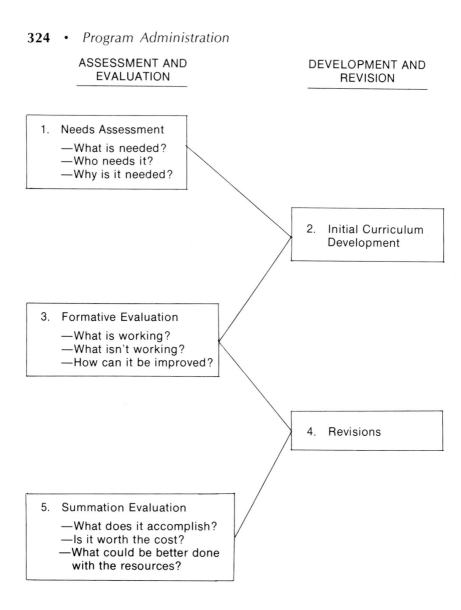

ASSESSMENT AND
EVALUATION

DEVELOPMENT AND
REVISION

1. Needs Assessment
—What is needed?
—Who needs it?
—Why is it needed?

2. Initial Curriculum
Development

3. Formative Evaluation
—What is working?
—What isn't working?
—How can it be improved?

4. Revisions

5. Summation Evaluation
—What does it accomplish?
—Is it worth the cost?
—What could be better done
with the resources?

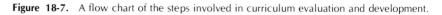

Figure 18-7. A flow chart of the steps involved in curriculum evaluation and development.

outside experts separate from accreditation); and (5) the utilization of a standardized curriculum evaluation scorecard.

Although structured evaluation procedures are important and should be conducted periodically, ongoing curriculum evaluation methods may be even more useful. The ongoing methods include such things as (1) hearing student comments, both positive and negative, about the various aspects of the curriculum; (2) informal discussions among faculty members; (3) feedback from parents and other members of the public; (4) attitudes of board members and administrators toward the curriculum as expressed through encouragement and budgetary support; and (5) the ongoing evaluation of student progress and special achievements.

One of the most useful approaches to evaluation of the curriculum and other aspects of the program is *cost-benefit analysis* in connection with budgeting. This procedure leads to a penetrating study of "what it's worth as compared to what it costs." Chapter 9 includes a section on this useful financial procedure.

One important aspect of curriculum evaluation involves the evaluation of individual courses or units of instruction, especially by the students in the class. Figure 18-6 shows a form that has been prepared for such use.

Figure 18-7 shows a flow chart that illustrates the steps involved in curriculum construction and revision. The flow chart has built into it the impetus to ask penetrating questions about curriculum effectiveness and how the curriculum could be improved.

BIBLIOGRAPHY

1. AAHPERD: Lifetime health related physical fitness test manual. Washington, D.C., 1980.

2. AAHPERD: Youth fitness test manual. Washington, D.C., 1976.

3. Anderson, W.G.: Descriptive analytic research on teaching. QUEST, *15*:1, 1971.

4. Anderson, W.G.: Videotape data bank. JOPER, *46*:31, 1975.

5. Austin, D.A.: Physical fitness reporting. JOPER, *51*:83, 1980.

6. Bain, L.L.: Description and analysis of the hidden curriculum in physical education. Doctoral dissertation, University of Wisconsin, 1974.

7. Bain, L.L.: Program evaluation. JOPER, *51*:67, 1980.

8. Barrette, G.T.: A descriptive analysis of teacher behavior in physical education classes. Doctoral dissertation, Teachers College, Columbia University, 1977.

9. Birdger, J.A.: Teacher evaluation with a computerized student questionnaire. Improving College and University Teaching, *16*:43, 1973.

10. Doyle, K.O.: Student Evaluation of Instruction. Lexington, MA., D.C. Heath & Co., 1975.

11. Greenberg, J.S.: How videotaping improves teacher behavior. JOPER, *44*:36, 1973.

12. Horine, L.: Faculty performance evaluation: one answer to accountability demands. JOPER, *52*:78, 1981.

13. Jensen, C.R., and Hirst, C.: Measurement and Evaluation in Physical Education and Athletics. New York, Macmillan, 1980.

14. Miller, R.I.: Evaluating Faculty Performance. San Francisco, Josey-Bass, 1972.

15. Morganegg, B.L.: An analysis of the pedagogical functions of physical education teachers. Doctoral dissertation, Teachers College, Columbia University, 1977.

16. Pflug, J.: Evaluating high school coaches. JOPER, *51*:76, 1980.

PART V
RELATED ASPECTS

Chapter **19**

FACILITIES AND
EQUIPMENT

Winston Churchill is reported to have said that "we shape our buildings, but afterwards they shape us." This statement can serve as a useful guideline for the planning of school facilities; those for physical education and athletics in particular have been developed with inadequate planning.

In light of today's spiraling costs combined with a tightened economic situation, facilities that provide for maximum effective utilization at the lowest cost have to be the rule rather than the exception. It is clear that such facilities cannot just happen; they have to be carefully planned and then managed with this concept in mind.

The administrator has two major concerns about facilities: facility management (priority of usage, scheduling, and maintenance and facility construction and/or renovation. Let us first discuss some important aspects of facility management.

MANAGING FACILITIES

One of the most important aspects of facility management is a clear definition of the kind of usage for which the facility can be available. The uses should be established into a system of priorities in order that the facility will serve its best purposes and that all concerned will know the relative priorities of its use. Following is a recommended priority system for physical education and athletic facilities.

1. Regular day-time classes and intercollegiate practices and contests.
2. Other activities sponsored and supervised by the department, such as intramurals, rehearsals, evening classes, and free play.
3. Official activities sponsored by other divisions of the school outside of the physical education/athletic department.
4. Activities sponsored by student groups or faculty and staff groups.
5. Activities sponsored by groups or agencies not affiliated with the school.

329

Facilities should be scheduled in order to get optimum use in accordance with the established priority system and to avoid conflict, misunderstanding, and disappointment due to errors. It ought to be clearly understood that scheduling must be done through the official scheduling office. On occasions when conflict or misunderstanding arises about the use of a facility, the information on the official schedule should consistently apply. Deviations from this procedure will contribute to confusion and personnel conflicts.

It is recommended that a simple scheduling form be used to record a scheduling commitment, and a copy be provided to the one initiating the request (Figure 19-1). It is also useful to maintain a current master sheet for each teaching station.

Facility maintenance keeps the facility attractive and protects it from deterioration. Maintenance should be an active consideration in facility planning and construction. If a facility is properly designed and well constructed, the maintenance costs will be minimal. Unfortunately, for many facilities, maintenance receives too little consideration in the planning and construction phase. This results in long-term maintenance problems which can become extensive. On the average, the lifelong maintenance costs of a build-

FACILITIES REQUEST FORM

Date _____

Area Requested   Rental Fee

Organization

Date(s) Requested   Time

Person in Charge

Mailing Address   Phone

PERSONNEL NEEDED:
  Building Supervisor   _____ cost
  Life Guard(s)   _____ cost
  Custodian   _____ cost
  TOTAL COST (rental fee
  and personnel)   _____

REQUEST APPROVED BY: _____

Figure 19-1. Sample form for the request of facilities.

ing amount to about three times the original construction cost, excluding the effects of inflation. With buildings that are poorly constructed or that have poorly selected materials, the maintenance costs run much higher. Highly durable and easily maintained materials on the exposed areas—both inside and outside—are the greatest single factor in the solution to the maintenance problem. Other important considerations include well-trained and conscientious maintenance personnel, adequate maintenance equipment located in strategic places for easy availability and use, and high expectations relative to maintenance among those associated with the use of the facility. Pride in the condition of the facility can make a major difference, and an administrator is in a good position to instill this kind of attitude.

FACILITY PLANNING AND CONSTRUCTION

Careful determination of facility needs for both the near-term and long-term is a responsibility primarily of those in administrative positions. Since the desired program is the basis for facility planning and the projection for facility needs, answers to the following questions are needed. What are the projections of future enrollment? Is the school likely to experience either consolidation or division? How many semesters of instruction in physical education will be required of all students? Is the instructional program to be broad in scope, with opportunities for the development of interests and skills in a large variety of activities? What will be the scope of participation in physical fitness and recreational activities for faculty and staff in addition to the participation by students? Will facilities be available for nonschool use, and if so, what kinds and how much? What will be the scope of the interschool athletic programs for men and women? What will be the scope of the intramural program? Will the program include dance activities in addition to sports and athletics? Will the program include aquatic or other activities that require specialized facilities? If the facility is for an institution of higher learning, will the program include professional preparation curriculum and research? What are the environmental and geographic factors that will affect the content of the program and the need for certain facilities?

Who Should be Involved

In any locality where school population growth is evident or where educational requirements are expanding, careful planning and timely construction of facilities is an important requirement, including the advanced acquisition of land. This can only be accomplished by involvement of the right people at the various levels within the educational system. It helps for an administrator to have clear insight into who needs to be involved and in what ways.

Following is a list of personnel who are ordinarily involved with planning and construction of facilities. Each situation differs in the amount of involvement of the personnel at each level.

College/University	*Public Schools*
Board of Trustees or Regents	School Board
Institutional Administrators	School Superintendent and Principal
Campus Planning Committee	State Specialist in Physical Education and
Office of New Construction	Athletics (optional)
Office of Building Maintenance	District Facility Coordinating
Architect	Committee (optional)
Consultant (optional)	Office of Facility Planning
Administrators of the College and	and/or Construction
Department where the facility will	Office of Building Maintenance
be used	Architect
Program Specialists	Consultant (optional)
Members of the Planning Committee,	Administrator and program specialist in
some of whom would come from	physical education and athletics
the above	Members of the Planning Committee,
Contractor	some of whom would come from
	the above
	Contractor

A *program specialist* is one who is actively engaged as a teacher and/or coach. This person will use the facilities and, consequently, is knowledgeable about the practical questions and problems of use. This makes his input especially valuable. One or more program specialists should be involved in every aspect of planning from beginning to end. This will help to ensure that the facilities will function as intended.

A *consultant* is a recognized specialist in the area for which the facility is being planned. Such a person is familiar with recently constructed facilities of this same kind and with the latest innovations in design and materials. A consultant can be especially helpful in suggesting to the planning committee the names of architects who are well qualified for the particular project; assisting the committee in analyzing alternatives and determining priorities; advising in connection with the public relations effort; and serving as a coordinator between the program specialists, the architect, and the contractor during the planning and construction stages.

The *architect* is not a draftsman or an engineer or a self-appointed planning specialist. He is one who has completed the required amount of education and apprenticeship and has become licensed by the appropriate state agency to practice architecture in the state. A licensed architect has certain ethical, professional, and legal responsibilities that are not necessarily assumed by lesser planning personnel. School administrators would be well-advised to always work with a fully licensed and reputable architect.

Developing the Idea

The idea of a new or revised facility develops through three important stages: *conception*, *presentation*, and *selling*.

Conceiving the need for a new or improved facility is the first step toward its accomplishment. The concept usually involves much discussion among those who have particular interest in the project or who understand the circumstances that would justify it. For example, if it seems that new tennis courts are needed, those directly concerned ought to thoroughly discuss the matter, carefully think about where the need fits in terms of priority and timetable, and what justification exists for the project. They should prepare themselves to defend the idea in terms of cost versus benefit.

After the idea has been conceived and thoroughly discussed by those immediately concerned, a proposal should be prepared for presentation to those in higher authority. Prior to, or in conjunction with, the formal proposal, informal approaches can be taken toward generating interest and support among administrative personnel and interested members of the community. Usually some discussion and exchange of information takes place over a period of time. This can provide valuable insight into what the formal proposal should contain once the idea develops to that point. Furthermore, it can pave the way for acceptance of the proposal.

For some projects, such as a group of outdoor tennis courts to be built on school property, little need may exist for public involvement. For certain other projects, however, say an expensive indoor swimming complex to be used by both school and community personnel, extensive public involvement and public support are essential. At this stage, a project steering committee should be organized, with one of its prime responsibilities being the public relations effort. The committee should apply those public relations principles and ideas explained in Chapter 11 that would be useful in the particular situation. This step is crucial because, if the public relations effort is not handled effectively, it will result in failure of the idea.

Preparing a Facility Program

A description of program needs should be written well in advance of the initiation of architectural planning to communicate the needs of the school program to the architect. The purpose should be to put into writing the current and anticipated school programs to be offered and determine the facilities required to house these programs at the optimum level. Here are some guidelines for preparing the facility program document:[15]

1. It should include all pertinent information to set the proper stage for further planning.
2. The information should be both concise and explicit.
3. It should state the optimal as well as the minimal program needs.
4. It should be realistic in terms of potential financing.
5. It should be both current and insightful in terms of present and anticipated future programming.
6. All aspects of facility needs should be considered, both indoor and outdoor; location of facilities affects both kind and amount of use.
7. A rough draft of the document should be reviewed by selected individuals and their ideas incorporated into the final copy.
8. It should take into account new trends that seem to have an element of permanency, such as (a) additional emphasis on opportunities for the

handicapped, (b) application of the community—school concept; (c) emphasis on the club sports movement, (d) equal opportunities for men and women; (e) emphasis on physical fitness and lifetime sports; (f) the weight training movement; (g) new products, materials and equipment; and (h) federal and state legislation that affects programming.

No matter how competent an architect might be, he cannot and should not be expected to know how to plan a building to adequately serve a group of specialists without considerable help and assistance from the specialists (clients) themselves. Thus, the underlying question of writing a program is how to transmit a large number of messages from the school staff to the architect, conveying the staff's wishes, needs, likes, interests, theories, and a multitude of other items, in such way that these items eventually become transformed satisfactorily into wood, concrete, and steel. The better this information is communicated to the architect, the more likely that the building will serve its purposes well and that the owner will be satisfied.

Often, the program is written before the architect is selected. The written program then should not dwell too much on shape or form or other specific aspects, but more on approximate size, kinds of use, special requirements, and particular features that are desired in the various components. Those working on such a program must know how they intend to use the building and for what purposes. This helps not only the architect and his associates, but also the school staff once the building is completed.

Because a written program is so important in transmitting information to the architect, the selected information presented here is taken from an actual written program for a physical education building.[3] To give the reader an overview of what is included in this particular 116-page program, the table of contents is listed.

Introduction
Certification
Space Requirements
Estimated Costs
Location of Building
Air Conditioning and Ventilation
Windows
Acoustical Requirements
Interior Surface Materials
Ceiling Heights
Location of Dressing Rooms
Location of Laundry and Issue Rooms
Elevator
Service Dock
Clocks and Class Bells
Audio, Radio and Television Equipment
Bulletin Boards and Display Cases
Room or Facility Descriptions

Figure 19-2 reproduces a single page in the *Space Requirements* section. Each area within the building is given a facility number. Figure 19-3 is a description of facility 49, taken from page 68 of the plan.

Dressing Rooms	Facility Number	See Page	Total Sq. Feet
Women's Physical Education and Intramural			
Locker and Dressing Room	42	61	10,000
Shower and Toweling Area	43	62	4,000
Lavatory and Toilet Area	44	63	2,000
Hair Drying and Make-up Room Area	45	64	500
Towel and Uniform Issue Room	46	65	600
Women's Faculty Locker, Dressing & Shower Area	47	66	1,500
Women's Swimming Instructor Shower and Locker	48	67	160
Men's Physical Education and Intramural			
Locker and Dressing Area	49	68	5,600
Shower	50	69	1,050
Toweling Area	51	70	1,050
Lavatory and Toilet Area	52	71	240
Towel and Uniform Issue Room	53	72	450
Men's Faculty Locker, Dressing, Shower,			
and Toweling area	54	73	1,970
Men's Swimming Instructor Shower-Locker Room	55	74	160
Intercollegiate Athletics			
Football Locker, Dressing & Shower Area	56	75	3,500
Other Sports Locker, Dressing-Shower Area	57	76	2,846
Coaches' Locker, Dressing & Shower Area	58	77	456
OTHER ROOMS (36 Total)			
First Aid Room	59	78	150
Swimming Pool Equipment Storage	60	79	576
Dance Property Storage	61	80	840
Costume Construction and Storage	62	81	600
Playfield Cart and Equipment Storage	63	82	250
Canoe and Trailer Storage	64	83	500
Ski Storage	65	84	180
Garage for Driver Training Car and Equipment	66	85	500
Health Department Storage-Room A	67	86	480
Health Department Storage-Room B	68	87	300
Women's Physical Education Department Storage,			
Room A	69	88	120
Women's Physical Education Department Storage,			
Room B	70	89	120
Recreation Department Storage	71	90	150
Intramural Equipment Storage Room	72	91	150
Gymnasium Equipment Storage	73	92	2,200
Gymnasium Supervision and Equipment Issue Room	74	93	200
Gallery, Swimming Pool A (40 seats @ 7 sq. ft. ea.)	75	94	280
Gallery, Swimming Pool B (1,000 seats @ 5 sq. ft. ea.)	76	95	5,000
Gallery, Gymnasium A (200 seats @ 6 sq. ft. ea.)	77	96	1,200
Gallery, Gymnasium B (200 seats @ 6 sq. ft. ea.)	78	97	1,200

Figure 19-2. Sample page from the "Space Requirements Section" of a written program for a new facility. (Courtesy of Brigham Young University.)

Information Sources

In addition to the ideas that school personnel already have, additional information can be obtained by several methods. One example is *field trips*, in which selected individuals travel to locations where similar facilities have

Facility 49
MEN'S LOCKER AND DRESSING AREA

Floor Area: 5,600 sq. ft.

Ceiling Height: Ten feet

Floor Material: Quarry tile

Wall Material: Ceramic tile

Ceiling Material: Moisture resistant and sound absorbent

General: Located adjacent to F. 50, F. 51, and F. 52;
   Lockers arranged on raised pedestal, no legs, solid base, with 106 inches, width for the aisle between the lockers;
   8 in. benches, 30 in. in front of lockers;
   360 dressing lockers, 12 in. by 15 in. by 60 in.; 50 of these to be designated as intercollegiate team lockers, 310 as lockers for physical education and intramurals;
   1,800 storage lockers, 12 in. by 15 in. by 12 in.;
   Lockers to be arranged on a 5 to 1 basis. All lockers to have louvred doors, perforated backs, and tiers; tops of lockers are to be slanted for cleanliness;
   Warm air is to be discharged under storage lockers section, forced upward through each locker (passing through perforations) and carried to the outside through central vents constructed in each locker section;
   Mirrors to be arranged on ends of rows of lockers;
   Two cuspidors and two drinking fountains, one set near toweling room, one set near entry.

Equipment needed in room:
   Benches in front of all dressing lockers;
   360 dressing lockers, 12 in. by 15 in. by 60 in., Worley Steel Lockers;
   1,800 storage lockers, 12 in. by 15 in. by 12. in., Worley Steel Lockers;
   Mirrors;
   2 cuspidors;
   2 drinking fountains.

Space utilization and importance to curriculum:
   Dressing rooms and lockers for all men's activities which will be held in this building.

Figure 19-3. A page from a written plan for a new facility. The information pertains to one area of the total facility. (Courtesy of Brigham Young University.)

recently been constructed. An on-site review of such facilities, combined with direct conversation with those who helped plan the facilities and those who use them, has tremendous potential for helping to sort out strengths and weaknesses. Returning with an adequate amount of useful photographs is fundamental to the success of the trip. Careful pre-trip planning should make sure that the right people are included and that the desired information is clearly identified in the form of a checklist. After completion of the trip, the photographs should be carefully reviewed and properly filed for future use, and the information gathered by use of the checklist should be adequately discussed and properly applied.

Sometimes architectural drawings of a similar facility elsewhere can be borrowed or reviewed on site. Borrowing a set of plans enables several people on the local scene to review them without the expense and time needed to take a field trip. Good ideas can be obtained from a review of plans that would not be obtained during an on-site inspection of the facility.

Other useful sources of information are textbooks and articles from periodicals on facility planning and construction. They include effective procedures to follow, desirable building features, and the advantages and disadvantages of various products. These sources of information are relatively accessible and inexpensive.

Selecting and Utilizing an Architect

Architects have often been criticized for their shortcomings in designing school buildings. Much of the fault, however, lies with school personnel. Often too much responsibility is left with the architect without enough involvement by school administrators and other employees. Even though the architect may be highly competent in architectural design and construction characteristics, he cannot be expected to understand all of the functional characteristics that are needed in a physical education building or athletic complex. He has not had first hand experience with utilization of such facilities and he certainly is not an expert on the program that the facilities are expected to accommodate. It should not be assumed that he is knowledgeable about the individual preferences of the school personnel.

Some architects do some truly wonderful things in both design and function, but even the best of architects needs all of the exact information available from and the preferences and opinions of the program administrators and subject matter experts. He needs the benefit of periodic reviews by those people to make sure that the plans develop properly. The school should get what it wants to accommodate its programs and not only what the architect wants. This places a lot of responsibility on both the architect and the school personnel to do cooperative, intelligent planning, and communicate thoroughly with each other throughout the course of the project.

Selecting the right architect is not a simple matter. One must consider knowledge and past experience as well as personality and ability to establish rapport. The client should interview prospective architects, view their work, inspect buildings they have designed, and confer with other clients they have served. An architect's ability to provide good service should be investigated from every standpoint.

The planning team that is selected to work with the architect should have a hand in his selection, because each member of the team will need to work effectively with him. In order to have the correct representation on the planning team, the following questions should be asked. Which areas or groups need to be represented? Which individuals are especially well prepared to make valuable contributions to the planning process? In addition to the need for planning expertise, the composition of the team has implications for public relations—both within and outside the school.

The planning team should include a committee composed of program specialists. This small group has the responsibility of working with the architect on details as the plan develops. Certain decisions must be made expediently in consultation with the architect. The chairman of the planning team should have a degree of leeway in doing this; however, "crisis-type" decisions should be avoided as much as possible.

Planning Checklist

The checklist presented on the following pages is intended to provide insight into the kinds of considerations that deserve attention in the planning process. It also serves, as a model for a checklist that could be utilized in an actual planning situation. In order to use the checklist, place the appropriate letter in the space indicated opposite each statement in the right hand margin: (A) the plans meet the requirements *completely;* (B) the plans meet the requirements *only partially;* (C) the plans *fail* to meet the requirements.[1] The material for this checklist is from Planning Facilities, a publication of the American Alliance for Health, Physical Education, Recreation and Dance, 1900 Association Drive, Reston, VA 22091. It is used by permission of the Alliance and of the Athletic Institute, 200 Castlewood Road, North Palm Beach, FL 33408.

General Considerations

_____ 1. The facility as planned is a part of a well-conceived and well-integrated master plan.

_____ 2. The facility has been planned to meet the total requirements of the program as well as the special needs of those who are to be served, both now and in the foreseeable future.

_____ 3. The plans and specifications have been carefully checked by all agencies and individuals whose approvals are required or desired.

_____ 4. The plans conform to state and local regulations and to acceptable standards and practice.

_____ 5. The plans have been prepared to accommodate possible future additions and expansions in the best manner possible.

_____ 6. Administrative offices, faculty offices, staff offices, conference rooms, work rooms, teaching stations, and service facilities are all properly interrelated and properly located for effectiveness and function.

_____ 7. Facilities for health services, emergencies, and first aid are adequate and suitably located.

_____ 8. The special needs of the handicapped have received adequate consideration.

_____ 9. The building is compatible in design and adequate in control as compared with the other buildings with which it relates.

_____ 10. Adequate attention has been given to making the facilities as durable, maintenance-free, and vandal-proof as possible.

_____ 11. Low-cost maintenance features have received the special consideration that is deserved.

_____ 12. Drinking fountains, restrooms, hair dryers, and other convenience facilities are adequate in number and properly located.

_____ 13. Provision is made for the repair, maintenance, replacement, and off-season storage of equipment and uniforms.

_____ 14. Noncorrosive metals are used in all damp areas such as dressing rooms and laundry.

_____ 15. Fire regulations and fire prevention have received adequate consideration. Also, fire alarm systems, both audio and visual, are adequate.

_____ 16. The facility contains adequate and well-placed bulletin boards, trophy cases, and display areas.

_____ 17. Adequate shower, dressing, and locker room facilities are furnished for students, staff members, guests, and game officials.

_____ 18. The proportion of space for different uses and the location relationships have received proper attention in the planning.

_____ 19. Adequate attention has been given to quiet areas for study and concentration.

_____ 20. The plan includes an adequate class signal system (bell or buzzer).

_____ 21. Adequate provision has been made for telephone service, intercommunication, both oral and written, mail service, and stereo.

_____ 22. The lock and key plan is suitable in terms of security and convenience.

_____ 23. The traffic-flow plan is well conceived and adequate, especially at stairways and exists.

Teaching Stations

_____ 1. Teaching stations are of optimum size to accommodate the desired number of students and the particular activities.

_____ 2. Teaching stations are designed with adequate safety zones between separate activity areas, and in connection with walls and fixed objects, smooth surfaces and padding are in locations where needed.

_____ 3. Each gymnasium has at least one smooth unobstructed wall for ball rebounding activities and adequate ceiling height (minimum of 18 feet for elementary schools and 22 feet for secondary schools).

_____ 4. Each teaching station has the desirable accessories, such as scoreboard, seating space, chalk board, bulletin board, floor markings, game standards, power operated partitions (where useful), public address system if needed, adequate spectator space for the activities planned for the area, and the standard equipment such as nets, mats, and the like.

_____ 5. Adequate storage closets and cabinets properly located and adequately secured.

_____ 6. Special instructional provisions as needed, such as television, instant video replay, phonographs and recorders, movie screens, and projection equipment.

_____ 7. Other instructional items are included where needed, such as wall mirrors, exercise bars, floor diagrams, acoustical drapery, and appropriate performance surface (different surfaces are needed for different kinds of activities such as basketball, tennis, weight training, modern dance, ballet, social dance, or gymnastics).

Walls

_____ 1. Provisions are made for wall surfaces to be of attractive, durable and maintenance-free materials.

_____ 2. Moveable and folding partitions that are power operated and controlled by switches.

_____ 3. Hooks and rings for nets and other attachments are properly placed, highly stable, and recessed for safety reasons.

_____ 4. Where moisture is prevalent such as in a natatorium, shower and dressing rooms, and laundry area, wall coverings are of moisture-proof or resistant materials. Special consideration is given in the case of walls that will be hosed down, such as shower rooms, steam rooms, and possibly, restrooms and dressing rooms.

_____ 5. Walls are free of protrusions and obstacles that interfere with traffic flow or create safety hazards. Corners are rounded and surface irregularities eliminated where desirable.

_____ 6. The wall texture and color of painted surfaces is the best it can be for attractiveness, lighting, and maintenance.

Ceilings

_____ 1. Ceilings in all instructional areas, offices, and meeting rooms are of the material that will provide the optimum acoustical effect.

_____ 2. Adequate consideration has been given to texture and color of ceiling materials.

_____ 3. Moisture-resistant ceiling materials are specified for moisture-prevalent areas.

_____ 4. Consideration has been given to adequate ceiling lighting, both direct and indirect, and both artificial and natural.

_____ 5. Overhead supported apparatus and equipment is secured to beams engineered to withstand stress.

Floors

_____ 1. Floors are made of appropriate materials for the particular activities to be conducted in each location. Performance effectiveness, safety, and maintenance are all considered. Carpeting is placed in areas where appropriate, taking into consideration acoustics, attractiveness, and maintenance.

_____ 2. Floor plates are placed where needed, and they are flush mounted and stable.

_____ 3. Appropriate consideration has been given to flooring material, texture, slope, and drains in shower and locker rooms, swimming pool decks, steam rooms, and other areas that will be hosed.

_____ 4. Nonskid surfaces and strips are placed where needed for safety, especially in wet areas and on stairways and ramps.

_____ 5. Highly durable and easily maintained baseboards are specified.

Electrical

_____ 1. Lighting intensity is in accordance with recommended standards.

_____ 2. Electrical control panels are properly placed and adequately secured.

_____ 3. Where appropriate, lights are controlled by key switches.

_____ 4. Adequate numbers of electrical outlets are properly placed.

_____ 5. Dimmer units are placed in instructional areas and elsewhere, as needed.

_____ 6. Natural light is properly planned in accordance with recommended standards.

_____ 7. Lights are shielded for protection from balls and other game implements.

_____ 8. Water-proof outlets are specified for moisture-prevalent areas and areas that will be hosed.

Temperature Control

_____ 1. Adequate provisions are made in all areas for heating, air conditioning, and ventilation.

_____ 2. Special consideration has been given to ventilation and individual temperature controls in locker rooms, dressing and shower areas, swimming pool, and other moisture-prevalent and odor-prone areas.

_____ 3. Proper ventilation is provided for such places as the wrestling room, equipment storage areas, research animal kennels, and other appropriate areas.

Other Considerations

_____ 1. Throughout the facility, adequate storage spaces are well located and properly designed.

_____ 2. Locker rooms are arranged for ease of supervision.

_____ 3. Provision is made for adequate control of access.

_____ 4. Adequate faculty accommodations are provided: shower and locker room, equipment and supply access, and lounge.

_____ 5. Food dispensary areas have received proper attention.

_____ 6. A well-defined program for laundering and handling of uniforms, towels, and equipment is included in the plan.

_____ 7. Shower heads are placed at appropriate heights for the ages of those being served. In the locker room, adequate attention is given to locker ventilation, placement of benches for convenience and ease of cleaning, height and size of lockers and width of aisle between lockers, in light of the grade levels being served.

Specialized Areas

In checking the plans, special consideration should be given to such specialized areas as the following:

_____ 1. Athletic training facilities.

_____ 2. Visiting team dressing room.

_____ 3. Dance studio.

_____ 4. Facility for ice activities.

_____ 5. Bowling alley.

_____ 6. Rifle range.

_____ 7. Indoor tennis courts.

_____ 8. A facility to accommodate a large number of spectators.

_____ 9. Research facilities.

Working with the Contractor

Once the plans are complete and the financial and other arrangements have been made to go ahead with the project, it is time to enter into an agreement with a contractor. As a general rule, a project should be put out to bid. All contractors who prepare bids must have access to exactly the same information about the project, so that the bids will be prepared on the same basis and can be logically compared against each other. When a project is put out to bid, the client has a moral obligation to accept the lowest bid unless there are justifiable reasons for doing otherwise. Sometimes, the bidding procedure includes an understanding that the client has the right to approve the subcontractors that the general contractor plans to engage. This assures that the client feels satisfied with all of the contractors who work on the project.

During the construction phase and beyond, the architect has a continuing responsibility to the client to make sure that the construction is done exactly according to the approved plan. To implement this, the architect works hand-in-hand with the contractor and performs his own periodic inspections to be sure that the conditions of the contract are adhered to from his point of view.

In addition, the school should assign an inspector for each major construction project. The inspector should be a school technician whose main responsibilities in connection with the project are to make sure the materials and workmanship are in accordance with the contractual agreement. He would also serve as a liaison between the contractor and client, and thereby, communicate any clarifications and decisions needed along the way. When the project is nearly completed, the inspector should be involved with the architect and the contractor in semifinal and final inspections. These inspections would result in a list of all of the items that are uncompleted or unacceptable. All of these items would have to be done to satisfaction before the final settlement would be made with the contractor and the architect.

On any large project, a number of changes are made during construction due to additional information that comes to light or the development of unforeseen circumstances. It is an advantage both to the client and the contractor to keep an open door for making such changes when they can be clearly justified. Whenever such a change is agreed upon, a change form should be completed and a copy kept by both the client and the contractor so that there is a written agreement explaining the change and the importance of circumstances associated with it. Actually, a change form should be viewed as a modification of the original contract.

Choosing the Type of Structure

In view of today's exorbitant and accelerating construction costs, the concept of maximum useful space for minimum cost is applicable, also keeping in mind the projected life span of the facility and the cost of maintenance. This requires careful analysis of the basic kinds of structure, the particular design features, and the materials used.

Conventional brick construction of school facilities has been by far the most prevalent and, in the majority of cases, is still clearly the best kind of basic construction. The particular features included in a conventional brick structure allow a wide range of choices, in which local needs and individual preferences can be easily accommodated. Practically all of the information presented in this chapter can be applied in conventional brick construction.

In the past few decades, considerable experimentation has been done and some practical use has been made of other forms of construction such as hard-shell domes and air-support structures. There is no question that such structures can provide large areas of space at less cost per square foot than conventional brick construction, therefore, these new forms of construction are worth serious consideration. Let us take, for example, the question of the advantages and disadvantages of air-support structures, since there has been a mild surge toward the use of these structures during recent years.

Pure air-support structures (Figure 19-4) and cable reinforced air-support structures (Figure 19-5) have certain advantages when compared with each other or with conventional construction. The cable reinforced structures have to have solid walls or some other kind of structure to which the cables can be attached. The advantages of the various kinds of air-support structures as compared with conventional construction are as follows: (1) The cost of air-support structures per square foot is only 25 to 35% that of conventional structures. (2) They are capable of providing a large span of unobstructed space. (3) They are relatively easy and fast to build; and the smaller structures can be put up and taken down during different seasons of the year. (4) The maintenance costs are relatively low. (5) They are relatively easy to light because of the penetration of natural light during the day and their ability to diffuse artificial light at night. (6) They are relatively fire-proof and highly earthquake resistant.

Some of the disadvantages are as follows: (1) The life of the air-support fabric is about 20 years, much less than that of conventional construction. This fact partially offsets the advantage of much lower initial construction costs. (2) In some environments, the architecture of air-support structures is considered unacceptable. (3) Temperature control has been a problem, especially in warm climates. Heat gain is a larger problem than heat loss. For this reason, air-support structures have proven to be more acceptable in colder than in hotter climates. In terms of acoustics, air-support structures are less than optimal, but in many cases, the level of acoustics is acceptable. (4) The potential for serious vandalism exists, but the fear of this has not been substantiated in cases where air-support structures have been built.

Additional Ideas

The park–school. This concept involves cooperative action between school and municipal authorities. It includes joint agreements as to the

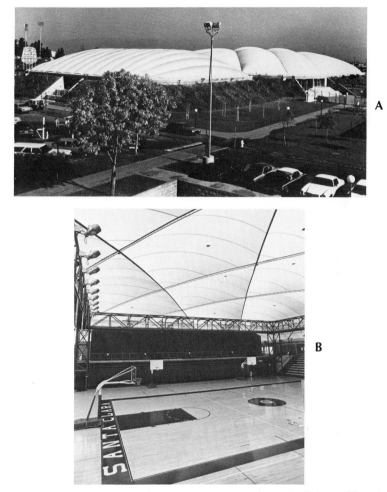

Figure 19-4. A structure at Santa Clara University supported completely by air-fill, with the top placed on a 16-foot concrete retaining wall surrounded by landscaped earth-fill. **A.** Exterior view; **B.** Interior view (Courtesy of Owens-Corning Fiberglass Corporation).

location, development, and use of the properties for both school and community purposes. In addition to the resulting economy in land ownership and costs of construction, operation, and maintenance, this cooperative approach fosters the desirable multiple use of areas and facilities.

In order to protect the interests of the cooperating authorities and to assure the most effective application of a park–school plan, a formal agreement should be enacted by the parties involved. Their uses of the facilities and their respective responsibilities for the purchase, development, operation, and maintenance should be spelled out.

Although the park–school (or sometimes called the community–school) concept has won wide acceptance in recent years, it still is not applied

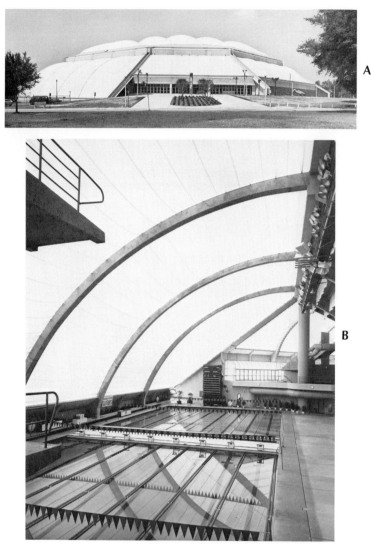

Figure 19-5. Air-supported structure at the University of Florida at Gainsville, with cable and metal beam reinforcement. Interior concrete walls form important elements of the support system. **A.** Exterior view; **B.** Interior view (Courtesy of Owens-Corning Fiberglass Corporation).

frequently enough. It should receive thorough consideration in every community and neighborhood.

Storage Space. Often, buildings are constructed with inadequate storage space or with storage space poorly located or poorly designed. Storage is an important element of the total operation, and it should receive adequate attention in planning and construction; however, storage space should be viewed practically. Consider, for example, that a building costs $75 per square foot. The question for administrators, then, is what kind of supplies and equipment and how much of them should occupy storage space at this kind of initial cost, plus interest on the original investment, plus the cost of maintenance.

Floor Surfaces.   A strong trend has been growing toward the use of carpet in a variety of areas. In some cases, short pile carpet is even used in activity areas. Some people have a bias against carpet because they view it as an expensive luxury; however, it often costs less than other floor coverings. The question of whether to use carpet should be analyzed in terms of relative initial cost, projected maintenance costs, acoustical advantages, and the positive psychologic influence it has on those who use the facility. It often makes people treat the facility with greater respect. Carpet should be used in all areas where it is practical and possible to do so.

In large foyers, shower rooms, or other areas where a hard surface is desired, one must decide whether to use concrete, terrazo, or some form of tile. Concrete is the cheapest in terms of initial cost. Terrazo has been found to be highly satisfactory with its combination of acceptability, initial cost, and maintenance cost. Tile comes in many forms and with a great variation in cost. The merits of any kind of tile should be carefully evaluated in any particular situation.

A decision must be made as to whether to install hardwood floors or some form of synthetic surface in gymnasiums. Hardwood floors have become expensive, and some fairly suitable synthetic surfaces can be installed at less initial cost. It is generally agreed, however that hardwood floors are still preferable in a gymnasium, unless the particular use of the area justifies a different kind of surface or the money is simply not available to afford them.

In outdoor areas, the use of *natural or artificial turf* depends on the availability of outdoor space, which in turn, influences the intensity of use. The initial cost for outdoor synthetic surfaces is high; but this kind of surface is necessary if the intensity of use is too great to be withstood by natural turf. In some locations, the cost of land is so high that it is more economical to own a smaller area that is prepared for high intensity use. Additional considerations to be taken into account are the type of surface preferred for the particular activities and the preference of those involved with the program.

Specialized Arrangements.   In *locker rooms* and *shower areas*, different arrangements can be considered, with each one having certain advantages and disadvantages. The various arrangements are illustrated in Figures 19-6, 19-7, and 19-8.

Principles of Planning and Construction

1. Each school or school system should have an overall campus plan. People to be involved with this plan should be competent and experienced not only in planning but in working with architects and contractors.

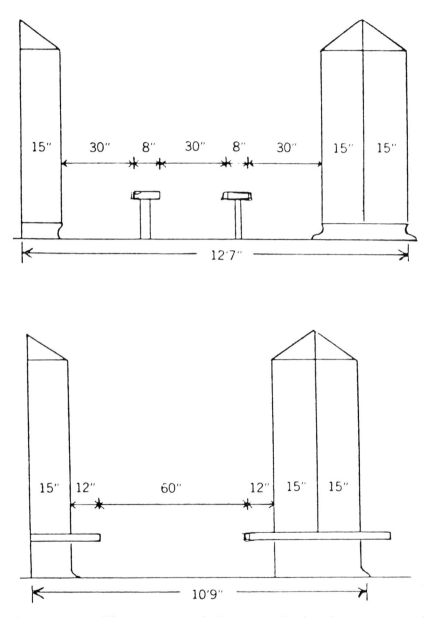

Figure 19-6. Two different arrangements for dressing room benches: isle mount (upper) and pedestal mount (lower). The pedestal mount has distinct advantages in terms of space utilization and traffic flow. (Courtesy of Boyd Jarman.)

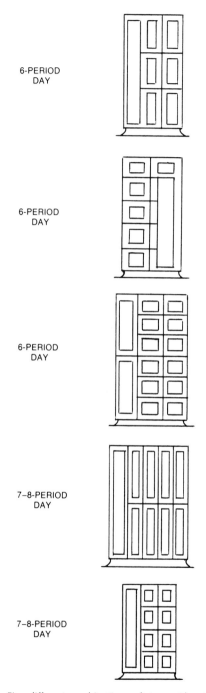

6-PERIOD
DAY

6-PERIOD
DAY

6-PERIOD
DAY

7–8-PERIOD
DAY

7–8-PERIOD
DAY

Figure 19-7. Five different combinations of storage/dressing locker arrangements, with the small lockers for storage of uniforms between classes, and the large lockers for clothes during class. (Courtesy of Boyd Jarman.)

Figure 19-8. Three different shower head arrangements: (A) post style; (B) stainless steel bank; and (C) wall mount. (Courtesy of Boyd Jarman.)

2. The functional capacity of a facility is of prime importance. Practically all other aspects rank below this important consideration.
3. Soundly conceived plans for areas and facilities are not achieved by chance or accident, but rather by thought and action of knowledgeable people who work well together.
4. When a building is ready for use, the true test of the planning occurs. If

the building works well, looks good, and wears well, then the planning team has accomplished its purpose.

5. Planning must be realistic in terms of the needs and financial situation of the community.
6. Facilities should be constructed of high-quality materials and workmanship in order to avoid expensive repairs and costly maintenance. Poor quality simply does not hold up under heavy use.
7. All planning and construction should conform to state and local regulations and acceptable facility standards.
8. Facilities should be designed so that they accommodate the needs of men and women equally.
9. The multiple-use concept should be carefully considered in the case of certain facilities. Application of this concept is basically an economy measure, which can greatly enhance the utility of the facilities.
10. Facilities should be designed so that the different components can be used independently without opening and supervising the entire building or complex.
11. Facilities should permit independent and simultaneous use for more than one activity within the same complex without encroachment or interference.
12. Adequate consideration should be given to possible future expansion of a particular facility, and the facility should be designed to accommodate this potential.
13. Relatively small offices designed for one faculty member are much preferred, because having more than one per office disrupts privacy and efficiency. An oversized office is highly conducive to housing two or more faculty members. The optimum size for one person is approximately 110 square feet.
14. The construction of an undersized teaching station is expensive because it forces the teaching of small classes every term for the lifetime of the teaching station.
15. Facility design and construction should accommodate easy and economical maintenance.
16. The special needs of handicapped persons should be taken into consideration in facility planning.
17. Desirable health and safety standards should be adequately considered.
18. Human traffic patterns for spectators and students should provide for movement through corridors and spaces with a minimum of congestion.
19. Initially, the planning should be pointed at the optimal or ideal in view of the particular circumstances. The reality of the restrictions will take over soon enough.

EQUIPMENT AND SUPPLIES

Although in this chapter much emphasis has been placed on facility planning and construction, administrators are generally more involved on a continuing basis with the purchase and management of equipment and supplies.

One of the most important guidelines in the selection of equipment and supplies is the same concept most people apply in their personal lives, "the best value for the money." Many of the purchases made for the school involve large expenditures; therefore, the one making the purchases must be thorough in his search for the right product from the vendor who will provide the best price and the best service.

Poor-quality equipment usually wears out quickly, is less perfect, and therefore, less desirable to use. Its short life-span is uneconomical in terms of the time and money required for ordering, transporting, and handling both the original item and its replacement. In certain instances, it is a good idea to investigate buying used equipment when investing in large and expensive items. Sometimes equipment used for demonstration purposes or that has been repossessed can be purchased at a considerable discount.

When purchasing clothing and protective equipment, proper fit and safety considerations must be given adequate attention. With certain items, such as footwear and the performance implements, their quality and condition can influence performance result.

Equipment must be kept secure. All items should have proper identification labels. Well-defined and sound procedures are needed for checking equipment in and out and monitoring its use. One of the best ways to control loss is to consistently use a check-out form. Figures 19-9 and 19-10 show examples of such forms.

Inventory

Inventory involves keeping an amount of stock that is adequate to avoid frequent shortages and resultant small orders, yet not so large that it occupies an inordinate amount of storage space. Stock, which represents money invested, must be properly secured in order to avoid loss. It should be reasonably protected from fire, dampness, exposure to the elements, or being damaged by rodents and insects; therefore, it should be stored in areas that are clean, properly ventilated, and protected from extreme temperatures and humidity.

Keeping current and accurate inventory records is an important element in equipment accountability. This requires the use of an appropriate inventory form, of which an example appears in Figure 19-11.

Storage and Care

Sporting goods suppliers have developed "equipment organizers" that can be transported directly from the issue room to the teaching station. *Nylon mesh bags* are highly useful for carrying balls and similar items to and from teaching stations, and the items can be stored in the same bag in the issue room. Mesh bags can be used for issuing clothing and the clothing can be laundered while still in the bag, thus eliminating the necessity of sorting

PHYSICAL EDUCATION ISSUE FORM

Name (print) _____
    Last   First   Middle

Locker No. _____   Homeroom _____

I hereby accept full responsibility for the following uniforms and/or items of equipment checked out to me:

Uniform Items	No.	Equipment (list items)	No.
Blouse or shirt			
Shorts			
Socks			
Leotard			
Swim Suit			
Towel			
Other			

Address _____Phone _____

Signature _____

* Note: Cross off items when returned.

Figure 19-9. A sample uniform and equipment checkout form for physical education participants.

and reassembling the issue. *Grocery carts* can be used for storage and transport of relatively light equipment items, and heavy-duty two-wheeled *wire carts* are available for the transport and storage of heavier items such as golf equipment. Inside storage rooms, appropriate hanging devices, storage bins, and shelves are essential.

Proper maintenance of equipment can keep the items in usable condition and extend their lifespan. Expensive equipment is hard to justify if it is not properly cared for and maintained. Equipment in poor repair results in disruptions and ineffectiveness in the program.

All those who use the equipment must clearly understand their responsibility for proper use and care, and their obligation for payment in the case of nonroutine damage. The time that items are to be returned and the check-in procedures must be clearly communicated.

Most equipment can be effectively cared for by simply using common sense. In cases where equipment requires specialized treatment or care,

ATHLETIC EQUIPMENT ISSUE FORM

Name _____ Sport _____ School _____

Address _____ Telephone _____ Locker # _____

LIST OF EQUIPMENT

Practice		*Game*	
Belt _____	Pants _____	Coat, sideline _____	
Cap _____	Pants, warm-up _____	Headgear _____	
Guards, knee _____	Shirt, warm-up _____	Jersey _____	
Headgear _____	Shoes _____	Pants _____	
Jersey _____	Socks _____	Pants, warm-up _____	
Pads _____	Stockings _____	Shirt, warm-up _____	
Pads, hip _____	Tights, wrestling _____	Shoes _____	
Pads, shoulder _____	Undershirt _____	Socks _____	
_____	_____	_____	
_____	_____	_____	

I am responsible for the articles listed hereon, which are charged to me, and agree that they will not be used for any purpose but the school games or authorized practice while in my possession.

Signature: _____

Date: _____

Figure 19-10. A sample form for the issue of athletic equipment.

INVENTORY FORM

Signature* _____Title _____

Date _____ Room of Location _____

Description	Quantity	New or Used	Condition of Equipment	I.D. # or label

* Signature of person accountable for the items

Figure 19-11. A sample equipment inventory form.

such instructions usually accompany the equipment at the time of purchase. If additional information or clarifications about care are needed, the distributor is usually the best source. Consistent interest in taking good care of equipment is often more important than special instructions. Following are some guidelines for the care of equipment.

1. The administrative head is the one finally accountable for all equipment and supplies in the organization.
2. Clear procedures should be established and followed relative to loss, theft, damage, or destruction.
3. Equipment should be discarded in accordance with the prescribed procedures and by authorized persons.

4. Accurate inventory and checkout records should be constantly maintained.
5. Procedures should be established to ensure proper use and maintenance.
6. Each individual to whom equipment and supplies are issued should be held accountable. A tight rein must be held on this procedure.
7. Sound procedures must be followed relative to the distribution and collection of equipment.
8. There should be an effective method of marking equipment and supplies as to ownership.

In managing equipment and supplies, an administrator should have positive answers to the following two fundamental questions. Do all of the employees consistently have all the supplies and equipment they need in order to be effective? Do the procedures provide adequate protection against loss, breakage, and misuse, and do they encourage conservation, economy, and efficiency?

BIBLIOGRAPHY

1. AAHPERD: Planning Facilities for Athletics, Physical Education, and Recreation. Reston, VA, 1976.

2. Anderson, G.M.: Athletic facility in an articulate enclosure. AIA Journal, 68 (6):184, 1979.

3. Brewster, S.: Specifications for a Physical Education Complex at Brigham Young University, Provo, UT, BYU Physical Plant Department, 1971.

4. Brooks, K.: Selecting the architect. American School and University, 49:49, 1976.

5. Bronzan, R.: Guidelines in facilities planning. Scholastic Coach, 46:36, 1977.

6. Ezersky, E.M., and Theibert, R.: Facilities in Sports and Physical Education. St. Louis, The C.V. Mosby, 1976.

7. Ersing, W.: Guidelines for designing barrier-free facilities. JOPER, 49:65, 1978.

8. Fieldhouse designed for the 80's. American School and University, 51 (4):82, 1979.

9. Flynn, R.: Focus on facilities in public schools. JOPER, 49:23, 1978.

10. Flynn, R.: Timely topics in facility planning. JOPER, 51:19, 1980.

11. Flynn, R.: What's happening in facilities. JOPER, 49:35, 1978.

12. Glading, J: The "big apple" beats the athletic facilities crunch. JOPER, 51:28, 1980.

13. Grant, N.: A facility goes underground. JOPER, 51:33, 1980.

14. Isaacs, L., and Frederick, S.D.: Physical education facilities for the handicapped. JOPER, 51:30, 1980.

15. Jarman, B.: Unpublished class notes. Brigham Young University, Provo, UT, 1981.

16. Kennedy, C.E.: Put independence and dignity into your pool. JOPER, 51:35, 1980.

17. Nalley, C.: A school–park relationship that benefits everyone. Athletic Purchasing and Facilities, *17*:24, 1981.

18. Penman, K.A.: Planning Physical Education and Athletic Facilities in Schools. New York, John Wiley and Sons, 1976.

19. Perry, F.C.: Pre-engineering buys more sports for less cash. American School and University, *48*:38, 1976.

20. Robison, R.: Fabric structures grow up. American School and University, *50*:46, 1977.

21. Scholastic Coach. The January issue each year emphasizes Athletics and Physical Education Facilities.

22. Servedio, W., and McLeon, W.: Problems of accessibility. JOPER, *51*:36, 1980.

23. Spencer, J.: Athletic Clothing Facts. Chicago, National Sporting Goods Association, 1975.

24. Theibert, R.: Time out for a re-evaluation of air shelters. Scholastic Coach, *9*:90, 1974.

25. Theunissen, W.: What's happening in facilities: the role of the program specialist. JOPER, *49*:27, 1978.

Appendices

PROFESSIONALLY RELATED ORGANIZATIONS

Members of a profession must know the organizations that relate to their profession and be at least generally familiar with the purposes, programs, and services of each. Knowledge about these organizations can serve at least two purposes:
1. It helps the administrator better understand how the organization can contribute to the profession as a whole and to the programs of any particular institution or school system.
2. It helps one to better know with which organizations to affiliate and for what reasons.

Appendix A. Professional and Service Organizations

Numerous professional and service organizations at the national level pertain to physical education and athletics. A brief description of each of these organizations is presented in alphabetic order. Some of the organizations have district and state subdivisions or affiliates. Many organizations pertain to a specific aspect of physical education and athletics. These organizations are listed in the last portion of the chapter.

AMATEUR ATHLETIC UNION (AAU)

The Amateur Athletic Union of the United States is America's largest, nonprofit, volunteer service organization dedicated to the encouragement and development of amateur sports and physical fitness. The AAU was founded in 1888 as a confederation of athletic clubs to restore and maintain integrity in amateur competition, to make facilities and opportunities for participation available to all, and to provide the best possible athletes to represent the United States in international competition. The AAU is sponsored solely by revenues from athletic events, fees for athletes' registration, sanctioning of meets, funding and contributions from business and industry, and the generosity of the American public.

The programs of the AAU apply to all of the American public regardless of age, sex, or race, through its nationwide membership of athletic clubs, schools, colleges, and many other organizations interested in amateur sports. It promotes the ideal of "sports for sports sake," protects the interests of the amateur athlete or team, establishes and maintains standards of amateurism, and sponsors a general athletic program open to all amateur athletes in the U.S. The AAU was first organized to try to maintain the pure image of amateurism in sports at a time when corruption was beginning to take hold of athletes and athletic events. The organization explicity defined amateurism and established clear-cut standards that outlawed practices detrimental to amateur sports. Sports clubs, educational institutions, and other bonafide athletic groups that qualified for membership in the AAU, were drawn together for the common purpose of promoting amateur athletics on the highest attainable level.

The AAU presently has 60 member associations, with more than 7500 member clubs encompassing all 50 states and the United States territories. Its 300,000 volunteers helped to sponsor local amateur athletic programs for various age groups. It is estimated that the AAU programs involve more than 25 million Americans each year. The AAU has development programs in 22 different sports. In addition, it sponsors the AAU junior olympics and is very much involved with arrangements for United States' athletes in international competition, including the world Olympic games.

The AAU publishes various pamphlets and brochures in addition to the monthly publication AAU News and the Annual Amateur Athlete Yearbook. The address of the main office is AAU House, 3400 West 86th Street, Indianapolis, Indiana 46268.

AAHPERD

The American Alliance for Health, Physical Education, Recreation and Dance is a voluntary education organization made up of 7 national associations and 6 district associations, with 54 state and territorial affiliates. The membership, which exeeds 55,000, is composed of health and physical educators, coaches and athletic directors, and personnel in safety, recreation and leisure services, and dance. The organization was founded in 1885 by a group of 49 people, mostly educators and physicians interested in promoting "physical training." Today, the membership network reaches into more than 16,000 school districts, over 2000 colleges and universities, and 10,000 community recreation units.

Following are the national associations that belong to the Alliance:

American Association for Leisure and Recreation (AALR) promotes school, community, and national programs of leisure services and recreation education.

American School and Community Safety Association (ASCSA) emphasizes safety in sports and other safety concerns such as injury control, highway safety, and first aid and emergency care.

Association for the Advancement of Health Education (AAHE) works for continuing, comprehensive programs of health education. Position papers are developed on such health topics as certification, drug education, and sex education.

Association for Research, Administration and Professional Councils and Societies (ARAPCS) coordinates the following special interest structures: Aquatics; College/University Administrators; City and County Directors; Outdoor Education; Facilities; Equipment and Supplies; International Relations; Measurement and Evaluation; Physical Fitness; Therapeutics; and Student Members.

National Association for Girls and Women in Sport (NAGWS) serves those involved in teaching, coaching, officiating, athletic administration, athletic training, club sports, and intramurals at the elementary, secondary, and college levels.

National Association for Sport and Physical Education (NASPE) provides leadership opportunity in physical education and sports development and competition, consultation, publications, conferences, research, and a public information program.

National Dance Association (NDA) promotes the development of sound policies for dance in education through conferences, convention programs, special projects, publications, and cooperation with other dance and art groups.

The AAHPERD holds a national convention each year. In addition, the 6 districts each hold a district convention annually, and the 54 state and territorial affiliates conduct annual conventions. The Alliance and its affiliates sponsor a large number of workshops, conferences, and clinics each year, all of which are aimed at professional development of its members or the solution of particular issues pertaining to the profession.

The Alliance publishes four regular periodicals: Update, Journal of Physical Education and Recreation, Health Education, and the Research Quarterly. More than a dozen newsletters are prepared and distributed regularly to provide information in specific areas of the associations; and the Alliance publishes 50 to 60 books and films each year. The titles are available in the AAHPERD publications catalog. The home office of the Alliance is located at 1900 Association Drive, Reston, Virginia 22091.

AMERICAN COLLEGE OF SPORTS MEDICINE

The American College of Sports Medicine is a nonprofit association with an international membership of more than 6000. Unlike most associations whose memberships are joined together by a single professional specialty, this organization represents over 40 different specialties. Among the objectives of the ACSM are the following: to promote and disseminate medical and other scientific studies dealing with the effects of sports and physical training on people's health; to initiate, promote, and correlate research in these fields; to establish and maintain a sports medicine library. ACSM has five regional chapters, and additional chapters are being developed throughout the United States as the interest of members dictates. Membership is open to any individual interested in sports medicine and who holds a graduate degree or who has become specialized in a field related to health, physical education, athletics, or the medical sciences.

The ACSM is a multidisciplinary professional and scientific society dedicated to the generation and dissemination of knowledge concerning the responses, adaptations, and clinical aspects of the human organism engaged in exercise and in recreational and competitive sports. The specific concerns include:

1. The basic physiologic, biochemical, biomechanical, and behavioral mechanisms.
2. The improvement of maintenance of functional capacities for daily living.
3. The prevention and rehabilitation in chronic and degenerative disease.
4. The evaluation and conditioning of athletes.
5. The prevention and treatment of injuries.

The College sponsors an annual national convention, several workshops in various geographic areas, lecture tours by selected sports medicine specialists, and position stands on important sports medicine topics and issues. The publications of the ACSM include the quarterly issue of Medicine and Science in Sports and the Sports Medicine Bulletin. It has also published the Encyclopedia of Sports Sciences and Medicine and a monograph series of sports and medicine. Its address is 1440 Monroe Street, Madison, Wisconsin 53706.

AMERICAN PHYSICAL THERAPY ASSOCIATION

This association has an individual membership of more than 30,000 individuals. It has 52 state chapters and 100 district chapters.

The APTA provides a variety of services to its membership in particular and to the profession in general. These services include the following: sets standards of practice, adopts and enforces ethical principles, and participates in the preparation and revision of the licensure examinations to assure quality physical therapy services for the public; accredits educational programs to assure the preparation of competent practitioners; guides and assists in the development of graduate education opportunities for physical therapists; promotes the exploration of new knowledge in physical therapy; holds an annual conference, conducts continuing education programs, and provides for the production and dissemination of publications to help transmit pertinent information; fosters the recruitment of minorities into the profession; speaks for the physical therapists in legislative and other health policy matters; conducts a public relations program; maintains a placement service; supplies information and advice to members, educational institutions, private and governmental agencies, and other associations.

The American Physical Therapy Association is a member of the National Health Council, the Coalition of Independent Health Professions, and the World Confederation for Physical Therapy. It publishes a monthly periodical entitled Physical Therapy, The Journal of the American Physical Therapy Association. It also publishes numerous information pamphlets, which are listed in its brochure of publications available upon request. The Association was founded in 1921. The home office address is 1156 15th Street NW, Washington, D.C. 20005.

CANADIAN ASSOCIATION FOR HEALTH, PHYSICAL EDUCATION AND RECREATION

This association is the Canadian counterpart of the United States' AAHPERD. The CAHPER is a national, nonprofit voluntary organization which, since its inception in 1933, has been concerned and engaged in providing and extending the benefits of physical activity to the citizens of Canada. Its particular objectives are stated as follows:

Acquire and disseminate knowledge pertaining to physical activity of human beings.

Stimulate interest and participation in physical activity by all Canadians.

Promote the establishment of acceptable programs of physical activity under the direction of qualified leaders.

Actively participate in the establishment and the improvement of standards of practice of all who are entrusted with the responsibility of leadership in the fields of physical activity.

Encourage relationships among professional groups concerned with human physical activity.

Cooperate with any and all local, provincial, national and international organizations which are committed to the improvement of the well-being of mankind.

The CAHPER issues a monthly periodical and a quarterly research bulletin. It also publishes numerous pamphlets and booklets on various topics of the profession. The national office is at 333 River Road, Vanier City (Ottawa), Ontario, Canada KIL 8B9.

NATIONAL ASSOCIATION FOR PHYSICAL EDUCATION IN HIGHER EDUCATION

As the only national organization devoted exclusively to the concerns of physical educators in higher education, NAPEHE

—works to encourage scholarly inquiry;

—disseminates research findings in the broad field of physical education and its related disciplines;

—provides a forum for discussion of major issues confronting physical educators in higher education;

—seeks to give direction to the professional through the preparation of position statements and other education means.

NAPEHE is the offspring of NAPECW and NCPEAM, the former women's and men's college physical education organizations. These associations have provided distinguished leadership to the profession for years. NAPEHE seeks to provide innovative leadership for the profession of physical education in higher education.

The NAPEHE sponsors a biannual publication of scholarly articles called Quest, a triannual newsletter, and printed proceedings of its annual convention.

NATIONAL ASSOCIATION OF COLLEGIATE DIRECTORS OF ATHLETICS

This organization serves intercollegiate athletics as a forum for its members to use in efforts to establish common standards and educational objectives among athletic directors in colleges and universities throughout the United States. NACDA disseminates information and guidelines pertinent to the immediate problems and issues confronting athletic directors.

NACDA sponsors an annual convention for the major governing bodies in intercollegiate athletics—NJCAA, NAIA, and NCAA institutions. This is the only meeting held regularly with the major governing bodies together in one place at one time. This yearly convention serves as a forum for discussing current issues affecting athletics and athletic administration.

NACDA has a quarterly publication entitled Athletic Administration. NACDA's home office is located at P.O. Box 16428, Cleveland, Ohio 44116.

NATIONAL ASSOCIATION OF INTERCOLLEGIATE ATHLETICS (NAIA)

The National Association of Intercollegiate Athletics is an autonomous athletic association made up of the intercollegiate athletic programs of 515 fully accredited 4-year colleges and universities. The fundamental tenent of the NAIA is that intercollegiate athletics is an integral part of the total educational program of the institution. This belief is strongly reflected in the governing documents, activities, and organizational structure of the Association.

Established in 1940 as the National Association of Intercollegiate Basketball, the NAIA (the name was changed in 1952) emerged from a "National Small College Basketball Tournament" inaugurated in 1937 in Kansas City, Missouri. The conversion of the NAIB to the NAIA in 1952 included the expansion of the program to include national championships in golf, outdoor track and field, and tennis. Football (two divisions), cross country, baseball, and swimming were added to the ledger in 1956, and wrestling (1958), soccer (1959), bowling (1962-1978), gymnastics (1964), indoor track and field (1966), ice hockey (1968), and volleyball (1969) are the most recent additions. The initial purpose of the NAIA—to provide national championship opportunities to colleges and universities competing below the so-called major level—has indeed been well served.

NAIA organizes and administers all areas of intercollegiate athletics at the national level, including rules and standards, and district and national sports competition. The address is 1221 Baltimore Street, Kansas City, Missouri 64105.

NATIONAL COLLEGIATE ATHLETIC ASSOCIATION (NCAA)

The NCAA was formed in 1906. It is the organization through which the colleges and universities of the United States act on matters to do with men's athletics at the national level (recently it has become involved with women's athletics). The association's membership exceeds 860 institutions, conferences, and affiliated organizations. It is devoted to the sound administration of intercollegiate athletics.

The services of the NCAA include the following:

Maintains a central clearing house and counseling agency in the area of college athletic administration.

Enacts legislation to deal with athletic problems.

Conducts research as a means of developing solutions to athletic problems.

Provides financial and other assistance to various groups interested in the advancement of intercollegiate athletics.

Represents the colleges in legislative and regulatory matters.

Administers group travel and medical insurance programs available to member institutions.

Provides a film/television production department.

Promotes and participates in international sports planning and competition by working with numerous national and international organizations.

Sanctions national intercollegiate competition and sponsors national college championship meets.

Compiles and distributes official statistics for intercollegiate sports.

Sponsors national rules committees for the various NCAA sports.

Provides other services to member institutions as requested.

The particular purposes of the NCAA are stated as follows:

—To uphold the principle of institutional control of, and responsibility for, all intercollegiate athletics in conformity with the Association's constitution and bylaws.

— To serve as an overall national discussion, legislative and administrative body for the universities and colleges of the United States in matters of intercollegiate athletics.

—To recommend policies for the guidance of member institutions in the conduct of their intercollegiate athletic programs.

—To legislate upon any subject of general concern to the membership in the administration of intercollegiate athletics.

—To study all phases of competitive athletics and establish standards therefor, to the end that colleges and universities of the United States may maintain their athletic activities on a high plane.

—To encourage the adoption by its constituent members of eligibility rules in compliance with satisfactory standards of scholarship, amateur standing and good sportsmanship.

—To establish and supervise regional and national collegiate athletic contests under the auspices of the Association and establish rules of eligibility therefor.

—To stimulate and improve programs to promote and develop educational leadership, physical fitness, sports participation as a recreational pursuit and athletic excellence through competitive intramural and intercollegiate programs.

—To formulate, copyright and publish rules of play for collegiate sports.

—To preserve collegiate athletic records.

—To cooperate with other amateur athletic organizations in the promotion and conduct of national and international athletic contests.

—To otherwise assist member institutions as requested in the furtherance of their intercollegiate athletic programs.

The NCAA home office is located at U.S. Highway 50 and Nall Avenue (P.O. Box 1906), Shawnee Mission, Kansas 66222.

NATIONAL EDUCATION ASSOCIATION (NEA)

The National Education Association of the United States was first organized in 1857 as the National Teachers' Association. The basic purpose of this early organization was to elevate the character and advance the interest of the profession of teaching and to promote the cause of popular education in the United States. The name of the association was changed in 1870 to the National Educational Association. In 1907, the National Education Association of the United States was incorporated under a special act of Congress approved in 1906.

Any person who is actively engaged in the profession of teaching or other educational work, or any other person interested in advancing the cause of education, is eligible for membership in the association.

The expressed goals of the NEA are to promote an independent, united teaching profession, professional excellence, and economic security for educators, and to provide leadership in solving educationally related social problems.

The organization has a membership of approximately 1.9 million. It puts out numerous publications in the form of periodicals, pamphlets, and books. A list can be obtained by requesting the publications brochure. The national office is the NEA building, 1201 16th Street NW, Washington, D.C. 20036.

NATIONAL FEDERATION OF STATE HIGH SCHOOL ASSOCIATIONS (NFSHSA)

The National Federation of State High School (Athletic) Associations was formed in 1920. At that time, it was decided that the welfare of high schools required that a more active part in the control of athletic activities be exercised by the high school administrators through their individual state organizations. This need prompted the formation of a national organization. In 1922, the Chicago meeting was attended by representatives from 11 states, and the name of the National Federation of State High School Athletic Associations was adopted.

The basic legislative body for this association is a National Council made up of one representative from each member state association. The executive body is the executive committee of 8 state Board of Control members. The Federation consists of 50 individual state high school athletic and/or activities associations and the association of the District of Columbia. Also affiliated are 7 interscholastic organizations from the Canadian provinces.

The NFSHSA is a service organization which assists schools and state associations in a variety of ways. The home office is at 11724 Plaza Circle, P.O. Box 20626, Kansas City, Missouri 65195.

NATIONAL INTRAMURAL-RECREATIONAL SPORTS ASSOCIATION (NIRSA)

The early growth of intramurals in America was unstructured, but as the intramural movement expanded, there was an increasing effort to share ideas and set standards for improvement. In 1950, William Wasson of Dillard University formed the National Intramural Association (NIA). This was the first national group devoted entirely to intramural sports. It came into being largely as a result of a Carnegie grant to study the intramural programs in black colleges.

In 1975, the NIA changed its name to the National Intramural-Recreational Sports Association (NIRSA). This name change reflects the expansion of the association and the profession itself to include intramurals, sport clubs, and other forms of campus recreation.

NIRSA is designed to promote and encourage the growth and development of intramural-recreational sports programs. It offers members the opportunity for professional interaction through national conferences and state and regional workshops.

The membership of NIRSA includes professionals, students, and institutions throughout the United States and several foreign countries.

Communication within the membership is maintained through periodic publication of the *NIRSA Newsletter,* Conference *Proceedings, NIRSA Journal,* and a *Directory.* Additional services offered to the membership include job placement, a media center, and consultant assistance. The headquarters are at the Dixon Recreation Center, Oregon State University, Corvallis, Oregon 97331.

NATIONAL JUNIOR COLLEGE ATHLETIC ASSOCIATION (NJCAA)

The NJCAA was conceived in 1937 in Fresno, California when a small number of junior college representatives met to organize an association that would promote and supervise a national program of junior college sports consistent with the educational objectives of junior colleges. In 1949, the Association was reorganized by dividing the nation into 16 regions, and later it was divided into 22 regions.

The Association was concerned only with men's sports until 1975, when it added a women's division. This division grew rapidly, and now, approximately 500 institutions are enrolled in the women's division and 575 enrolled in the men's division. The NJCAA sponsors championships in a large variety of sports for men and women junior college athletes. Its purposes and general function are essentially the same as those described for the NCAA and AIAW. The NJCAA is the junior college counterpart of those organizations. The national headquarters is located at P.O. Box 1586, Hutchison, Kansas 67501.

NATIONAL RECREATION AND PARK ASSOCIATION (NRPA)

A nonprofit organization dedicated to the improvement of people in the profession and the advancement of the profession itself; NRPA sponsors various publications, workshops, and institutes. It provides direct consultation and technical assistance for the improvement of programs, leadership, and facilities. The Association is also dedicated to the building of public understanding of the recreation field.

NRPA was formed in 1966 by the merger of five pioneer organizations in the park and recreation field: The American Association of Zoological Parks and Aquariums, the American Institute on Park Executives, the American Recreation Society, the National Conference on State Parks, and the National Recreation Association. The NRPA is presently subdivided into the American Park and Recreation Society, Armed Forces Recreation Society, Commissioners-Board Members, National Student Recreation and Park Society, National Therapeutic Recreation Society, and Society of Park and Recreation Educators. The NRPA publishes *Parks and Recreation* (monthly), *Leisure Research* (quarterly), and several books and pamphlets. The mailing address is 1601 North Kent Street, Arlington, Virginia 22209.

PHI EPSILON KAPPA

Phi Epsilon Kappa was founded in 1913 by the students and faculty at the Normal College of the American Gymnastics Union in Indianapolis, Indiana. This professional fraternity for physical educators was initiated to bind members together and to promote a friendly atmosphere among members of the profession.

More than 24,600 members have been initiated into this professional fraternity since its conception in 1913. Among its objectives are "to further the individual welfare of its members and to foster scientific research in the fields of health education, physical education, recreation education and safety education." Publications include the *Physical Educator,* and membership is available through the various collegiate chapters located in colleges and universities throughout the United States.

For further information contact Business Manager, 4000 Meadows Drive, Suite L-24, Indianapolis, Indiana 46205.

SOCIETY OF STATE DIRECTORS OF HEALTH, PHYSICAL EDUCATION AND RECREATION

The Society of State Directors of Health, Physical Education and Recreation was first organized in 1926 in New York City. The Society lists five basic purposes, among which are the following: "the promotion of sound programs of physical education including appropriate athletics at preschool, elementary, secondary, and post-secondary school levels; and to study problems affecting the quality of programs and to implement procedures for their solution."

The Society is composed of state directors of health, physical education, and recreation, and their associates. Associate memberships are available for those who have duties in one of these disciplines.

Over the years, the Society has issued numerous proclamations, resolutions, and proceedings which have had an impact on school, college, and community programs.

For further information, contact Secretary-Treasurer, The Society of State Directors of Health, Physical Education and Recreation, 9805 Hillridge Drive, Kensington, Maryland 20795.

U.S. OLYMPIC ORGANIZATION

Too little is known by sports administrators and the public in general about the purposes, objectives, organization, and procedures of the U.S. Olympic Committee. The following are stated as the committee's objectives:

Establish national goals for amateur athletic activities and encourage the attainment of those goals.

Coordinate and develop amateur athletic activity in the United States directly relating to international amateur athletic competition, so as to foster productive working relationships among sports related organizations.

Exercise exclusive jurisdiction, either directly or through its constituent members or committees over all matters pertaining to the participation of the United States in the Olympic Games and in the Pan-American Games, including the representation of the United States in such games, and over the organization of the Olympic Games and the Pan-American Games when held in the United States.

Obtain for the United States, either directly or by delegation to the appropriate national governing body, the most competent amateur representation possible in each competition and event of the Olympic Games and the Pan-American Games.

Promote and support amateur athletic activities involving the United States and foreign nations.

Promote and encourage physical fitness and public participation in amateur athletic activities.

Assist organizations and persons concerned with sports in the development of amateur athletic programs for amateur athletes.

Provide for the swift resolution of conflicts and disputes involving amateur athletes, national governing bodies, and amateur sports organizations, and protect the opportunity of any amateur athlete, coach, trainer, manager, administrator, or official to participate in amateur athletic competition.

Foster the development of amateur athletic facilities for use by amateur athletes and assist in making existing amateur athletic facilities available for use by amateur athletes.

Provide and coordinate technical information on physical training, equipment design, coaching, and performance analysis.

Encourage and support research, development, and dissemination of information in the area of sports medicine and sports safety.

Encourage and provide assistance for amateur athletic activities for those who are under-represented such as women, certain minority groups, and the handicapped.

The United States Olympic Committee consists of 31 national sports-governing bodies responsible for the organization and selection of team members for the sports on the programs for the Olympic and Pan-American Games, 11 multisport organizations, and the Armed Forces of the United States, from which directly or indirectly have come substantial numbers of members of the United States Olympic and Pan-American Teams, and representatives from the 50 states and District of Columbia. In addition, individual members include the International Olympic Committee members for the United States and the U.S.A. representative on the Executive Board of the Pan-American Sports Organization.

The United States Olympic Committee has two governing bodies: the House of Delegates, which is the larger body, and the Executive Board, which has the responsibility of conducting the business affairs. The *House of Delegates* consists of representatives from the 31 national sports-governing bodies and the various state Olympic organizations, plus the officers of the United States Olympic Committee and the representatives from the International Olympic Committee and the Pan-American Sports Organization. The House of Delegates meets annually to determine overall policy and to study and amend the constitution.

The *Executive Board* has charge of the ongoing business affairs of the United States Olympic Committee, and it interprets and implements the policies and procedures for carrying out the purposes and objectives as set forth in the act of Congress creating the United States Olympic Committee, and in the constitution, bylaws and general rules of the United States Olympic Committee. Included with the framework of the Executive Board are the United States Olympic Committee officers who form the administrative staff.

The United States Olympic Committee has within its structure numerous important committees which deal with a multitude of responsibilities in the areas of finance, eligibility, game management, and program developments. Two United States Olympic Committee Councils that sports educators ought to know about are The Educational Council and the Sports Medicine Council. *The Education Council* has the responsibility for developing and implementing, with the approval of the Executive Board, the various activities under the auspices of the United States Olympic Committee that are designed to promote the spirit of Olympianism and to encourage widespread participation of citizens of the United States in the Olympic movement. This includes sponsoring the annual United States Olympic Academy. In addition, the Council is responsible for selecting the United States delegates for the sessions of the International Olympic Academy in Olympia, Greece.

The *Sports Medicine Council* has the responsibility to promote research and encourage the practical application of information regarding all aspects of sports medicine. This involves the accumulation and evaluation of sports medicine information; the conduct of clinics and workshops for physicians, athletes, coaches, and trainers; the preparation of printed material; and the liaison of the sports medicine function of the United States Olympic Committee with government and nongovernment organizations.

Much additional insight into the overall organization and function of the United States Olympic Committee can be gained by reviewing certain publications of the Committee, particularly the Directory of Personnel. This explains the details of the organization and the constitution and bylaws, which explain all of the established regulations and procedures within which the Committee functions. These and other publications can be obtained from the United States Olympic Committee Headquarters, Olympic House, 1750 Overstreet, Colorado Springs, Colorado 80909.

Appendix B
Sports Organizations

While descriptions have been given of organizations concerned with the broader aspects of physical education and athletics, the organizations with more specialized interests are listed in this appendix with their current addresses and the periodicals they publish.

Amateur Basketball Association
of the United States of America

1750 Boulder Street, Colorado Springs, CO 80909

Amateur Fencers League of America

249 Eton Place, Westfield, NJ 07090. Publishes: *American Fencing* (bimonthly).

Amateur Hockey Association of the United States

7901 Cedar Avenue South, Bloomington, MN 55420. Publishes: monthly bulletin, plus an annual publication titled *Hockey/Arena Bix* magazine.

Amateur Softball Association of America

P.O. Box 11547, Oklahoma City, OK 73111. Publishes: *Balls & Strikes* newsletter (monthly), ASB *Official Guide* (annually).

Amateur Trapshooting Association of America

601 West National Road, Vandalia, OH 45377.

American Badminton Association, Inc.

1330 Alexandria Drive, San Diego, CA 92107. Publishes: *Badminton USA* (bimonthly).

American Bowling Congress

5301 South 76th Street, Greendale, WS 53129. Publishes: *Bowling Magazine* (monthly) and *ABC Newsletter* (monthly).

American Camping Association

Bradford Woods, Martinsville, IN 46151. Publishes: *Camping Magazine* (monthly), plus several books and pamphlets.

American Casting Association

P.O. Box 51, Nashville, TN 37202.

American Lawn Bowling Association

10337 Cheryl Drive, Sun City, AZ 85351. Publishes: *A.L.B.A. Bowls* (quarterly), plus several booklets and brochures.

American Water Ski Association

P.O. Box 191, Winter Haven, FL 33880. Publishes: *The Water Skier* (bimonthly).

Athletic Institute

705 Merchandise Mart, Chicago, IL 60654. Publishes: numerous books and pamphlets.

Babe Ruth Baseball, Inc.

1770 Brunswick Avenue, P.O. Box 5000. Trenton, NJ 08683.

Bicycle Institute of America

122 E. 42nd Street, New York, NY 10017. Publishes: *Boom in Bikeways* (three times a year).

Boys Baseball, Inc.

P.O. Box 225, Washington, PA 15301.

Ice Skating Institute of America

1000 Skokie Boulevard, Wilmette, IL 60091. Publishes: *ISIA Newsletter* (monthly) plus numerous pamphlets and brochures.

International Bicycle Touring Society

846 Prospect Street, LaJolla, CA 92037.

International Racquetball Association

P.O. Box 1016, Stillwater, OK 74074. Publishes: *Racquetball Magazine* (bimonthly).

International Softball Congress Inc.

2523 West 14th Street Road, Greeley, CO 80631.

League of American Wheelmen, Inc.

19 South Bothwell, Palatine, IL 60067. Publishes: *American Wheelman* (monthly).

Little League Baseball, Inc.

P.O. Box 1127, Williamsport, PA 17701.

National Amateur Baseball Federation

Route No. 1, Box 280B, Rose City, MI 48654.

National Archery Association of the United States

1951 Geraldson Drive, Lancaster, PA 17601.

National Baseball Congress of America, Inc.

338 South Sycamore, Wichita, KS 67201.

National Campers and Hikers Association, Inc.

7172 Transit Road, Buffalo, NY 14221. Publishes: *Tent and Trail* (four times a year).

National Field Archery Association

Route 2, Box 514, Redlands, CA 92372. Publishes: *Archery Magazine* (monthly), *Archery World* (bimonthly), *Bow and Arrow* (monthly), *Bowhunter Magazine* (bimonthly), plus numerous books and pamphlets.

National Golf Foundation, Inc.

707 Merchandise Mart, Chicago, IL 60654.

National Jogging Association

Suite 202, 1910 K Street N.W., Washington, DC 20006. Publishes *N.J.A. Newsletter* (eight times per year).

National Public Park Tennis Association

155 West Washington Boulevard, Los Angeles, CA 90015.

National Rifle Association

10418 N.E. 2nd Avenue, Miami, FL 33138.

National Skeet Shooting Association

212 Linwood Building, 2608 Inwood Road, Dallas, TX 75235

National Swimming Pool Institute

2000 K Street N.W., Washington, DC 20006.

President's Council on Fitness and Sport

400 Sixth Street, S.W., Washington, DC 20201. Publishes: *Fitness Newsletter* (monthly).

U.S. Field Hockey Association, Inc.

107 School House Lane, Philadelphia, PA 19144. Publishes: *The Eagle* (eight times per year).

U.S. Figure Skating Association

Sears-Crescent Building, Suite #500, City Hall Plaza, Boston, MA 02108. Publishes: *Figure Skating Magazine* (monthly).

U.S. Golf Association

Golf House, Far Hills, NJ 07931. Publishes: *The Golf Journal* (eight times per year), plus numerous pamphlets and booklets.

U.S. Gymnastics Federation

1225 North 10th Avenue, P.O. Box 4699, Tucson, AZ 85703. Publishes: *USA Gymnastics News* (bimonthly), plus several booklets on gymnastics.

U.S. Handball Association

4101 Dempster Street, Skokie, IL 60076. Publishes: *Handball Magazine* (bimonthly), *National Racquetball Magazine* (bimonthly).

U.S. Judo Federation

Box 519, Terre Haute, IN 47802. Publishes: *Judo-USA* (monthly), *USJF Handbook* (biannually).

U.S. Lawn Tennis Association

71 University Place, Princeton, NJ 08540. Publishes: *Tennis USA Magazine* (monthly), *USTA Official Yearbook* (annually), plus numerous booklets and brochures.

U.S. Ski Association

1726 Champa Street, Suite #300, Denver, CO 80201.

U.S. Soccer Federation

350 Fifth Avenue, Suite 4010, New York, NY 10018.

U.S. Table Tennis Association

12 Lake Avenue, Merrick, NY 11566. Publishes: *Table Tennis Topics* (bimonthly).

U.S. Volleyball Association

557 Fourth Street, San Francisco, CA 94107. Publishes: *USA Volleyball Review* (bimonthly).

Young Men's Christian Association of
the United States of America

National Council, 291 Broadway, New York, NY 10022.

Young Women's Christian Association of
the Unites States of America

600 Lexington Avenue, New York, NY 10022.

Appendix C
Coaches' Associations

National coaches associations exist for all the well-established sports. These associations are active in updating procedures for conducting sports events, advancement of the sport, and rule modifications. Some of the associations publish monthly or quarterly publications for their membership; for example, the National Football Coaches Association, the U.S. Track and Field Coaches Association, the National Soccer Coaches Association, and corresponding coaches associations for most of the other sports. These organizations are popular among the coaching specialists, because each organization enhances the advancement of the particular sport and serves a fraternal purpose for the coaches.

Appendix D
Selected Professional Periodicals

AAHPER Update	Published monthly by the AAHPERD. (Available through membership) 1900 Association Drive Reston, VA 22091	A national newspaper devoted specifically to news and features in the broad fields of health, dance, and safety. Focuses on news about the alliance and its seven associations.
Athletic Administration	Published quarterly. 21330 Center Ridge Road, Cleveland, OH 44116.	Issues and methods in athletic administration.
Athletic Journal	Published monthly. 1719 Howard St., Evanston, IL 60202.	Broad scope of articles on athletic administration, coaching, conditioning, and performance.
CAHPER Journal	Published bimonthly by the Canadian Association for HPER, 333 River Road, Vanier City, Ontario KIL 8B9, Canada.	Focuses on materials pertinent to the broad fields of health, physical education, and recreation. Publishes informational items of interest to members.
Canadian Journal of Applied Sport Sciences	Published quarterly by the Canadian Association of Sports Sciences, 333 River Road, Vanier City, Ontario KIL 8B9, Canada.	Manuscripts are published in the applied sport sciences including biomechanics, psychology, sociology, exercise physiology, and philosophy.
Coach and Athlete	Published seven times a year. Box 5642 1714 St. Johns Road, Baltimore, MD 21210.	Broad scope of articles on athletic administration, coaching, conditioning, and performance.
Completed Research in Health, Physical Education and Recreation	Published annually by the AAHPERD.	Annual compilation of research published in over 100 periodicals and abstracts of master's and doctor's theses in these areas.

International Journal of Physical Education (formerly Gymnasium)	Published quarterly by Verlag, Karl Kofmann, 7060 Schomdorf, Postfach 1360, Federal Republic of Germany.	Focuses on themes and topics dealing with teaching/learning processes. Other theoretic aspects of physical education and sport having an interdisciplinary value are published. Printed in English and German.
Journal of Leisure Research	Published quarterly by the National Recreation and Park Association, 1601 North Kent Street, Arlington, VA 22209. Members $8/yr; nonmembers $10.	Research articles of interest to professionals in the leisure sciences, motor development, play theory, sport sociology, and psychology. Contains book reviews and comment.
Journal of Sport Behavior	Published Quarterly by the U.S. Sports Academy, Mobile, AL 36688. $10/yr.	Publishes original, empiric investigations and theoretic papers dealing with studies of social behavior in the areas of games and sports. Includes articles of practical application as well.
Journal of Sport History	Published three times annually by the North American Society for Sport History. Address: Ronald A. Smith, NASSH Sec.-Treas., 101 White Bldg., Penn State Univ., University Park, PA 16802. $20/year members.	Publishes scholarly articles pertaining to all aspects of sport history. Additional thrust toward more hypothetic and theoretic sport historiography. Contains literature surveys, and book reviews.
Journal of Sport Psychology	College of HPER, Penn State Univ., University Park, PA 16802. Published quarterly by Human Kinetics Publishers, Champaign, IL 61820. $16/yr.	A cross-disciplinary journal that publishes theoretic papers, state of the art and synoptic reviews, position papers, and original reports of basic and applied research in sport psychology. Contains book reviews, research notes, and commentary.

Name	Publication Information	Description
Medicine and Science in Sports	Published quarterly by the American College of Sports Medicine, 1440 Monroe St., Madison, WI 53706, $18/yr.	Includes materials on athletic medicine, exercise physiology, growth and development, and clinical medicine.
NAPEHE Proceedings (formerly NCPEAM/NAPECW)	Published annually by the National Assn. for Physical Education in Higher Education. (Available to members at $25/). E. Ann Stitt, Tres., P.E. Dept., Calif. State Univ., Northridge, CA 91330.	Papers covering biomechanics and exercise, science, motor learning, sports, and professional preparation are published. Reports of general sessions and research abstracts are included.
Physical Fitness Research Digest	Published quarterly by the President's Council on Physical Fitness and Sport, Washington, DC 20201 (Free).	Each issue focuses on research pertinent to various phases of fitness and health.
Physical Fitness/Sport Medicine	Published by the President's Council on Physical Fitness and Sport	New scientific source designed for physical educators, physicians, coaches, athletic trainers and others. A comprehensive bibliographic service on the subjects of exercise physiology, sports injuries, physical conditioning, and the medical aspects of exercise.
President's Council on Physical Fitness and Sport	Publishes monthly the President's Newsletter. Washington, DC 20202.	Each issue focuses on articles relevant to various aspects of fitness and health.
Quest	Dept. of P.E., Univ. of California, Berkeley, CA 94720. Sponsored by the National Assn. for Physical Education in Higher Education. $25/yr (included membership); others at $12/yr.	Each issue represents a monograph on some particular subject of interest to college teachers. Scholarly manuscripts of a research, theoretic, and philosophic nature are published.

Research Quarterly	Published quarterly the the AAHPERD. 1900 Association Drive, Reston, VA 22091.	Publishes original research reports, review articles, and discussions dealing with human movement.
Scholastic Coach	50 W. 44th Street New York, NY 10036.	Broad scope of articles on athletic administration, coaching, conditioning, and performance.
The Journal of Physical Education	Published bimonthly by the National Physical Education Society (YMCA), 226 E. Washington Blvd., Ft. Wayne, IN 46802. $9/yr.	General manuscripts on various aspects of physical and health education, research, outdoor activity, and dance are published. Includes book reviews and announcements.
The Journal of Physical Education and Recreation	Published monthly (except Dec., July, and Aug.) by the AAHPERD, 1900 Association Drive, Reston, VA 22091. Prof. mem., $30 yr; $15 and $12.50 for students.	Publishes an array of articles, materials, and announcements pertinent to students and and professionals within physical education, sport, dance, and leisure studies. Articles range from the theoretic to how-to-do-it. Contains book reviews and special features.
The Journal of Sports Medicine and Physical Fitness	Official Journal of the International Federation of Sports Medicine. Published quarterly by Minera Medica. Corso Bramante 83-85, 10126, Torino, Italy, $30/yr.	Literature focuses on the medical aspects of sport and physical training. Contains original research papers, book reviews, editorial comment, and announcements.
The Physical Educator	Published quarterly by Phi Epsilon Kappan Frat. Ed. Office: School of HPER, Indiana Univ., Bloomington, IN 47401. $8/yr.	Publishes general manuscripts in the areas of physical education, recreation, and safety. Includes sections on comparative physical education, dance, teaching techniques, book reviews, and bibliographies.
The Physician & Sports Medicine	Published monthly by McGraw-Hill 4530 W. 77th St., Minneapolis, MN 55434. $26/yr.	Contains both research and practical information pertinent to the physician, coach, and trainer of athletic teams.

Appendix E
Current Issues for Discussion and Study

Following is a sampling of 19 current issues that relate to physical education and athletics. The statements can serve as a basis for valuable discussion or they can be used as assignments for students to analyze the points in favor of or against each issue.

An issue is a problem that has arguments pro and con, but is not immediately resolvable. The importance of an issue changes with circumstances; and over a period of time, an issue might lose its significance and no longer be of serious concern. Conversely, some issues remain unresolvable and alive. Certainly not all of the major issues are included here, but this list does contain a representative sampling.

1. Should interscholastic athletics be part of the junior high school program, and if so, how much emphasis should they receive?
2. Is it usually desirable for athletic coaches to major in physical education and teach in the physical education program, or is it better for physical education to have coaches teach other courses?
3. Should the school and the community consistently cooperate relative to design, construction, and use of activity facilities, both indoor and outdoor?
4. Should physical education be a required subject in the schools, and if so, at what levels?
5. Is it desirable for physical education teachers also to teach the health classes or should these be taught by someone else, and if so, who?
6. Should handicapped and injured students have equal opportunities for physical education even though it might be inconvenient and expensive to provide those opportunities?
7. Should handicapped and injured students be taught separately or should they be integrated into the regular physical education classes?
8. Is it desirable for female students to have opportunities in athletic competition at the various educational levels that are equal to the opportunities of male students?
9. Should restrictions from participation in athletics and physical education be used as a method of discipline in the schools or should participation in these programs stand on its own merit and not be considered a reward for acceptable behavior?
10. Is physical fitness the primary purpose and the primary justification for physical education in the schools?
11. Does participation in competitive athletics inherently contribute toward the positive development of the participants?
12. Should a greater portion of the physical education time and resources in schools be devoted to developing skills in lifetime sports?
13. Does dance logically belong in physical education or in fine arts; or should certain phases of dance be attached to each area?

14. Is the claim true that more physical education skills are learned through recreational programs than physical education programs, and is the teaching of skills a legitimate role of recreation programs?
15. Are posture improvement and weight control procedures important phases of physical education, and is the physical education teacher the one primarily responsible for these aspects of education?
16. Should physical education be graded on the same basis as other subjects in the school, such as A, B, C, D, E, or should the pass/fail or some other system be used?
17. Is it sound to claim that "no person has the right to neglect his physical fitness—it is part of his responsibility as a citizen to keep in good condition?"
18. Should competency tests be used in evaluating progress and success among physical education students in the public schools?
19. Should physical education in the elementary schools be taught by classroom teachers or by a physical education specialist?

Index

Page numbers in *italics* indicate figures.

384 • Index